The Cybersleuth's Guide to the Internet

Conducting Effective Free Investigative & Legal Research on the Web

by
Carole A. Levitt, J.D., M.L.S.
&
Mark E. Rosch

I F L
PRESS
www.netforlawyers.com

©2018 Fourteenth Edition, Revised
Carole A. Levitt, J.D., M.L.S.
Mark E. Rosch
Internet For Lawyers, Inc.
7820 Enchanted Hills Dr.
Suite A-215
Rio Rancho, NM 87144
info@netforlawyers.com
www.netforlawyers.com
www.facebook.com/Internet.For.Lawyers

Previous editions published under the title "Internet For Lawyers: How to Use the Internet for Legal & Investigative Research – A Guide for Legal Professionals."

Commitment to our readers: Internet For Lawyers is committed to providing the most credible and up-to-date information about the free and low-cost resources on the Internet that are useful for investigative and legal research. Because we are committed to serving our readers' needs, we welcome your feedback. We invite your comments about this book to iflpress@netforlawyers.com.

Since 1999, Internet For Lawyers has provided local and state Bar Associations around the country with professional and entertaining in-person, turn-key CLE programs for their members. Our seminars are popular with attendees and the substantial revenue those seminars generate is popular with our Bar partners. We also provide in-house training seminars for law firms and companies, as well as working with selected training companies.

Our programs focus on teaching legal professionals how to use the Internet and technology to practice law and research more efficiently and cost effectively.

Since 2015, we have also offered our Bar Association and law firm partners a catalog of turn-key CLE webinars. Some are based on our own presentations, others are presented by some of the best-known experts in their areas of law practice management, legal ethics, and technology. More information about offering these webinars through your organization or firm is available at http://www.cleseminars.com.

The information contained in this book is useful to any individual who needs to locate investigative or legal information on the Internet – not just attorneys. It is provided as a service to the community. While we try to provide the highest quality information, we make no claims, promises, warranties or guarantees about the accuracy, completeness, or adequacy of any of the resources discussed in this book. Readers should not rely solely on the content of this book as the basis of their online research efforts. The sites discussed in this book are meant to be descriptive as a starting point for readers' research efforts.

This information does not constitute legal advice.

Because legal advice must be tailored to the specific circumstances of each case, and because we do not solicit or accept any legal questions, queries, or requests for advice, nothing provided herein entails, should be construed as, or should be used as a substitute for the advice of competent counsel.

If you are in need of legal assistance, contact the State Bar Association of your state and ask if they have a lawyer referral program. To locate a Bar Association in your area, see the list of Web site links compiled at http://linkon.in/11fgatU.

Cataloging-in-Publication Information
Levitt, Carole A.
The cybersleuth's guide to the internet / Carole A. Levitt, Mark E. Rosch – 14th ed. revised
584 p. 2.76 cm.
Includes index.
ISBN 978-0-9713257-9-1
1. Legal research--United States--Computer network resources.
2. Legal research--Computer network resources.
3. Internet research
4. Internet searching—I. Rosch, Mark E. II. Title
KF242.A1L481 2018

Discounts are available for books ordered in bulk.

Special consideration is given to state bar associations, CLE programs, and other bar-related organizations.

Contact us at: IFL Press, 7820 Enchanted Hills Dr., Suite A-215, Rio Rancho, NM 87144; iflpress@netforlawyers.com, 888/393-6181.

ABOUT THE AUTHORS
CAROLE A. LEVITT, JD, MLS and MARK E. ROSCH

Carole Levitt and Mark Rosch, principals of Internet For Lawyers (their in-person CLE company) and CLEseminars.com (their webinar division), have been internationally recognized CLE seminar speakers--full-time since 1999. They have been best-selling ABA Law Practice Division authors since 2003. Their areas of expertise are: Internet investigative, legal, and social media research; social media ethics; Google search; and Google cloud Apps.

Together, Mark and Carole have authored hundreds of Internet research articles and co-authored six ABA Law Practice Division (ABA LPD) books and fourteen editions of *The Cybersleuth's Guide to the Internet.*

In 2013, they were both recipients of the "Fastcase Fifty" award, recognizing "50 of the smartest, most courageous innovators, techies, visionaries, and leaders in the law" and in 2014, they both became Fellows in the College of Law Practice Management, the international honor society that recognizes distinguished law practice management professionals.

Previously, Carole was a California attorney, a law librarian in Chicago and Los Angeles, and a Legal Research and Writing Professor at Pepperdine School of Law. She graduated with distinction from The John Marshall Law School (Chicago) and served on the school's law review. Since 2003, Carole has served on the ABA Law Practice Division's Publications Advisory Board and served on its Executive Council from 2006-11. Carole also recently authored Internet Legal Research on a Budget for the ABA LPD.

Mark blogs and tweets about legal technology issues, in addition to presenting seminars and writing books and articles. He developed Internet For Lawyer's website, blog, Facebook Business page, and its webinar division (CLEseminars.com). Mark is a graduate of Tulane University. He is active in the ABA Law Practice Division and serves on its Legal Technology Resource Center Board. Mark recently completed a three year term on the ABA TECHSHOW Planning Board and prior to that he served on LPD's Education Committee and its State and Local Bar Outreach Committee

Appreciation

The authors would like to acknowledge the expert editing of Tim Johnson, who just happens to be the same person who produced so many of our ABA LPD books when he worked at the ABA. Tim has been a wonderful supporter of ours ever since we first began our involvement with the ABA in 2003, and continuing to this day—15 years later.

Who Should Use This Book

The Cybersleuth's Guide to the Internet is meant to be a guide to free and low cost resources for any one who needs to conduct investigative and legal research on the Internet. The book starts off at the "beginning" laying out Web browser functions some Web users might be less familiar with. It then lays the groundwork of how search engines locate and retrieve the information we're searching for before it moves on to discuss more sophisticated search techniques and then how to apply those techniques to other Web sites to locate the information we're looking for.

Because the vast majority of sites discussed in this book are freely available on the Internet, many of these resources could be located through Web searches – if you had the time to conduct those searches, sift through all of the results, and test out the sites until you had culled down the millions of potential sites to a list of the most credible, relevant, and useful. That's where the authors of this book come into play: we've done the test searching and sifting for you so now you can learn about the most credible, relevant, and useful sites and how to quickly master them.

How to Use This Book

The Cybersleuth's Guide to the Internet is a reference book; it is not meant to be read cover to cover. We have tried to organize this book the way researchers think – by keeping like topics together. There are a number of concepts and search strategies that are applicable to numerous types of research we discuss in different chapters. Therefore, some strategies appear in more than one place in the book to keep the back and forth page flipping to a minimum.

Throughout the book we have adopted a number of conventions to distinguish different types of information.

- Web site names are **boldfaced** to make them stand out on the page when you're scanning for them.
- We italicize certain words to make them stand out from the site descriptions, including:
  - Text that appears on Web pages such as the labels on pull-down menus or search fields (e.g., *Search* or *Last Name*)
  - The word that describes an unlabeled icon or button
  - The *search terms*, *keywords*, or *phrases* that we enter into search boxes in our sample searches
- Because many of the Web site addresses for the sites discussed in the book are so long, we have used a URL shortening service to make them easier to type into your Web browser. So, while you'll see many URLs that look like this – http://linkon.in/9uihD4 – they really do point to the Web site described and will then display the actual URL.

We've made locating all of the Web sites in the book easy by creating a full index of more than 2,300 entries. Sites are indexed by site name (e.g., Google.com), type of site (e.g., Search Engine: Google), and type of information they contain (e.g., Bankruptcy Dockets: PACER).

For those of you who own prior editions of *The Cybersleuth's Guide to the Internet*, you will notice that we have deleted all legal research chapters that were unrelated to investigative research (e.g., statutes, ordinances, etc.). This means we retained information about case law databases (but only free ones) and dockets (free and low cost). We used the deleted chapters as the basis for the first edition of *Internet Legal Research on a Budget* in 2014 (American Bar Association Law Practice Division). The second edition of that book is coming soon.

The four things we can count on when it's time to revise *The Cybersleuth's Guide to the Internet* are:
  • many of the sites in the book have changed some features or functions
  • there are a number of new useful Web sites to add
  • some Web sites no longer exist
  • almost all screen shots of the sites need to be replaced

The 14th edition revised 2018 is no exception. The following list highlights some of the new information covered in this edition:

Archived Web Pages

- **Archive.org:** Deleted the URL for the keyword search beta feature because you can now link to it from the homepage.

- Added a 2017 case about the Patent and Trademark Appeals Board accepting pages printed from **Archive.org's Wayback Machine** as authentic evidence of prior art. *Johns Manville v. Knauf Insulation,* IPR2015-01453, paper 49 (PTAB Jan. 11, 2017)

Articles by or About Judges and Attorneys

- **Washington and Lee Law School's Current Law Journal Content (CLJC)** site is no longer online.

- **Google** *Scholar Articles*: Although we discuss using **Google** *Scholar* for case law, we added a reminder to use it to search for articles (in both law and non-law journals) and to use it to set up free *Alerts* if you want to follow a particular judge or attorney.

- The **ABA Journal's Blawg Directory's** keyword search is no longer confusing because its search box is now labeled *Search the Blawg Directory* instead of *Search ABAJournal.com.*

Attorney Directories

- **Avvo**: This directory can now be searched by entering an attorney name or law firm name into the left-hand search box (instead of just by practice area). **Avvo** joined the **Martindale Legal Marketing Network** in 2018 as part of **Internet Brands**.

- **FindLaw's** *Find a Lawyer* directory: We've noted a better URL to use (https://lawyers.findlaw.com) and described how to search the re-designed directory.

- **Justia's** *Find a Lawyer* directory: We expanded the description to explain ratings.

- **Martindale.com:** We expanded our discussion of how to search this directory and added new illustrations. We deleted the *Advanced Search* menu illustration because it no longer exists.

- **Superlawyers.com**: Added an "s" to the URL's *http*, to indicate the site's shift to a secure connection - so it looks like this: https://attorneys.superlawyers.com.

Bar Associations

- **ABA Division for Bar Services**: To locate links to state or local bar associations, see the **ABA Division for Bar Services** site (http://bit.ly/findabar). Deleted the **FindLaw** list because it is no longer on their site.

Briefs (U.S. Supreme Court)

- As of November 2017, the **Supreme Court of the United States'** official site (https://www.supremecourt.gov/) finally began hosting its merit and amicus briefs. We explain how to find briefs because the site doesn't provide a separate link to the briefs for easy access.

- The **ABA Preview of United States Supreme Court Cases** site (http://bit.ly/abasupctbriefs) has stopped offering briefs now that they are available on the Court's site. They offer briefs from 2004 through November 2017.

Case Law

- **Google** *Scholar Cases:* Replaced all **Google** *Scholar* pages and illustrations to reflect the re-design of the site (especially how to find the new Menu and its hidden links to the *Advanced Search* (and other links).

- **govinfo.gov** (this site does not capitalize the "g" in *govinfo*): Search or browse federal cases back to 2004 (and many other federal resources). In December 2018, **govinfo.gov** will replace its predecessor site, the **Federal Digital System (FDsys)**.

Deaths: See Vital Records

Dockets

- **PACER**: We revised the entire **PACER** section, expanding it from eleven pages to seventeen, and added all new illustrations because after 29 years of very few updates to **PACER**, major changes were made, effective December 9, 2017. Besides changing the "look and feel" of **PACER**, most of the major changes were made to the *Case Locator*, with new searching and sorting features.

- **RECAP Archive**: We revised most of **RECAP Archive's** descriptions, expanding our discussion from six pages to nine pages; this includes adding all new illustrations after **CourtListener** made enhancements in 2017, and in 2018, reintroduced *Alerts* and changed the "look and feel' of the docket sheet (with some new options for displaying the list of case documents).

- **Justia's** *Federal Dockets* database: We expanded the description and added new illustrations.

- **Supreme Court of the United States'** *Docket* database: The official site has made some changes, so we expanded the description from two pages to six to provide more keyword search examples and more search tips. The *Docket* database now includes *Briefs* (see the *Briefs* entry for details).

Driver License Numbers—See Investigative Databases (Fee-based): TLOxp.com

Duckduckgo.com

- **Duckduckgo:** We added a reminder that if you limit your **Duckduckgo** "bang" search to **Google**, be sure you are logged out of your **Google** account to remain anonymous.

Experts

- **Google** *Scholar*: Although we discuss using **Google** *Scholar* for case law, we added a reminder to use it to search for articles by and about experts and to use it to set up free *Alerts* if you want to follow a particular expert or topic. We also expanded the discussion and how to find the hidden *Advanced Search* link.

Google .com

- **Google** *Apps Launcher*: **Google** has removed the *Even More* link from the bottom of the Apps list, so to link to most products, you must use this direct URL https://www.google.com/intl/en/about/products

- **Google** *"Instant"* Search Results: **Google** no longer displays "Instant" Search Results. The list of predictive keyword suggestions is still displayed.

- **Google** *News* Database (https://news.google.com/): We explained the recent re-design and added illustrations. The keyword search results page now offers *Follow*, *Share*, and *Save* buttons on the right-hand column. Since mid-2017, it is no longer possible to re-sort results by date at this *News* database, but there is a work-around, which we explain.

- **Google** *Reverse Image Search*: Reverse Image Search results now also include a Best Guess for this image, which is a keyword that attempts to describe the image.

- **Google** *Scholar Articles*: See **Articles by or About Judges and Attorneys** and see **Experts**

- **Google** *Scholar Cases:* See **Cases**

- **Using Google As a Phone Directory or Address Directory**: We have added more search examples for this strategy.

Investigative Databases (Fee-based): TLOxp.com

- **TLOxp.com's Subscription Change**: On August 22, 2018, **TLOxp**, a fee-based investigative database, sent us an email that effective Aug. 23., 2018, "The last four digits of Social Security numbers will be masked. Driver license numbers will be masked." No explanation was given until we called and were informed that home-based subscribers were the only ones who were losing access to these two data points. This change comes despite TLOxp subjecting home-based subscribers to a rigorous site visit and review process before granting access to the service.

- **TLOxp's** *Vehicles Advanced Search* menu allows you to search by *Name* (Personal or Business), *Address*, *SSN*, *VIN*, or *Tag Number*.

Judicial Profiles

- **Ballotpedia**: We provided a new URL to view **Ballotpedia's** biographies of state and local court judges (http://bit.ly/stlocaljud) and described how the search has changed.

- **CourtListener**: On April 19, 2016, Michael Lissner announced that **Court Listener** launched its new *Judicial Database* (https://www.courtlistener.com/person) with profiles of 8,500 federal and state courts judges.

- **The Federal Bar Association** now allows even non-members to view the online profiles of federal judges that have appeared in past issues of its *Federal Lawyer* magazine. We describe how to search the profiles.

Oral Arguments

- We added information that older U.S. Supreme Court oral argument recordings (from 1955- 2009) are stored at the **National Archives and Records Administration's** building and that the **National Archives'** website offers online access but only from 10/1955 - 12/1972.

- **Oyez**: We added this website so you can access U.S. Supreme Court oral argument recordings online for free, back to 1955.

Social Media

- **Ethics Opinions**: Added Massachusetts Bar Association Committee on Professional Ethics Opinion 2014-5 (May 2014)

- **Facebook**: We updated information that **Facebook** has recently discontinued many of its "nonobvious" search features, such as searching by email address and phone number to locate someone's **Facebook** profile and we replaced illustrations.

- **LinkedIn**: Although **LinkedIn** still allows you to search without being logged into an account, we explained that the results list is now obscured by a pop-up that asks you to *Join or Sign In*. Also updated information about how to *Filter* and updated all **LinkedIn** illustrations

- **SearchisBack.com**: While this third-party site still allows you to submit **Facebook** "social graph" searches to **Facebook**, we explain how **Facebook** has disabled part of it.

- **Social-Evidence.com**: Deleted this site. It is no longer online.

Social Security Numbers (SSN)—See Investigative Databases (Fee-based): TLOxp.com and see Vital Records

Vital Records

- The cost to subscribe to the Social Security Administration's (SSA) **Limited Access Death Master File (LADMF)** has decreased.

- **FamilySearch.org**: To access this site you now must sign up for a free account. We added an illustration of a search result from the *Search Historical Records* database to show how to use its *Refine your search* feature. We also added some specific search tips to highlight some undocumented search/filtering capabilities.

- **Findmypast.com**: We added this genealogy website because it still offers a search of the *United States Social Security Death Index* <u>with</u> Social Security Numbers, but only for deaths through 2012. You must use this URL (https://linkon.in/findmypastssdi) and register for a free account.

- **Ancestry.com** offers searchable access to the *United States Social Security Death Index* (the predecessor to **LADMF**), but only from 1935-2014. You might find SSNs for some older deaths.

- **Findagrave**: Updated number of graves in database.

Wayback Machine: See Archived Web Pages

For those of you who own prior editions of *The Cybersleuth's Guide to the Internet,* you will notice that we have deleted all legal research chapters that were unrelated to investigative research (e.g., statutes, ordinances, etc.). This means we retained information about case law databases (but only free ones) and dockets (free and low cost). We used the deleted chapters as the basis *Internet Legal Research on a Budget* (American Bar Association Law Practice Division, 2014; http://linkon.in/1jbLQZn).

The four things we can count on when it's time to revise *The Cybersleuth's Guide to the Internet* are:
- many of the sites in the book have changed some features or functions
- there are a number of new useful Web sites to add
- some Web sites no longer exist
- almost all screen shots of the sites need to be replaced

The 14th edition is no exception. The following list highlights some of the new information covered in this edition:

"Answer" Sites

- Deleted **Jelly.co**
- Added **Quora.com**

Archived Web Pages

- **Archive.org:** Added new cases about the admissibility of evidence from Archive.org; added more illustrations; added information about affidavits; and expanded discussion about new keyword searching of home pages.

Bankruptcy

- **Inforuptcy**: The site no longer offers free dockets.

- **PACER:** Updated all screen shots; expanded discussion of how to search party names and use filters; explained difference between *Party Name* and *Party Role searches;* updated information about restored bankruptcy dockets.

- **Recap**: Described how to search **Recap** after **Court Listener** re-launched and improved the **Recap Archive**. You can now search bankruptcy court dockets on their own (with full-text keyword searching and more). Updated all screen shots.

- **Freecourtdockets.com**: The site does not appear to have been updated in several years. After receiving no response from the site owner when we wrote the 13th edition and now the 14th edition, we deleted the site from the book.

Birthdays

- **Birthdatabase.org** was offline for some time and now that it's back online, its free search no longer works. Instead, the site wants you to click on links to fee-based sites, so we suggest trying the free **Familysearch.org** site or visiting your public library to use their **Ancestry.com** subscription database for free.

- **SteveMorse.org**: We deleted this database because it had been pulling its information from **Birthdatabase.org**, which no longer provides birthdays.

Blawgs and Blogs

- **Google Blog Search**: Deleted because Google disabled it.

Browsers

- Updated introductory chapter to reflect Internet browsing with Google Chrome in Windows 10.

- Included some tips for browsing on iOS devices.

- **Opera**: Expanded discussion of private browsing techniques to include recently-released free Virtual Private Network (VPN) built into the **Opera** browser.

Business Research

- Added information about some public libraries offering free remote access to various business research databases, such as **Mergent**, **Morningstar Investment Research Center**, and **Business Source Premier**.

- **SearchSystems.net:** Added information about this site's links to business registries in the U.S. and other countries.

Directories & Search Engines

- Deleted **CompletePlanet,** which had offered links to over 70,000 topical search engines and directories on a variety of topics, because the site has been discontinued.

- Added **DMOZ** (http://www.dmoz.org), which claims to be "the largest, most comprehensive human-edited directory of the Web.

Discussion Groups

- **Google** *Groups:* Its usefulness has declined over the years, but is still keyword searchable.

Dockets

- **Freecourtdockets.com**: Deleted this site because it does not appear to have been updated in several years and we received no response from the site owner when we wrote the 13th edition and now the 14th edition.

- **Inoruptcy**: The site no longer offers any free dockets.

- **PACER:** Updated all screen shots; expanded discussion of how to search party names and use filters (such as *Attorney*); explained difference between *Party Name* and *Party Role searches;* updated information about restored dockets.

- **PacerPro**: Now includes dockets from the federal appellate courts.

- **Recap**: Described how to search **Recap** after **Court Listener** re-launched and improved the **Recap Archive** (with full-text keyword searching and more) and updated all screen shots.

EDGAR—See SEC Filings

Human Search Engines

- **Internet Public Library's Ask an ipl2 Librarian** service, which allowed you to submit questions via an online form, has now shut down and suggests that you check your public library to see if they offer chat.

Images

- **ImageToss**: Deleted because the site no longer exists.

Pay Investigative Research Databases

- **SearchSystems.net's Premium** investigative research databases: Updated screenshots.

- **TLOxp**: Made note of new URL (http://www.tlo.com/); Expanded information about how to search; added information about new databases, such as *Vessels*, *Utilities*, and *Relationships*; added information about expanded jurisdictional coverage (e.g., vehicle records have expanded to thirty-nine states and Puerto Rico from what had been twenty-two states and the District of Columbia; and detailed **TLOxp's** new (increased) pricing, monthly minimum "spend," and new required site visits for all users.

Oral Arguments

- **Court Listener**: Described how to search **Court Listener's** oral arguments database, which includes arguments from the U.S. Supreme Court and many U.S. Courts of Appeals.

People Meta-Search Sites

- **Radaris**: Added this site.

Real Estate

- The **Public Records Retriever Network** (**PRRN**): Public Records Retrievers no longer search public records in Guam and American Samoa but have expanded to search records in the Dominican Republic and Venezuela, among other countries, and have expanded from searching public records in 45 U.S. states to all 50.

- **RealEstate.com:** Deleted because it doesn't seem to provide information on all addresses.

Search Engines

- **Bing:** updated information about how:
  - to exclude words
  - home page was re-designed and now shows different Tabs
  - *Alerts* service is no longer offered – replaced by *Interests* (sort of)

- **DuckDuckGo**: Examine the new layout for results.

- **Google**:

  - **Alerts**: Documented a less-than-useful change to the process of creating a new Alert.

  - **News**: Find out how **Google** "broke" the *News* database

  - **Patents**:

    - **Google Patents Search:** We describe how to use the new interface and why the older interface, which **Google** still maintains, may still be useful for advanced searching. **Google** no longer hosts bulk downloadable versions of patent data (see the USPTO site at https://developer.uspto.gov/data instead).

    - **Google Scholar** offers an *Articles* search with an *Include Patents* check box, but it appears you can no longer obtain actual patent results (only articles about patents).

  - **Image Search**: Explained new *Save* feature in *Image* search results.

  - **Search Tools:** On the results page, this link is now labeled as *Tools.*

  - *Apps Launcher*: It now appears on the iPhone.

  - *Reverse Images*: Updated information about facial recognition.

- **Yahoo!:** Outlined recent acquisition by Verizon.

SEC Filings

- The SEC's **EDGAR** database has made some major changes, including a full-text search back to 1994, but only of "headers." In May 2017, we were informed that **EDGAR** plans to extend its four year "true" full-text search back to ten years soon.

- **Morningstar** (aka **Morningstar Investment Research Center**) is no longer offered free on the Web, but it can still be accessed for free by anyone who has a public library card, if your library includes **Morningstar Investment Research Center** in its remote database collection.

Social Media

- Cases: Added more cases about getting evidence from social media posts admitted.

- Even though **Facebook's** *Graph Search* is no longer available in the site's search box, we uncover a few new ways to continue to conduct these sophisticated relational searches.

- We've also added new ways to determine if a **Facebook** profile exists and how to search **Facebook Live** video.

- We explain the difference between "Deactivating" and "Deleting" a **Facebook** profile.

- **FindmyFBid.com**: Identify **Facebook** numeric profile IDs from vanity URLs.

- **GeoSearchTool.com**: Third-party site for conducting geographic searches for **Youtube** videos.

- **Instagram**: Added discussion of site's built-in search capabilities. Noted the demise of third-party search sites such as **Findgram**, **GramFeed**, **Websta**, and **WorldCam**.

Social Media (cont.)

- Jurors: A new court opinion concerning whether lawyers can research potential jurors.

- **LinkedIn**: Reviewed changes to search interface/function in the site's new design.

- **Pinterest**: Added site and discussion of its search functions.

- **SearchisBack.com:** Conduct sophisticated relational searches through **Facebook's** social graph.

- **Twitter.com**: More detailed discussion of searching for tweets, including hacking the search box to conduct searches for tweets near a specific location.

- **Social Evidence**: New software-as-a-service (SAAS) provider for monitoring/collecting social media posts for evidentiary purposes.

- **YouTube**: More detailed discussion of searching for videos, including conducting searches for videos posted near a specific location.

UCC Filings

- **National Association of Secretaries of State** (**NASS**) Web site: Updated URL.

Unclaimed Money and Other Financial Assets

- **The National Association of Unclaimed Property Administrators:** Updated coverage to include Kenya.

Vital Records (*See also* Birthdays)

- **Familysearch.org**: Updated information about search feature changes and updated illustrations.

- **Findagrave**: Updated number of graves in database.

- **Texas Marriage and Divorces**: Updated dates of coverage of these downloadable records at state's website.

Wayback Machine (Internet Archive at Archive.org)

- Added new case, *My Health v. General Electric Company*, No. 15-cv-80-jdp (W.D. WI December 28, 2015) at http://linkon.in/myhealthvge, where the court refused to take judicial notice of pages from the **Wayback Machine** without an affidavit to authenticate the pages.

- More details and screenshots about how to know when pages or sites have been excluded from the **Wayback Machine** from the start versus after they were collected.

- Added link to the **Wayback Machine's** Standard Affidavit

- Added information about new keyword searching feature, but only of homepages.

TABLE OF CONTENTS
AT A GLANCE

TABLE OF CONTENTS

Chapter One

INTRODUCTION TO THE INTERNET AND WEB BROWSERS

STARTING AT THE BEGINNING

This is a book about using the Internet for free (and low-cost) investigative and legal research. The information in this book can be useful to Internet searchers of all comfort and skill levels.

For those of you who are regular Internet searchers, and are comfortable with the functions of your Web browser, you can probably skip *Chapter One*.

For those less comfortable with searching on the Internet, *Chapter One* should not be skipped.

WHAT IS THE INTERNET?

The Internet is a worldwide group of public and private computers linked together in a network to share information. It is not owned or regulated by anyone—instead it is a free, universal, shared resource. The Internet began as a Department of Defense project in the 1960s to create a communications network that could survive a nuclear attack. For the first twenty years, only the government, universities, and large corporations used the Internet. Beginning in approximately 1993, it became more available to the public at large. Now there are numerous consumer uses of the

Internet, including communicating via e-mail, accessing shared information (news, research, stock quotes, etc.), participating in discussion groups, joining social networks, listening to music, and purchasing products (e-commerce), to name just a few.

WEB BROWSERS

The most common use of the Internet is to locate information by accessing the World Wide Web (WWW). The Web, as it is often referred to for short, is a collection of electronically linked files (Web pages) stored on millions of individual computers around the world. A website is an interconnected collection of these Web pages, usually created by the same individual or organization. A homepage is the first page of the site. website contents can range from plain text, graphics, and animation, to specialized formats used primarily to display highly formatted documents such as forms (PDF), full-motion video, or animation. A Web browser, such as Microsoft's Internet Explorer® (IE) or Edge, Mozilla's Firefox, or Google's Chrome, is the software that permits you to locate and view these Web pages. (Edge is Microsoft's newest browser, released for the Windows 10 operating system.)

Initially, Netscape Communicator/Navigator was the most popular browser among Web users. Over time, however, IE became the dominant browser with, at one point, more than 90 percent of those on the Web using it to access sites. Depending on which current statistics you believe, by early 2017 IE and Edge's combined share of the browser market was either 4.8% (http://www.w3schools.com/browsers/browsers_stats.asp), 4.18% (http://linkon.in/2ruDZNi), or 24.84% (http://linkon.in/2qQ6GCp). Meanwhile, by early 2017, Google Chrome's browser market share was either: 75.1% (http://www.w3schools.com/browsers/browsers_stats.asp), 58.35% (http://linkon.in/2qQ6GCp), or 52.81% (http://linkon.in/2ruDZNi).

By itself, as of this writing, statistics show Microsoft Edge usage at less than 2%.

Because of the growing popularity of the Chrome browser, we've elected to illustrate the anatomy and functions of Chrome (as available in the Windows 10 operating system). We will be using a personal computer, running Windows 10, for all screenshots, but will indicate when there are obvious differences for Mac users. Also, all browser and Web page functions that we describe are based on their use on a personal computer, so they may look quite different on mobile devices or not be available at all.

Downloading Chrome

Follow the directions at http://linkon.in/chromedownloadhelp to download Chrome on computers using Windows 10/8/7 (but not Windows Vista/XP/RT), Apple OS X version 10.9 or newer, or Linux. That page also includes information about using the browser with iPhones/iPads and Android devices. Once downloaded, Google Chrome will be automatically updated anytime it detects a new version of the browser.

Chrome's Address Bar/Omnibox

The white box at the top of the browser window has always been referred to as the "Address Bar" and it had, until a few years ago, been used only to reach a specific website by typing the site's address into it. The technical name for a website's "address," which consists of the entire *http* string, is "URL" (Uniform Resource Locator). The part after the *www* (e.g., "netforlawyers.com") is known as the "domain" name.

However, in the past few years, many browsers, including Chrome, have expanded the address bar's function. It now can also be used to keyword search the Web—simply by typing your keywords or phrases into the *Address Bar* and pressing your *Enter* key. With this expanded function, the *Address Bar* is also referred to as the *Omnibox*.

Another easy way to search is to use your cursor to highlight any text or image on a Web page, then right-click if using a personal computer (or *control+left click* if using a Mac), and click *Search Google for.* The highlighted words will display to the right of *Search Google for*.

Chrome's Tabbed Web Browsing

Chrome uses "tabbed" browsing, which gives you the ability to view multiple Web pages in their own respective tab, but within one browser window, as shown in the next illustration (where we are viewing the **Internet For Lawyers** website). Notice the other three tabs at the top: *Inbox, Google News,* and *USA.gov*.

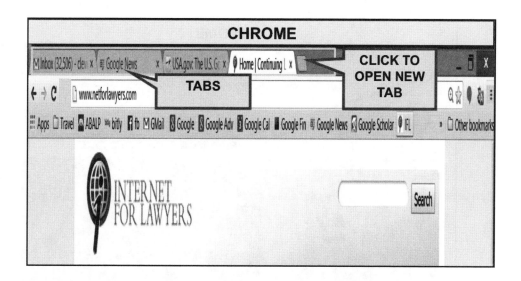

Tabbed browsing allows you to easily switch back and forth between the websites you are viewing by simply clicking on the corresponding tab. Note that if you click on a link on a Web page you're viewing and the subsequent page does not appear to open, there's a good chance that the new page has opened in a new tab. Check the top of your browser window to see if it's there.

You can open a new tab yourself to browse to a new Web page without closing the page you are currently viewing by clicking the box to the right of your active tab, as shown in the previous illustration (or press *Ctrl+t* for PCs or *command+t* for Macs). To close any tab, click the small *x* on the right-hand side of the tab you want to close (or press *Ctrl+w* for PCs or *command+w for Macs* while viewing the Web page in that tab).

Toolbar: Back, Forward, Reload this Page, Home, and Search

The *Toolbar* is located on the same row as the *Address Bar/Omnibox*. There are three tools on the *Toolbar* that are located to the left of the *Address Bar/Omnibox*: *Back, Forward,* and *Reload this page*. They assist you in moving around the Internet (see the next illustration). The *Back* arrow permits you to back up, one page at a time, to earlier pages (or websites) that you have visited in the active *Tab*, while the *Forward* arrow does the opposite.

Use the *Reload this page* icon when you are visiting sites that are not loading properly or where the information changes continuously, such as stock quotes and sports scores, to be sure you are viewing the most current data. To stop a page from loading, click the *x* in its *Tab*. This will close that *Tab*.

On the same row as the *Toolbar*, but located to the right of the Address Bar/Omnibox, is the Menu, which we will discuss in the next section.

You can use the *Menu* button to customize and control how Chrome functions. The *Menu* button is the last button located to the right of the *Address Bar/Omnibox.* If you hover over the *Menu* button, the words *Customize and control Google Chrome* pop up.

Once you click this button, you will then see a fly-out *Menu* that offers you various ways to customize and control your Google Chrome experience. We'll discuss each one in separate sections.

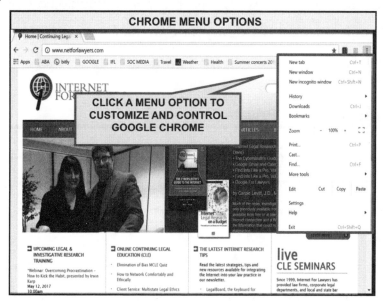

New Window

To open a new browser window (instead of a new *Tab*), you can either click *Menu>New Window,* or PC users can use the *Ctrl+n* shortcut, whereas Mac users would use the *Command+n* shortcut.

New Incognito Window (Private Browsing)

If you want to browse the Web without Chrome recording your browsing history (e.g., pages you opened and files you downloaded onto your hard drive), you should click the *Menu* button and then choose *New Incognito Window* (also referred to as "private browsing") from the drop-down.

In addition to your browsing history not being recorded, all cookies (temporary files) are also deleted after you close all *Incognito* windows. Although this is referred to as private browsing, websites you visited could still have recorded information about your visit. Files you downloaded to your device during *Incognito* session will remain on your device until you delete them. Even if you sign into your **Google** *Account* while browsing *Incognito*, your Google searches will not be recorded in your **Google** *Web History*. Note: the **Google** *Web History* stored in your **Google** *Account* only records the searches (the keywords) that you conduct at **Google** and not searches run on any other search engine. The **Google** *Web History* also does not list the pages you visit. To view your **Google** *Web History*, visit http://www.google.com/history when logged into your **Google** *Account*. To view your *Chrome Browser History*, visit chrome://history.

Virtual Private Network (Private Browsing)

While this book is not meant to address cyber-security issues, anyone using public Wi-Fi hotspots to connect to the Internet should be concerned about the security and privacy of the information they are sending back and forth over those connections.

There are many security options you can employ to better ensure that privacy and security, such as using services that encrypt your data in transit or Virtual Private

Networks (VPNs). As the name implies, Virtual Private Network products add a (virtual private) layer of security over the available public Wi-Fi network connection. Additionally, using a VPN can hide the actual location form which you are conducting your searches.

While there are many commercially available services that provide VPN service for a fee, for many casual, or even business users, the added step of having to install and configure VPN software may seem like too much. For some others, remembering to connect via the VPN software once it is installed is the hurdle between them and greater security.

The Opera Web browser alleviates some of these difficulties by offering users access to a free VPN. The Opera VPN has the added benefit of being "always on" until the user turns it off. See http://www.netforlawyers.com/content/opera-browser-free-virtual-private-network-vpn-0202 for more details.

Bookmarks

Once you locate relevant websites to which you plan to return, you can save them as "Bookmarks" (IE and Edge call them "Favorites") in your Chrome browser, so returning to them is a simple task. Adding *Bookmarks* is like creating a website address book—with speed dial. With just one click on the website name in your *Bookmarks* list, you will directly link to that site without needing to remember to type in the URL. It is perhaps one of the most useful features, aside from the *Find* function that we'll discuss later. You can add any page of a website as a *Bookmark*. You could link to either the homepage of a website (such as the U.S. Supreme Court's homepage) or a specific document that you use often at that website (such as a specific Supreme Court order), or both. (NOTE: Over time, pages and documents might be removed from the Web or Webmasters could change the URL where the page or document is stored. In those cases, your *Bookmark* would point to the old location, which may not hold the information it once did, or the Web page may no longer exist at all.)

There are three ways to add a *Bookmark* while you are viewing a site to which you want to return:

- Click on the *Bookmark this page* star (located at the end of the address bar); or
- Use the *Ctrl+d* shortcut for PCs or the Command+d shortcut for Macs; or
- From the *Menu* button, select *Bookmarks>Bookmark this page*, then click *done* in the *Bookmark added* pop up window (we don't recommend this since it's a three-step process instead of one)

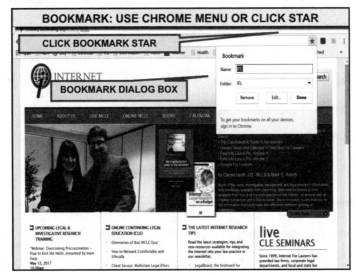

No matter which one of the three *Bookmark* options that you choose, a *Bookmark added* dialog box will pop up and automatically insert the web page name into the *Name* box. You have the option of giving your new *Bookmark* a different name (e.g., a shorter name or a more descriptive name) by clicking into the *Name* box, or you can accept the name of the Web page assigned by its designer. See the next section in this chapter for more editing options.

From the *Folder* drop-down menu, if you select *Other Bookmarks*, this simply places the bookmarked site at the end of your *Bookmark* list (on its own and not into a folder). Click *Done* to save your new *Bookmark*.

You would also use the dialog box (shown in the previous illustration) to *Remove* a *Bookmark* if you immediately change your mind about adding it or if you want to immediately *Edit* a *Bookmark,* beyond just changing the *Bookmark's* name as described earlier. The *Edit* button allows you to change the URL.

The *Folder* drop-down menu in the *Bookmark* dialog box offers several options to organize your new *Bookmark,* as shown in the next illustration and discussed next.

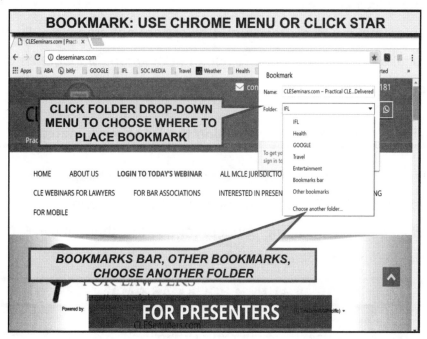

- *Bookmarks bar:* If you choose the *Bookmarks bar* from the drop-down, this allows you to add the new bookmarked site to the bar just below the Address Bar/Omnibox (we recommend this for sites you often visit); you can organize your new bookmarks into one of the folders you created previously by selecting it from the drop-down menu; or select

- *Choose another folder:* This allows you three different options:

  - First, you can place the new bookmarked site into one of the displayed Folders (and click *Done*).

  - Second, if you don't see the appropriate folder in the short list of Folders, you can click *Choose another folder* to see the full list of folders to choose which one you want to enter your new Bookmarked site into (and then click *Save*).

  - Third, you can create a new Folder by clicking either *Bookmarks bar* or *Other bookmarks* from the list and then clicking the *New Folder* button at the bottom of the list of folders (be sure to name it and click *Save*). You can also place your new *Bookmark* into a new sub-folder by clicking a folder from the list and then the *New Folder* button at the bottom of the list of folders and by following the above instructions.

You can name your Folders using any system that is useful to you, such as by jurisdiction (e.g., New Jersey), by subject (e.g., Medical), by types of materials (e.g., Public Records or Forms), or by a combination of a jurisdiction and a subject (e.g., California Statistics).

Unfortunately, *Bookmarks* and *Folders* are not automatically placed into alphabetical order. You will need to use the *Bookmark Manager* as described in the next section.

Organizing Existing Bookmarks Using the Bookmark Manager

To reorganize *Bookmarks* and *Folders* that are already in your *Other bookmarks* or the *Bookmarks bar,* you must click the *Menu* button>*Bookmarks*>*Bookmark manager* (or use the shortcut *Ctrl+Shift+o* for PCs or the shortcut *command+Shift+o* for Macs).

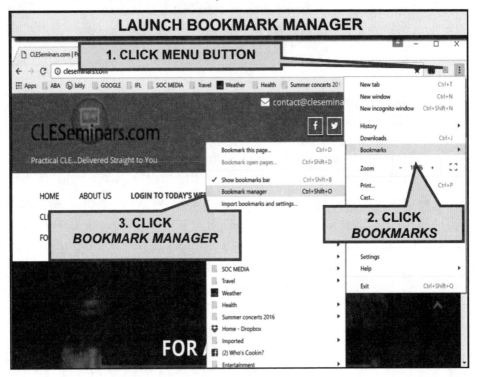

The next illustration shows the *Bookmark Manager.* If you click *Bookmarks bar* (in column one, or the left-most column), the *Folders* and *Bookmarks* you have already placed on your *Bookmarks bar* will fly out to the right (in column two). From here there are various ways to reorganize *Bookmarks* and *Folders.*

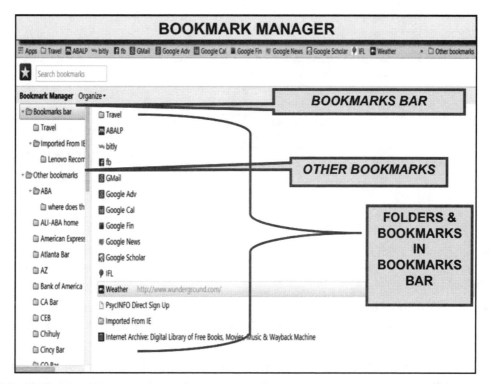

Whether you click *Bookmarks bar*, or *Other bookmarks,* or one of the *Folders* from the left column and then click *Organize* (at the top, next to *Bookmark Manager),* a menu will fly out to the right, with the following options to organize column one:

- *Add page*: This is how you would manually add a new bookmarked site and its URL.
- *Add folder*: This would create a new folder (not a sub-folder) at the end of the Bookmark list, which you would then name and later add Bookmarks into.
- *Cut*: This allows you to *Cut* a bookmark out of one folder and *Paste* it into another. (Note that there is also an option to *Copy* a bookmark from one bookmark folder and *Paste* it into another.)
- *Reorder by [alphabetical] title.*
- *Import bookmarks from HTML file.*
- *Export bookmarks to HTML file.*

Another organizing option is to right-click on an individual folder in the left column. A different menu will fly out to the right as shown in the next illustration.

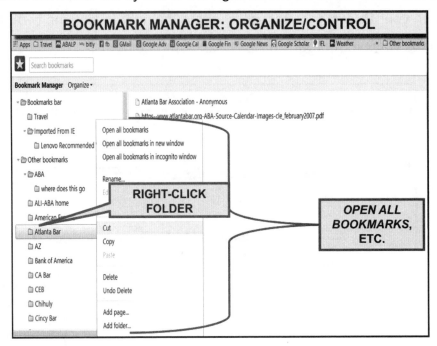

From this menu, you can:

- *Open all bookmarks*: This will open each Bookmark (from the folder you chose) in its own separate tab.

- *Open all bookmarks in new window*: This will do the same as *Open all bookmarks*, but the *Bookmark* tabs will open in a different browser window from the one you are currently using.

- *Open all bookmarks in incognito window*: This will do the same as *Open all bookmarks in new window*, but in a private browsing window (see our earlier discussion about *Incognito browsing* on page 8).

- *Rename* [the folder's title]

- *Cut* [the folder]: You can cut it permanently or you can paste it back in elsewhere as its own folder or a sub-folder.

- *Copy* [the folder]: You can copy the folder to paste it elsewhere so it exists in two different places (as its own folder or a sub-folder).

- *Delete* [the folder]: You can also Undo Delete [the folder].

- *Add page*: This is how you would manually add a new bookmarked site and its URL to a folder.

- *Add folder*: This will actually add a new sub-folder to the folder you have right-clicked. You will need to name this folder and later add Bookmarks to it. (You can also click an existing folder and drag and drop it into another folder so it becomes a sub-folder).

You can also organize the *Bookmarks* in a folder by:

- Left-clicking the folder (e.g., *ABA* in the next illustration) to display the bookmarked sites in that folder (they will appear in a column to the right of the folder column);

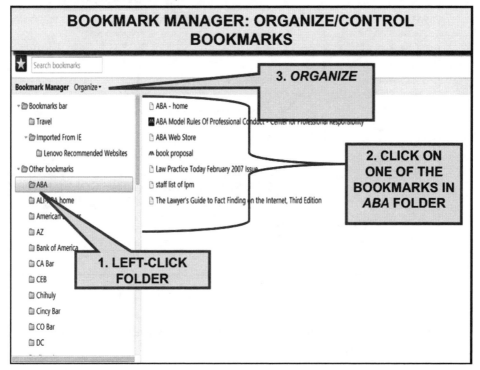

- clicking one of the bookmarks on the right (e.g., *book proposal*) and;
- then clicking *Organize.*

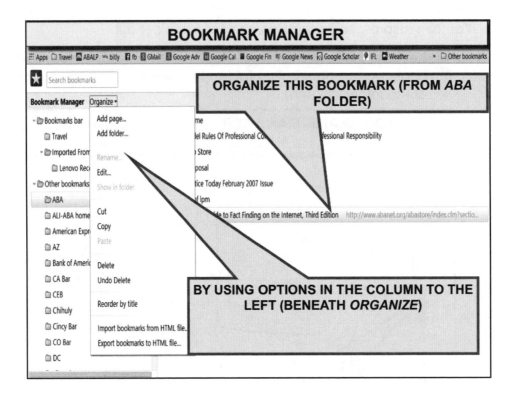

- *Add page*: This is how you would manually add a new bookmarked site and its URL.

- *Add folder*: This would create a new sub-folder within the folder you originally clicked on.

- *Edit* [the bookmark]: You can change the name or URL of the bookmark.

- *Cut* [the bookmark]: You can cut it permanently or you can cut it and (see next)

- *Paste* [the bookmark]: You can paste the Cut bookmark into an existing or new folder.

- *Copy* [the bookmark]: You can copy the bookmark to paste it into two (or more) places (in a folder or a sub-folder).

- *Delete* [the bookmark].

- *Undo Delete* [the bookmark].

- *Reorder* [the bookmarks] *by* [alphabetical] *title*.

- *Import bookmarks from HTML file*.

- *Export bookmarks to HTML file*.

You can also organize the *Bookmarks* in a folder by left-clicking the folder, which will display the bookmarked sites in that folder in a column to the right of the folder column (see next screenshot). Then, you can right-click an individual *Bookmark* to organize the individual *Bookmarks* in many of the same ways noted earlier, but in addition, you can:

- *Open in new tab*: This will open the one Bookmark in a separate Tab.
- *Open in new window*: This will open the one Bookmark in a separate Tab, but in a different browser window from the one you are currently using.
- *Open in incognito window*: This will do the same as *Open in new window*, but in a private browsing window (see our earlier discussion about Incognito browsing on page 8).

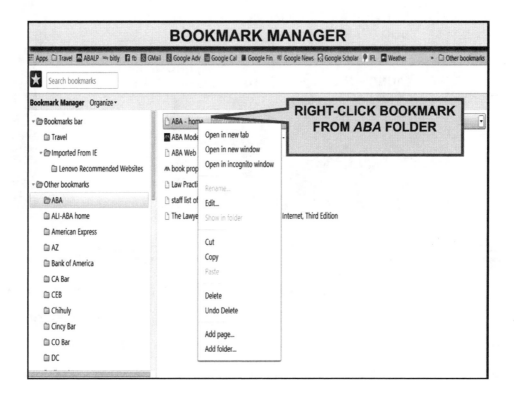

To launch (open in your Web browser) a *Bookmark* so you can visit a website, click *Other Bookmarks*>a specific folder>a specific *Bookmark*.

To close a site, click on the *X* in the upper right-hand corner of its *Tab*.

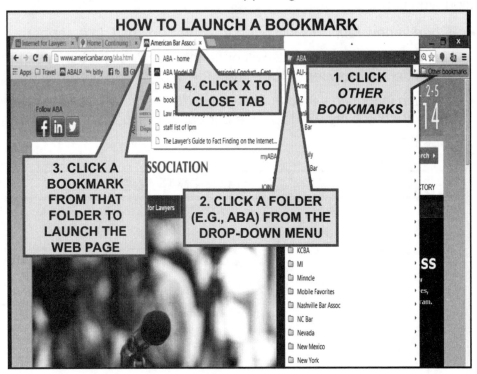

Bookmarks: Backing Up, Syncing, Exporting, and Importing

To avoid losing those *Bookmarks* that you've painstakingly saved and organized (in case your hard drive crashes), it is advisable to save them (i.e., back them up). There are two ways to do this. The first way is to sign into Chrome with your **Google** *Account*. That saves a copy of your *Bookmarks* and other browsing preferences to the cloud (i.e., to Google's servers instead of to your own computer or server) for you to use from any device. This gives you the added benefit of being able to access them for use across all of your devices (e.g., computers, mobile phones, tablets, etc.). (See https://support.google.com/chrome/answer/185277 for details on how to sign into Chrome with your **Google** *Account* and sync your settings across devices.)

If you don't already have a free **Google** *Account*, see

https://support.google.com/accounts/answer/27441 for details about creating one. The

second way is to save *Bookmarks* to removable media (e.g., an external hard drive or

flash drive), to your network, or even to a cloud-based storage space such as *Google*

Drive or *Dropbox*. To do this, click the *Menu* button>*Bookmarks*>*Bookmark manager*

(or use the shortcut *Ctrl+Shift+o* for PCs or the shortcut *Command+Shift+o* for Macs).

Then, select *Organize*. You will see two choices: *Import bookmarks from HTML file* or

Export bookmarks to HTML file. Choose *Export bookmarks to HTML file* and when the

Save As dialog box pops up (as shown in the next illustration) you can decide where

to save the *Bookmarks*.

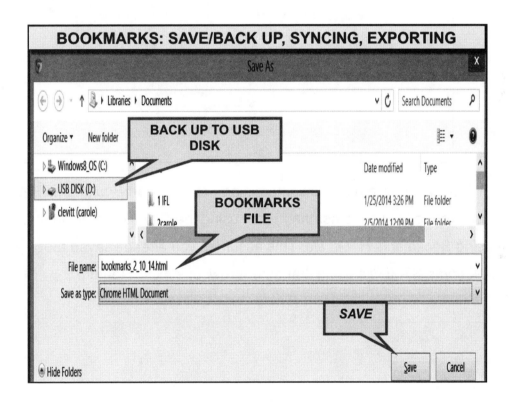

Now that you have saved your *Bookmarks*, you can import them into another

Web browser (like Edge, Internet Explorer, Firefox, Safari, or Opera).

Chrome also has an easy way for you to import *Bookmarks/Favorites* from

Microsoft Internet Explorer directly into Chrome by clicking the *Menu*

icon>*Bookmarks*>*Import bookmarks and settings*. The dialog box shown in the next illustration will then pop up and you can decide which items to import by unchecking the boxes you do not want and then clicking the *Import* button.

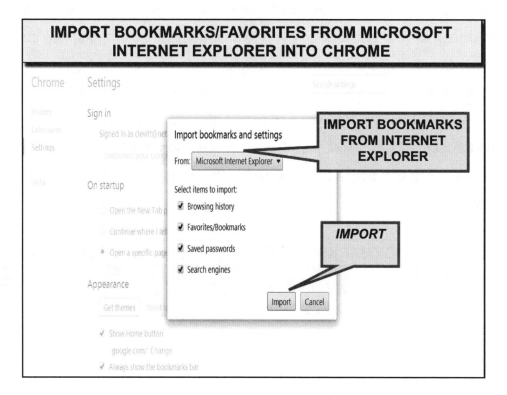

You would also use this same dialog box to import *Bookmarks*/*Favorites* into Chrome from a browser other than IE by using the *From:* drop-down menu and choosing *Bookmarks HTML file*. This assumes you already saved those *Bookmarks* to a *Bookmarks HTML file* using that other browser's export feature.

You can access a list of tabs you have recently closed by clicking on the *Menu* button and then selecting *History* from the list of options. Then you will then see a fly-out menu that is labeled *Recently closed*, which lists all of the tabs and sites you recently visited. Click on any one of the tabs to open that *tab* (or series of tabs) to quickly return to a site (or multiple sites).

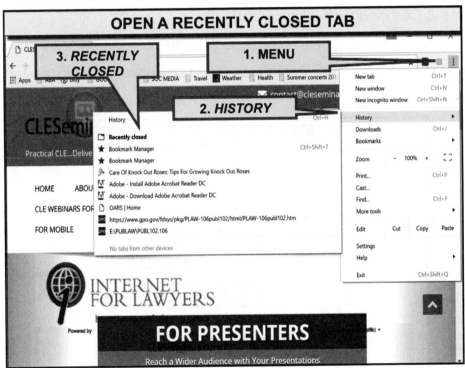

Notice that the tabs are not just to websites. Some of them are to the Google Calendar, Gmail, and even documents you opened in the browser. This is known as your *History*—but only a small portion of it, which we'll discuss in more detail later, on page 30.

The *Zoom* option on the *Menu* fly-out allows you to change the look of your browser window and the Web pages that appear in it.

To make pages easier to read, you can increase or decrease the size of a Web page's text by clicking the – *or* + signs. (PC users who prefer keyboard shortcuts can press *Ctrl+* or *Ctrl-* to zoom in or out of the Web page they are viewing, and Mac users can press *Command+* or *Command-*).

You can also hide all the browser Bars to increase the area of your browser window by clicking the *Full Screen* icon (it's not labeled, but it is located to the right of the *Zoom* plus sign).

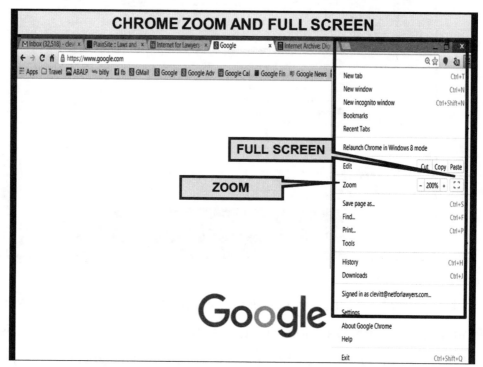

The next illustration shows what the full screen view looks like on a personal computer.

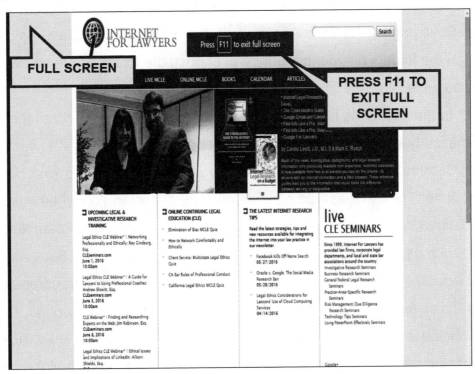

Note, to return to the screen view that shows your browser Bars, personal computer users can right-click anywhere on the screen to bring up a pop up that offers an *Exit full screen* option or click *F11* on their keyboard (depending on your keyboard, you may need to simultaneously click the *Fn* key). For Mac users, even in full screen mode, you will still be able to view the Chrome Menu icon. So, to return to the screen view that shows your browser Bars, simply click the Chrome Menu icon and then the arrows to the right of the *Zoom*.

Saving (Downloading) Web Pages

You can save/download Web pages by clicking Chrome's *Menu* button>*More tools*>*Save page as.* A *Save As* dialog box will pop up. In the *Save As* box, browse through the folders on your hard drive to choose the folder where you want to save the page as a file.

In the *File name* box, you can type a new file name or accept the one that was automatically inserted. In the *Save as type* box, you can choose how to save the page. Clicking the *Save* button in this dialog box adds the file to your computer's hard drive. Note: The *Save as type* choices will vary depending on whether you are saving a traditional Web page or another document format that has been uploaded to the Web, such as PDF or DOCX. To save a PDF, for instance, our *Save as type* choices were *Adobe Acrobat* (because we have Acrobat installed on our computers) or *All Files.* To save a Web page, the first *Save as type* choice is *Webpage, HTML Only.* This choice is used to download the material in a format easily accessible to your word processing software and allows you to later manipulate the text—for example, copy and paste it into one of your documents. It saves just the HTML code (the programming language used to create most Web pages), but not graphics, audio, or other files; most of the Web page's original formatting will be lost.

The second choice is *Webpage, Complete* which saves the HTML code and the individual components (the graphics, audio, and other files) stored in their own folder onto your hard drive and preserves the original formatting. This choice provides the most faithful re-creation of the page as it appeared when it was viewed on the Web and it will also give you a copy of the graphic or audio files that could be taken down by the site's owner and thus be no longer available to you on a subsequent visit to the Web page.

It is important to note that once you've saved a Web page in any of these formats to your own computer, with the right know-how you could alter the text, graphics, audio, or any content of the Web page (stored on your own computer) to say or show whatever you would like. So, if you'll need to use your copy later as proof of something that was posted on the Web page that might have been changed, it is important that you document the date and time you saved the page, what its contents were at that time, etc. Also, burning a copy of the saved file(s) to a DVD (where they cannot be easily changed) that shows the date on which you captured your copy of the page could be useful.

In the next section, we will discuss another way to save a copy of a Web page onto your hard drive that also retains all of the formatting and images.

Printing Web Pages

Chrome's *Print* feature allows you to print a hard copy (paper) or print to a PDF file on your hard drive.

After clicking Chrome's *Menu* button and *Print*, a *Print* dialog box will pop up for you to choose a print location. You can also reach this same *Print* dialog box with the keyboard shortcut *Ctrl+p* for PCs (or *command+p* for Macs). You could print to an attached or networked printer, or save to PDF. If you are signed into your Chrome account, you can also save to **Google Drive**.

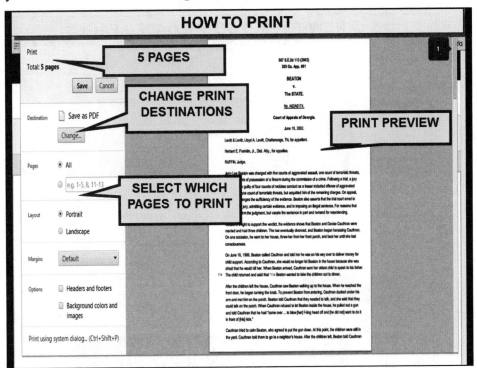

One important thing to note is that a Web "page" can be much longer than just one printed page or one screen. Therefore, clicking *Print* can deliver more pages to your printer than just the content you are viewing in your browser window, so be sure to look at the number of sheets of paper listed at the top. You can print *All* pages or limit the print to specific page numbers or a range of page numbers that you type into the *Pages* box. Look to the right of the *Print* dialog box to see what content will appear on which printed pages.

You can also opt to print a portion of a page or a frame by highlighting the portion first and then right-clicking if using a PC (*control+left click* on a Mac), and then clicking *Print*.

Copy and Paste Portions of a Web page

The easiest way to copy just a portion of a Web page is to highlight it, right-click if using a PC (or *control*-click on a Mac), and then click *Copy*. You can then paste it into your own document (or e-mail), using the shortcut *Ctrl+v* if using a PC or *command+v* if using a Mac.

Where's My Download?

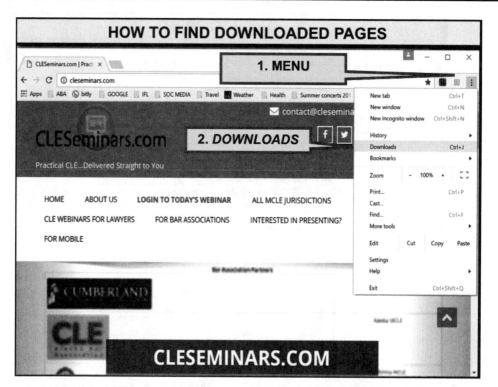

If you downloaded a Web page (or a document from a website) and can't recall where you downloaded it, click *Downloads* from the Chrome *Menu*. A *Downloads* page will appear with a reverse chronological list of files downloaded, a search box, and a three-dot icon (hidden behind the *Open downloads folder* drop-down menu in the next illustration).

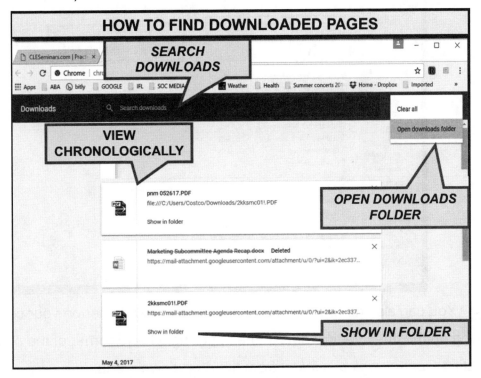

Each downloaded file on the list includes a *Show in folder* link which can be clicked to open the folder on your computer where the file is stored.

If you do not want to scroll through the reverse chronological list for the file you're trying to locate, you can use the search box at the top of the page to locate the file by searching for it by name.

You can also delete all your downloaded files from the list by clicking *Clear all*.

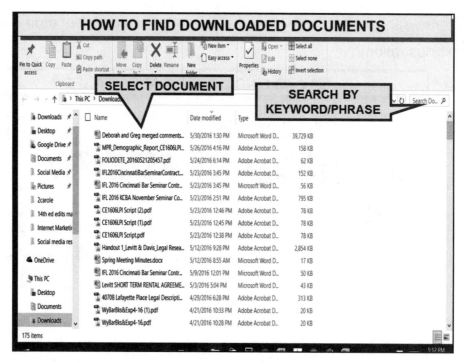

You can also go directly to the default download folder on your computer by clicking on the three vertical dots in the upper-right hand corner of the page and selecting *Open downloads folder* from the drop-down menu.

Once in the *Downloads* folder, you can use Windows' File Explorer capabilities to sort by *Name, Date,* or *Type,* or you can keyword search the downloaded files stored in this folder.

Using the Find Function to Search for a Word or Phrase in a Web Page or Document

Instead of manually scanning through a website to find a specific word/phrase, use Chrome's *Find* feature listed on its *Menu*. This will open a search box near the top of the browser window into which you can enter the keyword or phrase you are looking for. This will take you directly to the location on the Web page with that word/phrase and will highlight it. Clicking the down-arrow button next to the *Find* box takes you directly to the next place your word/phrase appears on that Web page (and highlights it). There is also an up arrow to return to the previous occurrences of your word/phrase.

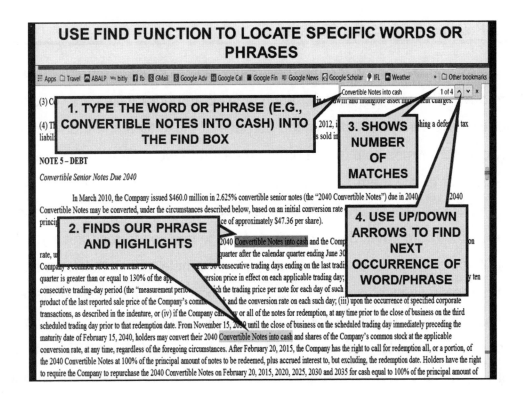

You can also use the keyboard shortcut *Ctrl+f* for PCs or *command+f* for Macs to access the *Find* function while viewing a Web page. This shortcut also works with almost any word processing document, such as a Word or WordPerfect document, an Excel spreadsheet, and even a PDF as long as it's not a scan.

If you are using Chrome on an iPhone, the *Find* function can be invoked by clicking the *Menu* icon (indicated by three vertical dots in the upper right-hand corner of the screen) and then clicking *Find in Page*.

As you are surfing the Internet, your browser saves temporary files on your hard drive. Three of the most common types of temporary files are "Cookies," "Cache," and "History." First, we'll explain the purpose of these files and then we'll look at how they can sometimes help, but at other times hinder you. Finally, we'll discuss how to use them or delete them.

Cookies: These are small pieces of information that (some) websites you visit write to your hard drive. Sites usually use these cookies to recognize you on a return visit. If you order products from Amazon, for example, notice that on a subsequent visit to the site it might welcome you back by name and you may not have to sign in again. This could be helpful because it saves you time. Some advertising banners can also write a cookie to your hard drive to track the effectiveness of a particular ad, while at the same time, that cookie could be used to track your movement around the Internet. This is not really helpful to you.

History: Chrome keeps a 90-day running list of sites you've previously visited. This is helpful if you need to find your way back to a site that you once visited but might have since forgotten its URL or name.

Cache: As you visit various websites, Chrome saves portions of the pages you visit in its cache files for future reference. On return trips to pages you've previously visited, Chrome checks its cache and compares the version found on the Web to the version stored in the cache. If there is no difference in the two versions, Chrome will display the copy stored on your computer, allowing the page to open faster. This too is rather helpful because it aids you to surf more quickly.

However, some people consider these temporary files to be a hindrance because over time they can take up a substantial amount of disk space and slow down your computer. Also, these temporary files provide a "Hansel-and-Gretel-like" trail of your Internet activity. Knowledgeable individuals could follow that trail if they gain access to your computer remotely (by hacking) or by using your computer when you are not around. For these reasons, it's a good idea to delete these files regularly.

To access your personal browser history, click *Menu>History* (or use the shortcut *Ctrl+h* for PCs and *Command+h* for Macs). This will open a new browser *Tab* that lists all of the places you have visited on the Internet (websites and also any cloud products such as **Google Calendar** or **Google Gmail**). Click on any of the history items to return to that location. They are listed in reverse chronological order. There is also a search box in the upper right-hand corner where you can keyword search your history.

Notice the link for *Tabs from other devices*. If you have also logged into Chrome on your mobile device or another computer, the history of those browsing sessions would be available on the computer you are currently browsing with.

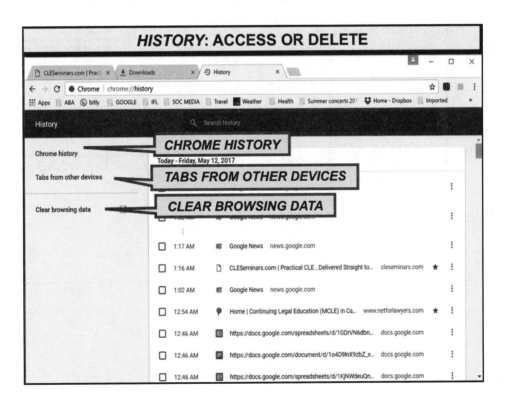

You can clear <u>all</u> of your browsing history by clicking *Clear browsing data*. If you only want to delete selected items, click into the checkbox to the left of the history item(s) you want to delete and then click *Remove selected items.* In the next section, we'll discuss another way to delete your browsing history and also other browsing data.

How to Delete Browsing Data (Cache, Cookies, and Web History, etc.)

Using Chrome's *Menu>More tools>Clear browsing data,* you can delete all types of browsing data, such as *Web history, Cache, Cookies,* etc. Even though you just learned how to delete *Web history* earlier, this tool allows you to delete in a different way: by date—from *the past hour* to *the beginning of time.* By clicking into one or more of the check boxes to the left of the browsing data options and clicking the *Clear browsing data* button at the bottom of the screen, you can delete one, multiple, or all types of browsing data stored in your browser.

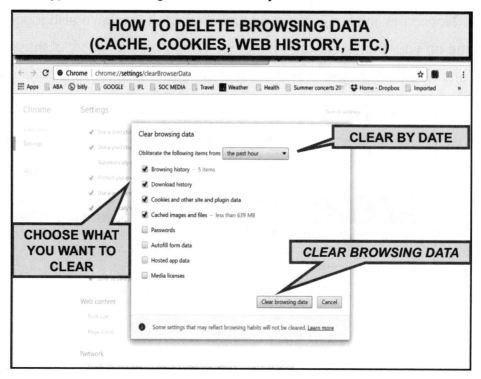

When using **Google** Chrome's *Omnibox* to search, the default search engine is **Google**, of course. However, you can switch to another search engine by clicking the *Menu* button>*Settings*>*Search*>*Set which search engine is used when searching from the omnibox*. From the drop-down menu, you can choose **Yahoo!**, **Bing,** or **AOL**. (No, that's not a typo. As of this writing, AOL is still an option.) You can also access a much larger list of potential sites to use as your default search, by clicking the *Manage search engines* button. (Note that this list includes alternative search engines like **DuckDuckGo**, as well as non-search engine sites such as **AirBnB** and **Amazon**.) Searching from the Omnibox gives you all of the same features as conducting a search from the Search box on the corresponding site. For example, if your browser's Omnibox is set to use **Google** to return search results, you can use all of the advanced search operators and instructions discussed in *Chapter Five*.

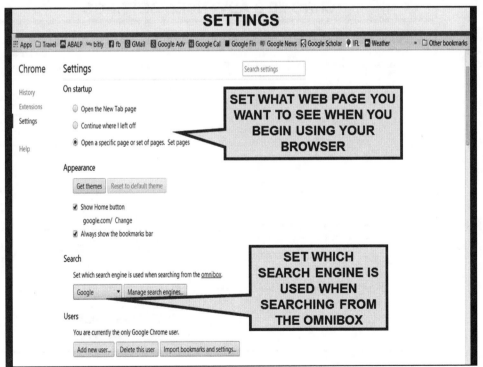

Setting the Default Startup Page

On the *Settings* page, you can also determine what Web page you want to see when you begin using your browser by clicking into the *Open a specific page or set of pages* radio button and then click *Set pages* in the *On startup* section. In the *Add a new page* box that subsequently pops up, type in the URL of the site you want to see as your opening page.

Using Chrome's Advanced Settings

Click the *Show advanced settings* link at the bottom of the *Settings* page to further customize Chrome. The next two illustrations display some of the choices. For example, you can *Enable Autofill to fill out web forms in a single click* or you can set font size from *Very Small* to *Very Large*.

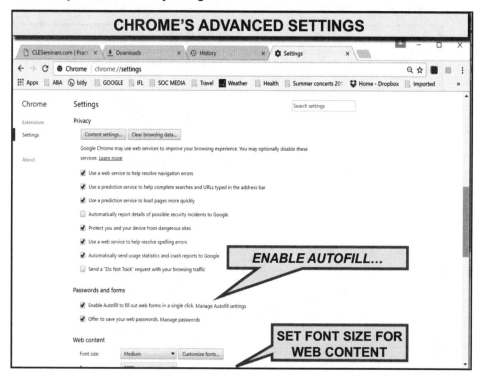

On the *Advanced Settings* page, you can also change where you want Web pages and documents to be downloaded (this sets a default location), or you can place a check mark in the box to the left of *Ask where to save each file before downloading* if you don't want to set a specific default download location.

E-Mailing Web Pages and URLs

You can share information you find on the Internet by e-mailing it to others. One way is to simply highlight the portion of the page you are interested in, or highlight the entire page (by using the *Ctrl+a* shortcut for PCs or the *command+a* shortcut for Macs), and then copy>paste it into the body of an e-mail message. Another way is to highlight>copy>paste the URL into an e-mail so the recipient can connect to the site with just one click on the URL. Finally, if you have previously downloaded a Web page or portion of a page to your hard drive, as discussed on page 24, it can be added to an e-mail as an attachment.

Chapter Two

RELIABILITY AND ADMISSIBILITY OF INFORMATION FROM THE INTERNET

Duty to Google/Due Diligence

Back in 1999, it might have been understandable that a district court would caution against relying on data from the Internet as "voodoo information." *St. Clair v. Johnny's Oyster & Shrimp*, 76 F. Supp. 2d 773, 775 (S.D. Tex. 1999), *available at* http://linkon.in/rIIpRx. Today, fortunately, many judges are not only admitting information from the Internet into evidence, but they are also themselves conducting Internet research to help make judicial decisions, as indicated by the following cases:

- In *Munster v. Groce*, 829 N.E.2d 52 (Ind. Ct. App. 2005), *available at* http://linkon.in/w4RQ0h, the court was incredulous that the plaintiff failed to "Google" the missing defendant (Joe Groce) as part of his due diligence process. The court stated, "We do note that there is no evidence in this case of a public records or Internet search for Groce ... to find him. In fact, we [the judge] discovered, upon entering 'Joe Groce Indiana' into the Google™ search engine, an address for Groce that differed from either address used in this case, as well as an apparent obituary for Groce's mother that listed numerous surviving relatives who might have known his whereabouts." The court upheld the defendant's claim of insufficient service of process and affirmed the dismissal of the case.

- In a similar case the court noted that with ready access to the Internet, the investigative technique of merely calling directory assistance to find a missing defendant has gone "the way of the horse and buggy and the eight-track stereo." *Dubois v. Butler*, 901 So. 2d 1029 (Fla. Dist. Ct. App. 2005), *available at* http://linkon.in/sx8qAS.

- In a tax sale case in Louisiana, an appellate judge upheld the trial court's nullification of the government tax sale where the trial court judge conducted an Internet search and determined that the tax-delinquent owner was "reasonably identifiable" and would have been locatable if the government had run a simple "Internet search" to locate the named mortgagee. (The government claimed to have conducted a public records search and a LexisNexis search.) Part of the basis of the appeal was whether it was appropriate for the trial court judge to have conducted an Internet search of his own. The appeals court stated, "Nevertheless, we find any error the trial court may have committed by conducting the Internet search is harmless, because the trial court's ultimate conclusion that the tax sale violated Dr. Weatherly's due process rights is legally correct." *Weatherly v. Optimum Asset Management*, 928 So. 2d 118 (La. Ct. App. 2005), *available at* http://linkon.in/rsLDNB.

- In 2011, the judge in *Fodor v. Doe*, 3:10-CV-0798-RCJ (VPC) (D. Nev. April 27, 2011), *available at* http://linkon.in/sFTMqW, conducted an Internet search of his own using Google to check the veracity of the plaintiff's claim that a blog posting at issue was the very first search result that came up in a Google search of the plaintiff's name. There is no indication that an appeal was filed alleging that the judge erred by conducting his own Internet search.

Not every court, however, agrees that it is acceptable for judges to conduct their own Internet research. For example, in *Felegi v. Astrue*, Civil No. 2:10-cv-02186 (W.D. Ark., December 16, 2011), *available at* http://linkon.in/2rZWa05, "Instead of further developing the record by recontacting Plaintiff's treating sources, the ALJ 'Googled' Plaintiff's illnesses and found her impairments were not disabling. Such a practice is prohibited."

In their article about the theory of judicial notice in the information age, Jeffrey Belin and Andrew Guthrie Ferguson state that the ease of accessing factual data on the Internet allows judges and litigants to expand the use of judicial notice. The authors seem comfortable with this expansion for certain types of information, such as government websites, mapping services, or official reporting agencies, because they deem them as accurate. But, the authors have significant concerns about taking judicial notice of other information on the Internet since the accuracy of information on the Internet is not uniform. *See* Jeffrey Bellin and Andrew Guthrie Ferguson, "Trial by Google: Judicial Notice in the Information Age," *Northwestern University Law Review*, Vol. 108, No. 4 (2014, Forthcoming), draft *available at* http://linkon.in/1bi9EEI.

Google search results (and the Internet in general), don't always have the answer (or the *right* answer). Sometimes you need to use traditional search methods, especially when a statute instructs you to use a specific search method or resource.

In a 2007 Pennsylvania case, for example, the court ruled that a Google search, which a county performed to locate someone who owed back taxes on a property, was insufficient and instead the county should have used the print telephone book. The court noted that if the county tax collectors had looked up the missing defendant's name in the telephone book, they might have been able to reach him because the phone number in the telephone book was correct while the phone number found by conducting a Google search had been disconnected. The court, taking a very literal approach, concluded that the county's service by publication was insufficient because, by law, it was required to search the countywide telephone book to find an address to mail notice of a tax sale to a delinquent owner. *Fernandez v. Tax Claim Bureau of Northampton County*, 925 A.2d 207 (Penn. Comm. Ct. 2007), *available at* http://linkon.in/vUfekn.

Wikipedia: Inherently Unreliable...Or Not?

Some judges still will not allow information located on the Internet into evidence because they believe it to be inherently unreliable. Information found on **Wikipedia** (http://en.wikipedia.org/wiki/Main_Page) sometimes falls into this category. *See Fleishman v. Cont'l Cas*, No. 09 C 00414 (N.D. Ill. November 22, 2011), *available at* http://linkon.in/fleishmanwiki.

However, some judges have allowed in evidence based on **Wikipedia** entries (see, e.g., *Tiffany v. eBay,* 600 F.3d 93, 96 n. 1 (2d Cir. 2010), *available at* http://linkon.in/tEho9o; *United States v. Lane*, 591 F.3d 921, 924 n. 1 (7th Cir. 2010), *available at* http://linkon.in/tvL3jO; *Brown v. Nucor*, 576 F.3d 149, 156 n. 9 (4th Cir. 2009), *available at* http://linkon.in/vebCXd).

We do not recommend taking information found at **Wikipedia** ("the free encyclopedia that anyone can edit") as absolute fact because anyone can create or edit entries on **Wikipedia** on any given topic. On the other hand, if someone uploads information that is incorrect, it is often the case that someone else will correct it. Therefore, some people find **Wikipedia** to be reliable. It's best to cross-check any information you find on the Internet by using at least two different sources.

Reliability of Information Retrieved from the Internet Archive Site

Getting information admitted into evidence that has been retrieved from the **Internet Archive** (http://www.archive.org; see page 134) can also be a challenge because, to quote the magistrate in *Telewizja Polska USA, Inc. v. Echostar Satellite*, Case No. 02C3293 (N.D. Ill. Oct. 15, 2004), *available at* http://linkon.in/FQ7ojz, "Admittedly, the Internet Archive does not fit neatly into any of the non-exhaustive examples listed in Rule 901; the Internet Archive is a relatively new source for archiving websites. Nevertheless, Plaintiff has presented no evidence that the Internet Archive is unreliable or biased." (See pages 143–146 for a full discussion of this case and why the **Internet Archive** was ultimately not allowed into evidence in this case.)

Reliability/Authenticity of Information Retrieved from Social Networking Sites

Getting information admitted into evidence that has been retrieved from social networking profiles has become another challenge for lawyers, especially if the owner of the profile uses a pseudonym. In *Tienda v. State*, No. 05-09-00553-CR (Tex. App.—Dallas, December 17, 2010) (do not publish), *available at* http://linkon.in/IhNLsK, a murderer appealed his conviction, arguing that the trial court erred in admitting evidence from his **Myspace** profile because there was no proof he had created and maintained that profile. He asserted that the profile had not been authenticated.

Meanwhile, the profile included the following information: the pseudonym "Smiley," which he was known by, and which witnesses testified about; photographs of the appellant, with one displaying his electronic monitor and another his tattoo;

references to the murder; and email addresses incorporating both the alias "Smiley" and his real name.

The Texas Appeals Court, in its 2010 decision, rejected his assertion and affirmed the trial court (that had admitted in the social networking evidence), explaining that:

> The inherent nature of social networking websites encourages members who choose to use pseudonyms to identify themselves by posting profile pictures or descriptions of their physical appearances, personal backgrounds, and lifestyles. This type of individualization is significant in authenticating a particular profile page as having been created by the person depicted in it. The more particular and individualized the information, the greater the support for a reasonable juror's finding that the person depicted supplied the information.

For an opposing decision, see *Griffin v. State*, 419 Md. 343, 19 A.3d 415 (2011), *available at* http://linkon.in/M2Gxl1. In that case, the court, stated:

> We agree with Griffin that the trial judge abused his discretion in admitting the MySpace evidence pursuant to Rule 5-901(b)(4), because the picture of Ms. Barber, coupled with her birth date and location, were not sufficient "distinctive characteristics" on a MySpace profile to authenticate its printout, given the prospect that someone other than Ms. Barber could have not only created the site, but also posted the "snitches get stitches" comment. The potential for abuse and manipulation of a social networking site by someone other than its purported creator and/or user leads to our conclusion that a printout of an image from such a site requires a greater degree of authentication than merely identifying the date of birth of the creator and her visage in a photograph on the site in order to reflect that Ms. Barber was its creator and the author of the "snitches get stitches" language.

A year after the 2011 *Griffin* decision, the Texas Criminal Appeals Court affirmed the 2010 Texas Court of Appeals *Tienda* decision, *Tienda v. State*, 358 S.W.3d 633 (Tex. Crim. App 2012), *available at* http://linkon.in/tienda2012. In addition to all the circumstantial evidence found in the content of Tienda's Myspace profiles (described in the 2010 Texas Court of Appeals *Tienda* opinion on page 41 and in the 2012 Texas Criminal Appeals Court *Tienda* opinion), the Texas Criminal Appeals Court also included data from the Myspace general "Subscriber Reports" associated with Tienda's accounts as circumstantial evidence.

The court noted that the State had taken the extra step (not taken in *Griffin*) to subpoena these general Subscriber Reports from **Myspace.com**, and then explained what the Reports showed: "[T]wo of the MySpace accounts were created by a 'Ron

Mr. T,' and the third by 'Smiley Face,' which is the appellant's widely known nickname. The account holder purported to live in 'D TOWN,' or 'dallas,' and registered the accounts with a 'ronnietiendajr@' or 'smileys_shit@' email address." The Texas Criminal Appeals Court held that, "[t]here are far more circumstantial indicia of authenticity in this case than in *Griffin*—enough, we think, to support a prima facie case that would justify admitting the evidence and submitting the ultimate question of authenticity to the jury." (For details on how to subpoena **Facebook** for the name of an account holder, see page 348.)

Although the Texas Criminal Appeals Court relied on circumstantial evidence, it laid out the three non-exclusive methods that the *Griffin* Maryland Court of Appeals thought were the best ways that social networking postings should be authenticated. We will state them here as they may be useful to you in your cases if you don't want to rely on the vagaries of circumstantial evidence:

- First, the proponent could present the testimony of a witness with knowledge; or, in other words, "ask the purported creator if she indeed created the profile and also if she added the posting in question." That may not be possible where, as here, the State offers the evidence to be authenticated and the purported author is the defendant.

- Second, the proponent could offer the results of an examination of the Internet history or hard drive of the person who is claimed to have created the profile in question to determine whether that person's personal computer was used to originate the evidence at issue.

- Or, third, the proponent could produce information that would link the profile to the alleged person from the appropriate employee of the social networking website corporation.

In 2015, *Griffin* was overruled by *Sublet v. State*, 113 A. 3D 695, 442 MD. 632 (2015), so Maryland now follows the *Tienda* court, *available at* http://linkon.in/sublettienda.

We have collected links to the full decisions and/or orders of these and a number of the other more often-cited cases that involve evidence from social networking sites at http://linkon.in/nvtPSa.

Chapter Three

WHO'S BEHIND A DOMAIN?

If you have visited your subject's website to find contact information, but none is offered or if you need to learn who's behind a website (or at least who the contact person is and their address and telephone number), visit **BetterWhois.com** (http://www.betterwhois.com). It searches multiple domain name registries. After typing in a domain name, click the *Search* button. Depending on the registry, you might be able to view the name, address, and phone number of the registrant and the administrator immediately or you might have to type in a verification code and be taken to a page that shows abbreviated information. If that happens, copy the URL that follows the *"For complete domain details go to"* instruction and paste it into your browser address bar. After you type in another verification code you can view the full details.

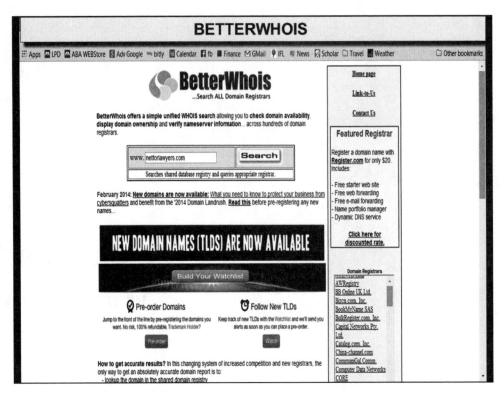

DomainTools (http://www.domaintools.com/) is a cyberforensics company that offers access to some of its search tools for free. Like **BetterWhois**, **DomainTools** searches through multiple registries and shows abbreviated information for free, but if you need to view the details or conduct other search types, you will need to subscribe ($49.95 per month). However, if you need to conduct reverse searches at **DomainTools**, you will need to pay separately per search (http://reversewhois.domaintools.com/). (Detailed results of reverse searches are no longer offered anywhere for free.)

You can use **DomainTools** to search or reverse search (http://reversewhois.domaintools.com/) by one or more of the following criteria to see what domains an individual owns:

- E-mail Address.
- Registrant (Owner) name.
- Whois Record: Note: you can narrow this search by selecting *Contains ALL These Words* or *Does NOT Contain These Words*. This is a full-text keyword search option so our search for *levitt* and *enchanted hills* (our partial address) brought back one correct result.
- Domain Name: Note: you can narrow this search by selecting *Contains*, *Begins With*, *Ends With*, or *Does Not Contain*.

- Extension (TLD).
- Note: you can narrow E-mail Address, Registrant (Owner), and Extension (TLD) searches by selecting Exactly Matching or Does Not Match.

The next illustration shows the results page for our reverse search of *carole levitt* to learn which domains she owns.

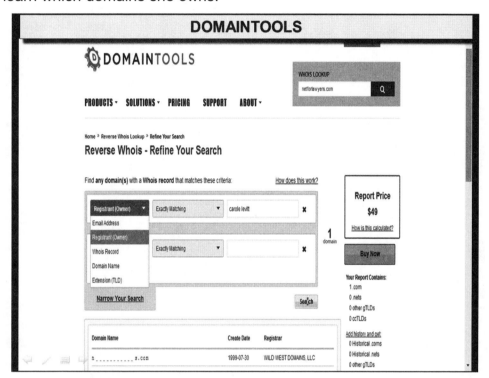

Reverse search pricing is based on the number of results returned by the search and whether you're interested in *Current Domains* or you want to also include *Historical Domains*. Prices start at $49 for results that include 1 to 10 *Current Domains*.

While there is, unfortunately, no single registry website that contains data on all domains, **BetterWhois.com** and **DomainTools** search a large number of the individual registries.

For a full list of ICANN-accredited domain name registrars, visit the **Internic** site (http://www.internic.net/alpha.html). Click the registrar's logo to visit a particular registrar's site and to search each one's database of registered domains.

Chapter Four

NAVIGATING TO INFORMATION ON THE INTERNET

Searchers use one of the following options to locate information on the Internet:

- A search engine (e.g., **Google**, **Bing**, or **Yahoo!**), to type one or more words or phrases into the search engine's search box.

- A Web browser (e.g., Internet Explorer, Safari, Firefox, or Chrome), to type a known website address (URL) into the browser's Address Bar. Note: The Address Bar has evolved (for many browsers) into an "Omnibox" (as explained in *Chapter One*), so it also doubles as a keyword search box.

- A directory, to click through the directory's topics and sub-topics until a relevant topic is found (or to type a keyword into the directory's internal search engine) and then click on the chosen topic for a list of websites.

DIFFERENCES BETWEEN SEARCH ENGINES AND DIRECTORIES

As part of the discussion about locating information on the Internet, the terms "search engine" and "directory" have come to be used interchangeably. However, while both types of websites will help us locate information on specific topics from other websites, they do so in very different ways.

As the name implies, search engines search the content of other Web pages to retrieve results relevant to the keywords we enter into their search boxes. Generally, search engines do not reach out and search live pages on the Internet for every search conducted. To return the majority of its results, a search engine automatically crawls the Internet, sending out "spiders" or "robots" (software programs) that capture the content of the individual Web pages of various websites at a particular point in time. The robot then builds an index of the content of those Web pages. When you conduct a search using a search engine, that search engine looks through its index for the Web pages that are most relevant to the word or phrase that you have typed into the query box.

If something new has been added to a particular site since the robot's last visit, it will not be reflected in your search results. That new information will only show up in search results after the search engine's spider visits the site again and the search engine adds this new information to its index. (While the major search engines are working towards returning results in "real-time," the majority of results are still drawn from these indices.)

After entering your keywords into the search box or Omnibox and pressing *Enter*, the Web pages that the search engine "thinks" are relevant to your search are then displayed in a results list. Sometimes search engine results will be right on target and other times completely irrelevant, even though they contain your exact search terms.

Each search engine has its own robot, which finds different pages on the Internet and treats the information about those pages uniquely when organizing results to any particular search. That said, it is important to point out that **Yahoo!** no longer maintains its own robot. Currently, **Yahoo!** retrieves its search results from a combination of **Google's** and **Bing's** robots. (As of this writing, **Yahoo!** is still in the process of being acquired by **Verizon** and merged with **AOL** into a new entity called **Oath**. It is unclear how **Oath** will generate results from its search engines—or even what the company's combined search engines might be called or if there will be an **Oath** search engine.)

A **Google** search results page may be divided into anywhere from one to four of the following types of results, depending on the search: "Organic Results," "Local Results," "Ads," and "Knowledge Graph" (to be discussed in the next chapter). Every results list will display *Organic Results* in the first column, but not every result will display any of the other three types. If there are any *Local Results* or *Ads* (as is the case in the next illustration), you might not see the *Organic Results* until you scroll down the page (see the illustration after the next one).

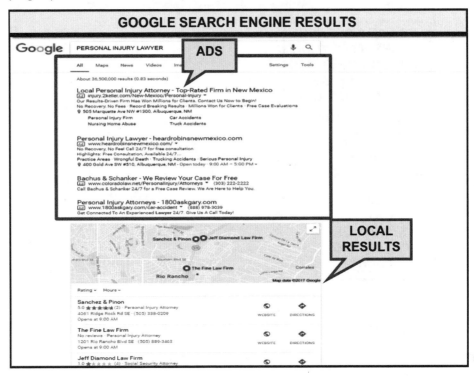

The *Organic Results* (shown in the next illustration), are determined algorithmically by the search engine based on the relevance of your search words to the words in the search engine's index (and hundreds of other criteria). *Organic Results,* as the name implies, are determined naturally and are not paid for or sponsored. They could also be influenced by your past search history (located in your browser history or, if you are logged into your Google account, stored in your Google account).

Similarly, *Local Results* are determined algorithmically by the search engine and cannot be paid for. In addition to *Local Results* showing you information about "what" you searched for, they also include information about the "where" (based on where you connected to the Internet). For example, when we searched for *personal injury lawyer* while connected to the Internet in Rio Rancho, New Mexico, our *Local Results* only displayed information about personal injury lawyers located in Rio Rancho (and the surrounding area of Santa Fe), as well as a map of their office locations (indicated by push-pins that correspond to the address listed to the left of the map). However, if we conduct the same search when we are connected to the Internet in another city, our results will be different because they will show *Local Results* for that city. This is possible because **Google** (and any website) can estimate our general location (usually down to the city or portion of a city) based on characteristics of your Internet connection.

Ads won't appear for every search. For instance, if you search a person's name, an ad will generally not appear, but if you search for practice area-related keywords like *malpractice attorney,* one or more ads will probably appear. *Ads* generally only appear at the top of the search results page now. Unlike *Organic* and *Local Results*, the position (i.e., the rank) of each ad in the *Ads* section is for sale to the highest bidder. There are a number of criteria that go into deciding which ads are placed where in the list, but generally, the more money an advertiser bids, the higher up in the list their ad will appear. *Ads* will not necessarily be local. All of the major search engines offer the ability to purchase *Ads*.

Search engines are useful for general Web searching (when you do not have familiarity with a specific website or a directory) or when you truly want to cast a wide net and not use a selective group of websites found at a directory. But not every Web page is searchable by a search engine—those that are not are said to be "invisible."

SEARCH ENGINES AND THE INVISIBLE WEB

The earliest search engines were not as powerful as the ones we are using today. Those early search engines could only recognize and index a small range of document types—mainly those coded in the Hypertext Markup Language (HTML). Documents posted on the Web in any other file format, such as PowerPoint, Excel, Word, or the Portable Document Format (PDF), were not indexed and, therefore, were invisible to people using search engines to locate information on the Internet. Because these files were "invisible" to search engines, they (and other non-indexed material) were referred to as residing on the "Invisible Web"—meaning all those documents were actually available on the Internet but only if you knew the exact URL to locate them. The documents that were readily retrievable via search engines were, conversely, referred to as residing on the "Visible Web." Fortunately, documents that were once invisible to all search engines are now visible to many and will be discussed later in *Chapter Five*.

Despite the increased function and power of contemporary search engines, there are still many types of documents that are posted on the Internet that remain un-retrievable (invisible) via search engines. Some may be un-retrievable because the search engines do not (yet) know how to access or process the information found on a publicly available source. Or, the search engines may not know that the pages exist for any of the following reasons:

- The information is created dynamically (e.g., information contained in a database; see page 113 for information on how to find databases).
- The pages were not submitted to search engines for indexing and no other sites link to them.
- The robot hasn't yet returned to the site or page for indexing, so it doesn't know something has been revised, added, or deleted.

Additionally, some websites may prefer to make their content available only to registered users (e.g., members of a particular association) or paid subscribers. These resources, being protected by a firewall or otherwise password protected, would never be accessible to a search engine's robot.

As a side note, if you own a website that is not included in the major search engines' search results, and you want it to be, then you should submit your site to be crawled by each search engine's spider. All of the major search engines provide a form on which you can submit your site's URL. Submitting your site adds it to the list of sites the search engine will crawl for inclusion in its indices. The submission pages for the three most popular search engines are as follows:

- **Google** (http://www.google.com/submityourcontent/index.html)
- **Yahoo!** (http://search.yahoo.com/info/submit.html)
- **Bing** (https://ssl.bing.com/webmaster/SubmitSitePage.aspx)

DIRECTORIES

Directories are comprised of website links that are hand selected by people who are (usually) subject specialists. They test and evaluate the sites before adding them to the directory. Therefore, the sites found in an online directory might be more reliable (or at least more selective) than ones found using a search engine. Directories also generally contain fewer sites than search engines.

Some directories only allow users to click through categories until they come to the level that holds the information they are looking for (e.g., *Government>Law>Legal Research>Libraries*). This practice is often referred to as "drilling down." Other directories add the ability to search through their collection of links with an internal search engine to point the users to the category (and specific sites) where they'll find the information they need. This is where some confusion between search engines and directories has arisen. The internal search engine of the directory is searching only through the collection of links assembled by the human editors of that directory, and not an index assembled automatically by search robots or spiders the way a Web search engine does.

As search engines have become more powerful, directories have fallen out of favor. In fact, **Google** shuttered its directory in the summer of 2011 and **Yahoo!** shuttered its directory in December 2014.

DIFFERENCES BETWEEN VARIOUS SEARCH ENGINES

You will often retrieve different results if you conduct the same search using different search engines—because no two search engines work exactly alike. Every search engine has its own spider that it sends out to retrieve information, and every spider treats the information it finds differently when building its respective index. Most general search engines allow users to retrieve information using:

- Keyword searching (e.g., "negligent")
- Phrase searching (e.g., "negligence per se")
- Boolean connectors, such as AND, OR, NOT (e.g., "negligent OR intentional NOT criminal") between search words and phrases

Many pay databases (and some free websites that have internal search engines) allow more flexibility in creating searches, including allowing the use of:

- Proximity connectors, such as NEAR or ADJACENT, inserted in between search words and phrases (e.g., "carole NEAR levitt")
- Field searching, such as entering keywords or dates into Title or Date fields (e.g., "negligence AND date 1999")
- Natural language searching (e.g., "What is negligence?")

Boolean Logic and Connectors: How to Connect Search Words and Phrases

Boolean logic refers to the concept of connecting keywords and phrases together to construct an effective and logical search.

The following words are Boolean connectors:

- AND—A search using the AND connector will result in all of the keywords or phrases showing up in the results list. Typically, **Google** and other major search engines will place the words very near to, if not even adjacent to, one another.
- OR—A search using the OR connector will result in either one or more (or all) of the keywords or phrases showing up in the results list.
- NOT—A search using the NOT connector excludes words or phrases from the search results when placed before the word you want to exclude. Some search engines and sites use AND NOT, or BUT NOT, or the minus sign (-) instead of NOT.

You will get vastly different results if you use the *AND* Boolean connector instead of the *OR,* or if you use the *NOT* connector instead of the *AND*, so be sure you understand the differences before you begin constructing your search.

While most major search engines support these three Boolean connectors, there can be some differences. For example, to exclude a search term (or phrase) at **Google**, you must precede the search term or phrase with a *minus sign* (-). **Bing** and **Yahoo!** seem to be flipping back and forth on how to exclude a search term (or phrase). They both currently accept the *minus sign*, while only **Bing** recognizes *NOT* (which must be in uppercase letters). (Recently both had accepted either the *minus sign* or *NOT*.) A peculiarity of **Yahoo!**, however, is that even if you use the *minus sign* to exclude a word or phrase from your search, they might still appear in the ads that accompany your search results. **Google**, **Bing,** and **Yahoo!** all require you to type the *OR* Boolean connector in uppercase letters. For more details on which search engines employ which Boolean connectors, see the comparison chart discussed on page 62 and enlarged on the last page of this book.

Boolean Connector "Defaults"

Each search engine has a "default" Boolean connector, with most defaulting to *AND*, so if you type more than one word (or phrase) into a search engine's query box and do not add a Boolean connector between each keyword or phrase, the search engine will add its default Boolean connector (behind the scenes) in between your keywords or phrases. However, some search engines and some websites' internal search engines default to *OR* (for example, **Twitter**). You can override a default by simply typing in the Boolean connector that you want to use in between each keyword or phrase.

Phrase Searching

Most search engines allow you to search two or more keywords as phrases by surrounding them with quotation marks (e.g., *"dog law"* or *"negligence per se"*). This is a more limiting search than a search employing the *AND* Boolean connector. The phrase search locates your terms in the exact order in which you have entered them and with no intervening words between the keywords you have enclosed in quotation marks. It also limits its search to the exact spelling of the words in the phrase. So, will a search for the phrase *"dog law"* find documents with either of the following phrases?

- *The law of a dog*
- *The dog in Western law*

The answer is *no*, because the quotation marks instruct the search engine to search for documents with both of the words *dog* **and** *law* next to one another and in that exact order.

Many researchers searching for documents that include a proper name conduct a phrase search for that name, such as *"carole levitt."* However, this will only retrieve results that refer to *Carole Levitt* spelled that exact way, in that exact order, and with no intervening words, such as middle names or middle initials. What is missing from this search then are documents on the Web that refer to *Carole Levitt* as: *Carole A. Levitt*; *Carole Ann Levitt*; *Levitt, Carole A.*; *Levitt, Carole*; *Levitt,* and *Carole Ann,* or that contain common misspellings of Carole's name (*Carol Levitt* or *Carole Leavitt*). A better search for proper names would be to use a Proximity connector between the first and last name, as we will discuss in the next section.

Proximity Connectors

Some search engines and websites' internal search engines allow you to use Proximity connectors to indicate that you want a keyword or phrase to appear close to another keyword or phrase in a returned document. The closer together keywords appear in a document, the more likely they are related to one another, which is probably more in line with how you intended them to be.

One of the Proximity connectors used by some free search engines and some websites' internal search engines is *NEAR*. There is no standard, however, for how near *NEAR* means. For example, placing the *NEAR* connector between words (or phrases) when using **FindLaw's** case law databases, means that the site will return results where the search terms are on the same page, "close together," while a different search engine might deem *NEAR* to mean within three words of each other or in the same paragraph.

Google, **Bing**, and **Yahoo!'s** help pages do not use the words "Proximity connectors," but placing an asterisk in between words at **Bing** and **Yahoo!** seems to work as a *NEAR*-type Proximity search, although we don't know exactly how "near" our words will be to each other. You cannot use multiple asterisks to try to control the number of words between each keyword. It appears that you can use the asterisk with keywords and/or phrases.

Google's help page explains that you can "Put a * in your word or phrase where you want to leave a placeholder." **Google's** example is: "largest * in the world".

As you'd expect, this search returns a list of some of the world's largest things (e.g., deserts, lakes, countries, armies).

Practically all pay databases, but only some free search engines, allow you to dictate the exact proximity between words, usually by using the Proximity connector *within*/n (e.g., *within2*, *within10* or *w/2*, *w/10*).

Google is one of the few free search engines that allows you to dictate an exact proximity separating your keywords, but most searchers do not know about it. **Google** uses the word *AROUND* for its Proximity connector instead of the usual "within" and it must be entered in uppercase letters, with the number of words that you decide you want your keywords to be from each other placed within parentheses. Your search would look like this:

carole AROUND(2) levitt

According to Dan Russell, **Google's** Uber Tech Lead for Search Quality and User Happiness, the AROUND feature has been around "for ... oh ... the past 5 or 6 years. [But it] turns out that nobody ever bothered to write much about it." Russell took the wraps off the feature in a fall 2010 blog post (http://linkon.in/dVc69f). Perhaps the reason "nobody ever bothered to write about it" is because there is NO documentation of the *AROUND* function in **Google's** "Web Search Help" section. There is a mention of the *AROUND* proximity search function in the "Web Search "Help Forums," but it didn't appear there until January 14, 2011.

When using the AROUND connector, in addition to instructing **Google** how close you want your words, you are also instructing Google to search for your keywords in any order and, as with any **Google** search, your keywords will be spelled the exact way you typed them but will also include common variations of their spellings. Thus, a search for *carole AROUND(2) levitt* could bring back any of the following results:

- Carole Levitt: no words between our keywords and the name spelled exactly as we typed it
- Carole A. Levitt: one word (the middle initial A) between our keywords and the name spelled exactly as we typed it
- Carole Ann Levitt (one word (the middle name Ann) between our keywords and the name spelled exactly as we typed it
- Carol Suzanne Levitt: one word (the middle name Suzanne) between our keywords and the name Carol was retrieved instead of Carole
- Alain Levit, Carol Lim: no words between our keywords and the name Levit was retrieved instead of Levitt
- Joseph Gordon-Levitt inexplicably performing Carole King's classic "You Make: two words (inexplicably performing) between our keywords

To conduct a more targeted search, try enclosing your search terms within quotation marks. This search instructs Google to return results where the keywords are spelled this exact way but still offers the flexibility of the proximity connector:

"carole" AROUND(2) "levitt"

For example, this search will capture results where *levitt* preceded *carole* and the names were spelled exactly that way.

As you can see in our previous example, proximity searching is especially useful for proper name searches where various documents on the Web could refer to the same person in a variety of ways, and it can also be superior to phrase searching and Boolean searching. For instance, if you had searched this proper name as *carole levitt* (which would have instructed the search engine to add the *AND* Boolean connector between the two names), this might have brought back results where the keyword *carole* was paragraphs away from the keyword *levitt*, thus bringing back irrelevant results such as *Carole Smith* and *Lloyd Levitt*. If you had searched this proper name as a phrase search (*"carole levitt"*), this may have been too narrow and missed some relevant results (ones with her middle name or middle initial, for example).

Searching with Wildcards

Most pay databases (and some websites' internal search engines) use the asterisk or the exclamation point to take the place of one or more characters in a search term. The asterisk and the exclamation point are referred to as "wildcards." A wildcard can be used at the end of a word to stem or extend the root of a word so that a search for *child** would find *child, child's, children*, and so on, or it can be used in the middle of a word to take the place of any character—this is useful when the same word is spelled different ways (e.g., a search for *mari*uana* would find *marijuana* or *marihuana*). Some sites also allow you to use multiple wildcards in the middle of a word to take the place of multiple characters.

However, **Google**, **Bing**, **and Yahoo!** do not use the asterisk as a wildcard to stem your search terms because they automatically stem words. For example, they will automatically search for the plural of a word when you enter the singular into the search box.

To complicate matters, **Google** <u>does</u> use the asterisk, but to take the place of one or more keywords (not characters) in a search, as explained earlier in the section about Proximity connectors (page 57). The Help pages at **Bing** and **Yahoo!** do not tell us if they use the asterisk to take the place of one or more keywords but using the asterisk seems to work.

Organizing Your Search with Parentheses

Parentheses are used to clarify a complex Boolean search or to change the "logic" of the Boolean logic. Unfortunately, of the major search engines, only **Bing** and **Yahoo!** recognize parentheses as a search parameter. Using parentheses at **Bing** and **Yahoo!** is optional, except when you are combining your *OR* search with another Boolean connector (even the "invisible" default *AND*). Failing to use parentheses will bring back results that make little sense. Here is a sample **Bing/Yahoo!** search:

"homeland security" (nevada OR oregon)

The parentheses (in the previous example) instruct **Bing/Yahoo!** as to which search terms to group together. So, your search results would include the phrase *"homeland security"* and *nevada OR Oregon. Because OR is actually an AND/OR,* using the parentheses will bring back any of these results:

- *"homeland security" AND Nevada*
- *"homeland security" AND Oregon*
- *"homeland security" AND Oregon AND Nevada*

Google does not recognize parentheses to group search terms. Since **Google** ignores most punctuation, we would expect a **Google** search for *"homeland security" (nevada OR oregon)* to return the same results as a **Google** search for *"homeland security" nevada OR oregon*. However, in our test searches, while the first two dozen or so results were the same, we did see small variations in the results through result 100.

Because **Google** prioritizes the *OR* connector over the *AND* connector, **Google** groups the keywords and connectors for the search for *"homeland security" nevada OR oregon* the same as **Bing/Yahoo!** treat the search keywords and connectors for the search for *"homeland security" (nevada OR oregon)*.

As we've discussed, each search engine offers some different features and different ways of implementing similar features. While every search engine offers help pages, they are often only somewhat helpful. For that reason, we have created a handy chart (http://linkon.in/8XULKZ) to illustrate a comparison between some of the most popular search engines—and to clarify some areas where the search engines' own help pages are vague or silent. The chart includes information on the search engines' *Default Boolean Connector*, *Other Boolean Connectors Recognized*, *Proximity Connector*, availability of *Cached Pages*, and more. It also includes direct links to each search engine's help pages. (See the back of this book for an enlarged, tear-out version of this chart.)

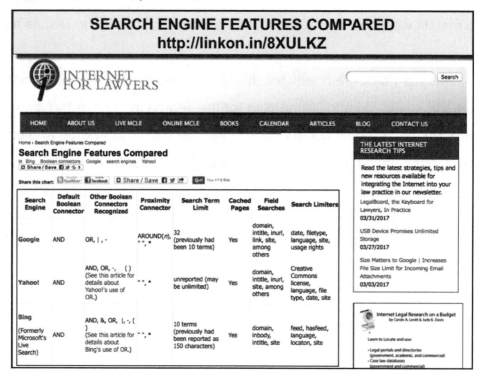

Chapter Five

SEARCH ENGINES: GOOGLE

There are literally thousands of search engines on the Internet—each of which claims to deliver the most relevant results. While we have not reviewed all of them, we have compiled a list of our favorite search engines and directories (in order of our preference). Google, which we'll discuss in this chapter, is our top pick for general research because:

- Many believe that **Google** delivers some of the most relevant results of any major search engine.
- Between two-thirds and three-quarters of all English language searches are run through **Google** in one way or another.
- A majority of the advanced search features found at many of the major search engines were first introduced by **Google** and later adopted by those other search engines.

In the next chapter, we'll discuss the combination of **Yahoo!** and **Bing,** which comes in a close second.

As we will discuss in the next chapter, while **Yahoo!** and **Bing** have made major advances in the past few years, we still feel that **Google** allows us to create the most targeted searches and consistently returns the most useful results. That said, no one search engine holds the best answer for every search. There are some occasions when we have found the precise answer we've needed using a search engine other than **Google**.

Google employs hundreds of factors to determine what it believes are the most relevant results for a particular search. This includes tailoring your search results based on your past web search history and pages you have visited. Some of this information is stored on your computer, as part of your browser "History" and some might be stored as part of your free **Google** Account (if you have one; and if you have a **Gmail** address you have one). See page 31 for information on clearing your browser History and https://support.google.com/accounts/answer/465 for information on deleting your **Google** Account History.

Other factors include the proprietary "PageRank" technology it employs to determine a Web page's relevance and importance based on each page's content, the number and types of other Web pages that link to it (inbound links), a limited number of HTML tags (e.g., Title) and page attributes (e.g., ALT), recency of content update, whether a page employs pop-up ads, and hundreds of other criteria. **Google** no longer documents how often its spider updates the entirety of its index. In the past, published reports indicated the index was updated about every 28 days. Some websites are spidered more frequently—with some spidered every day (or multiple times per day).

Google also offers many advanced features and search functions that help it return relevant results. **Google** pioneered many of these advanced features, and when we wrote the first edition of this book in 1999, **Google** was the only search engine that offered most of them. For instance, **Google** was the first major search engine to search and index many types of files (other than just HTML Web pages (such as Microsoft Word documents, and PDFs) that until then had been relegated to the "Invisible Web." (In other words, although the documents were on the Web, search engines could not locate them so they were invisible to researchers.)

In the intervening years, **Google's** basic and advanced search features have become the *de facto* search industry standards, as the other major search engines have developed and implemented similar features. So, as we discuss the use of these basic and advanced search features, we will use **Google** to illustrate those features and to "stand in" for those other search engines as well. Where there are significant differences between search engines, we will point those out.

Google's Boolean default connector is *AND*. Therefore, there is no need to type the word *AND* between keywords to connect them. **Google** will automatically do this behind the scenes for you.

Google is not case sensitive with regards to your search terms, so there is no need to capitalize proper names. (However, **Google** is case sensitive with regards to certain search "instructions" that are used to create more targeted searches, which we will discuss on page 78.)

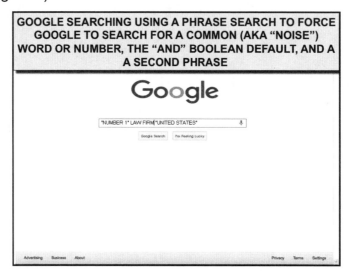

GOOGLE SEARCHING USING A PHRASE SEARCH TO FORCE GOOGLE TO SEARCH FOR A COMMON (AKA "NOISE") WORD OR NUMBER, THE "AND" BOOLEAN DEFAULT, AND A A SECOND PHRASE

Google automatically excludes common ("noise") words and also numbers (e.g., *the* or *1*) unless you enclose them in quotation marks (such as *"number 1"* seen in the previous illustration), or **Google** determines that the noise word is integral to your search terms (as seen in the next illustration).

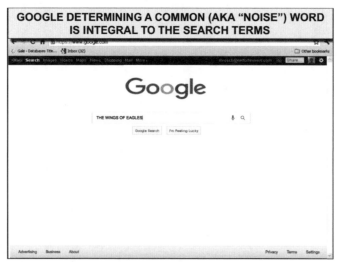

GOOGLE DETERMINING A COMMON (AKA "NOISE") WORD IS INTEGRAL TO THE SEARCH TERMS

For example, a search for the words *The Wings of Eagles* (without quotation marks) at **Google** returns a list of results where all of those keywords (including *the* and *of*) are boldfaced as part of the title of a John Wayne film.

Yahoo!, on the other hand, seemingly excludes no words from its search results but does not recognize when noise words are integral to the result. If you were to search for *the wings of eagles* at **Yahoo!** (without quotation marks), the results would include not just Web pages where the film's title appears but also Web pages that included all of those words—with the words **of** and **the** boldfaced as keywords but not in connection with any of the other keywords.

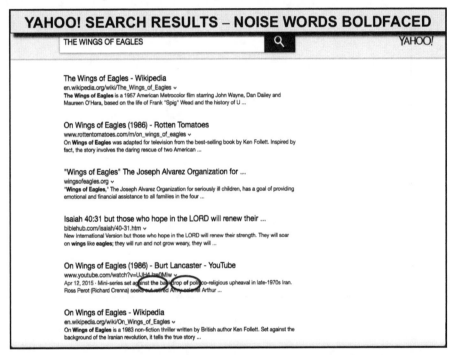

This exclusion rule can be overridden by enclosing your search terms in quotation marks or using the *Verbatim* filter as discussed on page 74.

There are four primary methods of searching **Google**, three of which are displayed on its homepage (as seen in the next illustration):

- *Google Search* (with a list of *Predictive Keyword Suggestions*)
- *I'm Feeling Lucky* (see page 75)
- *Voice Search* (see page 71)

Later, we will discuss the fourth searching method that is found on **Google's** *Advanced Search* page.

After you begin typing characters into the search box on the homepage, predictive keyword search suggestions begin to appear beneath the search box in a list. These are determined by some mix of preset **Google** "guesses" of popular searches, the searcher's prior Web search history, and the searcher's geographical location (based on **Google's** automatic detection of the Internet connection). It is unclear how these criteria are weighted in determining the list of suggestions, however.

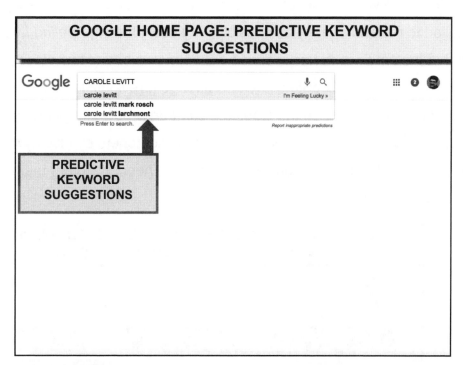

Note: In our test searches, when we used **Chrome** as our browser, the predictive keyword search suggestions list showed on both of our Windows 10 machines and on our Mac laptop. But, when we used **Firefox** as our browser, the predictive keyword search suggestions list failed to show on one of our Windows10 machines, despite having the same version of **Firefox** on both machines. In these same test seaches, the *Google Search* and *I'm Feeling Lucky* buttons were displayed at the bottom of the list of predictive keyword suggestions.

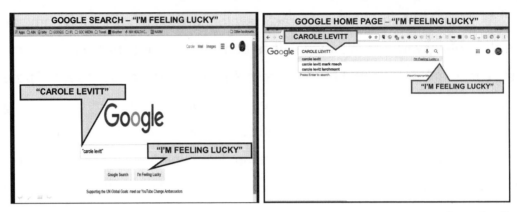

For those who run out of patience when they see too many results—feeling compelled to review as many as possible—try using the *I'm Feeling Lucky* button. (Note that the *I'm Feeling* Lucky option will appear in one of two place—either below the search box on the **Google** search homepage [previous, left illustration] or to the right of each search term on the *Google Instant* drop-down list, when you hover over each one [previous right illustration].) It rewards searchers by displaying just one site instead of a results list. It's often just the one they need. No other major search engine offers a similar function.

Voice Search: For those who would rather talk to their computers than type, **Google** has introduced **Voice Search**. (Using **Voice Search** requires either a built-in or added-on microphone.) To use **Voice Search**, click the microphone icon on the right-hand side of the search box and a *Search by Voice* will pop up. You will then be prompted to begin speaking your search query.

While the voice recognition of **Voice Search** is not 100 percent accurate, with careful enunciation we were able to get results for our *Carole Levitt* query. Even though the transcribed keywords did not include *Carole* with an *e*, results with that spelling were included further down the first page of results.

After you click *Google Search*, you will see a "traditional" results page (shown in the next illustration) or one that includes the *Knowledge Graph*, which we will discuss on page 74. Regardless of which results page is displayed, the default display of results is always *All.* The *All* results include all of the different types of resources in the full **Google** index. You can narrow down your search results to a particular type of resource by clicking one of the other filter links across the top, such as *News*, *Images*, *Videos, Shopping*, *More*, or *Tools.* (**Google** often experiments with its interface, so the order of these filters might vary on your results page.)

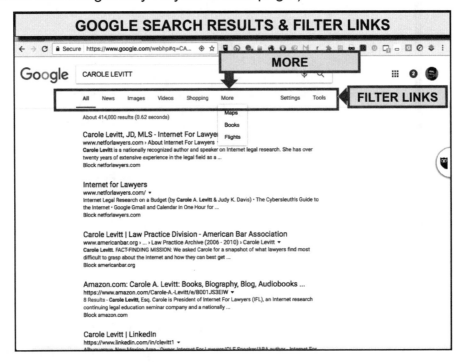

If you click the *More* link, a drop-down menu is displayed, from which you can narrow your search results further to:

- Maps
- Books
- Flights

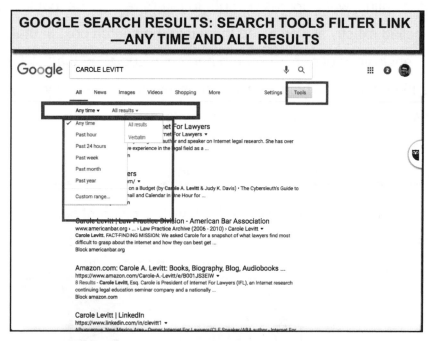

If you click the *Tools* link (on the **Google** *Search* results page), an *Any time* drop-down menu is displayed, from which you can narrow (or expand) your search results by time (or date or date range), such as by:

- *Any time* (this is the default)
- *Past hour*
- *Past 24 hours*
- *Past week*
- *Past month*
- *Past year*
- *Custom range*

The time filters aren't as useful as they first appear because most Web pages do not include a time or date. If that's the case, **Google** will either assign a date based on the date their web crawling robot found and indexed the page or based on a date mentioned somewhere in the text of the page (which could be days, weeks, or even years before the date the page was published to the Web). The time and date filters work much better in the **Google** *News* database because news articles always include a publication date. The date filters also work much better in the **Google** *Scholar* database because court opinions and periodical articles always include a publication date.

The *Tools* link offers a second drop-down menu, labeled *All results,* that offers a *Verbatim* option, which forces **Google** to return results that contain your search terms, spelled exactly as you typed them into the search box. In that way, it functions similar to enclosing your entire search phrase in quotation marks. The *All results* option is the default and brings back results that also include synonyms for your keywords and alternative spellings for your keywords.

Google Search Results: Knowledge Graph

As discussed earlier, **Google** displays two different search results, the traditional (shown previously) and the one with a *Knowledge Graph* (shown next).

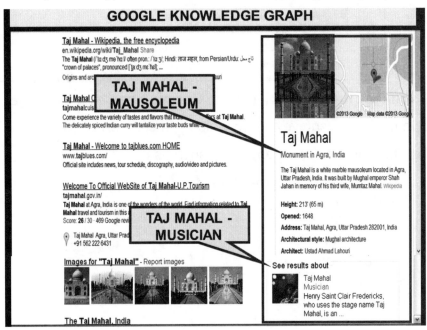

In an effort to "instantly get information relevant to your query," **Google** introduced its *Knowledge Graph* in May 2012 and placed it in a column on the right-hand side of the search results. However, it only appears for selected searches. The *Knowledge Graph* draws those results from a separate database of more than 500 million entries to help put search results for potentially ambiguous queries into context and to highlight information about people, places, and things of note. Results for a search for *Taj Mahal*, for example, would return categorized results for the monument in India, or a Grammy Award-winning musician, or possibly even a casino in Atlantic City, New Jersey.

Most of the major search engines offer *Advanced Search* templates, where users can create very sophisticated Boolean searches or search for information from very specific sources by entering information into the *Advanced Search* template or choosing options from various drop-down menus.

Although advanced type searches can be accomplished by entering specific search "instructions" into the search box on **Google's** homepage (as explained in more detail on page 78) or into the Chrome *Omnibox*, we find it more convenient to use the *Advanced Search* page template.

Throughout the first decade of its existence, **Google** had placed a prominent link to its VERY useful *Advanced Search* page directly to the right of the search box. The 2011–2013 redesigns of the homepage took that link away and pushed access to the *Advanced Search* page to behind the often-overlooked *Settings* link in the lower right-hand corner of the homepage or the *Settings* menu at the top right of your search results page (below the search box) once you run a search.

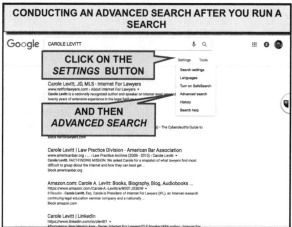

With this change, **Google** joined other search engines, such as **Yahoo!**, that hide their *Advanced Search* option. (We will reveal **Yahoo!**'s Advanced Search option hiding place later when we discuss some other search engines at more length in *Chapter Six*.)

You can also reach the *Advanced Search* page directly at http://www.google.com/advanced_search.

We'll use the **Google** *Advanced Search* page to illustrate how the tools on the *Advanced Search* template can be used to create more effective searches. It offers a query template that makes Boolean and phrase searching easier (as illustrated in the next image) by entering your search terms into one or more of the following search boxes: *all these words, this exact word or phrase, any of these words,* and *none of these words*. Note: If you enter more than one phrase into the *exact word or phrase* box, you will need to enclose each phrase in quotation marks.

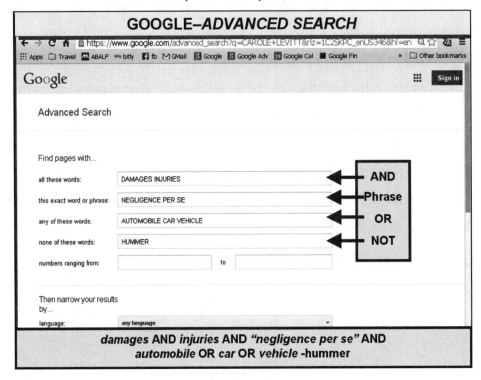

The *Advanced Search* template also offers more sophisticated search tools, such as the ability to search by:

- *Language* (returns pages written in any language or a specific language)
- *Region* (returns results from a specific country—choose any region to indicate all countries, or select a specific country from the drop-down list)
- *Last update* (returns results that were updated within a set time frame— selected from available options on a drop-down menu)
- *Site or domain* (returns results from a specific site or domain—discussed in detail later in this chapter, beginning on page 77)
- *Terms appearing* (returns results where your keywords appear in specific places of the referenced page—e.g., in the title of the page, in links to the page)
- *File type* (returns results in any file format or only a specific format – e.g., Adobe Acrobat PDF)
- *Usage rights* (returns results that are free to use or share; free to use or share, even commercially; free to use, share, or modify; free to use, share, or modify, even commercially, *or* not filtered by license *at all)*

The following is an example of a sophisticated *Advanced Search* where we entered one search term into the *all these words* search box and selected options from four different drop-down menus to narrow down our search results. We created a search for the word *negligence* in the *title* of a document where the document must be in the *Word file format*, is written in *English,* and for which **Google** has detected an update in the *past year*.

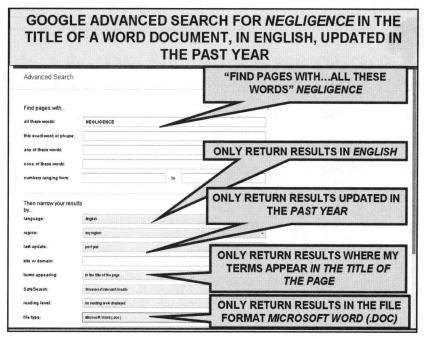

If you have ever had trouble locating information on a specific website/domain, but you are certain the information is on that site, you might have better luck using **Google's** *Then narrow your results by site or domain* search feature (located on the *Advanced Search* page) rather than a site's own internal search engine. Using the *Then narrow your results by site or domain* search feature, you can essentially superimpose the **Google** search engine over another website (assuming it's a site that **Google** has previously indexed).

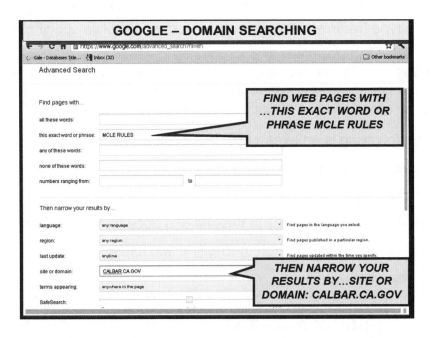

You can combine **Google's** *Then narrow your results by site or domain* feature with keywords and phrases entered into the *Advanced Search* page's query boxes to restrict a **Google** search to only a specific domain that you've specified. This is achieved by entering the URL of the site you want to search into the *Then narrow your results by site or domain* query box (see the previous illustration).

If you wanted to type the *site or domain* search "instruction" into the **Google** homepage search box instead of using the *Advanced Search page* (shown in the previous illustration), it would look like this:

site:calbar.ca.gov "mcle rules"

Note: The instruction, *site:* must be in lowercase letters. (All **Google** instructions must be in lowercase letters.)

Google used to offer the option to <u>exclude</u> an entire site or domain with the *Domain…Don't return results from the site or domain* instruction from a drop-down menu that accompanied this feature. Now, to exclude a certain domain from your search, you must type the instruction directly into **Google's** search box yourself (*-site:sitetoexclude.com*), as illustrated in the prior screen shot. The instruction *-site :* must be in lowercase.

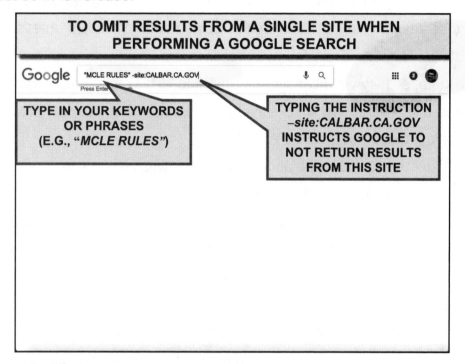

The ability to limit your results to a certain domain or site is accomplished in a very similar manner at **Yahoo!** and **Bing.** **Bing** and **Yahoo!** are also, once again, offering the ability to exclude a domain or site from results using the minus sign the same way it is used at **Google**.

Google has bundled a number of informational searches that retrieve details about a particular website into one search. Links to conduct these informational searches can be generated by first searching for *info:sitename*. The individual searches are:

- *Show Google's cache of* sitename
- *Find web pages that are similar to* sitename
- *Find web pages from the site* sitename
- *Find web pages that contain the term* "sitename"

Using Google's Advanced Search File Type Drop-Down Menu to Locate a Specific File Type

In 2001, **Google** began indexing file types created in Adobe's popular Portable Document Format (PDF). This marked one of the first significant steps to indexing anything other than HTML documents on the Web and was a boon to all Web searchers. They could now find the PDF documents that numerous government agencies, researchers, and universities posted to the Web. Up until 2001, these file formats could not be easily found by researchers because search engines did not index them, so they were considered "invisible." This moved many documents from the "Invisible Web" to the "Visible Web." (See page 52 in *Chapter Four* for more information about the "Invisible Web.")

Later in 2001, **Google** announced that it was also able to index files stored in file formats generated by the Microsoft Office suite (e.g., Word, Excel, and PowerPoint), all of which had been invisible up until then. Eventually, other major search engines like **Yahoo!**, **Bing**, and **USA.gov** added the ability to index these file formats as **Google** had done and return them in relevant searches. Using the *File Type* drop-down menu, which can be found on each search engine's respective *Advanced Search* page, allows you to limit a search to the file type you select.

In 2007, Microsoft introduced a new Extensible Markup Language (XML)-based file type that ends with the letter "x" to its Office suite. So now, in addition to the previous *doc*, *xls*, and *ppt* file extensions for Word, Excel, and PowerPoint (respectively), newer files are created with the *docx*, *xlsx*, and *pptx* extensions (respectively). Additionally, there are "macro-enabled" files that end in "m" (e.g., *docm*, *xlsm*, and *pptm*) that can also be posted online.

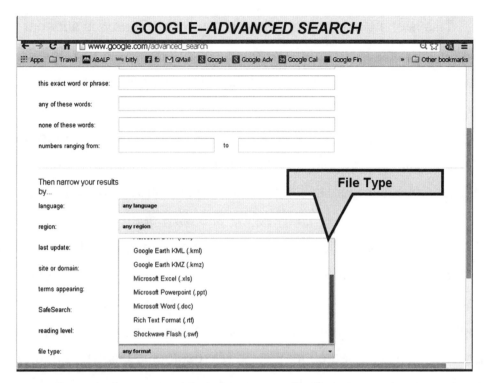

Because **Google** has not added these new file formats to the drop-down menu of file type options on its *Advanced Search* pages, this is one time where using the *Advanced Search* page presents a serious limitation in our ability to retrieve the most, yet still targeted, information. Selecting *Microsoft Powerpoint (.ppt)* from the **Google** *Advanced Search File Type* drop-down menu will **only** return results in the *ppt* file format **and not** *pptx*, *pptm*, or *.pps* file formats. The same is true for Word and Excel file type searches. In order to retrieve the alternate formats in search results, you will need to search for them specifically by typing your query along with the *filetype* instruction directly into the search box, like this:

"Mark Rosch" filetype:pptx

"Mark Rosch" filetype:pptm

(Note that *filetype* must be typed using lowercase letters.)

You can search for both filetypes by using the **OR** Boolean connector (discussed on page 55) to create a more sophisticated, targeted search (like the next example) to retrieve all of the file types in a single search.

"Mark Rosch" filetype:pptx OR filetype:pptm OR filetype:ppt

This is one place where **Yahoo's** *Advanced Search* is superior to **Google's**, because selecting *Microsoft Powerpoint (.ppt)* from the **Yahoo** *Advanced Search File Type* drop-down menu will return results in the *ppt, pptx,* and *pps* file formats and not just *pptx* or *pptm*.

It is also possible to conduct a *filetype* search at either **Google or Yahoo** without any keywords. For example, you can retrieve a list of all PDF documents uploaded to a particular website, regardless of their content, by structuring your search like this:

filetype:PDF site:www.deere.com

Bing no longer offers an Advanced Search template. The only way to retrieve specific file types in your search results is to type the *filetype* instruction directly into the search box on **Bing's** homepage. The strategies discussed in the previous paragraph, for conducting similar searches at **Google** and **Yahoo!**, also apply at **Bing**. Like **Yahoo**, a search for the old Microsoft office filetypes (e.g., *filetype:ppt*) also retrieves the newer filetypes (e.g., *pptx*).

Using Google's Advanced Search File Type Drop-Down Menu to Locate PowerPoint Presentations

PowerPoint presentations (once invisible on the Web, as noted earlier) can be extremely useful when looking for material on a "hot" topic that has been the subject of conference presentations. The individuals making these presentations could also make good expert witnesses. Similarly, you may be able to find presentations from a particular expert using this strategy.

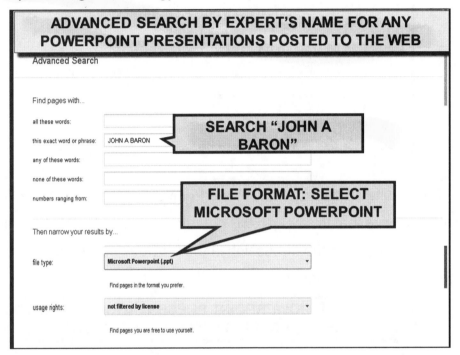

To do this, enter your search terms in the appropriate search boxes (e.g., *Find pages with all these words*, or *Find pages with this exact word or phrase*), and then select *Microsoft PowerPoint (.ppt)* from the *File type* drop-down menu. The illustration on the previous page shows how to limit a search to return only PowerPoint presentations about an expert, *John A Baron*.

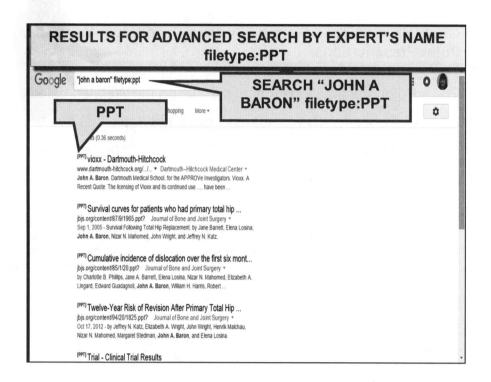

The results list displays only PowerPoint presentations that include your keywords. Beware that this search will not retrieve the newer PowerPoint file formats (e.g., *.pptx*, *.pptm*). See the discussion in the previous section for tips on how to retrieve those other file formats as well.

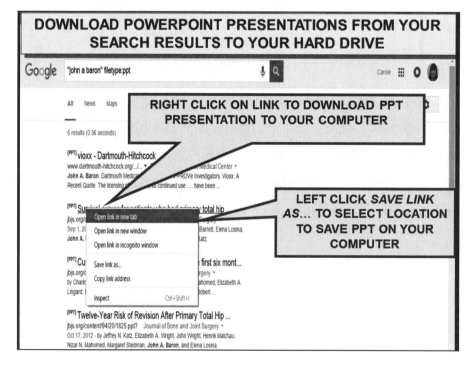

Once you've found a PowerPoint presentation that looks useful, you can download the file to your computer's hard drive, where you can then open it using PowerPoint. Depending on the web browser you're using, the version of that browser, the operating system of the computer you're using, and the version of that operating system it's running, how you interact with the PowerPoint file you find will vary. In some browsers, if you simply left-click the link, the presentation will automatically download to the default Downloads folder on your computer. If your browser is one where left-clicking will just open the slides in the browser, then you will want to right-click the link as shown in the previous illustration and then left-click to *Save link as* option in the subsequent drop-down menu. Downloading the presentation is a good choice because you can view it in the "editing" mode and read the presenter's notes (if there are any).

Using Google's Advanced Search File Type Drop-Down Menu to Locate PDFs

As mentioned on page 80, PDFs on the Web were once invisible. Advances in search engine technology mean that they now reside on the "Visible Web." website owners might post documents as PDFs in order to maintain the integrity, layout, or design of a document so that it looks the same regardless of the type of computer on which it is displayed. Some common examples of this include court forms, tax forms, client intake sheets, advertisements, and brochures.

For an illustration of the **Google** *Advanced Search File Type* search drop-down menu, see page 81.

Locating Other Types of Files, Specialized Databases, and Services from the Google Homepage

In addition to searching Web pages and other file types (as noted earlier), **Google** and other search engines have created specialized databases and products for you to search. For example, Google has created databases for *News*; *Finance*; and *Scholar*, as well as products such as *Gmail* and *Calendar*, to name just a few.

Unfortunately, **Google** hides them behind an unlabeled *Apps Launcher* button on the upper right-hand side of its **Web Search** homepage. Do not confuse this **Google** *Apps Launcher* with the *Chrome Apps Launcher* (located on the left side of the *Chrome tool bar*).

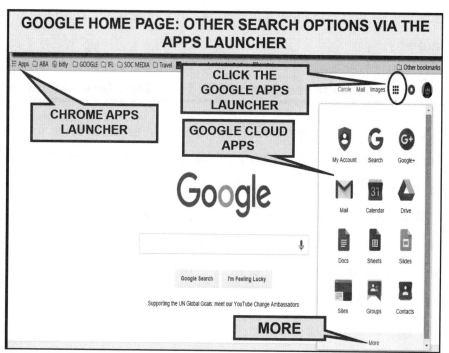

Google has apparently added so many file types, databases, and services that they will not all fit on the *Apps Launcher's* first pop-up, so you will need to click the *More* link at the bottom.

If we still don't see what we needed, we used to click an *Even more from Google* link on the subsequent *Apps Launcher* pop-up, but it has been removed. The only way to access "even more" (**Google's** apps, specialty databases, and other products) is by using the direct URL https://linkon.in/moregoogleprod and scrolling down past many large images advertising commercial products, like **Google Home,** until you reach the *See all products* section.

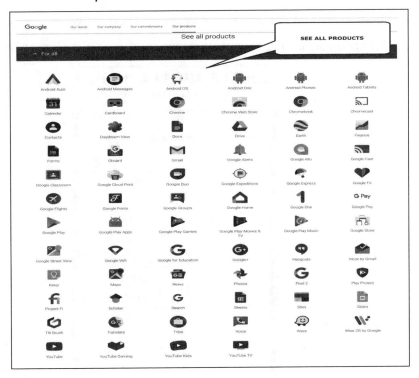

And even then, we've noticed that we aren't seeing "all products." For example, the *Alerts* product is not listed, despite still being available at https://www.google.com/alerts. Additionally, the *Image Search* is not listed here either, but at least it's easy to find on **Google's** homepage.

Some of the useful databases and services listed on the **See all products** page, which we will discuss later, include:

- Finance
- Scholar
- Groups

Note that the appearance of the *Apps Launcher* is not necessarily uniform across platforms (as seen in the previous illustration, which is from a laptop computer and in the next illustration, which is from an iphone) or even between devices of the same platform (if they are running different versions of the same operating system).

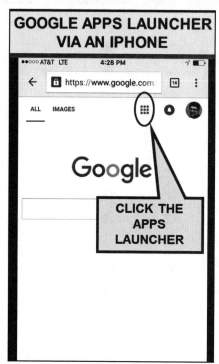

Depending on the search query, **Google** Web searches often also include a few news items as part of the results page—placing them at the top of the first page of results.

However, to search <u>only</u> news results, **Google** offers a *News* database search accessible from the *Apps Launcher* (or use this direct URL: https://news.google.com). The *News* database contains stories from thousands of news sources around the world. The majority of these sources are traditional newspapers and magazines, while an increasing number are reputable online-only sites and blogs. The *News* database used to index and return results from only the past 30 days of news. However, sometime in 2015, Google began making changes to the 30 days of news limit, first returning many years worth of news in our test results, then only returning a few days, and more recently returning a random number of days depending on our search (e.g., four days, eighteen dates, twenty-two days).

The *News* database displays the top stories for you to browse and also offers a search box for you to search for specific stories. **Google** removed the *Advanced Search* feature from the **Google News** database.

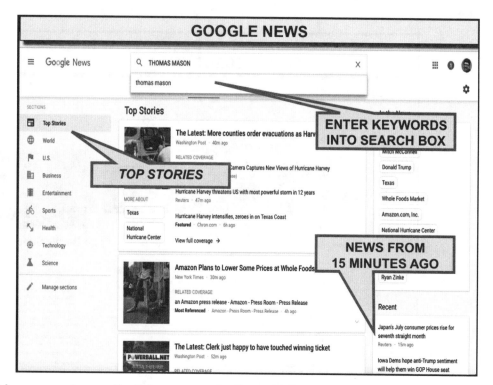

Your search results list appears in the middle column. Results are sorted by relevance.

Since mid-2017, it is no longer possible to re-sort results by date at this *News* database, but there is a work-around. Instead of using the *News* database at https://news.google.com, conduct a "regular" Web search at **Google.com** (http://www.google.com) and then filter to *News* as shown in the next illustration. .

SMARTER SHARED RIDES

Get $10 of Ride Credit with code:

DCRIDES234

Valid for new members only.

Expires 12/24/2019

Download the App

ridewithvia.com

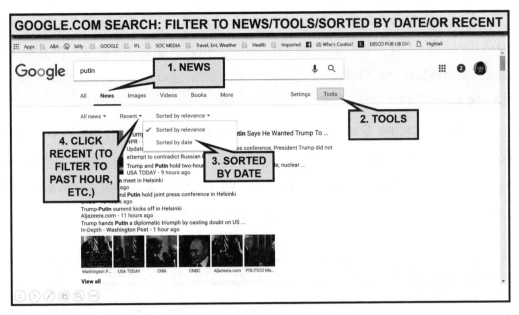

Note that in our test searches, news results retrieved in this manner display stories up to 60 (or more) days old in relevance order. To sort these news results by date, click the *Tools* button, then the *Sort by Relevance* drop-down at the top of the results, and then click *Sorted by Date*.

The results will then be sorted from most recent to oldest, but they will still be sorted by relevance, within each date. You can take relevancy out of the *Sort by Date* results by clicking the *Recent* drop-down arrow to sort by:

- Past hour
- Past 24 hours
- Past week
- Past month
- Past year
- Archives
- Custom range

Going back to the **Google News** database (https://news.google.com), the default page is *Top Stories*, but you can enter keywords into the search box to see stories you are interested in. After you enter a search and click on the results, you will notice some new features. The right-hand column (see next illustration) offers a *Follow* button and a *Share* button, but only if your search is a **Google**-recognized *Topic*.

For example, when we searched *Ruth Bader Ginsburg,* the first suggested result had the word *Topic* next to her name indicating she was a **Google**-recognized *Topic.* (To deploy the *Follow* and *Share* features, you must be logged into your **Google** Account.)

If you click the *Share* button (see the next illustration), this pops up a menu that allows you to share a story to social media by clicking *Facebook, Twitter,* or *Google+.* The *Share* menu also displays *Copy link.* You would click that if you wanted to paste a story's link into a document (or email) that you are writing.

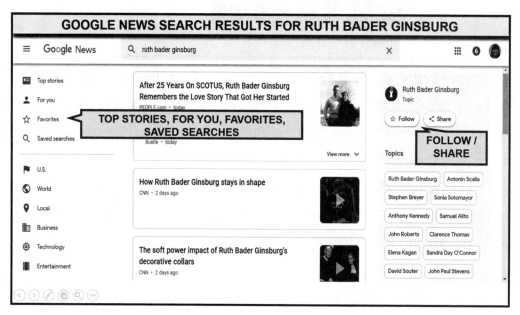

Clicking the *Follow* button in the right-hand column (see prior illustration) changes this button to a *Following* button and places that story's topic into your *Favorites* (see left-hand column on next illustration). When you later click *Favorites,* you will be able to view all your *Favorites* organized by **Google** into *Topics, Locations,* and *Sources* (see next illustration).

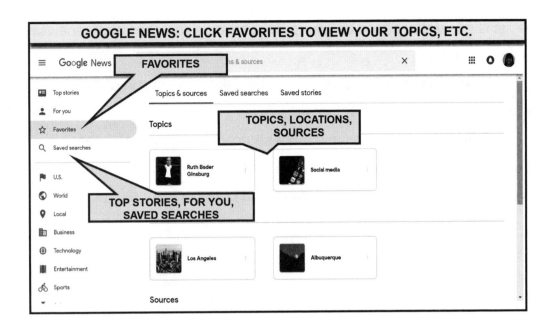

If you click one of those *Topics*, the *News* database results page shows only stories based on the *Topic* that you are *Following*.

To delete a *Topic*, first click *Favorite*s from the left-hand column (see prior illustration), then click one of your listed *Favorites* (see prior illustration). This retrieves a results page with stories from the topic you are *Following.* Click the *Following* button to the right of the story and it will change back to *Follow* and will be deleted from your list of *Favorites.*

Sometimes you will only see a *Save* button instead of the *Follow* and *Share* buttons. This happens if your search is not a "recognized" *Topic,* as explained earlier. If you click *Save*, this places your search (your keywords/phrases) into your *Saved searches* (see the left-hand column of the previous illustration). When you later click *Saved searches,* you will be able to view all your *Saved searches* and you can then click on one to re-run the search. Deleting a *Saved search* works in a similar manner to how we earlier described deleting a *Favorite*.

Clicking the *For you* link (see the left-hand column of the previous illustration) changes the results page to a list of stories on a page labeled *Recommended based on your interests*. It's not clear where those are coming from because there are stories listed on our results page that are not just the ones we are *Following,* but most likely the list is generated based on your previous *News* searches and/or news results you've clicked on.

To return to the *Top Stories* (see the left-hand column of the previous illustration), simply click *Top Stories*.

Other search engines and meta-search sites also find current news, such as **Bing.com** (http://www.bing.com/news), **Yahoo!** (https://www.yahoo.com/news) and **Dogpile** (http://www.dogpile.com/?qc=news).

Google Alerts (http://www.google.com/alerts) allows you to set up an alert service based on your chosen keywords (or phrases). You are then notified (via e-mail) when your chosen keywords (or phrases) appear online in one (or all) of the following: *News*, *Blogs*, *Web*, *Video*, *Books*, *Discussions*, or *Finance*.

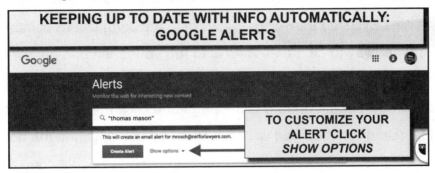

Before you begin, you must click the *show options* drop-down menu beneath the search box to display the source list and other customization options. The default source is *News*. **Google Alerts** now lets you select multiple options on the source list. Previously, you could only choose one. To set your **Google Alert** to include all of the sources, choose **Google Alerts'** *Automatic* option from the *Sources* drop-down menu. You can request notification on a *once a week*, *once a day,* or *as it happens* basis. Google will send *All results* or you can opt to receive *Only the best results*. Enter your e-mail address to receive Alerts in your e-mail in-box or select *RSS Feed* from the *Deliver to* drop-down menu to receive Alerts in your preferred RSS Reader.

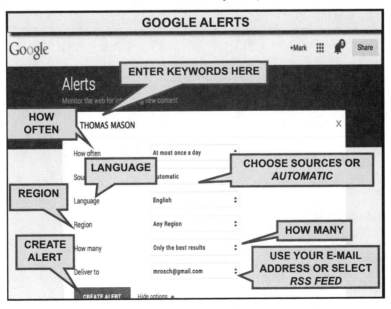

You can create very sophisticated *Alerts,* using any of the search syntax and instructions we have discussed. For instance, you could create an *Alert* for *"john a baron" filetype:ppt OR pptx* to be notified every time **Google** detects a new PowerPoint presentation uploaded to the Web that includes John A. Baron's name. You might also create an *Alert* for the search we described on page 82 with no keywords, *site:deere.com filetype:xls OR xlsx, to* be notified every time **Google** detects a new Excel spreadsheet uploaded to the John Deere company website.

Another way to create an *Alert* is to run your search at https://www.google.com, then on the results page, select *News* from the filter bar and from that *News* results page, scroll down to the bottom of the page and click the *Create alert* tab on the right-hand side. (Unfortunately, you will no longer see this option at the bottom of the **Google** *News* database search results at https://news.google.com, discussed in the previous section).

Yahoo! has discontinued its alerts, while **Bing** has limited its alerts to return just News results—renaming the feature *Interests*. (See page 122 for details about **Bing's** *Interests*.)

In 2006**, Google** launched the **Google News Archive** (http://news.google.com/newspapers). The purpose of the **Google News Archive** was twofold: First, it was meant to give access to the archival collections of hundreds of newspapers dating back approximately 250 years by scanning and publicly posting them on the Web. Second, the scanning project was reportedly meant to also fine-tune the optical character recognition (OCR) capabilities **Google** was employing in its **Google** *Books* project. **Google** stopped adding additional content to the **News Archive** project in the spring of 2011.

It has been reported that its database includes 60 million pages. Coverage dates and ranges vary by publication. **Google** does provide an alphabetical listing of all of the newspapers included in the **News Archive** along with the coverage dates for each paper. The earliest newspaper included on that list is the Newport, Rhode Island, weekly publication, *The Weekly Companion; and the Commercial Centinel* from December 15, 1798. While access to many of the **News Archive's** articles is free, others (mostly from newspapers such as the *Washington Post* Archives and the *New York Times* Archives) require a fee. Before you pay for news articles found by the **Archive**, see page 175 to learn about remote access to public library databases that include free news articles (and more).

In the previous illustration, note that you can browse a particular newspaper by clicking its link or clicking a letter to jump to that portion of the list. You can also keyword search the entire collection by entering your keywords into the search box at the top of the **Google News Archive** page.

If **Google** ever disables this page, you may still be able to search this collection using the domain search limiter (discussed on page 77) to return results from the **News Archive** collection in this manner:

- Berlin Wall site:news.google.com/newspapers.

Currently, this search syntax does return results from the **News Archive**. Our test searches during the writing of this book have yielded mixed results when the *Custom Range* filter is applied to these search results.

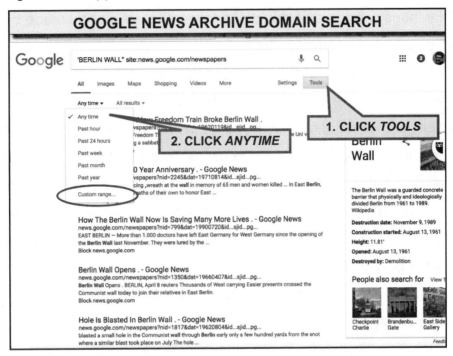

The **News Archive** search is apparently in flux. As we become aware of changes, we will post them to our website at http://linkon.in/1c1eWRO.

Using Google to Locate Blogs

Since 2001, personal "Web logs" (or "blogs") have become a popular and powerful means of expression and communication on the Internet. Many blogs are like a personal journal or diary. Others are used as an individual professional publishing platform for marketing purposes. Made up of short, frequently updated posts, blogs are arranged in reverse chronological order—with the newest posts at the top of the page. Many blogs present more of an attitude (or at least a personality) than a regular website.

The contents and purposes of blogs vary with the personalities of the "bloggers" who create them. Blogs can contain everything from links and commentary on current events, to news about a specific topic or company. A personal blog might resemble an online diary and include photos, poetry, essays, project updates, or fiction. Often these blogs are no more than a chronicle of what's on the mind of the blogger at any given time. Professional blogs might include current awareness items or commentary on a particular industry or area of law. Blogs (almost) always allow readers to comment and interact or provide feedback to the writer.

Blogs' ease of development and updating make it extremely easy for anyone, even those with limited technical ability, to create, host, and update their own website. Regardless of their content, though, blogs (as a collection of interconnected pages hosted publicly on the Internet) are websites. Blogs can be an excellent source of news or commentary on "hot" topics and public opinion regarding companies or their products, but not every search engine treats results from blogs equally. Blogs are such a useful source of information that **Google** created a separate searchable database of blog content.

Unfortunately, **Google** no longer maintains its original database of blogs. It has instead rolled blog results into "regular" *Web* and *News* search results (where they had already been included). Those blog results are primarily weighted towards larger commercial/news blogs (e.g., Huffington Post, Slate, Washington Post, Wall Street Journal), as opposed to the smaller, more personal blogs that had previously been included.

For information on using blogs for investigative research, see page 171.

Audio and video can be found online if you know where to look. **YouTube.com** (owned by **Google**) is obviously one of the largest repositories, but you can limit searches to video-only results right from **Google** Web search results by clicking the *Videos* tab that appears above the results list in the prior illustration.

The **Google Video** search (which can also be reached directly at https://www.google.com/videohp) returns a variety of results ranging from amateur and instructional videos to episodes of popular TV shows, music videos, and short films. Even though these videos can be posted anywhere on the Web, the majority of results in our test searches come from **YouTube**. **Bing** includes a *Video* tabs on its homepages to limit results just to videos. **Yahoo!** no longer offers this option.

Podcasts are a more recent development in delivering audio content via the Internet. You can think of podcasts as "radio delivered via the Internet." Instead of listening to a live broadcast, however, listeners download audio files to their computers or portable media players (e.g., a smartphone or tablet) to play them back when it is convenient. Like other kinds of content available on the Internet, podcasts are relatively easy to create and cover a wide array of topics. Most podcasts are saved in the MP3 format, allowing maximum portability and flexibility in playing back the audio content. A recent **Google** search for *podcasts* returned over 206 million results (compared to 79 million just two years earlier).

In the legal arena, some lawyers are creating podcasts for marketing purposes and to educate clients and potential clients on a variety of topics. (Legal podcasts are occasionally referred to as "plawdcasts," but the term has not gained the popularity of the term "blawg," which is used to refer to legal blogs.) As listeners, legal professionals can use podcasts to get up to speed or keep up to date on numerous legal and non-legal topics.

To find podcasts on all topics, you can use an online directory of podcasts, such as **iTunes** (available via the iTunes store; see http://www.apple.com/itunes) or **PodcastAlley.com** (http://www.podcastalley.com/).

For legal podcasts, see the **ABA's Blawg Directory** (http://www.abajournal.com/blawgs/topic/podcaster) or **Justia's BlawgSearch** (http://blawgsearch.justia.com/blogs/categories/podcasts /), or simply use a search engine. For example, to find a podcast about *copyright infringement*, we searched **Google** for *podcast, copyright,* and *infringement*. Over 813,000 results were returned. One of those results was the "This Week in Law" podcast (https://www.twit.tv/shows/this-week-in-law) hosted by IP attorney Denise Howell and others, along with a revolving panel of experts. She posts a new podcast each week on various intellectual property and technology law issues.

Once you have located podcasts that you find useful (or entertaining), you can either check back with the host site frequently to download new installments, or subscribe to the podcast via RSS. Similar to RSS feeds of text content, podcast RSS feeds alert you automatically when new content is available and even send the files to you automatically. These specialty RSS aggregators are sometimes called "podcatchers." Some of the more popular podcatchers include **iTunes** (http://www.apple.com/itunes) for Mac and Windows; **Juice** (http://juicereceiver.sourceforge.net) for Mac, Windows, and Linux; and **Feedly** (http://www.feedly.com), which was originally Web based, but is now also available for iOS and Android mobile devices.

For audio of a different kind, **FindSounds** (http://www.findsounds.com) is a specialty search engine where you can locate specific sounds to add sound to a video or live presentation.

Using Google to Locate Images

It is often useful to find out, in advance, what a person looks like, whether you are investigating that person or simply need to identify someone you are meeting for the first time (such as a new client) at a public place. Process servers could also conduct an image search before they serve their targeted person to be sure they've served the correct person. Entering the person's name into an image search engine can sometimes help you find his or her picture. You can also conduct an image search for places, concepts, or products by using the appropriate keywords to describe them.

Google has billions of images in its *Images* database. There are several ways to invoke an *Image* search at **Google**:

- Click the *Images* link on the top, right-hand side of **Google's** homepage. (**Bing** offers a similar link at the top of its homepage to conduct an image-only Internet search.)
- Click the *Images* filter displayed above the search results list after you run a Google search. (**Yahoo!** and *Bing* offer similar filters in the left-hand column and above their respective search results lists.)
- Use this direct URL: https://www.google.com/imghp
- Use **Google's** *Advanced Image Search* (https://www.google.com/advanced_image_search) for the most precise search. (Neither **Yahoo!** nor **Bing** offers *Advanced Image Searches* any longer.)

When you search by your subject's name, sometimes the results (see next screenshot) will include images of your subject with another person or even images of people without your subject but with whom they are associated. We've also seen results of images of our subject's book covers, images of presentations they have made, images of events they have attended, etc. These results could be useful if you are trying to link your subject to a particular person or event.

After receiving your results from one of the first three methods noted earlier, you can click *Tools* to filter results by *Size*, *Color*, *Type* (e.g., *face*, *clip art*), *Time*, and

Usage rights. There is also a *More tools* drop-down option that includes just one function beyond the default *All results*. The *Show sizes* option on this drop-down menu displays each image's size (in pixels) at the bottom of the image. If this option is not selected, the image's size is only displayed when you hover over a particular image.

Using the *Advanced Image Search* allows you to set any of the previously mentioned filters in advance of your search and to set a few additional filters, such as *aspect ratio*, *region*, *site or domain*, and *file type.*

When you click an image, you are then offered a number of options, including: (1) to visit the page where the image appears (and possibly obtain more information about the image) or (2) to view the image separately from all the other images. If you right-click on the image, you can download the image or search **Google** for the image. If you're logged into your **Google** account, you will also see an option to *Save* an image. You can see all of the images you've saved from previous searches at http://www.google.com/save.

See pages 421–422 for other image databases.

In the summer of 2011, Google introduced the ability to *Search by Image*. Rather than just typing a keyword or phrase into the search box on the **Google Image Search** homepage, you can click the camera icon in the search box (http://images.google.com) to upload a photo from your computer's hard drive (or drag and drop the image into the search box if you're using **Google's** Chrome Web browser), or enter the URL of an image on the Web.

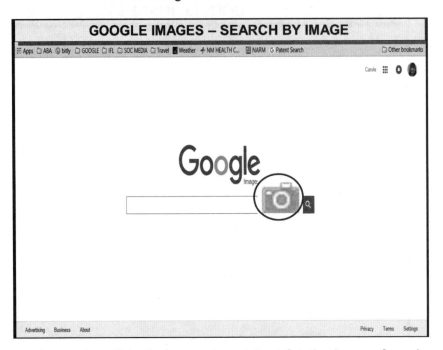

The search results will include exact matches for the image found on the Internet, as well as a collection of *Visually similar images* that may or may not be all that similar to your original image Search results now also include a *Best Guess for this image*, which is a keyword that attempts to describe the image.

When **Google** introduced this feature in 2011, they clearly stated that it did not use facial recognition. According to **Google's** blog (http://linkon.in/googlesearchwithimage), "The technology behind *Search by Image* analyzes your image to find its most distinctive points, lines and textures and creates a mathematical model. We match that model against billions of images in our index, and page analysis helps us derive a best guess text description of your image. *Search by Image* technology also includes the ability to match against images on the web so that we can show you similar images." Since that time however, **Google** has acquired, and further developed, facial recognition software such as **FaceNet** (http://linkon.in/googlefacenet). It is unclear whether **Google** is applying such facial recognition technology to return *Search by Image* results.

"Hidden" Search Engine Features Not Even Found Behind Google Menu's Even More

Google Dictionary: To use the **Google Dictionary**, type the word *define* followed by a colon and the word you want defined (all lower case, with no spaces) into the query box on the **Google** homepage (e.g., *define:clew*). Several definitions of the word are displayed, from various dictionaries (general and topical) and websites. Using the example of *clew*, definitions came from **Wordnetweb** (http://wordnet.princeton.edu), which is a "lexical database of English" created by a professor at Princeton, and **Merriam-Webster Dictionary** (https://www.merriam-webster.com/dictionary/clew) **Wordnetweb** gave a general definition of the word ("a ball of yarn or cord or thread") while the **Merriam-Webster** site gave a more specific definition relating to boats ("a lower corner or only the after corner of a sail").

Google Flight Status Search: You can quickly check the status of an airline flight by typing the name of the airline and a flight number into the **Google** search box. Results can include status, departure and arrival times, and gate information. Cancellation and diversion information is also included, when applicable.

Google Patent Search (https://patents.google.com) offers a searchable database of nearly 40 million granted U.S. and foreign patents and nearly 35 million applications from:

- U.S. Patent and Trademark Office (USPTO)
  - over 10 million patents back to 1790
  - over 4 million applications back to 2001
- European Patent Office (EPO)
  - over 1.5 million patents back to 1980
  - over 4 million applications back to 1978
- the Japanese Patent Office (JPO)
  - over 8 million patents back to 1994
  - over 18 million applications back to 1993
- State Intellectual Property Office of People's Republic of China (SIPO)
  - over 9.3 million patents back to 1990
  - over 7.2 million applications back to 1985
- World Intellectual Property Organization (WIPO)
  - over 3.7 million applications back to 1978
- German Patent and Trademark Office (DPMA)
  - over 4.6 million patents back to 1987
  - over 2.8 million applications back to 1987
- Canadian Intellectual Property Office (CIPO)
  - over 2.1 million patents back to 1978
  - over 940 thousand applications back to 1978

Google machine-translates foreign patents so that they can be searched in English.

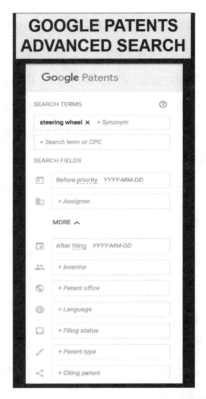

Once you run your search, you can filter your results by adding additional search terms, or other criteria, using the *Advanced Search* form that appears in the left-hand margin of the results page. Filters include:

- *Assignee* (name)
- *Inventor* (name)
- *Patent Office*
- *Filing Status* (*Grant* or *Application*)
- *Patent Type* (*Patent* or *Design*)

In 2012, **Google** created a tool to help locate prior art as a standalone search. In 2015, the **Prior Art Finder** was rolled into **Google Patent Search**.

If you're looking for prior art, you can broaden your search to include related scholarly articles from **Google Scholar,** by clicking the *Include non-patent literature* check box beneath the search box on the **Google Patent Search** homepage. This will retrieve patent applications and grants, as well as prior art from non-patent sources, such as from journals, magazines, etc., all in one interface. Note that this search does not retrieve case law results.

It should also be noted that **Google** still maintains its old search interface for the patent database at http://www.google.com/patents (aka http://www.google.com/?tbm=pts). Searching at this page only retrieves patent results.

One advantage to searching the patent database with the old interface is having access to that interface's **Advanced Patent Search** page (http://www.google.com/advanced_patent_search). This *Advanced Search* page offers different search filters than those available in the new interface, including field limiters such as:

- Patent Number
- Title
- Original Assignee
- Patent Type/Status
- Restrict by filing date

The *Advanced Search* page for the new interface offers the same limiters that appear in the left-hand margin of patent search results (discussed earlier).

Despite its name, this database also includes registered trademark images from 1870 to the present and applications from 1884 to the present.

Using Google As a Phone Directory or Address Directory

Entering the name of an individual and/or the city/state where that person resides is a surprisingly effective way of locating that individual's street address or phone number. Similarly, you can run a "reverse" search by entering a phone number into the **Google** search box to identify the number's owner or an associated address.

To conduct a reverse telephone search, we would ordinarily enter the phone number into the search box with dashes between the segments (*310-559-2247*) because **Google** tells us that it ignores punctuation. However, recent test searches show that **Google** is not ignoring punctuation in the case of a string of digits, like a phone number. In these test searches, we saw different results for a search for *310-559-2247* and *3105592247*. However, these test searches were inconclusive as to which search syntax works best. In some tests, we received more results for the *3105592247* search, in some we received more results for the *310-559-2247* search, and in some we received more results for the *310-559-2247 OR 3105592247* search. So, to retrieve results that include the most variations of ways phone numbers are listed at web sites, it's apparently necessary to run these multiple search types for the same phone number.

In order for **Google** to return phone number results, the information would have to be included in a publicly available Web page that **Google** has indexed. Google does not maintain its own database of addresses and phone numbers.

Until the summer of 2010, **Google** did maintain its own databases of listed residential and business phone numbers. Even though **Google** clearly listed the procedure for requesting the removal of one's information from these databases, it still received numerous complaints about their availability. **Google** cited these consumer complaints as the reason for the databases' removal.

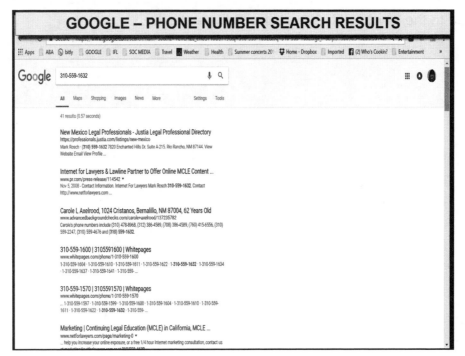

Yahoo! and **Bing** will return similar results for a phone number search. **Yahoo!** and **Bing** also do not maintain their own phone listings database.

Search engines can also be used to uncover alternative phone numbers, such as cellular phone and fax numbers. This isn't because there is a freely available database of these numbers. Rather, it's because people have been known to post these numbers publicly on the Web in a place where the search engines' robot can find them and add the information to their indices.

The key to locating this information is using the right combination of keywords and Boolean connectors. To use **Google** (or any other search engine) to locate the phone number of a specific person, begin by typing the person's *first* and *last name* into the *All these words* query box on the *Advanced Search* page. Then add the targeted keywords that describe the information you're looking for (e.g., *cell, cellular*) into the *Any of these words* query box. Because the people who include these numbers on a Web page want people to contact them, these numbers often include their name and the legend *cell* or *cellular* next to the number. This is why this search strategy can uncover those numbers if they've been posted publicly on the Internet. You may also be able to locate phone number information by including keywords related to the city or state where the individual lives.

As we discussed on page 53, search engines do not always index data found within databases because some databases are built in such a way that search engines <u>cannot</u> retrieve information from them. So, if you are not finding the information you need, consider that it might be "hidden" in a database that a search engine cannot penetrate. Nevertheless, you can still retrieve the information you need from a database by using search engines to locate the existence of a database that might contain your information. Then you can search the database to locate the "invisible" data within the database. The trick to helping the search engine locate the database is to type the word *database* into the search engine's search box and then add other words and phrases to describe the data you are seeking. For example, to find a database of all California State Bar members, we typed the phrase *California state bar* and the keywords *member* and *database* into **Google's** *Advanced Search* page, as shown in the next illustrations. The search engine then found the California State Bar's member database.

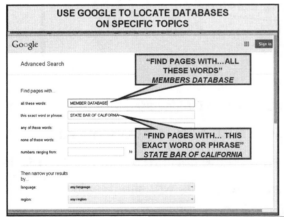

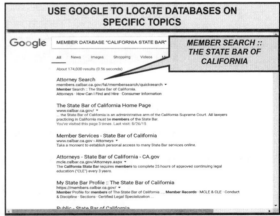

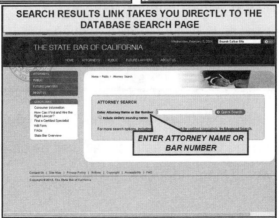

Taking the previous *California State Bar* example one step further, we can use very specific keywords and phrases to, for example, get information on Carole Levitt's license to practice law in California. If we type *Carole Levitt California* into the *all these words* query box on **Google's** *Advanced Search* page and *attorney search* into the *this exact word or phrase* box, the first search result returned is Carole's attorney registration record from the California State Bar's website (see next illustration).

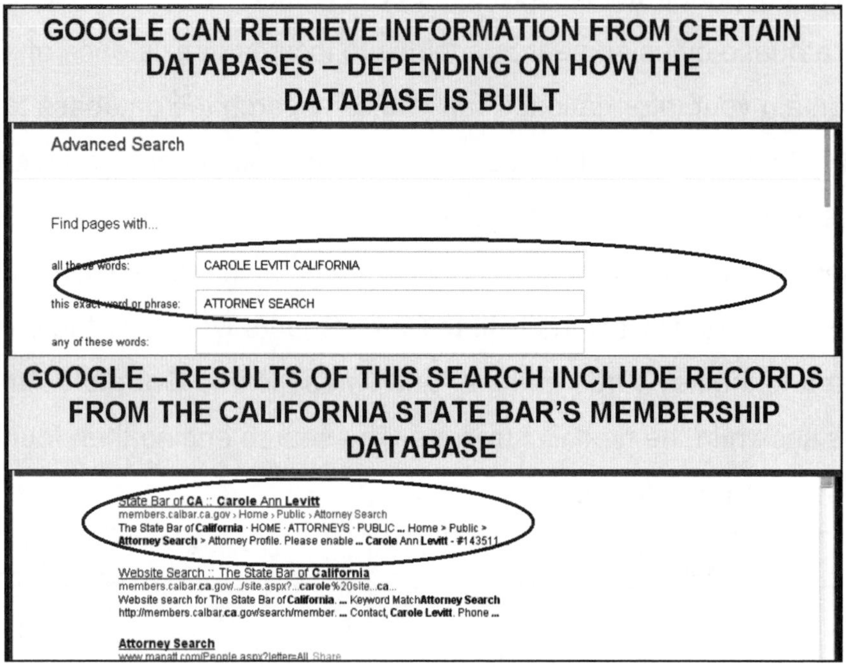

GOOGLE CAN RETRIEVE INFORMATION FROM CERTAIN DATABASES – DEPENDING ON HOW THE DATABASE IS BUILT

Advanced Search

Find pages with...

all these words: CAROLE LEVITT CALIFORNIA

this exact word or phrase: ATTORNEY SEARCH

any of these words:

GOOGLE – RESULTS OF THIS SEARCH INCLUDE RECORDS FROM THE CALIFORNIA STATE BAR'S MEMBERSHIP DATABASE

State Bar of **CA** :: **Carole Ann Levitt**
members.calbar.ca.gov › Home › Public › Attorney Search
The State Bar of **California** · HOME · ATTORNEYS · PUBLIC ... Home › Public ›
Attorney Search › Attorney Profile. Please enable ... **Carole Ann Levitt** - #143511

Website Search :: The State Bar of **California**
members.calbar.ca.gov/.../site.aspx?...carole%20site...ca...
Website search for The State Bar of **California**. ... Keyword Match**Attorney Search**
http://members.calbar.ca.gov/search/member. ... Contact, **Carole Levitt**. Phone ...

Attorney Search
www.manatt.com/People.aspx?letter=All Share

This search works for two reasons: (1) The California State Bar's membership database stores and displays information in such a way that **Google** can access it, and (2) the phrase attorney search appears on the California State Bar's results page when conducting a search for licensed attorneys at its website. Realistically, though, you wouldn't know in advance whether a database that would answer your question was built in such a way as to allow **Google** access.

New Google Search Tips and Tricks

To help you keep up with developments in **Google** Search, we blog extensively about new and upcoming **Google** features, as well as changes to existing features, at our Internet For Lawyers blog (http://linkon.in/waPq9r).

HUMAN SEARCH ENGINES

You can submit text questions online to the librarians at the **Library of Congress** (http://www.loc.gov/rr/askalib) in more than 30 areas of specialty. The **Library of Congress** also offers designated times when you can "chat" with the librarians live.

The **Internet Public Library's** *Ask an ipl2 Librarian* (http://www.ipl.org/div/askus) service, which allowed you to submit questions via an online form, has now shut down and suggests that you check your public library to see if they offer chat.

Quora (http://www.quora.com) describes itself as "a place where you can ask questions you care about and get answers that are amazing." Users can post any question they are interested in to be answered by other **Quora** users—some responders are world-renowned experts in their fields, senior executives in various fields, or other highly regarded individuals, while others are just well-informed on a particular topic. However, some responders might be none of these things. Whether the answers are amazing or not is up to you.

Yahoo! *Answers* (http://answers.yahoo.com) allows its users to submit text questions online to be answered by other **Yahoo!** *Answers'* users. Answering a question earns a user two points and asking a question "costs" five points (but you can "earn" 100 points just for creating a free account). (**Google** had previously offered a similar service but discontinued it at the end of 2006.)

FINDING "SPECIAL TOPIC" DIRECTORIES

The concept of a "Directory" refers to topical websites that are "human edited." The editors are experts who volunteer to curate a list of what they deem the most useful and credible websites in their field. There are fewer and fewer of these topical human-edited Web directories these days.

Yahoo! discontinued its human-edited directory in 2014 and **CompletePlanet** discontinued theirs in 2015. **DMOZ** (http://www.dmoz.org/), once known as the Open

Directory Project (ODP), which claimed to be "the largest, most comprehensive human-edited directory of the Web," closed in 2017.

Justia still maintains topical directories such as **LegalBirds**, a combination directory and search engine of law-related **Twitter** accounts (see page 447) and its **BlawgSearch**, a combination directory and search engine of law-related blogs (see page 447).

BRINGING IN YOUR OWN SEARCH EXPERT

At the end of an Internet research seminar, we often hear the following comment: "That was a great seminar. I really understand the Web better now and everything I can find on it. But where do I go now to find someone to do it for me?" The goal of our seminars is twofold: (1) to teach lawyers how they can use the Web for research on their own, and (2) for those lawyers who don't have the time (or inclination) to use the Web on their own, to inform them of what's available on the Web so they know what to ask for when handing a research assignment over to an associate, librarian, or paralegal. However, for many of you in a small or solo practice, there is no one else to take over the research task! Or maybe you have an assistant, but the subject matter or depth of research is out of that person's area of expertise. In either case, this is the time to seek expert research support.

For those determined lawyers who insisted that you "needed" us to locate the information you were missing, we formed our **Information For Lawyers** investigative research division (http://www.infoforlawyers.com) in late 2005.

The research focus is on the six information categories with which attendees and readers have repeatedly asked us to help them:

1. People Finding (e.g., missing witnesses, missing heirs)
2. Competitive Intelligence (e.g., profiling an opposing party or counsel, expert, prospective client)
3. Asset Searching (not bank accounts)
4. Company Background
5. Criminal Records (note: availability of information varies widely from jurisdiction to jurisdiction)
6. Legal Research
7. Social Networking Research

We have assembled a seasoned staff of research professionals to handle your requests. These degreed law librarians and lawyers have over 50 combined years of experience conducting research for attorneys at some of the country's most respected law firms and for large corporate clients. While no electronic search is absolutely complete, we have access to some of the most comprehensive pay databases available for locating information about people. Our experienced team reviews and cross-matches their results, combining them with other information they have located from sources available on the Internet, to deliver a dossier of information that can help make or break your case.

Pricing varies by project, but most are billed at $250/hour ($50 minimum). Per-search fees incurred when using pay databases are billed to clients (at cost, with no markup) in addition to the hourly fee.

Chapter Six

OTHER FAVORITE SEARCH ENGINES AND META-SEARCH SITES

Until recently, **Google** had very little competition from its rivals in the relevance of its search results, or the types and numbers of documents in its index, but **Yahoo!** and **Bing** have made impressive progress.

Beginning in mid-2004, **Google** claimed to index nearly 8.2 billion pages of the Internet (although it is important to note that there is no way to independently confirm this self-reported number). In late 2005, after attempting to refute **Yahoo!'s** claim of indexing more than 20 billion items, **Google** removed the reference to the size of its index from its homepage. (**Google** had not updated the number posted on its homepage since first claiming 8.2 billion pages in 2004.) Currently, the major search engines no longer display the number of pages in their respective indices.

While nobody knows the exact number of pages on the Internet, the Dutch website **WorldWideWebSize** (http://www.worldwidewebsize.com) has developed an intricate formula for estimating not just the number of pages on the "indexed Web," but also the number of pages in the indices of **Google** and **Bing**. (**Yahoo!** is not included since it now retrieves results from **Bing's** and **Google's** indices rather than maintaining its own—as explained later in this chapter.)

On a recent visit in the fall of 2018, the site estimated the following sizes for the indices of these two major search engines:

- **Google**—46 billion Web pages
- **Bing**—.165 billion Web pages (a precipitious 90% drop from the previous year's estimate)

The site recalculates its estimates daily.

Bing (http://www.bing.com)

In May 2009, **Microsoft** relaunched its search initiative with a new "decision engine" named **Bing**. At launch, **Microsoft** described **Bing** as being "designed to empower people to gain insight and knowledge from the Web, moving more quickly to important decisions." The idea was to present information to help users make decisions in four major categories—*Travel*, *Shopping*, *Health*, and *Local*—rather than just displaying a list of links.

Since then, **Bing** has evolved into delivering its results in a manner more similar to other search engines.

In July 2009, "**Microsoft** … acquire[d] an exclusive 10-year license to **Yahoo!'s** core search technologies, and **Microsoft** will have the ability to integrate **Yahoo!** search technologies into its existing web search platforms; **Microsoft's Bing** will be the exclusive algorithmic search and paid search platform for **Yahoo!** sites. **Yahoo!** will continue to use its technology and data in other areas of its business such as enhancing display advertising technology" (http://linkon.in/msftyahoo). Then, on February 18, 2010, **Microsoft** and **Yahoo!** announced that they "received clearance for their search agreement, without restrictions, from both the U.S. Department of Justice and the European Commission, and will now turn their attention to beginning the process of implementing the deal." As of May 2017, **Yahoo!** Is retrieving a mix of results from the **Bing** and **Google** indices. As of this writing, researchers can still search at either **Bing** or **Yahoo!**. In our identical test searches of both search engines, we found similar results for those identical searches, although some of the results were in a different order.

Bing has the following tabs on its homepage top bar for you to limit your search to various databases (or to use various services):

- *Images*
- *Videos*
- *Maps*
- *News*
- *MSN*
- *Office Online*
- *Outlook.com*

Bing had long hidden its *Advanced Search* functions, making them inaccessible until after you had run a search. In a redesign of their interface in late 2013, **Bing** eliminated its *Advanced Search* menu altogether but did not eliminate its *Advanced Search* functions—if you know how to invoke them. Luckily, many of the instructions used to invoke the *Advanced Search* in **Bing are** nearly identical to those used to invoke **Google's** *Advanced Search* functions: Enter the *Advanced Search* operators and instructions into the **Bing** search box on its homepage. For example, **Bing** recognizes the same *site:* instruction (to limit a search to a specific site or domain) as **Google,** and it recognizes the same *filetype:* instruction (to limit a search to a specific *filetype*) as **Google**. To limit your search to one of the following specific *filetypes* at **Bing**, your search would look like this:

- Microsoft Documents: *[keyword] filetype:doc OR [keyword] filetype:docx* (e.g., *climate change filtetype:doc OR climate change filtetype:docx*)
- Microsoft PowerPoint files: *[keyword] filetype:ppt OR [keyword] filetype:pptx*
- Microsoft Excel Spreadsheets: *[keyword] filetype:xls OR [keyword] filetype:xlsx*
- PDFs: *[keyword] filetype:pdf*

Bing also offers many of the same types of searches and Boolean operators as **Google**, except for one major difference: **Bing** recognizes parentheses as a search parameter while **Google** does not (see page 60 for details on organizing your search terms with parentheses).

Bing offers a type of *alerts* but it only runs your search through its *News* database. **Google Alerts**, on the other hand, allows you to run your search through several other specialized databases (in addition to its *News* database) or through its entire Index, as discussed in *Chapter Five.*

Bing has renamed its news alerts feature *Interests*. You must create (and sign into) a Microsoft Account before using it.

Once logged into your Microsoft Account, you enable *Interests* by turning them on at http://linkon.in/2qcXFr3. The majority of *Interests* displayed are general topics, such as *Business* and *US News*. You can receive updates on a particular company by clicking the *Add interest* link in the page's *Finance* section or on *Local News* stories by clicking the *Add interest* link in the *News* section. **Bing** does not offer options to retrieve national or international news, or general web searches like **Google** does with its *Alerts*.

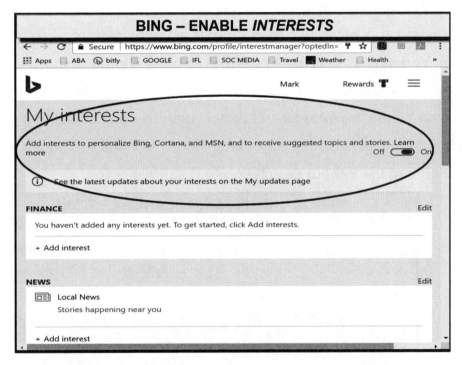

Yahoo! (http://www.yahoo.com)

Yahoo! was founded in 1994 as a directory of websites organized by category (and sub-category) rather than a keyword searchable index of pages. Through a series of highly publicized acquisitions and brand extensions, as well as a number of chief executive changes, the company has gone from the market leader to its 2016 acquisition by **Verizon**. (**Yahoo!** closed its directory in 2014.)

Since Microsoft's 2009 investment in **Yahoo!,** the search engine no longer maintains its own search algorithm or index, relying instead on a mix of results from **Bing** and **Google**. (See page 120 for details.)

However, as of this writing, **Yahoo!** is in the process of being integrated by **Verizon. Verizon** has announced plans to combine **Yahoo!** with **AOL** into a new company called **Oath.** Most statements from **Verizon** and **Oath** executives have focused on **Yahoo!** as a media and content producer and advertising platform. It is unclear if a search engine will play a prominent role in the company's future.

For now, the **Yahoo!** search engine is still available.

When you visit **Yahoo!,** you can conduct a search using the search box at the top of the page. But to limit your search to specific file types, specialized databases, and services (other than traditional websites), you can click on one of the many tabs either on the top Bar or beneath the search box. The tabs in the Bar on the top include: *Mail, Flickr, Tumblr, Answers, Groups, Mobile, View, More.* If you click *More,* then the additional options duplicate many of the ones that appear below the search box, including: Politics, Celebrity, and Style. Options for limiting results just to *News,* and *Finance,* among other topics, also appear below the search box.

Access to conduct an image search has been removed from both lists on the homepage, but it reappears on the search results page (in a Bar beneath the search box) and can also be conducted at http://images.search.yahoo.com.

Neither **Yahoo!** (http://www.yahoo.com) nor **Yahoo! Search** (http://search.yahoo.com) offer a link to the site's *Advanced Search*. You can still access the *Advanced Search* page directly at http://search.yahoo.com/web/advanced.

Yahoo! offers many of the same search features and functions as **Google**. The following are some of the different features found at **Yahoo!** (or some of the same features, but implemented differently by **Google**):

- *Yahoo! uses the asterisk (*) as a Proximity connector. (See page 57* for a full discussion of Proximity connectors.) To conduct a proximity search at **Yahoo!**, separate search terms with the asterisk (e.g., Mark * Rosch). Using the asterisk in this way (at **Yahoo!**) indicates that you want the first keyword to be separated from the second keyword by one, or more than one, word. The asterisk essentially takes the place of the missing word(s) in such a search. While **Yahoo!** still recognizes the asterisk as a proximity connector, results for most of our test searches were no different when comparing searches for identical keywords conducted with and without the asterisk.

- Like *Google, Yahoo!* has also discontinued the link search which returned a list of Web pages that linked to a Web page you defined in your search.

- One search feature available at **Yahoo!** that is not available at **Google** is the ability to organize your searches using parentheses. See page 60 for more information on organizing your search terms with parentheses.

- Like **Google**, **Yahoo!** can locate phone numbers or addresses in the publicly available Web pages in its index. Note that, also like **Google**, searches on **Yahoo!** for phone numbers entered with the dashes return different results than searches without the dashes. So, a search for 423-752-9237 is different than a search for 4237529237.

- **Yahoo! Answers** (http://answers.yahoo.com/) allows users to submit text questions online to be answered by other **Yahoo! Answers** users. **Yahoo! Answers** users earn points through participation. For example, answering a question earns a user two points and asking a question "costs" five points (but you can "earn" 100 points just for creating a free account). **Google** had previously offered a similar service but discontinued it at the end of 2006).

Yahoo! has even created a sparse (more **Google**-like) search interface known as **Yahoo! Search (**http://search.yahoo.com). It features just a search box with local weather information below it and *Trending Now* topics at the bottom of the page.

META-SEARCH SITES: SEARCHING A "SEARCH ENGINE OF SEARCH ENGINES"

Meta-search sites function like a "search engine of search engines"—submitting your search to multiple search engines at once. They do not maintain their own index, but instead rely on the indices of other search engines from which they draw results.

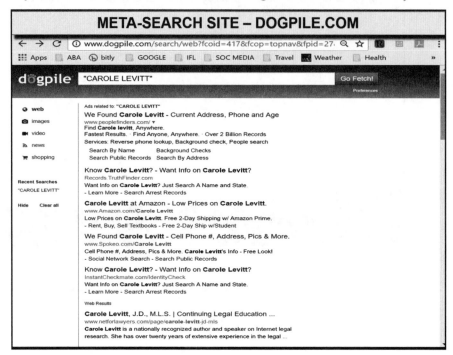

Dogpile (http://www.dogpile.com) is one of the best-known sites in this category. Even though **Dogpile** is once again submitting its queries to **Google**, as well as **Yahoo!** and other search engines, we currently prefer **Yippy** (http://www.yippy.com) and **DuckDuckGo** (http://duckduckgo.com) because they offer features that make them stand out from **Dogpile** (as described in the section beginning on page 130).

Yippy.com (http://www.yippy.com—formerly Clusty.com; formerly Vivisimo.com)

Unlike other meta-search sites, **Yippy** creates a set of topical folders listed in the left-hand column, labeled *Top x Results* (where *x* is some number of results). A small number (in parentheses to the right of each folder's name) indicates the number of results in that folder. Folders can be expanded to show their contents by clicking on the plus sign (+) to the right of the folder. Folders may contain links to resources or sub-topical folders related to the topic of the main folder. Previously, the site referred to these groupings as *Clusters* or *Clouds*.

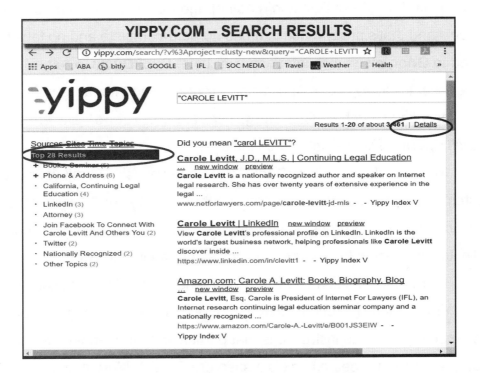

Additionally, **Yippy** offers specific details about how many results each source (to which it submitted your query) returned for your search. This level of information can be useful in case one of the search engines displays zero results, which may mean it is too busy processing other search requests or otherwise does not respond to **Yippy's** query. This information is accessible by clicking the *details* link above the search results (circled, to the right, in the previous illustration). None of the other meta-search sites offers a similar feature.

Another useful feature is **Yippy's** *Preview* option for links on a search results link. Clicking the *Preview* link that accompanies any result opens the requested pa within the results list page—without opening a new tab or otherwise navigating away from the results list.

Although **Yippy** claims it submits its queries to Ask, Open Directory, Gigablast and others, in our test searches **Yippy** results come mostly from news sources.

DuckDuckGo (http://www.duckduckgo.com)

Despite having a slightly sillier name than **Yippy**, **DuckDuckGo** focuses on search and search results with few added frills. Like the earliest versions of the **Google** interface, **DuckDuckGo's** homepage features a search box and a search button—and that's pretty much it. It has no auto-complete and no tabs like those added to **Google's** search interface over time. **DuckDuckGo** retrieves its results using the publicly available Application Programming Interfaces (APIs) of over 400 sites, including search engines **Bing**, **Yandex**, and **Yahoo!**, and crowd-sourced sites like **Wikipedia**. The default search includes results from all of these sources.

You can also use **DuckDuckGo** to anonymously submit your search to just one search engine, using special instructions they call "*Bangs*." Typing an exclamation point in the search box opens a drop-down menu that lists these *Bangs*. For example, *!g* limits your search to **Google** or *!b* limits your search to **Bing**.

More of these instructions can be found at http://duckduckgo.com/bang.html. When using *Bangs* to send a search to a particular search engine, you can use all of the search syntax and instructions that particular search engine recognizes (e.g., **Google's** proximity search as discussed previously). More than 9,000 *Bangs* are available.

Additionally, **DuckDuckGo** enhances users' privacy by not collecting or passing along information about the searches you perform. It does not store search history, IP addresses, or user agents. Additionally, the site does not pass along the phrases you've used in a search to the site you visit when you click on a lts list. Keep in mind however, that once you visit a site from the results n collect information about your activity on their site—including your IP

If you limit your **DuckDuckGo** *Bang* search to **Google**, be sure you are logged out of your **Google** account to remain anonymous.

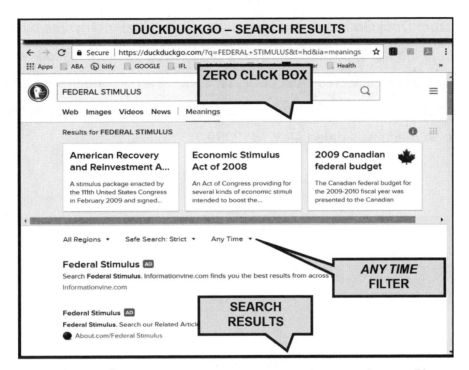

Many **DuckDuckGo** search results include an *"Instant Answer"* box at the top of the results list meant to provide the answer to your query without the need to click a link to read some other page. *Instant Answer* results are often compiled by human volunteers.

The site mostly delivers on its primary promises of relevant results with little clutter and increased privacy (as described earlier in this section).

DuckDuckGo minimizes clutter and spammy results by automatically eliminating millions of pages marked as "parked" or "spam" by its robot. It also places a lot of weight on content and links from crowd-sourced sites (where the content is created by potentially large numbers of users) because those sites are continuously being reviewed by the site's users. **DuckDuckGo** ranks those results above algorithmically generated results. However, these attempts to reduce the number of extraneous results can also lead to less discovery of useful investigative or background research information that is often found in "random" sites on the Internet. **DuckDuckGo** recognizes many of the connectors and instructions recognized by other search engines, such as the *minus sign (-)* to exclude a word or phrase, and the *filetype:* instruction to limit results to a specific type of file (e.g., PDF). (See page 80 for more details on the *filetype:* instruction.)

DuckDuckGo has also added a time filter (labeled *Anytime* by default) that appears at the top of the search results list, between *Instant Results* and the *Ads.* In our test searches, it works most of the time, however, in one test search one of the results incorrectly displayed after we selected the *Past Month* option from the *Anytime* drop-down menu was dated *May 14, 2009*.

Chapter Seven

FINDING OLDER VERSIONS OF
WEB PAGES THAT HAVE BEEN
DELETED OR REVISED

To find older versions of Web pages that have been deleted or revised, use **Google Cache**, **Yahoo! Cache**, **Bing Cache**, and **The Wayback Machine** (also known as the **Internet Archive** or by its URL, **Archive.org**).

Cached Pages at Bing, Google, or Yahoo!

If a page listed in **Bing**, **Google**, or **Yahoo!** search results is no longer available (e.g., you receive the dreaded "404 error" message when you click on it), you may still be able to access a version of that page that the search engine has stored on the search engine's own server for future reference and/or retrieval. This "cached" version is a copy of that particular page as it appeared at the time of the search engine robot's last visit to that page. Note that none of these search engines offers cached versions of all pages in its search index. They also don't make it obvious where to find the links to these cached versions.

Neither **Bing**, **Google**, nor **Yahoo!** displays their *Cached* link on the search results page any longer. To access the links to a *Cached* page you must click on the down-arrow (or triangle) next to the URL for the page you're interested in accessing. (See the next illustration.) This will open a pop-up window containing the *Cached* link.

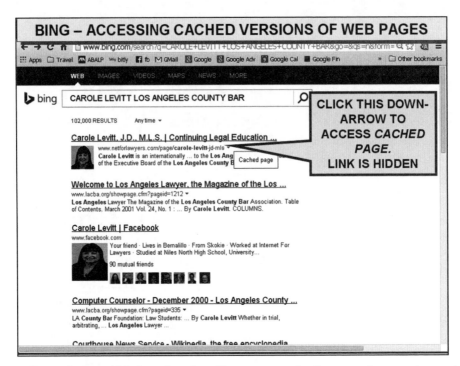

Bing, Google, and Yahoo! only offer access to the most recent version of a page that has been captured in their respective cache. All three include the date on which the cached copy was made (Google also includes the time).

Cached Pages at the Internet Archive's Wayback Machine

To find old versions of revised or deleted Web pages, you can also try the **Wayback Machine** (http://www.archive.org), which is an archive of nearly 300 billion old Web pages from 1996 to date. Unlike the traditional search engines we've discussed, which offer access only to the most recent cached versions of the old Web pages they've captured, the **Wayback Machine** offers access to all of the versions of any Web page it has ever captured.

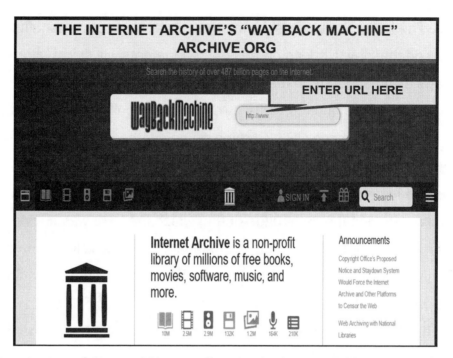

To locate any of these old pages that you're interested in, you must enter the URL of the specific site (or page) into the search box on **Archive.org's** homepage and hit the *Return/Enter* button on your keyboard.

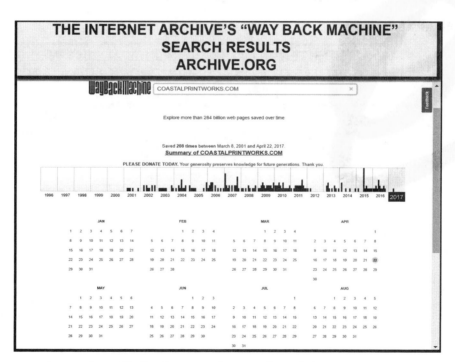

The search results will display a calendar list of the most recent captures of the URL for which you searched that are available in the **Wayback Machine's** collection. Each blue dot on the calendar represents a day on which the searched URL was crawled. The larger the blue dot is, the more *snapshots* of content from that URL were captured on that day. Clicking on any of the blue dots will display the version of that Web page as it appeared on the date selected.

The timeline at the top of the calendar graphically depicts the distribution of all captures for the searched URL. Clicking on any of the years in the timeline will then display all of the captures for the searched URL for the year selected. Above the timeline is a legend listing the number of times the searched URL has been crawled by **Archive.org** and the date range during which the URL was crawled. Note, however, that in our test searches, occasionally, when we clicked on a year where no captures were displayed in the timeline, the **Wayback Machine** would still display a cached page from the its collection.

The **Wayback Machine's** ability to store information from the pages it collects has increased over time. The site has always done a pretty good job collecting the text content of Web pages. However, the **Wayback Machine** has not always done as good a job capturing non-text content such as images, animations, or movies, as seen in the 2001-captured page of www.coastalprintworks.com, shown in the next illustration.

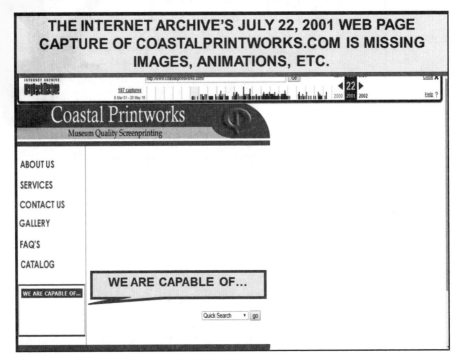

A more recent capture of the same website's homepage, seen in the next illustration, shows how the **Wayback Machine** now captures these non-text elements.

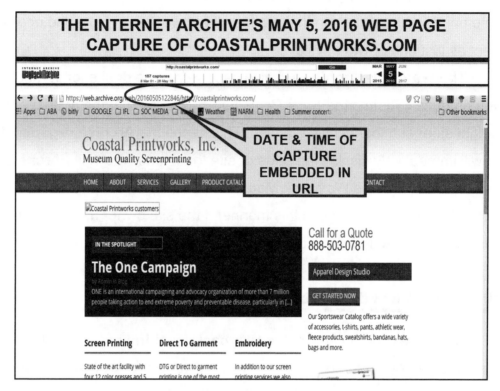

In addition to including the date on which a particular page was captured, the URL of a page displayed from the **Wayback Machine's** collection also includes the time that particular page was captured (as seen in the previous illustration). Together, this information could be used as a *de facto* third-party verification of the content of the page as it would have appeared on that date. Note that the time is Pacific Time and is expressed in a 24-hour clock format.

Clicking on a link on a page in the **Wayback Machine's** collection will take you to an archived version of the page you have requested—if one has been captured. Because the **Wayback Machine** does not capture every page of a site on every visit, clicking a link will take you to the next available version of the page you have requested. That page might have been captured the same day as the page you started on, or it might have been captured on some other date. So, it's important to note the date that the subsequent page was captured.

Archive.org had always stated that "it generally takes 6 months or more (up to 24 months) for pages to appear in the **Wayback Machine** after they are collected." However, since a January 2013 update of the site, we have been consistently able to locate pages in the collection that are less than two weeks old—and occasionally as recent as just one or two days old.

The **Wayback Machine** will also capture a page or site for immediate archiving if you enter its URL into the *Save Page Now* box located at the bottom of the page (on the right side) at http://archive.org/web. This sends the **Archive.org** robot to the URL and will immediately display the page or site to anyone who visits **Archive.org** and enters the URL into the **Wayback Machine's** search box. (Note that the **Archive.org** robot will not capture a page in this manner if the site owner has used the *robots.txt* exclusion explained in the next section.)

Full-Text Search of the Wayback Machine

Since the site's inception, the **Wayback Machine** has attempted several times to develop a keyword for its collection search. None ever worked well enough to become a permanent addition. In late 2016, that changed when the **Wayback Machine** added full-text search capability—sort of. The **Internet Archive's** full-text search of the **Wayback Machine** was in beta for a few years. It is now accessible from the search box on the site's homepage (https://www.archive.org).

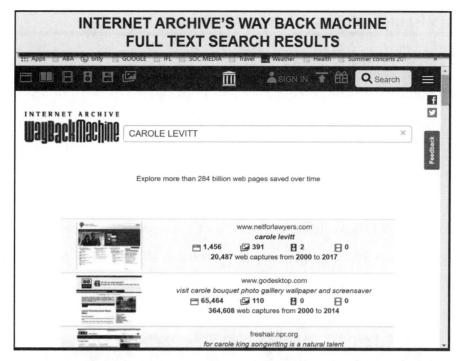

The **Internet Archive** announced the keyword search feature in a blog post (http://linkon.in/2qg25NP), describing it this way:

> With this new beta search service, users will now be able to find the <u>home pages</u> [emphasis added] of over 361 million websites preserved in the **Wayback Machine** just by typing in keywords that describe these sites (e.g. "new york times"). As they type keywords into the search box, they will be presented with a list of relevant archived websites with snippets containing:
>
> - a link to the archived versions of the site's homepage in the **Wayback Machine**
> - a thumbnail image of the site's homepage (when available)
> - a short description of the site's homepage
> - a capture summary of the site
>   - number of unique URLs by content type (webpage, image, audio, video)
>   - number of valid web captures over the associated time period

So, while you can conduct a keyword search through the collection, only the homepages of those sites are searchable and not pages or documents deeper within the site, which is why we said "sort of" at the outset of this section.

The **Wayback Machine** does not contain copies of every page on the Web—or even (in some instances) all of the content of the pages that it has captured.

By placing a special instruction for the **Archive.org** robot in their site's *robots.txt* file, any verified website owner can request that their site be excluded from the **Wayback Machine**. Most major social networking sites like **Facebook**, **Myspace**, and **LinkedIn** block **Archive.org** from collecting the content of user profiles in this way. (**Twitter** allows **Archive.org** to collect the contents of user profiles.) This is the message you will see if you search for someone's **Facebook** profile at **Archive.org**.

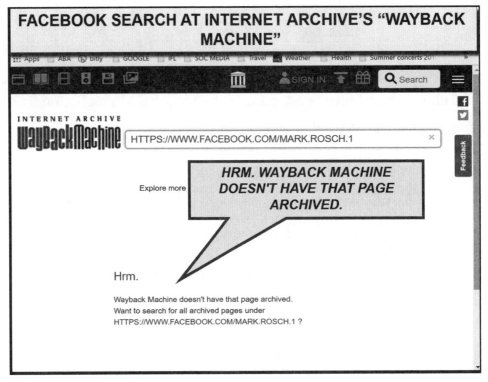

FACEBOOK SEARCH AT INTERNET ARCHIVE'S "WAYBACK MACHINE"

For a site that already has had their pages captured by the **Wayback Machine,** the site owner can ask that their pages be removed This action not only stops the collection of its pages going forward but also instructs **Archive.org** to permanently remove any pages that had previously been collected. (Web site owners can accomplish the same thing by making a request to **Archive.org** via e-mail at info@archive.org.)

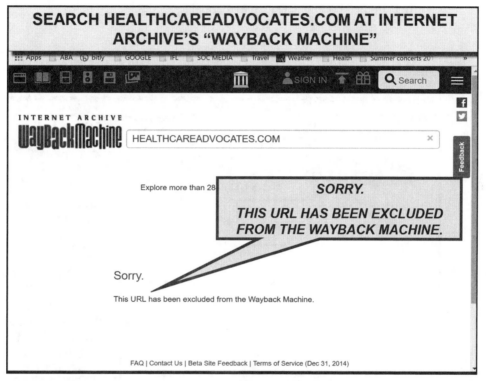

Note the differences in the two messages displayed in the two preceding illustrations. The first message indicates that pages (or the entire site) were never collected by the **Archive.org** robot. The second message indicates that the site owner requested their pages be removed by contacting **Archive.org** via email, or they added the *robots.txt* exclusion after pages from their site had been collected by **Archive.org**. After the **Archive.org** robot detected the addition of the robots.txt exclusion instruction, it stopped collecting pages from that site and deleted the pages it had previously collected.

As mentioned earlier, some older pages in the **Wayback Machine's** collection do not include images, animations, or other memory-intensive elements. While the **Wayback Machine** has gotten better over time about collecting these elements, it still has trouble collecting content from dynamic Web pages. (A dynamic Web page displays varying content based on the actions or input of the site's visitor.) The **Archive.org** site explains it this way:

> There are many different kinds of dynamic pages, some of which are easily stored in an archive and some of which fall apart completely. When a dynamic page renders standard html, the archive works beautifully. When a dynamic page contains forms, JavaScript, or other elements that require interaction with the originating host, the archive will not contain the original site's functionality.

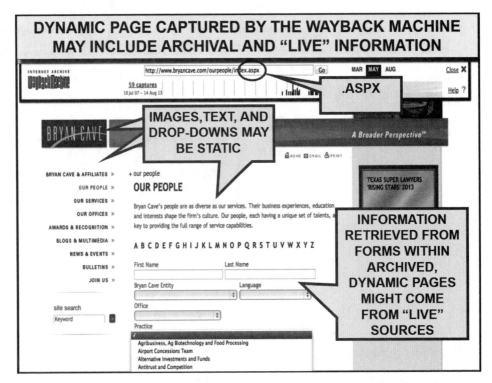

For some dynamic pages, this means that when they are displayed from the **Wayback Machine's** collection, features like search boxes or pull-down menus might not function as they did on the live version of the site. Other types of dynamic pages in the **Archive.org** collection might display a mix of archived, static content served from the **Archive.org** servers and current content served from the displayed site's own server. If you suspect that a page you're viewing might be dynamic, drawing both archived (static) and current (dynamic) elements, you might want to seek the advice of an expert in forensic Web page analysis.

Admissibility of Information from the Wayback Machine

Getting information from the Internet admitted into evidence should be no different than getting other traditional evidence admitted. Like traditional evidence, it too must be (1) relevant, and (2) authentic in order to be deemed admissible. While a judge makes the determination whether evidence is relevant and can be heard by the jury, it becomes the jury's responsibility to ascertain authenticity after an attorney makes a prima facie showing of genuineness. Relevancy is generally the easier of the two hurdles to overcome.

Proving the authenticity of Web page evidence might be straightforward when information is still posted on a party's own website, but it can prove to be problematic if the information you wish to get entered into evidence is no longer available at the original website and instead is only available via **Archive.org**.

Cases Admitting Evidence from the Wayback Machine

A Federal Magistrate Judge's Memorandum Opinion and Order in a *Motion in limine* hearing is widely cited as an example of a court allowing copies of Web pages from **Archive.org** into evidence. *Telewizja Polska USA, Inc. v. Echostar Satellite*, Case No. 02C3293 (N.D. Ill. Oct. 15, 2004), *available at* http://linkon.in/FQ7ojz. In that written (but not officially published) Memorandum Opinion, the magistrate rejected the plaintiff's claim that Web pages from the **Internet Archive** website were not properly authenticated and further rejected the plaintiff's attack on the **Internet Archive** website as an unreliable source. The magistrate stated that Federal Rules of Evidence Rule 901 requires only a prima facie showing of genuineness and leaves it to the jury to determine the true authenticity.

As to admissibility, many court opinions prior to *Telewizja* had indicated that hearsay objections to Internet evidence could be overcome, but none had addressed hearsay in terms of the **Internet Archive**. In the *Telewizja* Memorandum Opinion, the magistrate rejected the plaintiff's contention that the archived Web pages s[…] **Internet Archive** constituted hearsay, holding that they were not "statemer[…] rather they were merely images and text showing what a website once loo[…]

(The plaintiff had alleged they were "double hearsay," no less.) The magistrate also found that the website pages were an admission by a party-opponent and were admissible under the "best evidence" rule.

This would seem to be a worthwhile precedent to cite when trying to get Web pages retrieved from **Archive.org's** collection admitted into evidence—if the U.S. District Court judge hadn't overruled the magistrate. However, the overruling Judge did not create a written opinion, and the only reason we know about it is that an attorney told us. In our attempt to verify this, we sifted through the extensive docket for this case on **PACER** (Public Access to Court Electronic Records, discussed in *Chapter Thirteen*), but we were not able to locate the judge's order overruling the magistrate.

The only source we have found that mentions the judge's overruling the magistrate has been **Wikipedia**, the online encyclopedia to which anyone can make a contribution, discussed in *Chapter Two* (see http://en.wikipedia.org/wiki/Wayback_machine#Telewizja_Polska).

We do not recommend taking information found at **Wikipedia** as absolute fact. Cross-checking and verifying information found on the Internet is important. (Some courts have allowed information found at **Wikipedia** into evidence (e.g., *Allegheny Defense Project v. United States Forest Service*, 423 F.3d 215, (W.D. PA 2005), *available at* http://linkon.in/M2CE5S, while others have not (e.g., *Palisades Collection v. Graubard,* Docket No. A-1338-07T3 (NJ Superior Court April 17, 2009), *available at* http://linkon.in/2rieAb9. See page 43 for additional cases on this topic.)

Finally, we resorted to one of the oldest (and non-cyber) research methods— we picked up the phone and called the prevailing attorney who represented Telewizja Polska. He confirmed that the judge had indeed overruled the magistrate during the course of the trial but that there was no written opinion. (Although the ruling would probably be in the transcript, we did not download the transcript due to the expense. The attorney we spoke to also did not have a copy of the transcript because the case wasn't appealed).

Despite the fact that the judge apparently overruled the Magistrate in *Telewizja* and did not admit the printout of pages from the **Wayback Machine**, there was no written opinion. So, many courts continued to cite to the Magistrate's decision to allow in similar evidence because the decision was written. For example, in *SP Technologies v. Garmin International,* No. 08 C 3248 (N.D. Illinois, September 30, 2009),*available at* http://linkon.in/2svNivv, the court relied on *Telewizja* to admit printouts from the **Wayback Machine**, explaining:

> According to Plaintiff, the Web site has not been authenticated pursuant to Federal Rule of Evidence 901. That rule, however, requires only "evidence sufficient to support a finding that the matter in question is what its proponent claims." FED. R. EVID. 901(a). Here, Defendant has attached an affidavit from a manager at the Internet Archive, who explained how that Web site saves old web pages and that Defendant's Exhibit D was created in 1999. (Butler Aff. [182].) Plaintiff's argument amounts to a suggestion that the printout of this Web site would be admissible only if a person with direct knowledge of the Web site's existence in 1999 testified that the printout was a true and accurate copy of the contents of the Web site on that date. Such a high standard is not required for other types of evidence, and is beyond what Rule 901 requires. See *United States v. Harvey*, 117 F.3d 1044, 1049 (7th Cir. 1997) (Rule 901 "requires only a prima facie showing of genuineness and leaves it to the jury to decide the true authenticity and probative value of the evidence"). The court therefore notes Plaintiff's concerns about the reliability of the printout, but nevertheless concludes that the printout is admissible as evidence and denies the motion to strike. Accord *Telewizja Polska USA, Inc. v. Echostar Satellite Corp.*, No. 02 C 3293, 2004 WL 2367740, at *6 (N.D. Ill. Oct. 15, 2004) (admitting evidence from the Internet Archive when accompanied by an affidavit from an Internet Archive official).

In *Keystone Retaining Wall Sys. v. Basalite Concrete Prods.*, Case No. 10-CV-4085 (D. Minn., December 19, 2011), *available at* http://linkon.in/HIC0gB, the court rejected the argument that pictures from the Internet Archive were not sufficiently authenticated and stated, "The Internet Archive has existed since 1996, and federal courts have regularly accepted evidence from the Internet Archive." Id. at 34, n. 9. The court did not cite *Telewizja.*

In *Johns Manville v. Knauf Insulation* IPR2015-01453, paper 49 (PTAB Jan. 11, 2017), available at http://linkon.in/2r4ozBR, the Patent and Trademark Appeals Board accepted pages printed from the **Wayback Machine** as authentic evidence of prior art.

Not every court will take judicial notice of pages from the **Wayback Machine**, but will instead require an affidavit to authenticate the pages. For instance, in *My Health v. General Electric Company,* No. 15-cv-80-jdp (W.D.WI December 28, 2015), *available at* http://linkon.in/2s02XH6, the court ruled:

> The Wayback Machine is a third-party archive. Although information about historical websites is commonly used in this sort of litigation, its evidence is not so reliable and self-explanatory that it may be an appropriate candidate for judicial notice. The Seventh Circuit has approved of requiring a "knowledgeable" Internet Archive employee to authenticate Wayback Machine submissions before a court considers them. *Specht v. Google Inc.,*747 F.3d 929, 933 (7th Cir. 2014) ("[T]he district court reasonably required authentication by someone with personal knowledge of reliability of the archive service from which the screenshots were retrieved."). The court will not take judicial notice of information established by submissions that require authentication. If properly authenticated and supported with affidavits, GE may submit this evidence in support of a motion for summary judgment, but it is not so unequivocally reliable that the court should take judicial notice of it.

Cases Not Admitting Evidence from the Wayback Machine

Another unreported federal case in which the court would not admit Web pages obtained from **Archive.org** into evidence is *Novak v. Tucows,* No. 06-CV-1909, 2007 U.S. Dist. Lexis 21269 (E.D.N.Y. March 26, 2007), *available at* http://linkon.in/novaktucows. As part of his reasoning for this denial, the judge cited the *St. Clair* opinion (which we discussed earlier, in *Chapter Two*) and its characterization of information located on the Internet as "voodoo information."

How to Obtain an Affidavit from the Wayback Machine

Details for the process to obtain **Archive.org's** "Standard Affidavit," verifying printouts of pages from their collection, can be found at https://archive.org/legal/. **Archive.org**'s "Standard Affidavit" can be located at https://archive.org/legal/affidavit.php.

The site charges a minimum of $250 per request for an affidavit to authenticate specific pages printed from its collection. There is an additional $20-$30 charge per individual page, dependent on the type of content on that page. Notarizing the affidavit requires another $100 payment.

Archive-It (http://www.archive-it.org) is a subscription-based web archiving service from the **Internet Archive,** "that helps organizations to harvest, build, and preserve collections of digital content." It includes a keyword searchable collection of over 5 billion Web pages from state and local government agencies, public and private libraries, academic and court law libraries, and other institutions. The site has partnered with more than 400 entities in 48 U.S. states and 16 countries.

Initial keyword search results return collections with matching keywords. It is then necessary to select a specific collection in which to search. Content owners must subscribe to the **Archive-It** archiving and storage service in order to be included. Public availability of pages in any particular collection will vary.

Chapter Eight

INTRODUCTION TO INVESTIGATIVE RESEARCH

Whether you are conducting investigative research to locate a missing person or to gather background information about a person or company, there is a wide variety of free and low-cost resources to help you. We'll begin with some definitions of the various types of information you will be using to conduct investigative research. In subsequent chapters, we will take a close look at how to use specific websites for investigative research.

Note that these chapters are geared more to lawyers in the private sector; government lawyers and law enforcement personnel often have more access to certain investigative information than private lawyers.

Publicly Available Information

Much of the information that you find on the Internet to use for investigative research is referred to as "publicly available" information. It is information that you voluntarily provided to a private entity, which then made it public, or it is information that you voluntarily published in a public place. For example, if you provide your phone number and address to certain private entities—such as the telephone company—that information becomes publicly available via their published directories, unless you specifically opt out of being included. If you publish information on the Internet at an online community, social networking site, your website, or your blog, this is now publicly available information (unless the site is password protected). If someone else wrote about you, such as in a news or magazine article, or on their blog or website, this information could also become publicly available.

Some companies make a business of scraping publicly available information off the Internet to create vast databases of this information that they then resell to marketing companies or investigative research database vendors, who in turn sell it to subscribers. All of these bits of information, which might seem innocuous on their own, once aggregated into one database, can be searched to create a complete dossier about a person.

"Public Records" vs. "Publicly Available" Information

"Public records" refers to records filed with a governmental agency. They often offer the best way to find and investigate people and companies. The definition of what constitutes a public record varies from jurisdiction to jurisdiction. What is considered public in one state may not be considered public in another.

The availability of public records also varies from jurisdiction to jurisdiction. Just because a record is considered public does not mean that it must be made available on the Web (whether for free or pay-for-use). In some instances, records that are available online from one county office might not be available online from the equivalent office in another county, even in the same state.

In jurisdictions that do not provide Web access to their public records, you may be forced to resort to using a commercial pay-for-use database, using "snail mail," or visiting the offices of the repository agency in person to retrieve copies of those records. Some jurisdictions provide Web access to their information but require online payment to access it. Some states, such as Florida, not only have a plethora of free public records information on the Web (such as liens, judgments, trademark owner names, corporate records, and annual reports), they also provide the actual images of the full public record (http://www.sunbiz.org).

Public Records and "Personally Identifiable" Information

In the realm of public records, your name, Social Security Number (SSN), date of birth, address, and phone number are referred to as "personally identifiable information." (See the discussion beginning on page 489 for sources of "personally identifying" information.) Sometimes this type of information is completely shielded from public access and at other times it is partially redacted. So, not all parts of certain public records are available to the public.

Public Records and "Sensitive" Information

Some public records contain sensitive information. Sensitive information is any information in a public record that, if released, could cause embarrassment, bias, or harm (such as a divorce decree that includes children's names or a bankruptcy record that includes bank names and account numbers). This information is often redacted, thus portions of public records can become private. (See next section.)

Private Records

Some entire records filed with government agencies are considered private, such as tax returns and driver's license information. In other cases, as noted earlier, only portions of some records are considered private. Private records can be accessed if the subject of the record consents or if there are laws providing for exceptions, such as the Driver's Privacy Protection Act discussed in the next section.

Public or Private Records? Driver's License Records

In 2000, the U.S. Supreme Court, in *Reno v. Condon*, 528 U.S. 141 (*available at* http://linkon.in/ABDb7U), deemed driver's license records, which had up until that point been considered public records, to now be private under the Driver's Privacy Protection Act, 18 U.S.C. 2721 (DPPA), (*available at* http://www.law.cornell.edu/uscode/text/18/2721). However, under 18 U.S.C. 2721(b), the DPPA does allow access to driver's license information, without the licensee's consent, if you can meet one of the fourteen specified "Permissible Uses." Lawyers will generally be able to meet the fourth permissible use, while insurance companies can meet the sixth and private investigators can meet the eighth:

> (4) For use in connection with any civil, criminal, administrative, or arbitral proceeding in any Federal, State, or local court or agency or before any self-regulatory body, including the service of process, investigation in anticipation of litigation, and the execution or enforcement of judgments and orders, or pursuant to an order of a Federal, State, or local court.

> (6) For use by any insurer or insurance support organization, or by a self-insured entity, or its agents, employees, or contractors, in connection with claims investigation activities, antifraud activities, rating or underwriting.

> (8) For use by any licensed private investigative agency or licensed security service for any purpose permitted under this subsection.

Access to driver's license records varies from state to state. Some states only require you to provide a name, while other states require you to also provide a date of birth or other identifying information. The more information that states require from the researcher, the less accessible the records become. **BRB Publications** has compiled a comprehensive book, *The MVR Access and Decoder Digest*, detailing how to access driver's license information, driving histories, VIN (Vehicle Identification Numbers), and registration information for vehicles and vessels in the United States (on a state-by-state basis), Guam, Puerto Rico, the Virgin Islands, and Canada. (To purchase the book, see https://brbpublications.com/books/detail/538.aspx?Id=538.)

Some of the pay-for-use investigative research database vendors offer driver's license databases, but to search them, you must select one of the DPPA-permissible uses (noted earlier) from the database's drop-down menu. **TLOxp** (http://www.tlo.com) only offers current driver's license information for two states (Florida and Texas). (See *Chapter Twenty-Eight* for more information about **TLOxp**.)

"Proprietary" Information

Proprietary information is a catchall category for information that investigative research database vendors purchase from sources they typically won't divulge. This could range from entities that capture your address, such as a utility company or a local restaurant that delivers food to your home, to a magazine you subscribe to.

Chapter Nine

USING A GENERAL SEARCH ENGINE OR A PEOPLE META-SEARCH SITE TO FIND OR INVESTIGATE PEOPLE

We usually begin searching for information about people by running their names through a general search engine, such as **Google**. This process is often just referred to as "Googling." Even though it is very hit or miss, it is often worth the time. Of course, if you are trying to find a missing person, be sure to first ascertain whether your subject is still alive before wasting time Googling your subject. See page 290 for details on ascertaining whether your subject is no longer alive.

Proper name searching can be a challenge, not only because so many people have the same name but because people often use variations of their names. Some people always use their full name (first, middle, and last names) while others never use their middle name, and then there's always nicknames, not to mention misspellings and name changes when someone gets married or divorced.

If the subject always uses the same variation of his/her name, search it as a phrase (by enclosing it in quotation marks). For example, if Carole Ann Levitt always goes by "Carole Levitt," search it that way, or if she always goes by "Carole Ann Levitt," search it that way. But, if she sometimes goes by "Carole Ann Levitt" and at other times goes by "Carole Levitt," or "Carole A. Levitt," it's best to connect her first and last name with a Proximity connector so your results include all variations of her name. **Google** is the only free search engine that provides a Proximity search. See pages 58–60 for details on how to search **Google** using its Proximity connector.

Note that search results from Google and the other major search engines will typically include alternate spellings of a person's name if you do not use quotation marks. For instance, a search for *Carole Levitt* will also bring back results for *Carol Levitt* or *Carole Leavitt*. This can be helpful if a proper name was misspelled by a source but at other times it can be distracting if the results are for a different person entirely.

Using People Meta-Search Sites to Find or Investigate People

People meta-search sites (also referred to as "people information aggregator sites") are different from search engines (such as **Google**) because they do not create and maintain their own index for searching but instead submit your search to other sites that mostly focus on information about people. The meta-search site then summarizes the information into a results list, which sometimes includes photos, with links to the originating sites.

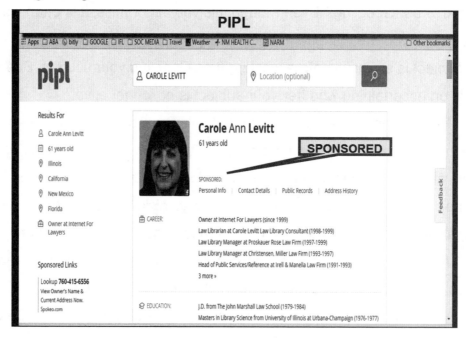

Pipl.com (http://www.Pipl.com; pronounced "people") is the most useful people meta-search site and is still available for free. The search box on **Pipl's** homepage can be searched by name, e-mail address, username, or phone number. Adding a location is optional, but helpful. Search results could include people who share the same name and variations of your subject's name. Once you select the name that appears to belong to your subject, the summary result (as shown in the next illustration) is displayed in a format akin to a resume, showing a photo of your subject and, in this case, a history of your subject's *Career* and *Education*, *Usernames*, *Phones*, *Additional Names* (aliases), *Places* (of residence), people your subject is *Associated With*, and links to the subject's other social media profiles (e.g., **LinkedIn**, **Facebook**, **Twitter**). You never know what you'll find using **Pipl**. For our test search, we also found links to articles authored by Carole, information about professional association offices she held, and even her childhood street name.

The information appears to have been scraped from multiple sites so it saves you the time of searching each site one by one. Click on any of the results, including photos, to visit the originating sites, most of which are free to access. If you click on the *Sponsored* links, however, you will be taken to pay-for-use sites.

Many of the free people meta-search sites we used to rely on have gone out of business (e.g., **123People.com**), or are now fee-based (e.g., **ZoomInfo.com** at http://www.zoominfo.com and **Spokeo.com** at http://www.spokeo.com), or primarily exist to send you to a pay-for-use site (e.g., **Zabasearch.com** at http://www.zabasearch.com) that shows an address and phone number for your search target and then tries to sell you an **Intelius** report (geared to the general public).

Intelius (https://www.intelius.com) is a fee-based consumer investigative research site that we do not recommend that lawyers pay for because it contains less fresh information, at a higher price, than the investigative research sites that lawyers can subscribe to, such as **TLOxp** at http://www.tlo.com (see pages 496–509). However, **Intelius** does provide some "teaser" information for free (see page 512), which could be useful.

Radaris (http://radaris.com), like **Intelius**, primarily exists to send you to a pay-for-use site and provides "teaser" information that can be useful. After you identify the correct result and view the free "teaser" information, be aware that if you then click on *Full Profile*, you will be presented with various reports and pricing plans that go as high as $49.95. We were less than impressed with the **Radaris** results for our test search of *Carole Levitt* because none of the results with the heading *Carole Levitt* were for "our" *Carole Levitt*. The correct result was the one with the heading of *Carole L Axelrood,* a name she used for only four years. It wasn't until after we scanned the *Known as* and the *Related to* sections of each result that we were able to conclude that the *Carole L Axelrood* result was the correct result. The names *Carole L. Levitt, Carole Rosch, and C Levitt* were listed in the *Known as* section of the *Carole L Axelrood* results and the names *Robert Levitt* and *Sally Levitt* (her parents) and Mark Rosch (her husband) were listed in the *Related to* section. Only if you knew enough about *Carole Levitt* would these clues have helped you to select the *Carole L Axelrood* result as the correct result.

One thing that impressed us, though, was that **Radaris** listed *Robert Levitt* and *Sally Levitt* as being relatives. We've rarely (if ever) seen that connection made at other databases.

Chapter Ten

HOW TO QUICKLY FIND PUBLIC RECORDS AND PUBLICLY AVAILABLE INFORMATION SITES

Directory Web Sites

The following are some of the most useful directories for finding sites that contain free public records and publicly available background information, with the most useful listed first:

- **Search Systems** (http://publicrecords.searchsystems.net)
- **Portico** (http://linkon.in/porticopubrec)
- **BRB Publications** (https://www.brbpublications.com)
- **Black Book Online** (http://www.blackbookonline.info)

Search Systems

Search Systems (http://publicrecords.searchsystems.net) provides over 55,000 links to free (and some pay) searchable public records resources and publicly available information sites. On its homepage, notice that **Search Systems** also offers *Premium Databases* and a search box labeled *People Search*, both of which are pay databases that we will discuss later (see page 514).

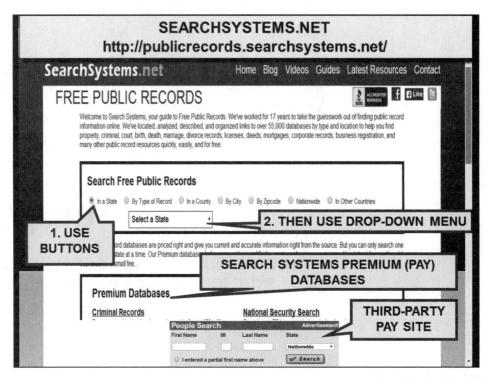

To find a specific public record or publicly available information site, click one of the following categories' radio buttons (shown in the previous screenshot): *In a State, By Type of Record*, *In a County*, *By City*, *By Zipcode*, *Nationwide*, or *In Other Countries*. Our sample search shows that we clicked the *In a State* radio button, at which point a drop-down menu appeared to *Select a State*. Each category's radio button offers either a different drop-down menu with choices relevant to that category or a search box for you to enter your query (e.g., if you choose the *By Zipcode* radio button, you would enter a Zipcode into the search box).

As you scroll down the homepage, there are other ways to search (see the next screenshot): *Search By Category* (such as *Birth Records*, *Court Records*, etc.)*, Search By State* (select a state from the alphabetical list)*, United States Nationwide* (such as *Adoption Resources*, *Campaign Contributions*, or *Census Records), United States Territories, Canada Nationwide* (or select a province from the alphabetical list), or by continent (select a continent from the alphabetical list).

SEARCHSYSTEMS.NET

Search By Category

Attorneys	Death Records	Property Records
Birth Records	Deeds & Mortgages	Recorded Documents
Corporations & Companies	Divorce Records	Registered Offenders
Court Records	Licenses	Unclaimed Property
Criminal Codes	Marriage Records	Uniform Commercial Code
Criminal Records	Missing Persons	Vital Records
Criminal Wants & Warrants	Outer Space	Voter Records

Search By State

Alabama	Kentucky	North Dakota
Alaska	Louisiana	Ohio
Arizona	Maine	Oklahoma
Arkansas	Maryland	Oregon
California	Massachusetts	Pennsylvania
Colorado	Michigan	Rhode Island
Connecticut	Minnesota	South Carolina
District of Columbia	Mississippi	South Dakota
Delaware	Missouri	Tennessee
Florida	Montana	Texas
Georgia	Nebraska	Utah
Hawaii	Nevada	Vermont
Idaho	New Hampshire	Virginia
Illinois	New Jersey	Washington
Indiana	New Mexico	West Virginia
Iowa	New York	Wisconsin
Kansas	North Carolina	Wyoming

United States Nationwide   United States Territories

Canada Nationwide

Alberta	Northwest Territories	Prince Edward Island
British Columbia	Nova Scotia	Quebec
Manitoba	Nunavut	Saskatchewan
New Brunswick	Ontario	Yukon
Newfoundland & Labrador		
Africa	Central America and Caribbean	North America

Regardless of which state you choose, each of the state pages is set up the same way (as shown in the next illustration). First, down the middle of the page, there will be explanations about the state's *Public Records Act*, *Court System*, *Criminal*

Records, and *Vital Records.* Then there will be drop-down menus on the left-hand side (*Montana Counties, Montana Cities*, *Montana by Topic,* and *Montana Licenses*) that allow you to filter your search.

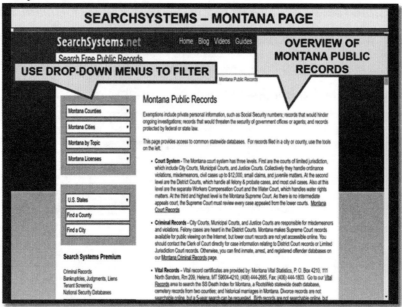

The state page continues with an alphabetical list of the *Most Popular* public record links (and publicly available information sites) in that state, followed by an alphabetical list of additional *Public Records* links in that state. Each public record entry is annotated and indicates if it's a *Pay Site*. Click any entry to visit its website.

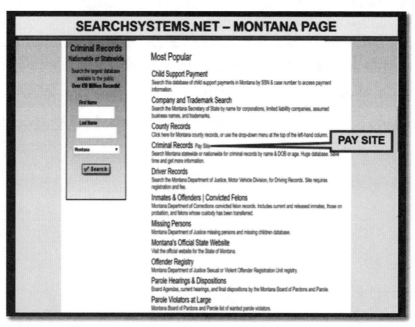

Portico (http://linkon.in/porticopubrec) links to public records sites and to publicly available information sites. It seems to offer more publicly available information sites than **Search Systems**, so if you aren't finding what you need at **Search Systems**, visit **Portico**. Links are arranged topically, then jurisdictionally. For example, after you click the topic *Real Estate,* a list of states appears. Choose a state and you will see links to statewide and/or county real estate assessor sites.

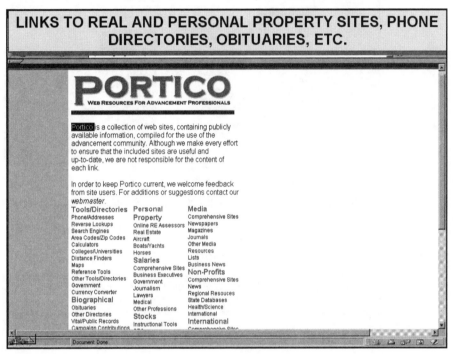

BRB Publications

BRB Publications (https://www.brbpublications.com) offers an extensive collection of free links to numerous sources for locating public records, including civil records, criminal records, driving records, real estate records, legislation, and state occupational licensing boards. Click *Free Public Record Searches* (shown in the next illustration) to view the links or use this direct URL: http://linkon.in/brbsearchpubrec.

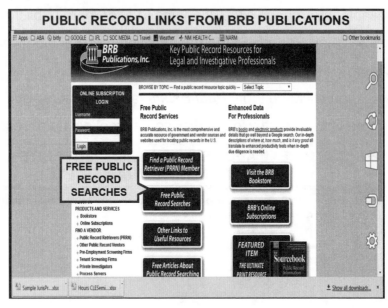

The next illustration shows the California free public record search page. Click a California county from one of the two left-hand columns to go to that county's public record sites or use the links down the middle for California state agency sites.

To locate a public record retriever who can physically retrieve copies of records not available online, click *Find a Public Record Retriever Number* (*PRRN*) *Member* from the homepage. Then, on the resulting page, use the drop-down menu to select a state and county to search by county, or just a state to return all companies who search in that state. To see results, you will need to click the *Go* button.

If you want more information and more links, **BRB** offers a subscription database product, its *Public Record Research System* (*PRRS*), at http://linkon.in/brbprrs. The database, which is updated weekly, details how to access records from more than 26,000 government agencies and institutions. The cost is $129 annually or $11.95 monthly. Ad hoc access is also available for a single month for $12.95.

Black Book Online

Black Book Online (http://www.blackbookonline.info) is sponsored by Crime Time Publishing, a publisher of books. It is geared toward private investigators and is owned by a Los Angeles-area private investigator. The site provides links to a variety of databases (e.g., telephone directories, reverse lookups, business information, court records, skip tracing resources, and death records).

At the top of its homepage, you can search **Black Book Online** by a subject's name. Adding a city or state is optional. Scrolling down the homepage, you can search the site's collection of public records resources using the *Find Free Public Record Lookups* search box. Scrolling even further down the homepage you can browse alphabetical lists by public record type or by state. Most of the sites and databases found at **Black Book Online** are free.

Each entry includes useful annotations about the site or database, as shown in the next illustration.

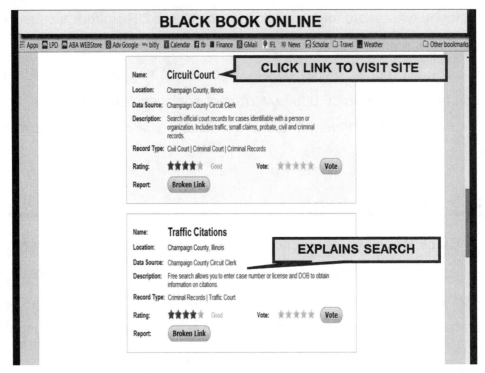

Some of the sites seemed a bit suspect at first, such as the *Spy Dialer Free Cell Phone Number Search Tool*, which allows you to enter a phone number (either cell phone or landline at **Spy Dialer's** site (http://www.spydialer.com) to learn who owns that number. Search results can include *Hear Voicemail*, *Name Lookup*, and *Photo Lookup*. Selecting the *Hear Voicemail* option (which is not available for all results) connects to the phone number you enter and retrieves the owner's voicemail greeting so you can hear (through your computer's speakers) whose phone it is (assuming they identify themselves). Note that the site returned voicemail messages for only two of the five phone numbers we searched.

The site claims its search is "sneaky…but legal." However, it is not as stealthy as it once was. Now, if you are using one of the two free options, the recipient of the phone call will see a phone number (not yours) in their caller ID when **Spy Dialer** connects to the phone. If the phone's owner calls that number, they will hear a message that informs them that they have been "spy dialed," but it does not identify who "spy dialed" them. The pay option leaves a Caller ID number that "is super-stealthy and can't be connected to," according to the site.

Free users are limited to three "spy dials" per day. You can get up to 100 "spy dials" over a 30-day period if you upload your phone's contact list to the site for them to add to their database (not recommended). A $9.95 membership also gives you 100 "spy dials" to use within 365 days.

Chapter Eleven

SEARCHING USENET (DISCUSSION) GROUPS, FORUMS, MESSAGE BOARDS, AND BLOGS, TO FIND AND INVESTIGATE PEOPLE

When you need to find, or investigate a person, Usenet (discussion) group postings, forums, message boards, and blogs (personal Web logs) were once good options because they included all kinds of personal information, rumors, and public opinion. While they still may be useful, social media sites have largely replaced them as a source for this kind of information.

Searching Usenet (Discussion) Groups

Google maintains **Google Groups** (http://groups.google.com), an archive of over 800 million full-text searchable Usenet "postings" (also referred to as "messages") sent to public Usenet groups since 1981 and posts from other online discussion and message boards. The database can be keyword searched using *Search for groups or messages* search box at the top.

There are numerous sites available that offer access to databases of Usenet postings, including:

- **Binsearch** (http://binsearch.info)
- **BinZB** (http://binzb.com)

Unfortunately, most of these focus on the newer types of posts that include downloadable media and not the older text/e-mail messages. Also, none are very user friendly, and they require either a paid subscription to a Usenet provider or the use of newsreader software to read the posts.

BoardReader (http://www.boardreader.com) searches thousands of message boards and forums. (The terms, used interchangeably, refer to online discussion sites where people can hold conversations by posting messages.) The *Advanced Search* is no longer on the homepage. You have to click on the magnify glass icon that appears next to the search box on the homepage (as shown in the next illustration).

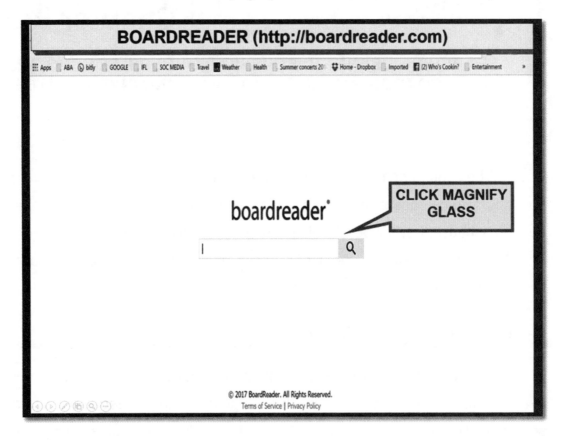

The *Advanced search* menu (as shown in the next illustration) takes two more steps to appear: first you click a gear icon and then click the *Advanced Search* link (not shown in the next illustration). Now you can create a more sophisticated search by entering your keywords into the search boxes labeled *with all the words, with the exact phrase*, or *without the words*. You can also limit your results to a certain *Language*, *Date*, or *Domain* (or a combination of any of these three options), and then sort by *Relevance* or *Freshness*.

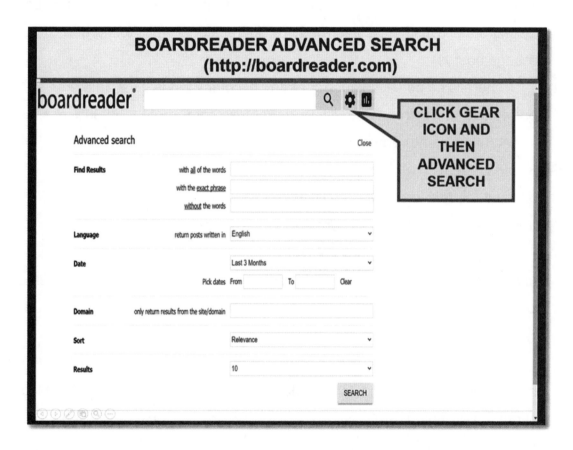

Blogs (short for personal "Web logs") are similar in their look and feel to traditional websites but are less formal in tone and content. However, some might remind you of groups, forums, or message boards, if they allow visitors to post comments. Blogs usually contain more personal information about the blogger (and the people the blogger is posting about), as well as the blogger's opinions about various people and topics. Thus, blogs can be a more useful and voluminous source of background/investigative information than traditional websites, groups, forums, or message boards.

There is no definitive answer as to how many blogs exist. In March 2018, it was reported that **WordPress** (http://www.wordpress.com) more than 30% of sites on the Internet (https://venturebeat.com/2018/03/05/wordpress-now-powers-30-of-websites/; posted March 5, 2018). And, in August 2018, its users published over 77 million new posts and readers left over 7.8 million new comments (https://wordpress.com/activity/posting/; retrieved on September 5, 2018).

You can keyword search **WordPress.com** hosted blogs at http://en.search.wordpress.com. This search includes only those blogs hosted at **WordPress.com** and not blogs that use **WordPress** software but are hosted elsewhere.

Google created a separate search engine to locate information posted to blogs that were published both on its blog platform (Blogger.com) and on other blog platforms. Unfortunately, **Google** disabled its Blog Search. It has instead rolled blog results into "regular" Web and News search results (where they had already been included). Those blog results are primarily weighted towards larger commercial/news blogs (e.g., Huffington Post, Slate, Washington Post, Wall Street Journal), as opposed to the smaller, more-personal blogs that had previously been included, thus making the results less useful for finding or investigating people.

Tumblr.com (https://www.tumblr.com) allows you to keyword search its 347 million blogs, but you will have to look closely to find the search box in the upper left-hand corner because it is faint and hard to notice until you click into it. What you don't have to look closely for is its sign-up page, which stands out in the middle of the homepage. Don't be fooled into thinking you must sign up to search **Tumblr**.

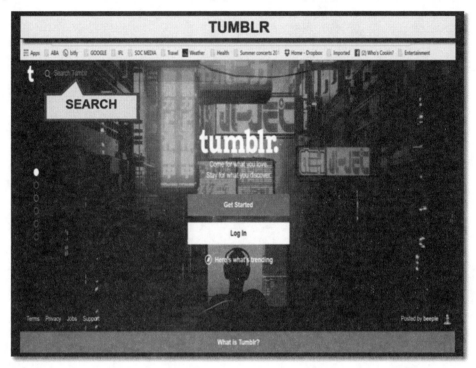

To keyword search law-related blogs, which are sometimes referred to as "blawgs", see **Justia.com's BlawgSearch** (http://blawgsearch.justia.com). You can also browse through its list of *Most Popular* blawgs, browse by *Categories*, view its *Featured Blawger*, or click on its *Recent Search Terms* to learn which topics are the most popular with searchers at **BlawgSearch**.

The ABA Journal's **Blawg Directory** is another source for locating useful blawgs (http://www.abajournal.com/blawgs). It can be keyword searched (use the search box on the upper-right side) or browsed by *Topic, Author Type* (e.g., consultant, judge, etc.), *Region* (by court, state, or country), *Law School*, and *Courts*. Also, see the ABA Journal's annual **Blawg 100** list posted every December (http://www.abajournal.com/blawg100).

For those interested in creating their own blogs, see, for example, **Google's Blogger.com** (http://www.blogger.com), **Movable Type** (http://www.movabletype.org), **WordPress.org** (http://www.wordpress.org), or to create a legal-specific blog, see **Justia** (http://www.justia.com/marketing/law-blogs) or **LexBlog** (http://www.lexblog.com).

Chapter Twelve

USE YOUR PUBLIC LIBRARY CARD FOR REMOTE ACCESS TO EXPENSIVE PAY DATABASES FOR FREE

Remote Access to Expensive Pay Databases for Free from Your Public Library

Many public libraries (from the smallest to the largest) provide free remote access to useful and current databases, which would be very costly if you had to pay to use them. Most of these databases are full-text and updated regularly (some as often as daily). There are two tricks to accessing library databases: (1) you must have a library card (and sometimes a pin number), and (2) you must know where to find the databases on your library's website. Look for links to *Research* or *Homework* or *Databases*—or similar labels. In this chapter, we do not provide URLs to any of the databases that public libraries offer because you do NOT access the databases directly; you access them through your library's website.

If you don't know your public library's URL, enter the name of your city or town and the keyword *library* to locate a link to your local public library.

Public library remote databases cover such topics as business, news, finance, law, science, medical, and more. These databases can be used for finding background information about clients, the opposition, a company, a product, or a topic about which you need to get up to speed.

Each public library decides which databases it wants to subscribe to, so it will vary from library to library as to what is available to library patrons. The next illustration is an example of the remote access databases from the Oklahoma County Metropolitan Library System (http://www.metrolibrary.org/research), which can be browsed alphabetically, or by audience (e.g., senior, child), or by category. If you know the name of the database, you can enter it into the search box.

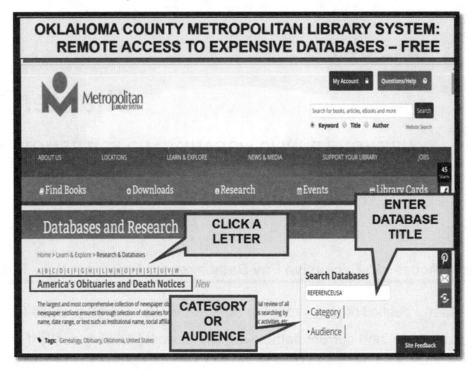

Newspaper databases are usually full-text and can range from the **New York Times** to many other national, international, and regional/local newspapers (some of which might include obituaries and advertisements). For example, the Oklahoma County Metropolitan Library System's library patrons can remotely access the following newspaper databases:

- **Access NewspaperARCHIVE**: Search tens of millions of U.S. and international newspapers with coverage going back more than 400 years.

- **America's Newspapers**: Search over 1,700 newspapers and other news sources including college/university newspapers, magazines, newswires, and radio and TV transcripts from across the U.S.

- **MasterFILE Premier:** Contains the full text of thousands of general reference magazines and publications that cover a wide range of subject areas including business, health, education, general science, multicultural issues, and more.

- **Newsbank - The Oklahoman** (1981–present): full-text archives of The Oklahoman newspaper, exclusive of paid advertisements, from 1981–present.

- **Newspaper Source Plus:** full-text access to thousands of U.S. and international newspapers and over one million radio and TV transcripts from sources like ABC News, CBS News, CNBC, CNN, Fox News, MSNBC, National Public Radio, PBS, and more.

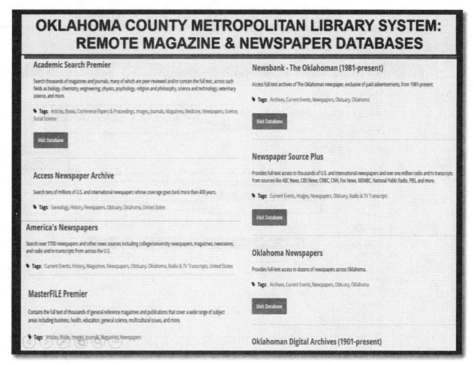

Most library remote databases include articles from hundreds (if not thousands) of magazines. Also offered are a variety of business directories, such as:

- **Gale's Business Insights: Essentials**, which includes company background information, broker reports, and more.

- **ReferenceUSA** (or the similar **AtoZdatabases**), which provides addresses and phone numbers for businesses and also background reports on private and public businesses. In addition to business information, **ReferenceUSA** and **AtoZdatabases** are useful databases for people-finding research. Both databases include names of millions of U.S. people, with their phone numbers and addresses. **ReferenceUSA** also offers a Canadian version to which some U.S. libraries also subscribe.

To begin a **ReferenceUSA** search (after you have visited your public library's website and entered your library card number), you can choose categories from the left-hand column to create a customized search form for each search (shown in the next illustration).

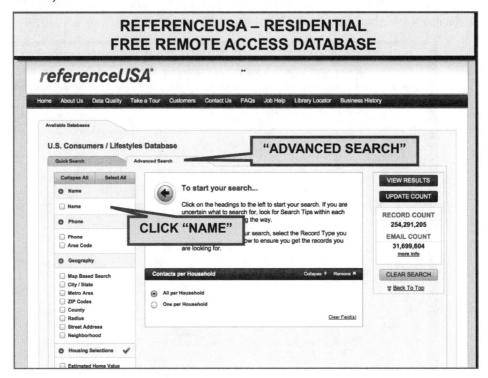

The next illustration shows the results, which include an address, phone number, and a *Show Neighbors* feature, similar to the one at **WhitePages.com** (see pages 308—310). We sometimes prefer to use **ReferenceUSA** over **WhitePages.com** because it does not distract us with any advertisements for pay databases and the neighbor feature includes the contact information (without having to do a second look-up as we do at **WhitePages.com**).

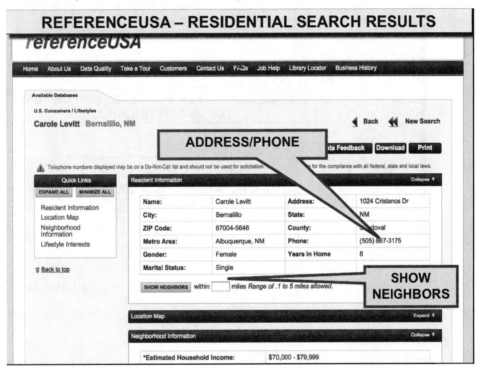

ReferenceUSA's Business database also allows you to create a custom form for each search as shown in the next illustration. While you can search by a company or executive name, you can also create more targeted searches. For example, if you are looking for an expert (or a list of potential clients) in a particular industry and in a particular metropolitan area, you can create a custom search form to meet this need by selecting *Keyword*, *SIC* (Standard Industrial Classification) *NAICS* (North American Industry Classification Systems), which are government-created numbering systems for each industry, and *Metro Area* from the left-hand side column of categories (shown in the next illustration). We have searched for *Silk screening* to locate that industry's SIC code number. Then we selected that SIC code from the list and added the *Metro Area* of *Los Angeles-Long Beach-Anaheim, CA* to construct our search. (Note that you can either click multiple SIC codes from the drop-down list to search for more than one code at a time, or you can copy and paste codes into the boxes below the the drop-down list.)

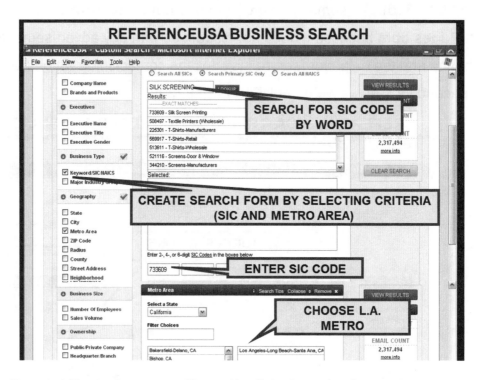

In the next illustration, you will see the list of results that meets our search needs. You could download this list (into an Excel spreadsheet, for instance), print the list, or review the details of any or all the companies.

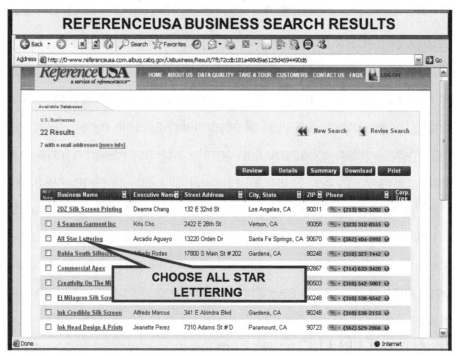

The next illustration shows you a portion of the company profile, which includes the business name, address, phone number, and all kinds of business details such as number of employees, revenue, credit rating, and much more. Be aware that the information comes from many sources (public records, publicly available information, and self-reported by the company owner or an employee) and could be incorrect. You can scroll through the entire report or you can jump to a specific category by selecting it from the left-hand column.

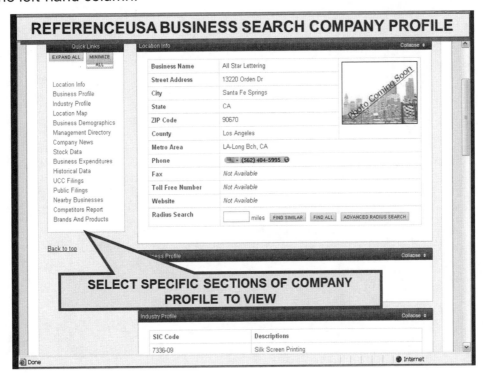

One of our favorite databases to conduct due diligence and background information is **General OneFile** (a Gale publication), which includes news and periodical articles, press releases, and news wires, on a wide range of topics. (Note that **General OneFile** is sometimes referred to as **Infotrac**.)

While most databases that public libraries subscribe to are offered remotely, some can only be used at the library. One of the most common of these databases is **Ancestry.com Library Edition**, which offers public library visitors free access to the same data found at the fee-based **Ancestry.com** site. See *Chapter Sixteen* for details on searching **Ancestry.com**.

Chapter Thirteen

COURT DOCKETS AND CASE DOCUMENTS (COMPLAINTS, BRIEFS, ETC.) AS INVESTIGATIVE RESEARCH TOOLS

Court docket sheets, and especially the case documents (when they're attached to the docket sheet), can be useful investigative/due diligence tools. Case documents could include complaints, answers, motions, opinions, orders, etc. All of these documents can be used to discover the following information: (1) how litigious someone is, (2) if someone has a criminal background, (3) if there is a bankruptcy in someone's past (see *Chapter Fourteen* for details about bankruptcy dockets), or (4) an address for a missing person if you can find a docket with an address where the person was recently served. Of all the case documents, the complaint is the most enlightening for your investigative/due diligence purposes because it provides background information about the matter and details the allegations. However, you will need to explain to your client that allegations are simply that and are not proven facts. But if you see a litany of complaints filed against the same company or person and they repeatedly list similar allegations, you might be able to see a pattern of behavior about which you can warn your client.

Some state and local courts place their docket sheets, or a summary of the docket sheet, online at the court's official site, while other courts place nothing online at all. In addition to the docket sheets, some courts place images of the case documents online. Sometimes they are available for free and other times you will need to pay for them.

This chapter will focus primarily on free and low-cost federal court docket sites but we will also give some examples of state and local court dockets.

All of the following sites, except for **PACER,** either offer free access to federal dockets and case documents or are a hybrid model of free and pay:

- **PACER** (https://www.pacer.gov) is the federal government's pay docket database for all U.S. District (Civil and Criminal), U.S. Bankruptcy, and U.S. Courts of Appeals' cases. Dates of coverage vary from court to court. Many dockets also include the underlying case documents. (See the full discussion on pages 185–202.)

- **RECAP Archive** (https://www.courtlistener.com/recap) offers free access to millions of assorted dockets and case documents from U.S. Courts of Appeals, U.S. District Courts (Civil and Criminal) and Bankruptcy Courts. (See pages 203–211 for details.)

- **PacerPro (**https://www.pacerpro.com**)** uses a hybrid pricing plan that offers some information for free and some for pay. It originally only included access to U.S. District (Civil and Criminal) and Bankruptcy Court dockets/case documents, but now includes the U.S. Courts of Appeals. See pages 214–219 for more information.

- **Justia** (http://dockets.justia.com) provides free access to U.S. District Court dockets (Civil only) and U.S. Courts of Appeals dockets, back to 2004. Some dockets include free case documents. See the full discussion on pages 212–214.

- The **U.S. Supreme Court** offers free dockets at its official site (http://linkon.in/ussupctdoc). See page 220 for details.

- **FindLaw** offers a free U.S. Supreme Court docket database (mostly summaries, but there are some case documents for older cases) at its **Supreme Court Center** site, but only through the 2009 term (http://linkon.in/aWDAO3). See pages 224 for details.

The following commercial pay sites offer better search features and alert services than the sites noted earlier. Additionally, they offer access to federal and selected state and local dockets/case documents, while the earlier sites offer only federal:

- **Westlaw's CourtExpress** (http://linkon.in/westcourtexp). To learn which courts are covered, see http://linkon.in/ctexpmap.

- **LexisNexis CourtLink** (http://www.lexisnexis.com/courtlink). "CourtLink® lets you conduct a single search across the full text of more than 168 million federal and state court dockets and documents in a single click. Then easily filter the results by date, litigation area, geography, court, and more to pinpoint the information you need."

- **Bloomberg Law Dockets** (http://linkon.in/bloomdocs). At its public website, **Bloomberg** does not offer information on court coverage, but its U.S. coverage is similar to **Lexis's** and **Westlaw's.** In addition, **Bloomberg** also states it covers international dockets ("U.K., the Cayman Islands, Dubai, the E.U., Hong Kong and more").

PACER (PUBLIC ACCESS TO COURT ELECTRONIC RECORDS): PAY FEDERAL DOCKETS AND CASE DOCUMENTS

PACER (http://www.pacer.gov) is the federal government's court docket database. Many lawyers are familiar with **PACER** because they file federal court documents using its *CM/ECF* system *(Case Management/Electronic Case Files)*. Because we are interested in using **PACER** for research purposes only and because *CM/ECF* is for electronic filing, our discussion of **PACER** will not include *CM/ECF*, but instead will focus on searching **PACER's** *Case Locator* database, which includes over 51 million cases and 310 million party records (https://linkon.in/pacerusserssearch). As of April 2018, 50,000 users access the *Case Locator* daily to perform over 500,000 searches daily and 10 million searches monthly (https://linkon.in/pacerusserssearch).

Almost all federal courts participate in **PACER** (13 courts of appeals, 94 district courts, 90 bankruptcy courts, and other specialized tribunals). **PACER's** *Case Locator* database includes the case's docket sheet, its underlying case documents (but not necessarily for all cases), transcripts, and the written opinions. Dates of coverage vary from court to court, with some courts going back to the 1950s. (Although **PACER** wasn't launched until 1988, some courts uploaded older dockets once they joined

PACER.) Coverage dates are indicated at each court's **PACER** site and on the *Court Information* page, but that page is only accessible after you log into **PACER** and click the *Court Information* tab at the top of the page. Newly filed cases will usually appear on **PACER** within 24 hours.

Some documents are completely unavailable to the general public, such as pre-2003 bankruptcy case documents (however, we found case documents for various pre-2003 bankruptcy cases) and criminal case documents pre-October 31, 2004. (See page 237 for more details about **PACER** bankruptcy court searching and an illustration of the *Bankruptcy Court* search page.) In addition, not all case information is available to the public. For example, various personal identifiers are removed or redacted before the record becomes public, including Social Security Numbers or taxpayer-identification numbers, financial account numbers, the name of a minor, dates of birth, and home addresses in a criminal case. It is the attorney's responsibility to inform clients that case files may be searched and obtained electronically by anyone and it is the attorney's responsibility to ensure that the earlier listed private information is not included in the case files. (For specific redaction rules, see Fed. R. App. P. 25(a)(5); Fed. R. Civ. P. 5.2; Fed. R. Crim. P. 49.1; or Fed.R. Bankr. P. 9037.)

> "At login to *CM/ECF*, a message reminds attorneys of their responsibility to redact this private information from the documents they file, and the most recent version of this reminder also requires attorneys to acknowledge that they have read the notice and complied with the redaction rules. Filers cannot complete the login process without checking the acknowledgment in this recent version (http://linkon.in/pacerredact)."

Speaking of redaction, in an April 5, 2010 **Federal Judicial Center Study** of **PACER**, the Center identified 2,899 documents with one or more un-redacted Social Security numbers among the almost ten million documents filed in federal district and bankruptcy courts within a recent two-month period, despite the Federal Rules of Procedure (Civil, Criminal, and Bankruptcy) requiring redaction (or truncation) of full Social Security Numbers. This accounted for approximately one out of every 3,400 court documents, with a greater number found in bankruptcy documents (http://linkon.in/HonEvF).

In August 2014, **PACER** updated its docket system – removing dockets from five courts. After an outcry from the legal community, in October 2014 the judiciary restored the docket sheets from all but one of those courts (the Central District of California Bankruptcy Court) to **PACER**. When we tested PACER in 2016 to see if the Central District of California Bankruptcy Court dockets were restored, they were.

PACER: Major Changes to Case Locator

After 29 years of very few updates to **PACER**, major changes were made, effective December 9, 2017. Besides changing the "look and feel" of **PACER**, most of the major changes were made to the *Case Locator*, with new searching and sorting features. The *Case Locator* is your key to conducting investigative/due diligence research at **PACER** because it's the only way to search the dockets of all federal courts simultaneously (but not the U.S. Supreme Court).

PACER: How to Begin a Case Locator Search

Start from the **PACER** homepage (http://www.pacer.gov) to choose one of the following three options:

- Register: click the *Register* tab to create an account
- Login: click the *Login* tab to e-file
- Find a case: click the *Find A Case* tab to begin a docket search

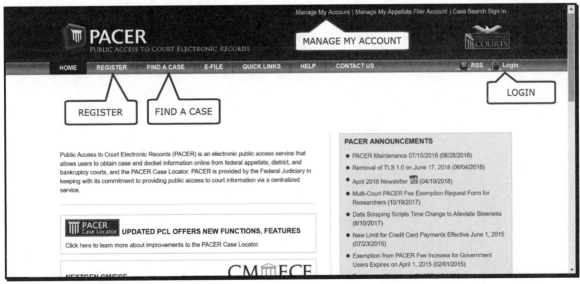

After you click *Find A Case,* you are given two choices. Your first choice is to *Search the PACER Case Locator* and your second choice is to *Search Individual Court*

Websites. If you want to conduct a national federal docket search, click *Search the PACER Case Locator*. Once you make that choice, you are required to log in. Then you are presented with a *Quick Searches* page.

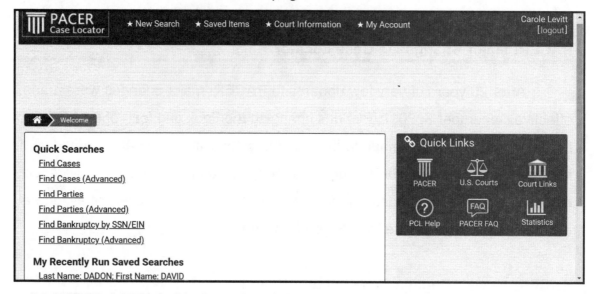

The *Find Cases* link is the "basic" search, and should have been labeled *Find Cases* (*Basic*) to to be consistent with the *Find Cases (Advanced)* label. Nevertheless, the *Find Cases* and the *Find Cases (Advanced)* options are both used when you know the case number or the case title.

After you click *Find Cases* to perform a basic search (shown in the next illustration), enter a *Case Number* or a *Title*, and choose a *Court Type* or leave it set at *All*. Notice you can switch to an *Advanced Case Search* by clicking the link on the right.

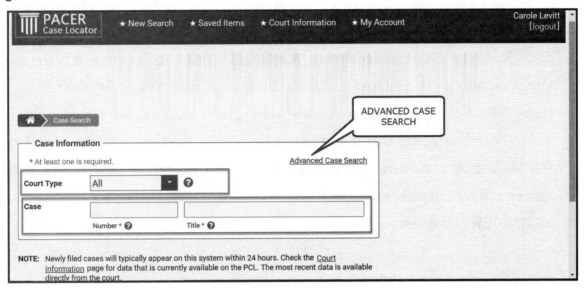

If you click the question mark to the far right of *Court Type*, a pop-up box explains that *All* is the default setting for court types, but that you can narrow your search to one *Court Type* (*Appellate*, *Bankruptcy*, *Civil*, *Criminal*, or *Multidistrict*). To make the choice, click the down-arrow to the right of *All*. You cannot search two, three, or four *Court Types* together; you can only search one *Court Type* or *All*.

If you click the question mark to the right of *Number*, a pop-up box shows sample case number formats.

If you click the question mark to the right of *Title*, a pop-up box explains wildcard searching like this: "the case title search is a 'starts with' search where a wildcard is assumed at the end of the search string…. Example: a search for john doe v will result in all cases with the case title John Doe v." This means that your results could include cases such as *John Doe v Acme*, *John Doe v. Brown*, etc. **PACER's** explanation provides another example: "A search for case title *Acme, Inc.* will result in all cases with the case titles starting with *Acme, Inc.*" This means that your results could include cases such as *Acme, Inc and Robert Brown v. Young*.

You can also add a wildcard (*) to the end of any word to extend it. For instance, a search for *Dav* Dado** could include cases such as *Dadon, Dave*; *Dadon, David*; *Dadon, David J*; *Dadones, David J*; *Dadoun, David J*; etc. In this example the wildcard extended beyond the first name and brought back results including middle initials. This is a very broad search and could bring back irrelevant results (and could be a costly search because the $3.00 cap does not apply to name search results). You can also use the * to take the place of a single character (e.g., *Sm*th* will bring back *Smith* and *Smyth*). Remember, a wildcard is assumed at the end of the search string, so our *Sm*th* example could also bring back *Smithers* or *Smethers*. Note: Wildcard searching also works in some of the searches we will soon discuss: in a *Title* search in a *Find Cases (Advanced)* search, a *Party* search in a basic *Find Parties* search, or a *Party* search in a *Find Parties (Advanced)* search. Also note, names are not case sensitive, so it doesn't matter if you use upper or lower case in any **PACER** searches.

PACER: Find Cases (Advanced)

Once you have chosen *Find Cases* (to conduct a basic search) and have been brought to the basic *Case Search* page, you can switch to an *Advanced* search from this page by simply clicking the *Advanced Case Search* link. Or, if you are not on the basic *Case Search* page, click the **PACER** *Case Locator* logo on the top of any page at **PACER** to return to the *Quick Search* page and select the *Find Cases (Advanced)* option (or one of the other search options listed).

The main difference between the basic *Find Cases* option and the *Find Cases (Advanced)* option is the ability to also select a *Region* and *Date Range*. You can enter specific date ranges into the *Date Filed* or *Date Closed* search box or you can click *Prior Month*, *Prior Six Months*, or *Prior Year*. You could enter a start date only and results will include dates from that date to the present. Another option is to enter an end date only, and results will include dates on or before that date.

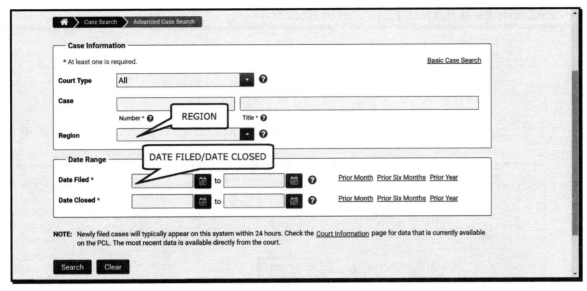

Depending on which *Court Type* you choose, different *Region* options appear in a pop-up box when you click the down-arrow to the right of the *Region* search box. For instance, if you choose *Court Type Appellate*, the *Region* list of choices is limited to the 1st through the 11th Circuit, the Federal Circuit, and the District of Columbia Circuit. However, if you leave the *Court Type* at the default *All*, the *Region* drop-down list expands to also display: the Federal Claims Court; each District Court (e.g., the Alabama Middle District Court), and the name of each State, which allows you to search all the federal *Court Types* in a specific state. To choose one *Region*, simply click into the check-box to the left of that *Region* and to add more *Regions*, click into each of the check-boxes to the left of their *Region* (as shown in the next illustration).

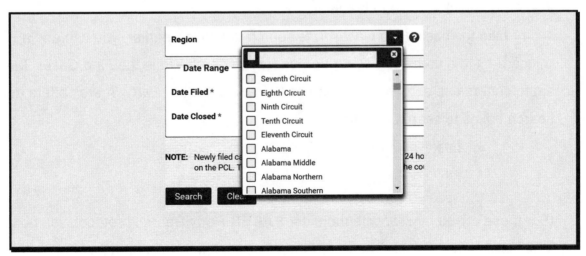

Choose the *Find Parties* option to search by a name if:

- you wanted to locate a case but didn't know its case number or full case title, but you knew one of the party's names, or
- you wanted to conduct background or investigative research about a specific party

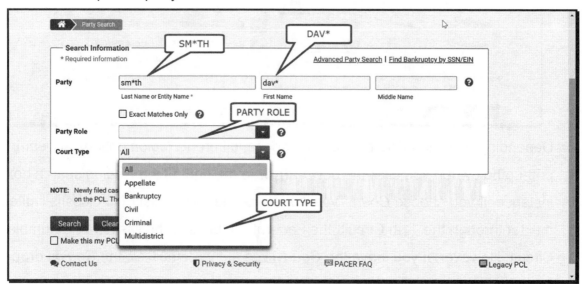

If we use the basic *Party Search* form (shown in the previous illustration) for background or investigative research, we typically leave the *Court Type* set to the default *All* to find cases involving our subject in any and all federal jurisdictions. But if you want to narrow the search, you could select just one *Court Type*, just like we did in the basic *Find Cases* search earlier.

Like the basic *Find Cases Title* search described earlier, you can add a wildcard (*) to a name in a *Party Search* (*sm*th dav**). While the *Find Cases Title* search offers one search box to search by case *Title*, the *Party Search* offers three search boxes to search by name:

- *Last Name or Entity Name*,
- *First Name*, and
- *Middle Name*.

(For those of you familiar with the older **PACER** Party Search protocol, you no longer enter Last Name, First Name (e.g., *levitt, joseph*) into one search box and you no longer have to separate them by a comma.)

If you are unsure of your subject's first or middle name (or its spelling) or if you want to create a broad search, you would search by last name only. If you check off the *Exact Matches Only* box (not offered in the *Find Cases' Title* search), you will be overriding the automatic wildcard (*) search and will be searching only the name you've entered.

To conduct an *Entity Name* search when you are unsure of the full name, use one or more wildcards. For example, to search for an entity that you think begins with the word *Stevens* and contains the word *Lake*, you could enter *Stevens* Lake** into the *Last Name or Entity Name* search box. Our search produced these two results:

- *Stevensville Lake Hotel* (adding the wildcard * after *Stevens* extended *Stevens** to *Stevensville* and a wildcard was assumed at the end of the search string, adding an additional word, *Hotel*, after *Lake*.)

- *Stevens Lakeshore RV Center* (adding the wildcard * after *Lake* extended *Lake** to *Lakeshore* and a wildcard was assumed at the end of the search string, adding two more words, *RV Center*, after *Lakeshore*.

Before **PACER**'s update in December 2017, a *Party Name* search was both a party name and an attorney name search, although this was not noted on the search box label. To display only party names or only attorney names in your results list, you then had to click a *Filter Results* tab and choose *aty* (attorney) or any of the thirty or so types of parties, such as: *pla* (plaintiff), *dft* (defendant), or *intv* (intervenor). Now, however, you can limit your search in advance to one of the thirty Party Roles (including attorney) once you click the down-arrow to the right of *Party Role* (see the previous illustration) to view the pop-up list (not shown).

PACER: Find Parties (Advanced)

You can create an even more targeted party name search by clicking the *Advanced Party Search* link on the upper right side of the basic search form (see the previous illustration). Or, if you are not on the basic *Party Search* page, click the **PACER** *Case Locator* logo on the top of any page at **PACER** to choose the *Find Parties (Advanced)* option).

The *Find Parties (Advanced)* option offers additional search boxes just like the *Find Cases (Advanced)* option does, such as *Region*, *Date Filed*, and *Date Closed*.

However, the *Find Parties (Advanced) Region* search is a bit different from the *Cases (Advanced) Region* search. When you choose the *Appellate* or *Civil Court Type* in a *Find Parties (Advanced) Region* search, another drop-down menu appears (see the next illustration), which offers you a way to narrow your search even further—by *Nature of Suit* (*NOS*). (The *NOS* is a numerical/topical classification system for federal civil litigation cases. It is used to assign a case type code (such as *1110 Insurance*) to each filed complaint and provides an easy way to identify and search for dockets with the same or similar case types across federal jurisdictions.) You can choose to search more than one *NOS* simultaneously.

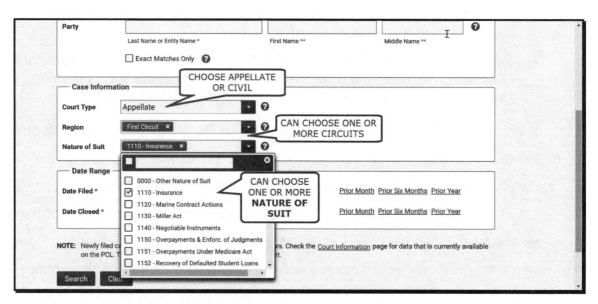

If you choose *Appellate*, the *Region* drop-down menu allows you to narrow your search to one or more Circuits. If you choose *Civil* (not shown), the *Region* drop-down menu allows you to narrow your search to one or more courts (e.g., First Circuit, Alabama Middle District Court) or regions (e.g. Alabama).

If you choose the *Bankruptcy Court Type*, you are offered these additional search options (shown in the next illustration):

- A *Four Digit SSN* (Social Security Number), which must be used in combination with a *Last Name*,
- A full *SSN or EIN* (Employer Identification Number),
- A *Chapter* search, and
- *Date Range*: *Date Dismissed* and *Date Discharged*.

When you are unsure where a subject might have filed bankruptcy, **PACER** is particularly useful because you can search all the bankruptcy courts together.

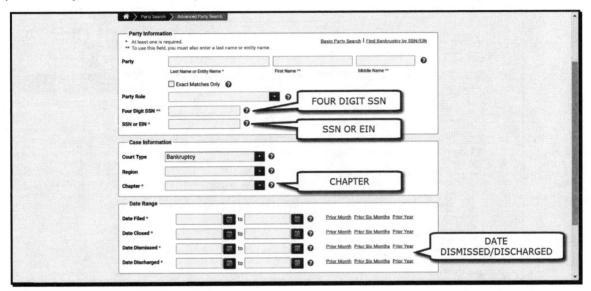

The next illustration shows **PACER** *Case Locator's* list with twenty-one results from a *Party Search* of *Last Name: Dadon* and *First Name: David*. The results list is sorted by *Party Name* and also displays five more columns of information. Even though we did not add a wildcard (*) to the end of *Dadon*, our results brought back more than *Dadon* (e.g., *Dadones*) because a wildcard is assumed at the end of the search string (*Dadon* and *David* are each a "search string"). If we had checked off *Exact Matches Only*, then our results would have been limited just to *Dadon, David*.

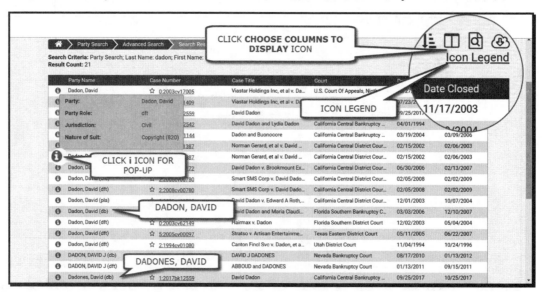

If you click on the *i* (information) Icon, a pop-up shows you it's a *Civil* case and that the *Nature of Suit* is *Copyright (820)*. To avoid clicking the *i* Icon for each case to learn more information about the case, you can click the icon in the upper right side that looks like two columns. (If you click the *Icon Legend* in the upper right side of the previous illustration, it explains that this two columns Icon stands for *Choose columns to display*.) In other words, you can add more columns to the results list to see more information about all the cases in your results list.

The next illustration shows what happens after you click the *Choose columns to display* icon: a *Search Result Columns* box pops-up from which you can choose which columns to display by checking or unchecking the check-boxes (e.g., *NOS*, *Bankruptcy Chapter*, *Date Dismissed*, and *Date Discharged*.

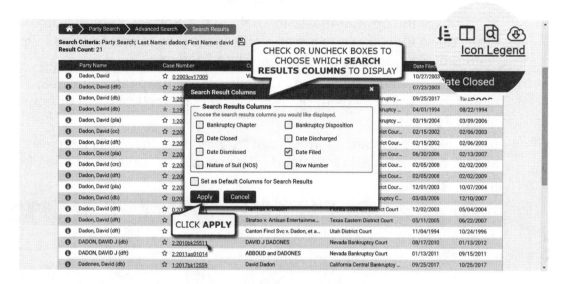

Date Filed and *Date Closed* were displayed in the original results list, so they were already checked off when the *Search Results Column* box popped-up. Remember to click the *Apply* button so your new columns get added to your results display. You can also click into the *Set as Default Columns for Search Results* box to make these choices your personal default results display for all searches. (You can always change them again later.)

If you want to re-sort your results display, follow these steps and see the next illustration:

1.   Click the *Sort Search Results* Icon (**PACER's** former sorting feature could be invoked by simply clicking each column heading.)

2.   A *Sort Results* option box pops up.

3.   Click the down-arrow to the right of the *Sort Field Party Name*. A list drops down for you to choose one of the following to sort by: *Case Title*, *Court*, *Nature of Suit*, *Bankruptcy Chapter*, *Date Filed*, etc.

4.   Then choose the display *Direction*: *Ascending* (alphabetically A-Z or oldest to newest if by date) or *Descending* (alphabetically Z-A or newest to oldest if by date).

5.   NOTE: You are informed that "*Sorting search results executes a new search for which a fee is charged.*" (Previously, re-sorting had been free.)

6.   Click *Apply*.

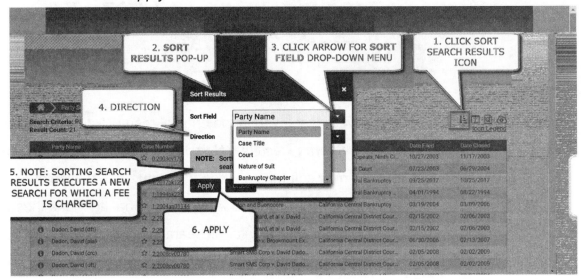

Many of **PACER's** new *Case Locator* features are invoked by clicking on various links and icons, which we'll explain. Fortunately, **PACER** included an *Icon Legend* to help interpret them. To display the *Icon Legend*, click the *Icon Legend* link (shown in the next illustration).

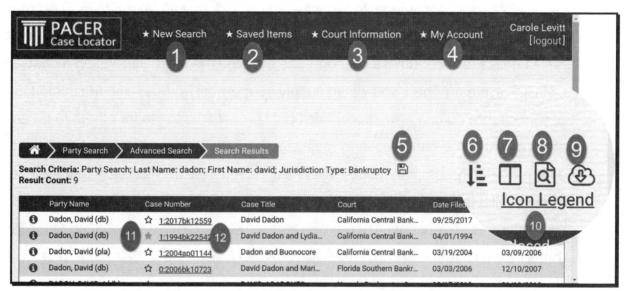

To invoke any of these features, click the following links and icons:

1. *New Search* link to begin a new *Case* or *Party* search (a fee will be charged)

2. *Saved Items* link to view your saved searches and saved cases

3. *Court Information* link to learn date coverage of each court

4. *My Account* link (then click *Change Client Code*, *Manage my account*, *Billing History*, or *User Options*)

5. *Disk icon* to save your search (e.g., your search string and other parameters) to *Saved Items*

6. *Down arrow with four horizontal lines icon* to *Sort search results*

7. *Two columns icon* to *Choose columns to display*

8. *Magnifying glass icon* to *Refine the Current Search* (a fee will be charged)

9. *Down arrow within a bubble icon* to *Download Search Results* (this will download your search results list; we suggest downloading the results list to CSV to view the results in Microsoft Excel)

10. *Icon Legend* to pop-up a written explanation of each icon

11. *Star* to save a case to *Saved Items* (the star will turn from white to yellow) or click a starred case again to remove it from your *Saved Items* (the star will turn back to white)

12. Click any *Case Number* to view the docket and, if available, its case documents

Using *CM/ECF*, each attorney of record (including pro se litigants) receives free e-mail docket alerts with hyperlinks back to the court documents.

To access documents in this way, you would log into your *CM/ECF* account with your court-issued *CM/ECF* filing login. (The **PACER** login does not work for this e-mail notice service, unless the court has adopted the *Next Generation (NextGen) CM/ECF* system.) Then, you would supply your e-mail address and the docket number of your case. You can also supply additional e-mail addresses for others to receive alerts as well. You can choose to receive an e-mail alert for each new event related to a filing or a daily summary notice of all filings. One free copy of each document is made available to each attorney of record and to any secondary addressee listed under the e-mail information screen. Visit the *CM/ECF Frequently Asked Questions* (https://linkon.in/efilefreecopy) and click *How do I receive my "free copy" of a document?* for more information.

Non-parties can also receive notices for cases they are interested in (for free), but they must register for a **PACER** ID and password, as well as a *CM/ECF* filer ID and password, and be an approved registrant in a federal court. To view any case documents, the non-party would be assessed the same fees as other **PACER** users.

Some courts now provide free automatic case notification through RSS feeds. Visit http://bit.ly/pacerrss to learn which courts have implemented RSS. Once there, click *Court Links* (on the left-hand side of the page) and then select the court's RSS feed icon, if there is one for the court you are interested in. Once you subscribe to a court's RSS feed, you will receive notice of all activity in all cases from that court (not just a case that you specify), a summary of the documents filed, links to the document, and the docket report. You can sort the feed results by date or case title. You must log into **PACER** and pay the usual costs to retrieve the document or docket report.

PACER: Audio Recordings

Digital audio recordings of court proceedings are available online for twenty-six federal district and bankruptcy courts (http://bit.ly/pacerrecording). The cost is $2.40 per proceeding. (Previously, it cost $26.00 to order a CD.)

PACER: Federal Court Opinions

Even though court opinions are "free" at **PACER**, you still need an account to search for an opinion, and you are charged for the initial docket search.

If you want to search opinions for free, and by keyword or citation and other criterion (and do not need the docket), see *Chapter Twenty-Seven* to learn about **Google Scholar**, member-benefits **Fastcase** (and its App) and **Casemaker,** or the *United States Courts Opinions Collection* at **govinfo.gov**.

PACER: Public Access Terminals to View and Print

PACER public access terminals are provided free at federal courthouses (but only for filings in the courthouse where the terminal is located). Viewing documents is free, but printing is priced at the usual $0.10 per page (http://bit.ly/pacerfreeview). The charge for copies from paper case files at the clerk's office is $0.50 per page.

PACER: Mobile Access

To search the **PACER** *Case Locator* using a mobile device (e.g., iOS—iPads and iPhones and Androids—version 2.2 and higher), you can go directly to pcl.uscourts.gov. The mobile search interface mirrors the web-based interface.

PACER: Firm Billing

PACER now offers a **PACER** Administrative Account (PAA) so firms can receive just one invoice for multiple users' accounts (http://bit.ly/paceradmin). The administrator of a PAA can:

- Choose whether to add existing users to the PAA (or leave some users outside the PAA)
- Set up new users and receive their login information immediately
- Activate and deactivate users
- Update user information
- Set the Client Code field as a requirement before a user can begin a search

PACER: Help

If you need help, visit http://www.pacer.gov/help.html to find out how to call or e-mail the **PACER** Service Center. A link to *Frequently Asked Questions* is also available from that URL. **PACER** also offers a free User Manual (http://bit.ly/PACERUserManual), which was updated December 2017.

There are free training modules on how to use the basic functions of *CM/ECF* (http://bit.ly/pacertrainingmod) and a training site populated with actual case documents filed between Jan. 1, 2007 and July 1, 2007 from the New York Western District Court (http://bit.ly/pacertraining). Unfortunately, the training modules and training site do not include the *Case Locator*, but the free User Manual does.

COURTLISTENER'S RECAP (PACER SPELLED BACKWARDS): FREE FEDERAL DOCKETS AND CASE DOCUMENTS

In 2009, in an effort to allow free access to millions of U.S. Federal District and Bankruptcy Court **PACER** case documents, a team at the **Center for Information Technology Policy** at **Princeton University** and **Harvard University's Berkman Center** created a software extension that volunteers could add to their browser, which would automatically download any document that they paid for from **PACER**, to a free alternative archive. The extension and alternative archive were named **RECAP** (https://www.recapthelaw.org) and the site's tag line was: "Turning PACER Around." The case document archive was hosted at the **Internet Archive**. In addition to offering free documents, **RECAP** also created more user-friendly file names than **PACER** by including the **PACER** court, case number, and docket entry number as the file name (https://free.law/recap/features/).

In May of 2014, the **Free Law Project** took over **RECAP** (The **Center for Information Technology Policy** at **Princeton University** remained as a partner.) Then, in August 2016, **Free Law Project** retired the recapthelaw.org website and moved all the old content to a new site, with a new URL: https://free.law/recap.

In November of 2016, **RECAP** was relaunched by **CourtListener** as the **RECAP Archive** and given a new URL: https://www.courtlistener.com/recap. The **Free Law Project** and the **Center for Information Technology Policy at Princeton University** remained as partners.

CourtListener: Enhancements to the RECAP Archive (2016 and 2017)

In 2016, **CourtListener** made several enhancements to the **RECAP Archive**, such as:

- converted many scanned case documents into keyword-searchable documents by applying Optical Character Recognition (OCR) software
- added more robust search features, including full-text keyword searching and field searching (discussed later in this chapter)
- expanded the **RECAP** Archive coverage to U.S. Courts of Appeals' dockets and case documents (originally, the Archive included only federal district and bankruptcy dockets and case documents)

In 2017, **CourtListener** made several more enhancements to the **RECAP Archive**, which they explained, as follows:

> After nearly a year of work, and with support from the U.S. Department of Labor and Georgia State University, we have collected every free written order and opinion that is available in PACER. To accomplish this, we used PACER's "Written Opinion Report," which provides many opinions for free. This collection contains approximately 3.4 million orders and opinions from approximately 1.5 million federal district and bankruptcy court cases dating back to 1960. More than four hundred thousand of these documents were scanned and required OCR, amounting to nearly two million pages of text extraction that we completed for this project. All of the documents amassed are available for search in the RECAP Archive of PACER documents and via our APIs. New opinions will be downloaded every night to keep the collection up to date. As a backup and permanent repository, we are continuing our partnership with the Internet Archive*, where we are in the process of uploading a copy of every opinion that we download. (http://bit.ly/recapfreectops.)

(*Note: On February 16, 2018, we learned that **RECAP** had reduced the frequency of its docket uploads to the **Internet Archive**. Instead of uploading daily, **RECAP** had switched to quarterly uploading. Unless that changes, be sure to search dockets at the **RECAP Archive**, and not the **Internet Archive**.)

In June 2018, **CourtListener** re-introduced its *Alert* service after a two-year hiatus (which we'll explain later in this section).

As mentioned, **PACER** users can install a software extension to their **Firefox** or **Chrome** Web browser to automatically donate any document that they paid for from **PACER** to **RECAP**. The extension is available for download at https://free.law/recap (shown in the next illustration).

Once you have downloaded the **RECAP** extension, each time your search results are displayed at **PACER**, **RECAP** will display a small *R* icon next to the document link if a free version of any of the documents is already available from the **RECAP Archive**. Over time, this can save you considerable fees. And, once you pay for a **PACER** docket sheet or case document, it is automatically transferred to the **RECAP Archive** for free public use. The **Free Law Project** also requests monetary donations to support the **RECAP Archive** and its other projects, which are to "Gather and curate the latest opinions from more than 200 courts daily, making them searchable in our collection of nearly 4M opinions. Host the largest archive of oral argument audio in the world, with nearly 1,000,000 minutes of recordings" (https://free.law/donate).

To visit the **RECAP Archive**, use this direct URL: https://www.courtlistener.com/recap. Although **RECAP** requires you to use **Firefox** or **Chrome** to upload a document, you are not required to use only those browsers to search the **RECAP Archive**.

At the *Advanced RECAP Search* page (https://www.courtlistener.com/recap), you can conduct a full-text, keyword search of the **RECAP Archive** case documents that have been OCR'd. At **PACER** (and many of the other free or hybrid docket databases discussed in this chapter), you cannot full-text keyword search case documents; you are only able to keyword search through short descriptions of each case document listed on the docket sheet. So, it should be apparent why **RECAP** provides a huge advantage to researchers. However, not all **RECAP Archive** documents have been OCR'd yet.

To search the **RECAP Archive**, enter one or more keywords (or phrases) into the top search box and click the *Search* button to the right of the search menu box.

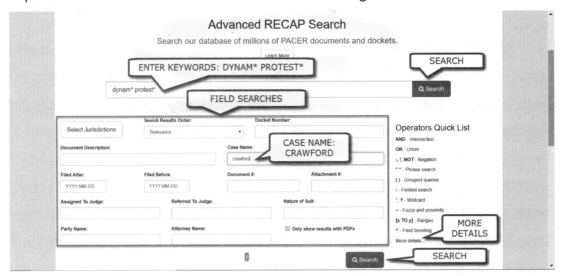

You can create a more sophisticated keyword/phrase search by using one or multiple advanced query techniques displayed in the *Operators Quick List* found on the right side of the search menu shown in the previous illustration. To learn how to invoke these *Operators* (often called "connectors" at other websites and search engines), *Wildcards*, *Fielded searches*, and other search techniques, click the *More details* link beneath the *Operators Quick List*.

You can also enter more information into one or more of the various *Fielded search* boxes located below the large keyword/phrase search box if you want to refine your search (see previous illustration). The *Fielded Searches* allow you to refine your keyword/phrase search by adding more information, such as *Docket Number, Document Description, Case Name, Filed After:YYYY-MM-DD, Filed Before:YYYY-MM-DD, Document #, Attachment #, Assigned To Judge, Referred To Judge, Nature of Suit, Party Name,* and *Attorney Name* (this can also include law firm name). Click the *Search* button on the bottom right-hand side of the search menu (see previous illustration) instead of the one to the right of the search box.

Instead of refining your keyword/phrase search by adding information into *Fielded Search* boxes, another search option is to leave the keyword/phrase search box empty and conduct a *Fielded Search*-only search (you can enter information into more than one *Fielded Search* box). For example, entering an attorney name (or law firm name) into the *Attorney Name Fielded Search* box is a good way to do background research about the cases handled by attorneys (or law firms) whom you may be opposing or considering hiring. You could refine this search even more by entering dates into the *Filed After* or *Filed Before Fielded Search* boxes. After you are done entering information into the *Fielded Search* boxes, click the *Search* button on the right-hand side at the bottom of the page to run the search.

In addition to *Fielded Searching*, the *Advanced **RECAP** Search* page also allows you to display *Search Results Order* by: *Relevance, Newest First,* or *Oldest First*; or you can check the box to exclude items not in **RECAP** (see previous illustration).

In our sample search (see previous illustration), we are trying to find a case discussing the dynamics of protesting and the party name *Crawford*. Instead of entering the word dynamics and protesting into the full-text keyword search box, we'll enter the root of each word and add the asterisk (*) as a *Wildcard* to retrieve cases with words beginning with the letters we entered.

You can see in the previous illustration that we entered *dynam** (this could retrieve *dynamic/dynamics/dynamically/dynamite*) and then *protest** (this could retrieve *protest/protests/protested/protesting*, etc.). The asterisk will also work in the beginning or middle of a word. To find *Smith* or *Smyth*, you would enter: *sm*th*.

After entering our keywords, we then used the *Fielded Search* boxes and entered the party's name (*Crawford*) into the *Case Name* box. (We could have used the *Party Name Fielded Search* box instead.) However, if we had entered the party name into the top full-text keyword search box, our results could have included the name *Crawford* anywhere in the document, from a judge to an attorney, to a witness, so it's much better to use the *Case Name* or *Party Name Fielded Search* boxes if you want to limit the results to a party to the suit. You can only enter one party name into the *Party Name Fielded Search* box, but you can enter multiple party names (e.g., *crawford sussman*) or the full case title (e.g., *crawford v sussman*) into the *Case Name Fielded Search* box. (The *Party Name* and *Attorney Name Fielded Search* boxes were added in March 2017.)

The next illustration shows our search result, *Sussman v. Crawford*. Keywords are highlighted in yellow. Notice the variations of the word *protest** and *dynam**. You can *Refine Your Query* by using the options in the left-hand column and then clicking *Search* (not shown) at the bottom left-hand side of the page to re-run the query. These are the same options as noted earlier (*Docket Number*, *Document Description*, and so on).

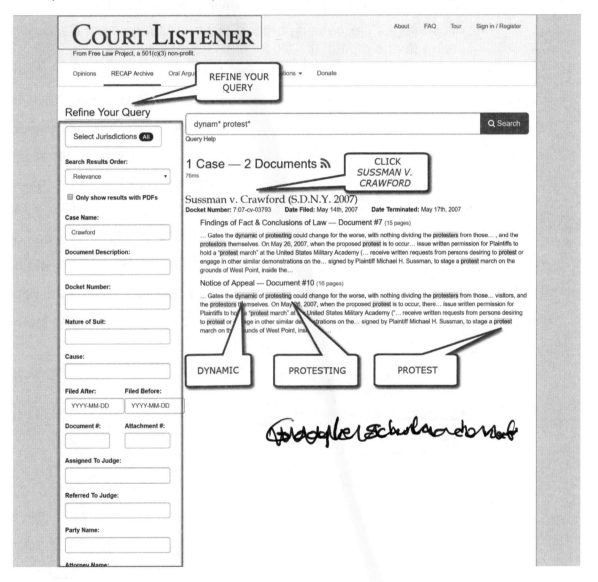

When searching the **RECAP Archive**, you are warned that the docket is unofficial and may be incomplete or out-of-date, so if you need to view complete dockets, check **PACER**.

They have all of the free opinions.

209

If you want to view a particular docket sheet, click the case name (see the next illustration). A list of all the case documents will be displayed, but you can display the list of documents in a variety of other ways, such as by:

- *Date Filed*: Enter the date(s) into one or both of the boxes to the right of *Filed*.
- *Documents*: Enter one or more document number(s) of only the documents you are interested in retrieving into the boxes to the right of *Documents* (we chose to display only documents 10 and 11).
- *Ascending* or *Descending* order: Click the *Ascending* or *Descending* button (to the right of the *Documents* boxes).

Notice the words *Download PDF* and the down-arrow to the right of the description, as in *Document Number 10* (shown on the next illustration). This indicates the document can be downloaded now if you click the down-arrow. Once you do, a drop-down menu appears that allows you to download it from **CourtListener** or the **Internet Archive**. These will be free downloads. But, the drop-down menu also displays a choice to buy it from *PACER,* which will not be free. Clicking it will take you to the log-on page of **PACER**. If you only see a *Buy on PACER* button to the right of the description, as in *Document Number 11* (see the bottom of the next illustration), this indicates the document is not available from **CourtListener** or the **Internet Archive** and must be purchased at **PACER**. Clicking it will take you to the log-on page of **PACER**.

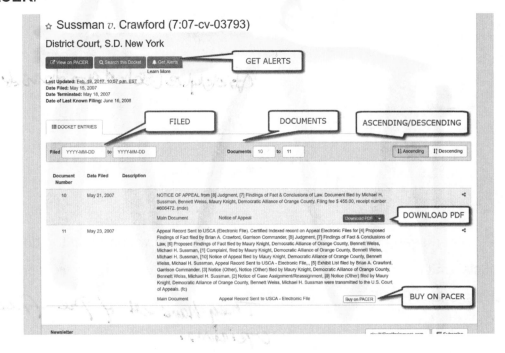

Notice the *Get Alerts* button on the top of the page. Before **CourtListener** relaunched **RECAP** in 2016, users had the option to set up alerts for specific cases to be advised via e-mail or RSS feeds every time a new document was added to that case's docket sheet. This option disappeared for two years but returned in June 2018.

CourtListener explains its *Alert* service this way:

> **RECAP** *Alerts* are a way of keeping up with cases in the **PACER** federal court filing system. These alerts monitor tens of thousands of cases across the country for new docket entries and send an email whenever new entries are acquired. In the last 24 hours, 20,622 dockets and 42,136 docket entries were updated. For active cases, this means that alerts will come any time from about a minute after the content is posted to PACER (for a case of national importance), to an hour or two, for a case of lesser importance in a jurisdiction that does not regularly provide public updates via their RSS feed. For closed cases, we get new content and can send alerts when we do client work on those cases or when a **RECAP** extension user shares a docket with us.

Once you have retrieved a docket from **RECAP**, you can create a **RECAP** *Alert* by clicking the *Get Alerts* button on the top of the page. If you don't already have a free account, you will be prompted to register for one before you can actually set up an *Alert*. You'll begin receiving *Alerts* as soon as a new docket entry is added to the docket. You can disable a **RECAP** *Alert* by clicking the *Disable Alerts* Button. Any user of **CourtListener** can monitor five dockets for free alerts, users who install the **RECAP** Extension can monitor 15, and users who make monthly contributions to **Free Law Project** can monitor as many as they want (within reason).

Two caveats about *Alerts*: First, **RECAP** is not able to offer complete coverage of everything being filed in **PACER** because some courts do not provide RSS feeds and others only provide partial feeds. This coverage gap applies to the federal Circuit Courts and a variety of other courts listed at https://www.courtlistener.com/help/alerts/. Second, the *Get Alerts* button will appear on every Docket sheet, even if that court is one of those that **RECAP** lists as not providing an RSS feed (or only providing a partial feed). So, before you set up an *Alert,* be sure that court provides an RSS feed and can even participate in **RECAP's** *Alert*s.

Justia's *Federal Dockets* database (https://dockets.justia.com/) is more limited in scope than **PACER** and **RECAP** because it does not provide access to bankruptcy dockets. It does provide access to the dockets of the U.S. Federal District Court, the United States Court of International Trade, the United States Federal Claims Court, and the U.S. Courts of Appeals (including the U.S. Court of Appeals for Veterans Cases). Another difference from **PACER** and **RECAP** is that case documents are only available for some dockets at **Justia** (and even then, some documents may be missing from a docket). However, **Justia** was the first site to offer free federal dockets, with a database back to 2004.

The database is no longer displayed prominently on **Justia's** home page but can be accessed by scrolling all the way to the bottom of the home page (http://www.justia.com) and selecting *Dockets and Filings* from the left-hand column titled US Federal Law. Or, use the direct URL (https://dockets.justia.com/; see the next illustration).

The database is poorly documented (possibly because it is still in beta mode, and has been for many years), so we have run many test searches to assist you in using it. At the *Search* page (see the previous illustration), you can search by one or more of the following criteria:

- *Party Name*
- *Judge*
- *Filed In*: Select one of these choices: *Federal Appellate & District Courts – All*; *Federal Appellate Courts – All*; *Federal District Courts – All*; one specific circuit court of appeals (e.g. Ninth Circuit); one specific circuit court of appeals, along with all its district courts (e.g., Ninth Circuit Appellate and District Courts - All); or one or all of a state's federal district courts (e.g., California Central Federal District Court or California Federal District Courts - All); or one of the national courts (e.g., U.S. Court of Federal Claims).
- *Type* (this refers to **PACER's** *NOS* designation, such as *Contract*)
- *Show* (choose either *All Case Filings* or *Only Case Filings with Downloadable Opinions or Orders*)
- *Cases Filed* (select *All Dates* or enter a date range)

In addition to searching, you can scroll past the search menu to browse by: *Type of Lawsuit* (**PACER's** NOS designation), *Cases by Circuit*, *Cases by State*, or *Most Recently Filed* (not shown in the next illustration).

Our search for the *Party Name Rich Yi* and Filed In Seventh Circuit brought back one result (as shown in the next illustration), where *Rich Yi* is one of many defendants in *Brown v. City of Chicago* et al. While many of **Justia's** docket results provide only a summary of the docket sheet, some include the full docket sheet. Also, if you see a gavel icon (as shown in the next illustration), this indicates its full docket sheet and a link to its available documents will be displayed for free. Some dockets include all the case documents. This would be indicated by a yellow star icon (this docket does not include a yellow star icon).

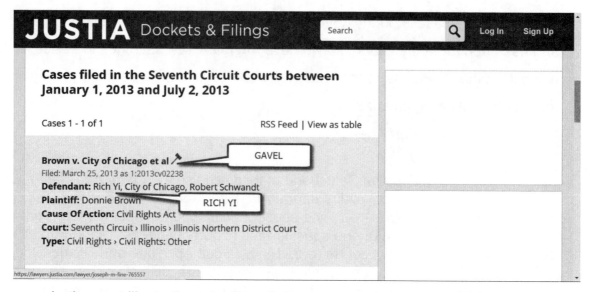

In the next illustration, **Justia** only has one case document (#5) available. To download this document, click its docket entry number (e.g., #5). When **Justia** does not have the complete docket sheet or any (or less than all) of the case documents, you can scroll down past the available case document(s) and **Justia** points (not shown in the previous illustration) users to **PACER** (discussed earlier in this chapter).

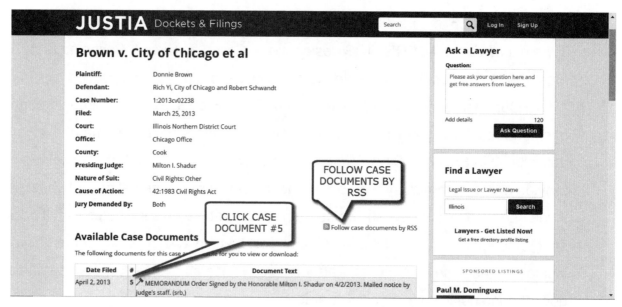

You can also opt to receive free RSS feeds of filings that meet your search criteria by clicking the *RSS* icon to the left of *Follow case documents by RSS*.

Hybrid (Free and Pay) Federal Dockets and Case Documents (Federal Appellate, Bankruptcy, and District Courts) from PacerPro

In addition to providing access to dockets, **PacerPro** (https://www.pacerpro.com) is also a docket management tool. We won't go into too much detail about that here, since we are focusing on investigative research, but we have been told that the site can save you time and money by taking advantage of some of its unique features (such as downloading all or multiple case documents at once—which **PACER** doesn't allow). **PacerPro** provides access to federal district, appellate, and bankruptcy court dockets and case documents for free to paid subscribers if they are already available in **PacerPro's** archive. Free accounts are limited to two bulk downloads monthly from the archive. When you request information that is not available in their archive, they will retrieve information from **PACER**—using your credentials (which you provide in advance to **PacerPro**). You will then be charged by **PACER**. This is why we label **PacerPro** as a hybrid pricing model (pay and free).

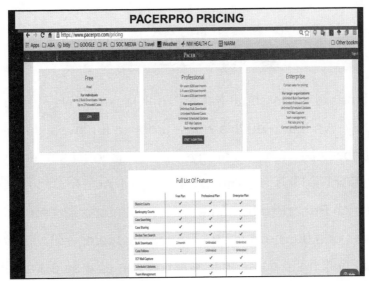

At first, we were not comfortable providing our **PACER** credentials to **PacerPro**, but after interviewing Gavin H. McGrane, **PacerPro's** CEO, our concerns were assuaged when we learned that **PacerPro** stores and transmits our **PACER** credentials in a secure manner using industry-standard encryption methods. Pricing is noted in the next illustration. (The Court of Appeals is missing from this illustration because **PacerPro's** site is a bit out-of-date, but it is included in the subscription.)

Even if you only want a free account, you will still need to join **PacerPro** (and at the moment, provide your credit card number—but we've been told this is an error and will be removed).

The homepage of **PacerPro** allows you to search by case number or by name, as shown in the next illustration.

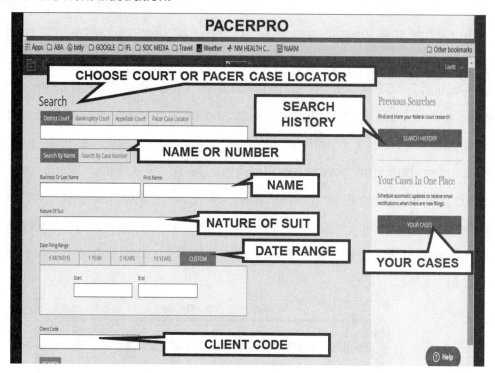

Last time we wrote about **PacerPro**, it lacked a way to search all federal courts simultaneously. We indicated this was a problem for investigative/due diligence research purposes because it's always best to conduct a nationwide search. **PacerPro** has solved this problem by adding a **PACER** *Case Locator* tab.

To search **PacerPro** by name, you can enter a last name only, or a last name and first name, or a business name. The name search will retrieve both parties and attorneys that match the name entered. You can also select a date range tab (*6 Months* and so on) or select the *Custom* tab and enter a specific *Start* and *End* date range.

Your search results include a graph feature, a *Refine by* feature, and a sorting feature that could be useful to quickly learn some background information about your subject's litigation history. For example, as you review the next illustration, you can quickly notice that our subject, who we thought was involved only in California litigation, is (or was) involved in litigation in several other states. We also can review the *Refine by* column to learn the *Type* of lawsuits our subject is involved in (e.g., a Civil case in the District Court) and the *Location* (the state and number of lawsuits per state). As we scroll down this *Refine by* column, we also learn the *Nature of Suit* (such as three Bankruptcies, two Securities, etc.), the *Role* (e.g., whether our subject was a defendant, plaintiff, etc.), and *Year Filed* (including the number of suits per year).

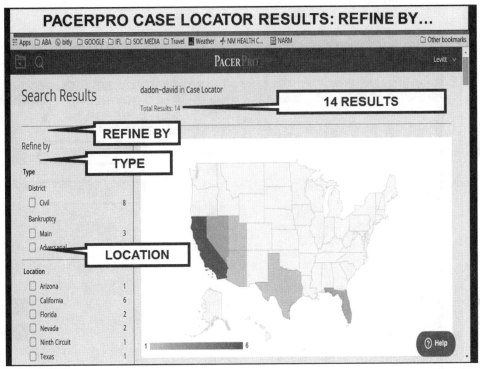

As shown in the next illustration, after you search by name and retrieve a list of matching cases from **PacerPro**, you can:

- *Share* dockets with as many people as you want (this sends an e-mail to the recipient, with the docket displayed).

- *Follow* a case to be alerted when new documents are added to the docket.

- *Download a report* to keep track of what you searched and when, with links to the dockets.

- Re-sort entries from *Most recent activity*, *Most recent filed*, *Title A-Z*, or *Title Z-A*.

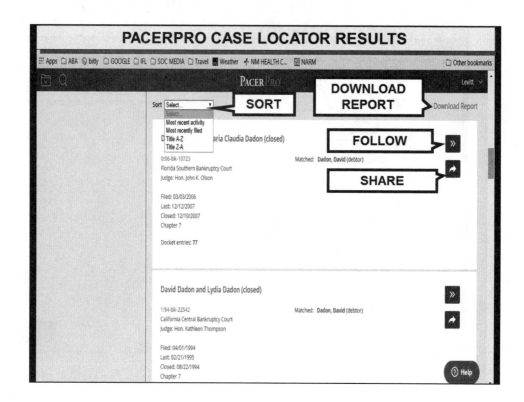

See the next illustration for some other useful **PacerPro** features, such as the ability to:

- Retrieve a docket or case document for free if you see the *Free* notation or learn that you will need to pay if you see the *Pacer fees apply* notation.

- Print the entire docket and all the case documents by choosing *Select All* or *Deselect All* (you can also choose less than all by selecting specific documents).

- Filter by keyword or phrase to search the case document descriptions and even use Boolean connectors, AND, OR, NOT (which must be in upper case as shown) or proximity connectors (e.g., ~3 means within three words).

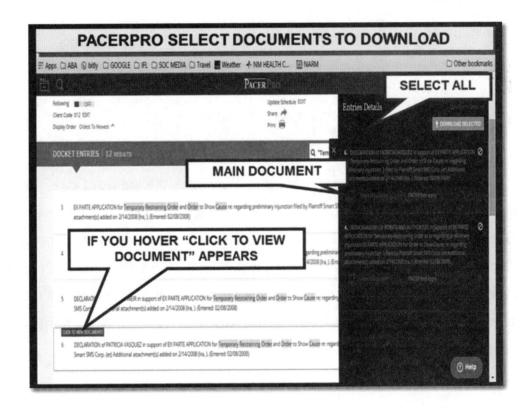

The U.S. Supreme Court does not participate in **PACER's** *CM/ECF* system or its *Case Locator*, but it has had its own docket database for some time at its site, **Supreme Court of the United States** (https://www.supremecourt.gov/). However, electronic filing was not required until November 13, 2017 when the Court amended Supreme Court Rule 29 and added Section 7:

> 7. In addition to the filing requirements set forth in this Rule, all filers who are represented by counsel must submit documents to the Court's electronic filing system in conformity with the "Guidelines for the Submission of Documents to the Supreme Court's Electronic Filing System" issued by the Clerk. (See http://bit.ly/sctrule29.)

The Court explained:

> The Supreme Court's new electronic filing system is now in operation. While paper remains the official form of filing, all parties who are represented by counsel must also submit electronic versions of filings through the system. Most documents that are submitted electronically will be made available on the Court's public docket free of charge. Filings from pro se parties are submitted only on paper but will be scanned and made available electronically on the Court's docket. (See http://bit.ly/sctelecfile.)

The Supreme Court's docket system provides the status of cases filed since the beginning of the 2001 Term (both pending and decided). Up until November 2017, the U.S. Supreme Court's docket database did not include any case documents (e.g., petitions, motions, briefs, etc.) unless it was an important/controversial case. But, as of November 2017, it began including copies of briefs in the docket report (which we will discuss in the **U.S. Supreme Court Argument Transcripts, Argument Audio, and Briefs** section, which comes after this section).

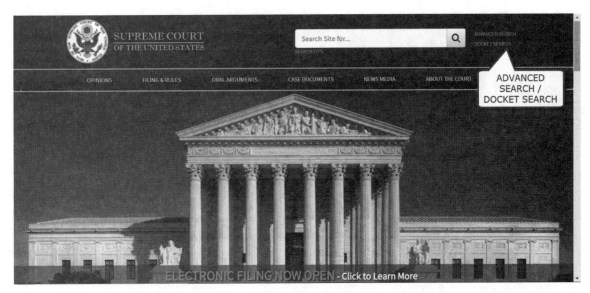

To search, click *Docket Search* located near the top, right-hand side of the home page (as shown in the previous illustration). Then, you are presented with a simple search box and informed that you can search for a docket by: docket number, a case name, or even other words or numbers included on a docket report. Searching with other words that might be included on a docket report comes into play when you don't know the case name or docket number of a case, but you know something about the case. For an example, let's say you knew that the Hudspeth County Conservation and Reclamation District was involved in a water rights case, but you didn't know the case title. You could search *Hudspeth County Conservation* to see if there was a docket entry that included those words. That search retrieved the docket sheet for *Texas v. New Mexico and Colorado*, which included this docket entry: *Brief amicus curiae of Hudspeth County Conservation and Reclamation District No. 1 filed* (see next illustration).

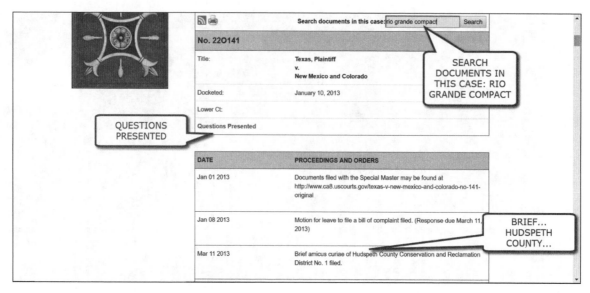

Once you retrieve the relevant docket report, notice that you are offered the ability to enter keywords into the *Search documents in this case* search box (as shown in the previous illustration). This is a full-text search of any of the documents in the docket report that are available for this case, but remember, very few case documents are available in the Court's docket database. Our search for *Rio Grande Compact* retrieved four documents, including a *Motion for Divided Argument*.

The *Questions Presented* can be found using two different methods: If you already retrieved the docket you were searching for, the first method is to simply click the blue *Questions Presented* hyperlink on the docket report (as shown in the previous illustration). Once the hyperlink is clicked, a PDF file setting forth the *Questions Presented* in the case will appear.

The second method is shown in the next illustration: Click *Advanced Search* on the homepage. Then a search menu appears where you can enter keywords into the *Search for* box, and then place a check mark into the *Questions Presented* check-box. This will retrieve all *Questions Presented* that include those keywords. There are many other options on this menu to keyword search, such as *Opinions, Argument Transcripts, Argument Audio,* etc. You can click into one or more of their check boxes to expand your search to these other documents. Not all documents are full-text searchable, however. For instance, we checked the *Argument Audio* box and entered the keyword *cake* (to find the *Argument Audio* for *Masterpiece Cakeshop, Ltd. v.*

Colorado Civil Rights Comm'n). We got no results, but a search for a partial party name search (*Masterpiece Cakeshop*) retrieved the *Argument Audio* for that case.

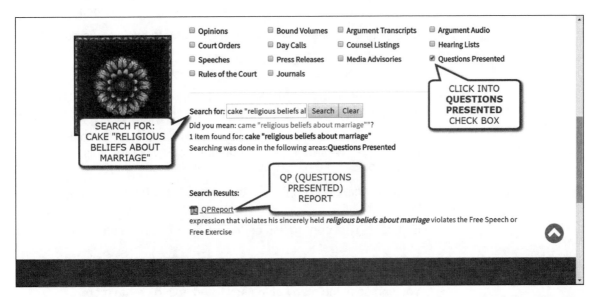

To learn how to create a sophisticated *Advanced Search*, click the *Search Tips* link on the homepage beneath the search box (see the first illustration in this section) or use this URL: https://www.supremecourt.gov/search_help.aspx. You will be instructed:

> To use this search page, you can look for a single word. Or, use the next two lists of tips to refine your search to find more specific results. In all these examples please note that the searches are case insensitive, so searching for *Supreme Court* is the same as searching for *SUPREME COURT*.
>
> - Look for two or more words at once by just separating them by a space or using the AND operator.
>
>   Example - type Supreme AND Court or simply Supreme Court to find documents that have both the word supreme and the word court anywhere.
>
> - Look for a phrase.
>
>   Example: type "Supreme Court" in quotes to find the exact phrase Supreme Court. The search is not case-sensitive.
>
> - Look for words that are close to each other by using the NEAR operator instead of the AND operator. When you use NEAR, the closer together the words are, the higher the rank of the page, so the higher it appears in the list of search results.
>
>   Example - type Rehearing NEAR denied to match documents where the word rehearing and denied are within 50 words of each other.

- Look for synonyms or similar words by using the OR operator. Note that if you don't use the OR operator and search using multiple words, a boolean AND operator is assumed.

  Example - type Order OR Journal to find documents containing the word Order or the word Journal, but not necessarily both.

- Limit your search by using the NOT operator to exclude words.

  Example - type surfing NOT Internet to find all instances of surfing, as long as Internet is not in the document.

- Use double quotes if you want to use AND, OR, NOT, or NEAR literally.

  Example - type "Search will not find" to find documents with the phrase Search will not find. Without the double quotes, this query would use the NOT operator to exclude the word find.

- Look for words that begin with the same letters by using a single asterick (*). [sic]

  Example - type cert* to find certify, certiorari, certification and so on.

More advanced searches

- You can combine many of the just listed tips to create more specific searches such as:Using multiple operators: Use parentheses around each combination of *NEAR* and combine them into a more complicated search such as: (*Supreme NEAR Court*) *AND* (*Capital NEAR Case*) would return items where the word *Supreme* is near the word *Court* and where *Capital* is also near the word *Case*. This would differ from *Supreme NEAR Court NEAR Capital NEAR Case* because that would require all four words to be in close proximity to each other.

U.S. Supreme Court Argument Transcripts, Argument Audio, and Briefs

As of November 2017, the **Supreme Court of the United States** site (https://www.supremecourt.gov/) finally began hosting its merit and amicus briefs on its official site, but the site doesn't provide a separate link to the briefs for easy access.Instead, briefs are listed on the docket report (click the blue link to view the brief). For pre-November 2017 briefs back to 2004, you will need to use other sites that we will discuss later in this chapter.

While the **Supreme Court of The United States'** site has included oral argument transcripts back to 2000 for some time, Heritage Reporting Corporation took over the project beginning in the October Term 2017. They are maintained on the Court's site and are posted on the same day an argument is heard by the Supreme Court (http://bit.ly/sctoralargtran). "Same-day transcripts are considered official but subject to final review..." (http://bit.ly/sctoralargtran). The transcripts are browsable by *Term* and then *by Date Argued* but can also be full-text keyword searched by clicking *Advanced Search* from the Court's home page, checking off the checkbox next to *Argument Transcripts*, and entering keywords into the *Search for* box (as shown in the previous illustration).

The Court's site also includes *Argument Audio* back to 2010; and "are available to the public at the end of each argument week...on Fridays after Conference" (http://bit.ly/sctoralargaudio). You can either download the *Argument Audio* or listen to them on the Court's website. The *Argument Audio* are browsable by *Term* and then by *Date Argued* but can also be full-text keyword searched as explained earlier in the section on *Argument Transcripts,* but just check off *Argument Audio.*

U.S. Supreme Court Dockets, Argument Audio, and Briefs From Other Sites

Older oral argument recordings (from 1955- 2009) are maintained by the National Archives and Records Administration. There is no indication if they will eventually be posted to the Court's site. There are two collections of recordings. You will be able to listen to some sound recordings online by searching the **National Archives Catalog** site (https://catalog.archives.gov/advancedsearch), but for others you may need to contact or visit the National Archives and Records Administration location (National Archives at College Park, Motion Pictures (RDSM), 8601 Adelphi Road, College Park, MD 20740-6001; Phone: 301-837-3540; Fax: 301-837-3620; or Email: mopix@nara.gov).

- *Sound Recordings of Oral Arguments - Black Series, 10/1955 - 12/1972* (https://catalog.archives.gov/id/77820785): scroll down the page and then click the *Search within this series* tab. There are 41 pages of records (with twenty results per page), which you can browse through or search by entering a party name or full case title into the search box. You will be able to listen to many, if not all, of these online.

- Audio Recordings of Oral Arguments, 1955 – 2012 (https://catalog.archives.gov/id/105447): this collection does not appear to be available online, so you will need to contact the National Archives.

Two other sites provide free access to many of the Supreme Court's oral arguments. The first is **Oyez** (http://www.oyez.org/cases) with oral arguments back to 1955. The second is **CourtListener,** which downloads the latest oral arguments from the Supreme Court at the end of each day to create a searchable archive (https://www.courtlistener.com/audio). In addition, **CourtListener** also downloads the latest oral arguments from the Courts of Appeals (First through the Ninth Circuits, the Court of Appeals for the D.C. Circuit, and the Court of Appeals for the Federal Circuit) at https://www.courtlistener.com/coverage/#oral-arguments. You can search for the audio version of an oral argument by entering full or partial party names into the *Advanced Oral Argument Search* box (https://www.courtlistener.com/audio) and/or by entering information into one (or multiple) of the following field search boxes: *Jurisdictions, Docket Number, Case Name, Argued After:YYYY-MM-DD, Argued Before:YYYY-MM-DD*, and *Judge*. Dates of coverage are not detailed for any of the courts.

As mentioned earlier, for pre-November 2017 briefs you will need to use non-official sites (all free), as noted in this next section.

The **ABA Preview of United States Supreme Court Cases** site (http://bit.ly/abasupctbriefs) offers briefs from 2004 through November 2017. For briefs after that date, the site now refers you to the Supreme Court's official site. To view briefs from 2004-2016, click the links on the left column. Click the links on the right side of the page to view briefs from the 2016-2017 and 2017-2018 terms. Then, select from the alphabetical list of party names. Or, to quickly find your case from the long list, we would recommend you use your *Find* function (*control f* for PCs and *command f* for Macs) and enter the party name into *Find* box to be taken directly to the listed case. You can then choose any of the briefs to view full-text.

SCOTUSblog (http://linkon.in/scotusblogbriefs) offers an archive of merit and amicus briefs back to 2007. However, it offers some additional features such as *Proceedings and Orders* (the docket sheet) and the ability to set up free alerts to receive updates by e-mail about a particular case's docket.

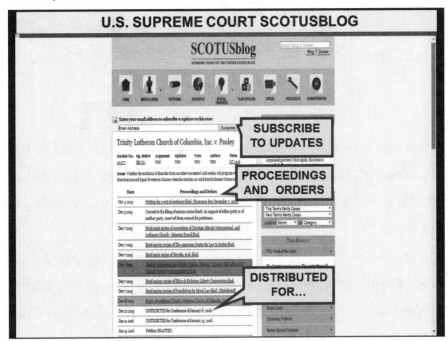

To use **SCOTUSblog** (http://linkon.in/scotusblogbriefs), choose a Term to view the list of cases for that Term. They will be listed in *sitting order* (*sitting* refers to the date of the oral argument). But if you prefer to view the list of cases alphabetically instead of by date argued, click the link *View this list sorted by case name*. Once you find the case, click on its title. Then you will see the *Proceedings and Orders*, listed from oldest to newest, as shown in the previous illustration. You can choose any of the briefs to view full-text.

Historical dockets (1999 to 2009) and briefs can be found at **FindLaw's** *Supreme Court Center*, but not through its homepage because there doesn't appear to be a link any longer. You will need to use this direct URL: http://linkon.in/flussupctdoc.

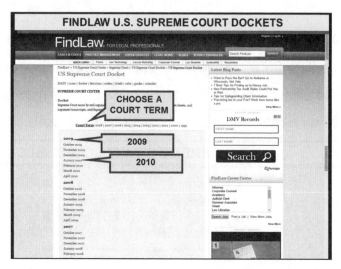

FINDLAW U.S. SUPREME COURT DOCKETS

Once you arrive at the docket page, there are some links to months in 2010 but when you click the links, there are no dockets. It appears that **FindLaw** stopped adding dockets at the end of 2009. (See page 227 for more details and some caveats about this site.)

Once you find the *Court Term* that interests you, choose a month to view the dockets list. **FindLaw's** docket database is actually a summary of the official docket. Each docket (see next illustration) displays the *Question* and the *Counsel of Record*; links to PDFs of the decisions from the Supreme Court and lower court, links to the Supreme Court's full, official docket sheet; links to briefs, and, when available, links to a written transcript or audio of the oral argument. However, many of the links in **FindLaw's** docket database often do not work, especially those to the Court's official site, because the Court has either taken them down or changed their URLs and **FindLaw** has not kept up with the changes.

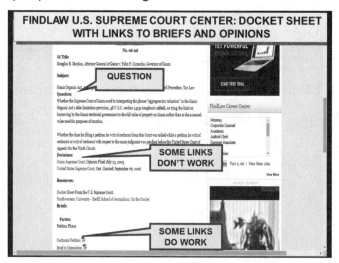

FINDLAW U.S. SUPREME COURT CENTER: DOCKET SHEET WITH LINKS TO BRIEFS AND OPINIONS

U.S. Supreme Court and U.S. Courts of Appeals Oral Arguments from CourtListener

Another site to access the Supreme Court's oral arguments (and also many U.S. Courts of Appeals' oral arguments), is **CourtListener**. This site offers a robust search engine where users can search by *Keyword, Jurisdiction, Case Name, Judge, Argued After* (date)*, Argued Before* (date)*,* and *Docket Number* (https://www.courtlistener.com/audio). To find out which circuits of the U.S. Courts of Appeals are included, see https://www.courtlistener.com/coverage/#scraped-jurisdictions.

Pay Dockets and Case Documents: Federal (Appellate, Bankruptcy, and District Courts), State, and Local from Westlaw CourtExpress.com, LexisNexis CourtLink.com, and Bloomberg Law Dockets

Even with the free, hybrid, and/or low-cost docket research options available, there are many reasons lawyers might still want to subscribe to pricier commercial pay docket databases, such as **Westlaw CourtExpress.com, LexisNexis CourtLink.com**, or **Bloomberg Law Dockets**. First, these pay sites offer much more sophisticated searching. In addition to the party name, docket number, NOS, and date searching, these commercial sites allow you to search by lawyer name, judge name, subject, and even full-text by keyword through the underlying case documents. They also offer more than just federal dockets. Various state and local court dockets are available from them. **Bloomberg** also offers international dockets. You can order copies of case documents from the commercial docket vendors if they are not available online. The documents can be mailed, sent by Federal Express, e-mailed, or faxed.

These commercial docket databases also offer automated case tracking and alerts about a specific case or all cases involving a specific party, lawyer, judge, NOS, and so on. Based on your search criteria, these databases can alert you via e-mail whenever a new docket is filed in a particular court or when a new document is added to a particular docket sheet. Their archives sometimes also go back farther in time than **PACER's** or state and local courts' official sites.

Courthouse News Service (http://linkon.in/cthsenewsdoc), while not a full docket database, offers a *Report* (a daily list) of new civil complaints filed in over 1,600 federal, state, and local courts. They charge $100 per geographic segment per month for their *Report*. For example, Alabama has three segments, consisting of North, South and Federal, so the total monthly charge would be $300. The complaints cost extra and not all of them are always available for download. If they are available, a *Download* link will be included at the end of the complaint's description in the *Report*. You can request **Courthouse News Service** send a runner to the court to obtain the complaint, but they don't send you the complaint directly; instead they'll add the case with the download link to the next *Report* that comes out and you download it from there. Subscribers to **Courthouse News Service** have told us that the **Service** has access to some courts that the other pay databases do not. **Courthouse News** also has an e-alert service, (which they call a *Dinger*) that will alert you when a party name you specify appears in a new complaint.

For information about which state courts offer online public access to court dockets and documents, visit the **National Center for State Courts** (**NCSC**) *Privacy/Public Access to Court Records State Links* and choose a state (http://tinyurl.com/statedockets).

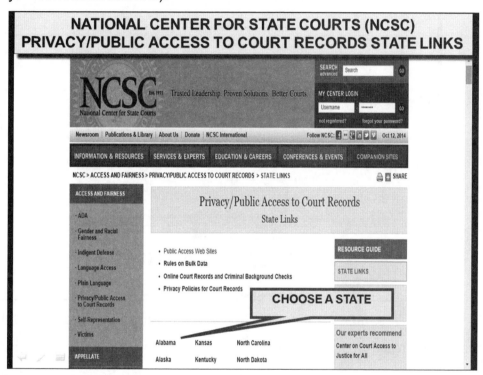

As shown in the next illustration, the **NCSC** *State Links* lists each state and describes the state's docket databases. Note, however, that the list is not complete. We found many docket databases missing from this list—but it's a start.

Another resource for determining whether a court has a docket database is **Search Systems** (http://publicrecords.searchsystems.net), which you can scan by state or county (see pages 159–162 to learn how to use **Search Systems**).

Official state and local docket databases vary as to what search capabilities and amounts of information they each offer and whether they are free or pay. For instance, in California, the state does not offer a way to search all the county superior (trial) courts' docket databases simultaneously. You would need to visit each county separately to learn if they had a docket database, determine if it's free, and then search each, one by one. In New York, however, there are statewide county docket sites (http://linkon.in/nywebcts) where you can search all counties simultaneously (or select just one county or multiple counties) for the following courts:

- **WebCivil Local**: contains cases from all the local Civil Courts in New York State (61 City Courts, the District Courts in Nassau and Suffolk Counties, and the New York City Civil Courts). You may search for cases by Index Number, Party Name, Attorney/Firm Name or Judge, and produce calendars for a specific Attorney/Firm or by Judge or Part.

- **WebCivil Supreme** (note: in New York, the Supreme Court is actually the trial court): contains information on both Active and Disposed Civil Supreme Court cases in all 62 counties of New York State. You may search for cases by Index Number, Party Name, Attorney/Firm Name or Justice, and produce calendars for a specific Attorney/Firm or by Justice or Part. Sign up for eTrack case tracking service and receive email updates and appearance reminders for cases you wish to follow. (See next illustration.)

- **WebCriminal**: provides information on pending criminal cases with future appearance dates for selected New York State Courts of criminal jurisdiction. You may search for cases by Case Number or Party Name and produce calendars by Court and Part or Judge

Once you retrieve your list of results, click the *Index* (docket) *Number* to view *Case Details* or click the *M* (found in the last column) to view *Motion Details*. The case documents are not available—just the docket.

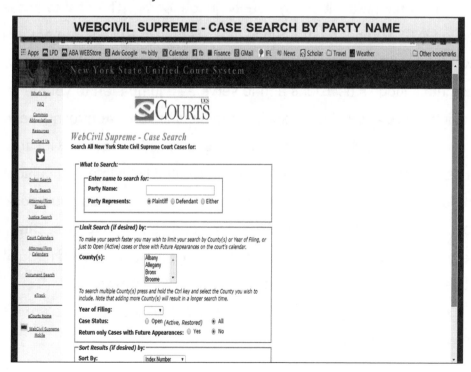

In California, Los Angeles County's Superior Court offers a docket database, **LA Court Online**, but the **NCSC** site failed to list it until recently. You can only search free at the Los Angeles County's Superior Court's docket database if you know the docket number (http://bit.ly/lasuperfreecaseno). To search by party name at the court's site (at **LA Court Online**) costs $4.75, with additional charges to download any of the case documents (http://bit.ly/lasuperparty).

Fortunately, a free party name (and attorney and judge name) search site has recently launched, **Plainsite.org** (http://linkon.in/plainsitefreedockets), which includes the docket sheet, but does NOT include the actual case documents. For a detailed article about **LA Court Online** and **Plainsite.org**, see (http://linkon.in/netforplainsite).

Even though it is, technically, a case document, one document you won't find in California county court dockets is a judge's Tentative Ruling. They are found online at the court's official site, but only for a brief period of time. Over the course of several years, two lawyers in Orange County, California, collected and archived thousands of these Rulings and created a database, **Bench Reporter** (http://www.benchreporter.com). You can search **Bench Reporter's** Tentative Rulings through multiple counties simultaneously by keywords and phrases. You can further refine your search with filters, by county, judge, or tag. The cost to access the collection is $39.00 per month. Since most Tentative Rulings are not available anywhere else, **Bench Reporter** has the potential to be a very useful database to gain insight into a judge's decisions and to serve as a jump-start to your legal research. For a detailed article about this database, see http://linkon.in/tentrulingsbench.

If, after reviewing all of the finding resources for state and local court dockets discussed in this section, you still have not located links to a particular state or local court docket database, enter the court's name and the words *court docket* (e.g., *los angeles court docket*) into a general search engine (e.g., **Google**, **Bing**, or **Yahoo!**) or leave off the word *docket* to find the court's homepage and scan through the court's site to see if it offers a docket (or case summary) database.

As noted on page 229, some state and local court dockets are also available on the commercial pay sites.

Chapter Fourteen

LIABILITIES: BANKRUPTCIES, UCC FILINGS, JUDGMENTS, AND LIENS

Bankruptcy

When you are conducting due diligence on a person or company, you should research whether they have ever filed for bankruptcy. This will give insight into their ability to handle their finances, which would be important if you are advising a client about entering into business with someone, for instance. This information is available from the Federal Bankruptcy Court portion of **PACER (Public Access to Court Electronic Records**; http://pacer.psc.uscourts.gov), the government's low-cost federal docket database discussed in *Chapter Thirteen*. Sometimes, it's enough information to just know that your subject has declared bankruptcy. Other times, when you need more information, you might want to review some of the case documents; however, the underlying case documents aren't always available.

After we discuss using **PACER** for bankruptcy research, we will discuss both free and pay-for-use bankruptcy databases, as well as one bankruptcy database that offers hybrid placing. Then, we'll briefly discuss how to find databases to learn if any UCCs, judgments, and liens have been filed against your subject.

Searching PACER Bankruptcy Courts

We have already described how to use **PACER** on pages 185–202, so we will only discuss how to search bankruptcy courts in this section. Please review the earlier **PACER** section before you begin your bankruptcy search. Because you can never be sure where your subject might have filed bankruptcy (or how many times and in what year), it is better to search all bankruptcy courts simultaneously instead of searching one bankruptcy court at a time. You can do this by using the **PACER** *Case Locator*. All bankruptcy courts participate in **PACER**. But, the dates of the earliest cases filed vary from court to court. For example, in sites that we visited, one court's earliest filed cases dated back to as early as November 1, 1974 (Indiana Southern District Court), whereas some other courts did not start filing cases until 1992. Fortunately, the dates of the most recent cases filed were the same for each court and were only one day behind the current date.

In August 2014, **PACER** removed all U.S. Bankruptcy Court cases that had been filed in the Central District of California prior to May 1, 2001, because the systems used by that court were not compatible with the new NextGen system being implemented by **PACER**. Although the docket sheets for the removed cases were eventually restored, the case documents were not. The commercial vendors, **Bloomberg**, **Lexis**, and **Westlaw**, preserved some of these removed docket sheets and case documents in their archives. For any case documents not available from a commercial vendor or **PACER**, you will need to order them from the court at 855-460-9641 or from the National Archives (both for a significant fee).

After you have logged into **PACER** and have reached the *Case Locator's Quick Searches* page, click *Find Bankruptcy by SSN/EIN* or *Find Bankruptcy (Advanced)*.

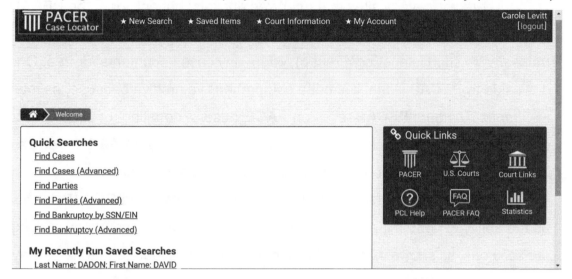

If you choose *Find Bankruptcy by SSN/EIN*, you can search by: (1) a *Four Digit SSN* (Social Security Number), which must be used in combination with a *Last Name*, or by (2) a full *SSN or EIN* (Employer Identification Number).

If you choose *Find Bankruptcy (Advanced),* as shown in the next illustration, you can search by one or more of the following criteria, such as: (1) *Party* (personal or entity), (2) *Party Role*, (3) *Chapter*, and (4) Date Ranges: *Date Filed, Date Closed, Date Dismissed,* and *Date Discharged*.

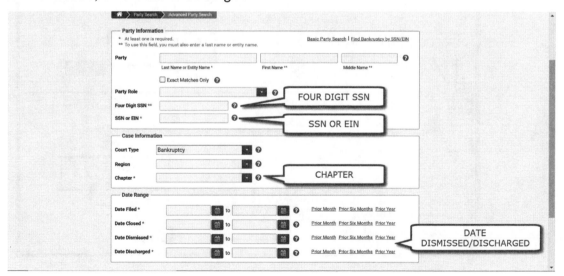

After you choose a case from the list of results, **PACER** will show you a summary of the available documents. You can choose to view: *Aliases, Associated Cases, Attorneys, Case Summary, Claims Register*, etc.

There are several sites that offer free dockets, but only one, the **RECAP Archive**, recently re-launched by **CourtListener** (https://www.courtlistener.com/recap), offers any case documents for free. One downside to **RECAP** is that it is not a comprehensive archive because, as mentioned in *Chapter Thirteen*, **RECAP** relies on **PACER** users "donating" dockets and case documents to **RECAP** when they have purchased them from **PACER**. See pages 203–211 to learn more about how to search the **RECAP Archive**.

CourtListener made many search improvements to the **RECAP Archive**, such as the ability to now limit a **RECAP** search to just bankruptcy courts by clicking *Select Jurisdictions*, as shown in the next illustration. (This is a feature that had always been available at **PACER**.) As explained in *Chapter Thirteen*, **RECAP** offers more advanced search options than **PACER**, such as searching by *Party Name*, *Attorney Name*, and *Keyword*.

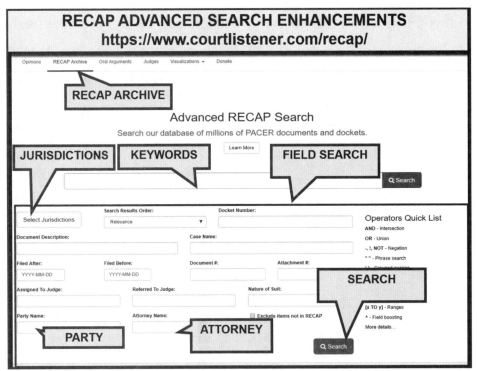

As soon as you click *Select Jurisdictions,* a menu pops up that allows you to click the *Bankruptcy* tab. Then, another menu displays all the *Bankruptcy Appellate Panels* and *Bankruptcy District Courts,* as shown in the next illustration. From this menu you can check one, multiple, or all (click the *Check All* tab at the top) of the displayed courts. Remember to click *Apply* at the bottom of the page.

Bankruptcy dockets and the underlying case documents can also be searched for a fee at various commercial vendors. They offer more sophisticated search options than **PACER**, such as full-text searching through the underlying case documents, and alerts.

- **Westlaw CourtExpress** (http://linkon.in/courtexp)
- **LexisNexis CourtLink** (http://www.lexisnexis.com/courtlink)
- **Bloomberg Law Dockets** (http://linkon.in/bloomdocs)
- **Inforuptcy** (http://linkon.in/inforuptcysearch): Last time we wrote about this site, it had been a free docket search site, but users had to pay for case documents. The site no longer offers any free options. However, it might be useful for bankruptcy practitioners who are looking for a case management system.
- **PacerPro (**https://www.pacerpro.com**)** uses a hybrid pricing plan that offers some docket information for free and some for pay. See pages 214–219 for details on searching this site.

Some pay investigative databases indicate if someone has declared bankruptcy, but do not provide the docket sheet or case documents. Examples of these investigative databases are **TLOxp** (http://www.tlo.com/about-tloxp), **Accurint** (http://www.accurint.com), and **Westlaw Next's PeopleMap** (http://linkon.in/peoplemapinfo). See *Chapter Tweny-Eight* for details about these databases.

UCC Filings, Judgments, and Liens Databases

To continue your research about a person's or company's finances, and in particular their liabilities, you might want to search for any UCC (Uniform Commercial Code) filings, judgments, or liens filed against them. These records will indicate, for example, if your subject is a debtor or secured party in a business transaction, has had a judgment entered against them, or failed to pay taxes.

As an aside, these documents are one more place to find a person who is evading you—if they include an address or other personally identifying information. Unfortunately, most states are redacting more and more personally identifying information from these documents, and thus they might be less useful in finding an evasive person.

In addition, these documents might be useful to help you identify where someone banks—assuming your subject deals with the same institution for all (or some) of their financial needs (from banking, to obtaining mortgages, etc.).

There are two categories of liens: voluntary and involuntary. Voluntary liens are placed against a property or a person when the owner voluntarily pledges property (real or personal) as consideration for a mortgage or another obligation. Examples of voluntary liens are:

- Deeds of trust or mortgage liens
- Notes
- Builder's or mechanic's liens
- Contracts for sale
- UCC Filings (usually UCC-1 Financing Statements)

Involuntary liens are sometimes referred to as adverse filings. In this case, the person or company did not pledge something as consideration. Instead, there has been an adverse judgment filed against the person or their property if:

- they defaulted on an obligation to pay a lender or a governmental entity, such as a failure to pay taxes; or
- they were on the losing side of a lawsuit and a judgment was filed against them.

Examples of involuntary liens are:

- Federal or state tax liens
- Mechanic's and materialman's liens
- Abstracts of judgment

Liens, judgments, and UCCs can be filed at the federal, state, or county level, so you need to search in many different places to cover all of these possibilities. For example, there are both federal and state tax liens, as well as both county and state judgments. It will vary from jurisdiction to jurisdiction whether the records are online and whether they are free or pay. The amount of information provided at each database will vary from jurisdiction to jurisdiction. In some jurisdictions there will be summary information only, while in others the image of the actual record is displayed. The search protocol will also vary from jurisdiction to jurisdiction.

The next illustration shows an example of a free government database to search liens, judgments, UCC Filings, and more, for McHenry County, Illinois (linkon.in/mchenryland), where you can search by *Party Name*, *Recorded Date Range*, and *Document Type* (select *All* or choose one).

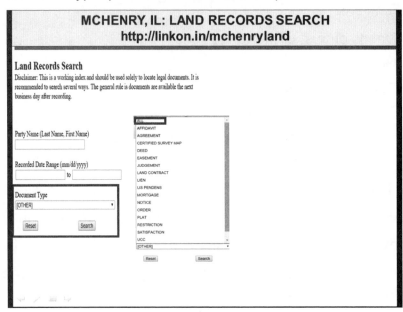

The next illustration shows search results from a McHenry County, Illinois, government *Land Records Search*. Note that the results page includes a variety of liens, from federal and state tax liens, to mechanic's liens and municipal liens. However, only summary information is displayed instead of the actual image of the record and the party's address is not included.

MCHENRY, IL DIRECT LIEN SEARCH RESULTS

McHenry, IL DIRECT SEARCH

Land Records Search

Search Criteria: Party Name = JONES and Document Type = LIEN

Search returns only 200 records. It is possibly that there are more records matching the search criteria. You need to narrow your search with more specific criteria.

Recorded Date	Document Name	Last Name	First Name	Party Type	Document Type
08/15/2014	2014R0027286	JONES	TIM J	PARTY AGAINST	REL FED TX LIEN
08/15/2014	2014R0027286	JONES	DANA L	PARTY AGAINST	REL FED TX LIEN
07/23/2014	2014R0024138	JONES	TIMOTHY J	PARTY AGAINST	MECH LIEN
07/23/2014	2014R0024138	JONES	ANTOINETTE	PARTY AGAINST	MECH LIEN
04/21/2014	2014R0012429	JONES	TIMOTHY	PARTY AGAINST	ST INC TAX LIEN
04/21/2014	2014R0012429	JONES	DANA	PARTY AGAINST	ST INC TAX LIEN
12/19/2013	2013R0058720	JONES	ROBERT J	PARTY AGAINST	MUNICIPAL LIEN

Search Systems' (http://publicrecords.searchsystems.net) free public records directory is a good resource to locate whether any state, federal, or local UCC, judgments and liens databases (and many other public record databases) are available on the Internet. If you are looking for links to UCC databases, for example, select *By Type of Record* from **Search Systems'** homepage and then *Uniform Commercial Code.* As shown in the next illustration, **Search Systems** lists links to each state's UCC database and describes whether they can be searched by name, by lien number, and so on. Notice that **Search Systems** alerts you in advance if you will encounter a *Pay Site* (e.g., see the *Arkansas* entry) even before you click on the link.

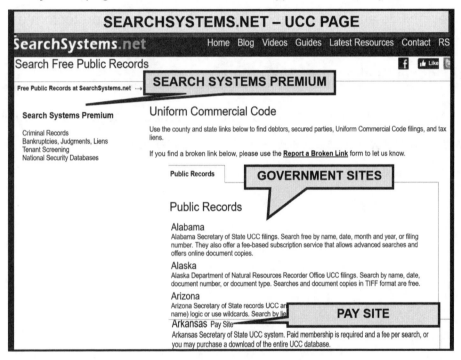

If a free search is not available in the jurisdiction you need to search, or if you need to conduct a multi-jurisdictional search (e.g., an "all state" UCC search), or a multi-type record search (e.g., search UCC, judgment, and liens records simultaneously) in one or more states or counties, you will need to use a pay database. **Search Systems Premium** (shown on the left-hand side in the prior illustration) offers a nationwide *Bankruptcies-Judgments-Liens* database search (for $5.00) where you can search over 100 million records by *Individual Name*, *Business Name*, or *SSN/Tax ID*. Many other pay databases (discussed later in *Chapter Twenty-Eight*) also offer these multi-jurisdictional and multi-type record searches. There is no way to run these types of searches for free on the Internet. See *Chapter Ten*, pages 159–162, for more details on how to use **Search Systems**.

BRB Publications (http://linkon.in/brbstandcountyliens) has also compiled a list of links to liens, judgments, UCC Filings (and other records) by state and county. See pages 163–165, for more details about **BRB**.

Many of the state records discussed in this chapter are filed with the Secretary of State. If you need to search a specific state's (and the District of Columbia's) UCC filings, visit the **National Association of Secretaries of State (NASS)** website (http://linkon.in/nassucc) and select a state from the *UCC Filings* drop-down menu. It does not include any U.S. commonwealths, territories, or protectorates.

Other Docket Background Searching

To get a full picture about your subject's background and their litigation history, you will need to conduct docket searches beyond bankruptcy dockets. See *Chapter Thirteen* to learn more.

Chapter Fifteen

LOCATING ASSETS

Using Asset Searches to Find People and Investigate Backgrounds

There are two main reasons to search for assets. The first reason is fairly obvious: to locate a person's assets so you can gather information about a person's financial worth. For example, in a divorce action, we need to locate assets for proper division of property. In another case, we might need to ascertain whether a defendant has assets or is judgment-proof. This could help us decide whether to file a lawsuit in the first place. The second, and not so obvious reason, to search for a person's assets is that their assets could lead us to their location. For example, certain types of assets, such as real estate, airplane, and automobile records typically contain current addresses. So, if you need to find a witness or you need to serve someone, finding records of their assets could prove useful.

Locating Bank Accounts and Balances

One of the questions we get most often is, "What site or database can I use to locate someone's bank accounts or other financial information?" And our answer is, "none." Furthermore, federal and state laws have placed severe limitations on the ways financial information can be collected and disseminated. The Fair Credit

Reporting Act (FCRA; 15 U.S.C. §1681 *et seq*, *available at* http://linkon.in/1wh5vaB; see pages 489–491) and the Gramm-Leach-Bliley Act (GLBA; 15 U.S.C. § 6801 *et seq.*, *available at* http://linkon.in/1Eqrhx0; see pages 491–494) are two of the primary federal laws that protect financial privacy. An example of a state law that protects financial privacy is California's Consumer Credit Reporting Agencies Act (Cal. Civ. Code, §1785.1-1785.36, *available at* http://linkon.in/calconsumeract).

Some asset search companies indicate that they can obtain financial information about your target—and remain compliant with the laws we just noted—by searching non-bank entities to which financial information may be reported during commercial transactions. These include third-party services used by retailers to verify checking accounts when a purchase is made by check.

However, asset search companies such as **TeleCheck** (http://www.firstdata.com/telecheck/) and **Certegy** (http://www.askcertegy.com/), are classified as "consumer reporting agencies" by the Federal Trade Commission (FTC), and are subject to the FCRA. Similarly, **ChexSystems** (http://www.consumerdebit.com), which compiles information about consumers' handling (or mishandling) of deposit accounts (e.g., checking, savings, debit cards), clearly states that it is a "consumer-reporting agency under by the federal Fair Credit Reporting Act (FCRA)."

In August 2013 and January 2014, **Certegy** (http://linkon.in/1s0lmuI) and **TeleCheck** (http://linkon.in/1vPA3lZ), respectively, were fined $3.5 million because they "did not follow proper dispute procedures…[and] failed to follow reasonable procedures to assure maximum possible accuracy of the information it provided to its merchant clients, as required by the FCRA." Note that the violations had nothing to do with unauthorized access, searching, or sale of data in their files. With this level of FTC oversight, it is difficult to see how asset search companies could be legally searching the files of **Certegy**, **TeleCheck**, or similar companies to provide attorneys with their targets' financial information.

In the past, some private investigators would telephone a bank pretending to be the target of your search to obtain information about your target's bank account. This practice, known as pretexting, is not legal. If a lawyer does the pre-texting, it would also be a violation of Rule 4.1 of the Model Rules of Professional Conduct ("In the course of representing a client a lawyer shall not knowingly: (a) make a false statement of material fact or law to a third person").

Some attorneys have told us that they use investigators who can still obtain information for them about hidden or undisclosed bank accounts and that they [the attorneys] don't ask too many questions about how the investigator got the information," because the attorneys "don't want to know. The problem with this "head in the sand" approach is that it does not protect the attorney if any laws were broken in the collection of the information, especially if the investigator used pretexting (which involves misrepresentation). As noted earlier, an attorney who uses misrepresentation could be disciplined under Rule 4.1 of the Model Rules of Professional Conduct, but also note that a supervising attorney could be held responsible for the investigator's misrepresentation under Rule 5.3 (b)-(c)(1) (*available at* http://linkon.in/1x6ln16) states:

> With respect to a nonlawyer employed or retained by or associated with a lawyer:...
>
> (b) a lawyer having direct supervisory authority over the nonlawyer shall make reasonable efforts to ensure that the person's conduct is compatible with the professional obligations of the lawyer; and
>
> (c) a lawyer shall be responsible for conduct of such a person that would be a violation of the Rules of Professional Conduct if engaged in by a lawyer if:
>
> (1) the lawyer orders or, with the knowledge of the specific conduct, ratifies the conduct involved;...

So, to obtain bank account information you would need to obtain a signed authorization from the target, obtain a court order, or already have a judgment (assuming the bank account information was relevant to the matter). Of course, there is always the possibility that your target has hidden assets that even the target's own attorney is not aware of, making it nearly impossible to find these assets.

Now that we've got that out of the way, let's look at some of the sources for locating information about assets—legally.

Trying to trace real estate assets for a divorce client? Trying to find a person's whereabouts by finding their home address—assuming they own a home? If you don't know where the person lives or if you want to conduct a nationwide search to trace their real estate assets held anywhere, a pay database search is required. But if you only need to target one county or city, you might be able to do a free search if that county or city's assessor, recorder, or treasurer records are available for free online and are searchable by owner name. However, many jurisdictions only offer free address searching, which brings you back to pay databases if you need to search by owner name. (See *Chapter Twenty-Eight* for information regarding pay databases.)

Search Systems (http://www.searchsystems.net), **Portico** (http://indorgs.virginia.edu/portico/assessors.html), and **BRB Publications** (http://linkon.in/1nTLiKc) are public record directories that each link to hundreds of free state and local assessor's, recorder's and/or treasurer's offices that are on the Web. Be aware that none of these sites lists every available resource in every jurisdiction, but we find that **Search Systems** usually links to more jurisdictions than the other two directories. After you visit **Search Systems'** homepage, you can quickly view property records (as shown in the next illustration), by clicking into the *By Type of Record* radio button, choosing *Property Records* from the drop-down menu, and then from the *Select a State* drop-down menu, *choose a state*. After that, a list of counties from that state will be listed with links to their property records.

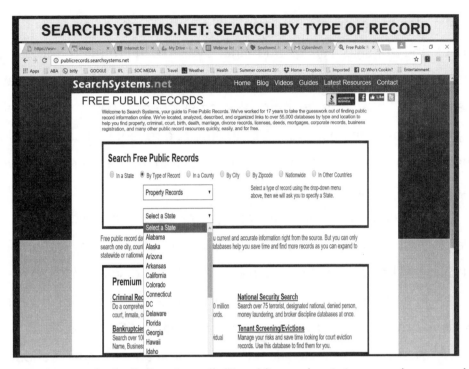

SEARCHSYSTEMS.NET: SEARCH BY TYPE OF RECORD

Because not every jurisdiction has digitized its real estate records, you might need to hire someone to search at the government agency where they are filed. The **Public Record Retriever Network (PRRN)** (http://www.prrn.us/content/Search.aspx), which bills itself as the "largest trade organization representing professionals in the public record industry," offers a searchable database of the organization's more than 500 vendor/members who offer services searching numerous types of public records in all fifty U.S. states plus D.C., Canada, Bermuda, Puerto Rico, and the U.S. Virgin Islands. The database is searchable by state or company name. Some member companies also list search capabilities in the Dominican Republic and Venezuela, among other countries. (Also, see *Chapter Twenty-Eight* for more information on pay investigative databases.)

Note that some jurisdictions only provide a property's assessed value, which will most likely be well below the market value, so if you are trying to ascertain your target's financial worth by way of the market value of the target's property, you might try searching by address at **Zillow.com** (http://www.zillow.com). **Zillow** gathers information from a variety of public records and publicly available sources to display recent real estate sales prices and current "for sale" listings, as well as estimated sales and estimated rental values (these estimates are called ("Zestimates").

Zestimates are generated automatically, partially based on recent real estate sales prices and "for sale" listings and other available information, without an actual inspection of the property to learn about its current condition, renovations, etc. Because of this, further research and cross-checking as to the actual market value of a property may be necessary. For example, a recent test search yielded a Zestimated market value approximately one-third less than the traditionally derived property appraisal of the same property.

You can retrieve information by searching with as little as an *Address*, *Neighborhood* name, or a *ZIP Code*. You cannot search by the property owner's name at **Zillow**. The property owner's name also is not displayed in the resulting record.

In addition to locating property valuation for a specific address, you can also retrieve broader data covering neighborhoods or ZIP Codes.

Searching for a specific address returns an information sheet about the house, from square footage to number of bedrooms/bathrooms, and the Zestimates for that property (sale and rent) as shown in the next illustration. The information sheet also lists *Facts and Features*, property tax information, "Zestimated" sales price trends for the property and the neighborhood, a list of recent nearby home sales in the area, the date of the last sale and the sales price, names of the local schools and their ratings. You can also manipulate an interactive graph to show Zestimates and taxes paid (and other items) over the past ten years. If the owner claimed his/her property, you might see the owner's description of the home (in the *What I Love About The Home* section) and a photo of the home.

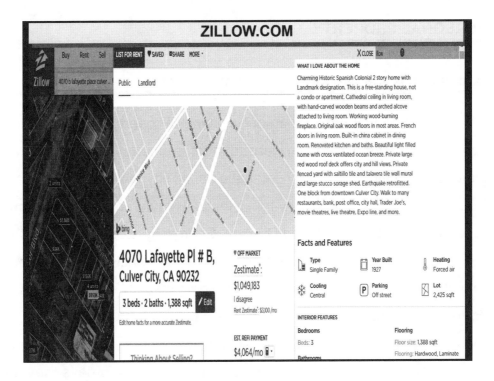

If you click on the map above the Zestimate, you can either view a full-size map of the neighborhood or a "bird's-eye" view of the property and other surrounding properties. If you close the information sheet, you can view an aerial map of the neighborhood, which points to the property you searched.

Registration (which is free) gives you access to additional features, such as the ability to track value information on specific homes. Registered users can also post a *Make Me Move™* price for other site visitors who might be interested in purchasing their home or post the home as for sale or rent by clicking the *More* drop-down menu above the map. (Zillow maintains "registration" and "claiming" processes to help confirm the legal owner of the home before users can input data about a specific address.) Registered owners can also describe their property any way they wish and make changes to the information provided by **Zillow**, even changing the listed square footage, for instance. All of this can automatically increase or decrease the Zestimate, even if the owner inserts false information.

Unclaimed Money and Other Financial Assets

The National Association of Unclaimed Property Administrators (NAUPA) sponsors the **Unclaimed.org** website (http://www.unclaimed.org). It links to the individual unclaimed property databases of all fifty states, the District of Columbia, Puerto Rico, Guam, the U.S. Virgin Islands, Kenya, and the Canadian provinces of Alberta, British Columbia, and Quebec. Searching is done by using the owner's name.

Some jurisdictions' search results display details about the unclaimed property (e.g., the amount), while others do not. Some also show the owner's address. If these addresses are current, these databases can be useful for locating a specific person (besides finding their money). Additionally, we have heard from people who have had success collecting debts from others, who claimed not to have the means to pay, by locating forgotten/unknown funds or other valuable property belonging to the debtor.

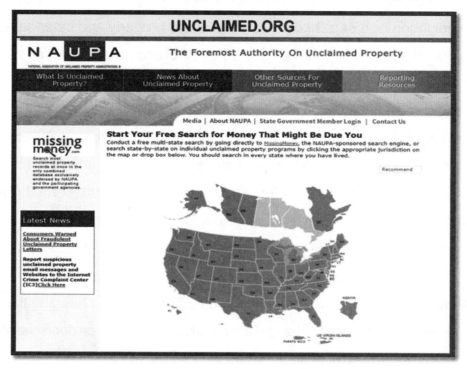

NAUPA also sponsors a free multi-jurisdictional database, **MissingMoney.com** (http://www.missingmoney.com), which only covers Alabama, Alaska, Alberta Canada, Arizona, Colorado, District of Columbia, Florida, Idaho, Indiana, Iowa, Kansas,

Kentucky, Louisiana, Maine, Maryland, Massachusetts, Michigan, Minnesota, Mississippi, Missouri, Montana, Nebraska, Nevada, New Hampshire, New Jersey, New Mexico, New York, North Carolina, North Dakota, Ohio, Oklahoma, Pennsylvania, Puerto Rico, Rhode Island, South Carolina, South Dakota, Tennessee, Texas, Utah, Vermont, Virginia, West Virginia, and Wisconsin. Using the search option on the homepage requires you to enter a *Last Name* and your *Resident State* or *Province*. (A *First Name* is optional.) Results are returned from all participating jurisdictions. Once your basic search results are displayed, you can narrow down your results by adding an *Initial* [of your target's middle name], *City,* or select a single *State* or *Province* from the *Search all states and provinces* drop-down menu. An *Advanced Search* option is also offered where you can search up to three additional previous last names (e.g., former or maiden names) and choose to continue to search *All Participating States or Provinces* or limit your search to up to four *States or Provinces* (cities can also be added). Data are refreshed weekly.

Aircraft Registrations/Ownerships

Landings.com (http://linkon.in/landingsdata) and the **FAA Registry Aircraft Inquiry** site (http://registry.faa.gov/aircraftinquiry) can both be used to verify pilot certifications and discover aircraft registrations/ownerships. In addition to using these sites to locate aircraft assets, they are useful for locating addresses of the owners and pilots if you need to contact them (or serve them).

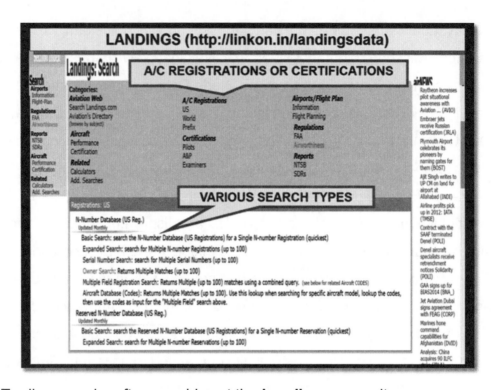

To discover aircraft ownerships at the **Landings.com** site (http://linkon.in/landingsdata), click *U.S.* or click *World* under *A/C Registrations.* You then have a variety of search options to choose from, such as *Owner Search* (in the format of *Last Name* [space] *First Name* or a *Basic Search*, where you can search by the U.S. aircraft *N-Number* ("N" stands for the FAA-issued registration number). U.S. registration information is updated monthly. When conducting *World* searches, you will need to search country by country. Each country's update cycle varies.

The **FAA Registry Aircraft Inquiry** site (http://registry.faa.gov/aircraftinquiry) offers two advantages over the **Landings** site: (1) it is updated daily, and (2) even if a plane has been deregistered and/or exported out of the United States, you can view information on the last U.S.–registered owner name and the country to which it was exported (if you click the N–Number in the results list). For aircraft ownership, search the database by *Name, N–Number, Serial Number, Make/Model*, etc.

To verify 600,000 pilot certifications at **Landings.com** (http://linkon.in/landingsdata), click *Pilots* (see previous illustration). Typically, you will be searching by *Name*, but you can also search by other criteria, such as by *Region*, *Country*, *City*, or *ZIP Code* if you need to know, for example, the names of certified pilots in a certain geographic area. Also, to narrow down a name search of a common name, add more criteria to the name search. The database only contains information on "pilots who have a current Medical Certificate."

At the **FAA Registry** site (https://amsrvs.registry.faa.gov/airmeninquiry), you must supply the following information about yourself before you can conduct a pilot certification search: your *Last Name*, *Employer*, *Street*, *City*, and *Country*. (*State* and *ZIP* Code are required for addresses in the United States.) Because the searcher's personal information is not required at the **Landings.com** site, we would prefer using that site to the **FAA** site. However, when we searched the same name at both sites, we obtained differing results, indicating that a search at both sites might be necessary.

Ownership information regarding domestic commercial and recreational vessels that are five net tons or larger, which are documented by the United States Coast Guard (USCG), is available in an online database (http://linkon.in/boatsearch) at the **Office of Science and Technology National Marine Fisheries Service** site (**NMFS** but informally known as **NOAA Fisheries**). This database is a copy of the USCG vessel database. You can only search by the vessel name or number, but search results will provide the owner's name and address.

To search by owner name for domestic commercial and recreational vessels that are five net tons or larger, you will need to subscribe to a pay-for-use investigative database, such as **TLOxp**. (See *Chapter Twenty-Eight* for details about how to subscribe.) At **TLOxp**, you can also search by the owner's address, Social Security Number, etc., as shown in the next illustration.

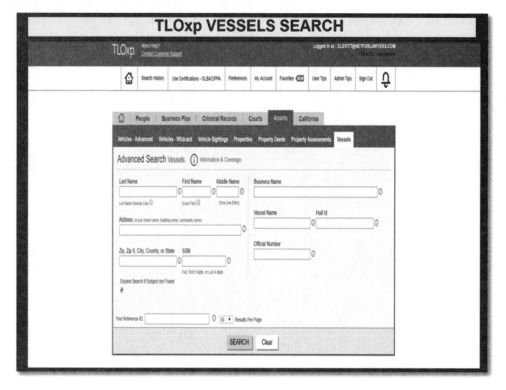

Registrations of vessels less than five net tons are handled at the state level (usually by the Department of Motor Vehicles or by the Department of Fish and Wildlife). Which agency handles these registrations varies from state to state, as does whether this information is available for free on the Internet. Public record portals like

Search Systems (http://publicrecords.searchsystems.net) or **BRB Publications** (http://www.brbpub.com/free-public-records) will be useful in helping you determine the right agency in the state you need to search.

Intellectual Property (Patents, Trademarks, and Copyrights)

In a hunt for people's assets, do not overlook intellectual property that they may own—patents, trademarks, and copyrights. In addition to searching intellectual property sites to locate assets owned by your target, the address listed on the record might be useful if you need to contact or serve your target.

Patents

The **U.S. Patent and Trademark Office (USPTO)** offers a full-text searchable database of patents back to 1976, which you can use by clicking the *Quick Search* option at http://patft.uspto.gov.

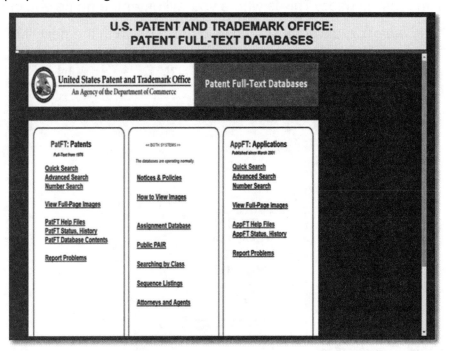

Patents from 1976–present can be field searched using the *Advanced Search* menu (http://linkon.in/usptoadvsearch). If you field search, be sure to run two different searches: the first by the *Inventor's name,* and, in case your subject was ever assigned a patent, a second search by *Assignee Name.* New patents are added each Tuesday.

Another place to search for patents is at **Google Patents Search** database (https://patents.google.com). **Google Patents Search** can be more useful than the **USPTO** site, for two reasons: First, despite its name, it also includes registered trademark images from 1870 to the present and applications from 1884 to the present. So, you can conduct a search of patents and trademarks together. Second, if you are trying to search for patent assets outside of the U.S., **Google Patents** offers a searchable database of 30 million foreign patents (in addition to its 10 million U.S. patents back to 1790). Fortunately, **Google** machine-translates foreign patents into English.

Google Patents maintains two search interfaces. First, we'll explain the new interface and then the old one. Searching by inventor or assignee's name often is a two-step process in the new interface. You first enter the name into the homepage of **Google Patents** full-text search database. If you receive too many results from your full-text search, your second step is to use the filter column that appears on the left side of the results page. This is where you will enter the name you originally searched into the *Inventor* or *Assignee* search field box (shown in the next illustration).

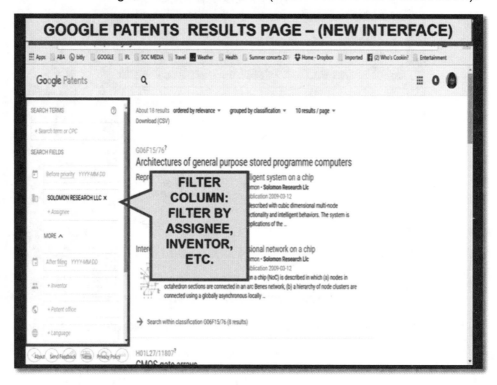

To avoid this two-step search process, you can use **Google's** old patent search interface to conduct a one-step *Inventor* or *Assignee* search. The old interface offers a direct URL to its *Advanced Patent Search* page (https://www.google.com/advanced_patent_search), where you can enter a name into an *Inventor* and *Assignee* field box (shown in the next illustration).

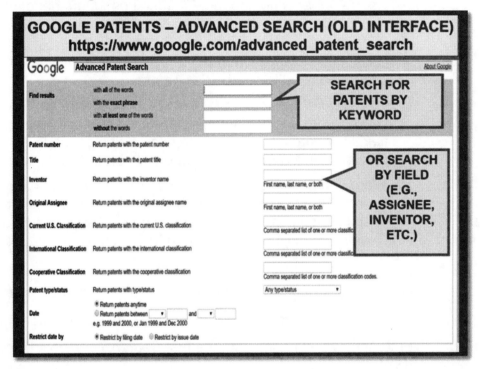

For more detailed information on searching **Google Patents**, see pages 108–110.

Use the **USPTO's TESS (Trademark Electronic Search System)** to search by a trademark owner's name (http://www.uspto.gov/trademarks/). There are over 4 million pending, registered, and dead federal trademarks. Scroll down to click the *TESS* button on the *Trademarks* homepage. On the subsequent page, you are offered three ways to search:

- *Basic Word Mark Search (New User)*—can only search word marks; cannot be used to search design marks

- *Word and/or Design Mark Search (Structured)*—can be used to search word (including names) or design marks via a form to specify fields to search; but in order to search design marks you must use relevant Design Search Codes listed at http://linkon.in/1pRvZwN

- *Word and/or Design Mark Search (Free Form)*—can be used to search word or design marks by entering field codes (provided) in the search box; in order to search design marks, you must use relevant Design Search Codes listed at http://linkon.in/1pRvZwN

To search by owner name, you can use either of the first two search forms listed earlier, but we prefer the second one, *Word and/or Design Mark Search (Structured)*. Enter the owner's name into the first *Search Term* box. If you know the full name, enter it as a phrase using quotations marks, and then, from the *Field* box drop-down menu, select *Owner Name.* If you know the first and last name but you are unsure if your target uses a middle name or initial, do not conduct a phrase search. Instead, you can enter the first name into one *Search Term* box and the last name into another *Search Term* box and then click the *Operator* drop-down menu to select *AND* or *NEAR* to connect the names. You can also search by last name only.

The **Design Search Code Manual** (http://linkon.in/Ztg0yd) provides a detailed list and explanation of *Design* codes, categories, and terms used to describe design (image) marks, and it can also be helpful when searching for non-word marks.

"The United States Copyright Office, and the position of Register of Copyrights, were created by Congress in 1897. The Register directs the Copyright Office as a separate federal department within the Library of Congress, under the general oversight of the Librarian" (https://www.copyright.gov/about). However, there is a movement to take this role away from the Librarian of Congress, by way of the Register of Copyrights Selection and Accountability Act of 2017, H.R.1695, 115th Congress (2017-2018), which passed in the House on March 26, 2017 (http://linkon.in/locregofcopy).

The **U.S. Copyright Office's** searchable *Public Catalog* (http://cocatalog.loc.gov) consists of one integrated catalog (instead of what had been three separate databases. You can search over 20 million records for registered works and recorded documents back to January 1, 1978. The catalog includes registrations and pre-registrations for books, music, films, sound recordings, maps, software, photographs, art, multimedia, periodicals, magazines, journals, newspapers, etc. Also included are records for assignments, transfers, and miscellaneous documents relating to copyright ownership.

The catalog defaults to a *Basic Search*, shown in the next illustration, where you can search by *Title*, *Name*, *Keyword*, *Registration Number*, *Document Number*, or *Command Keyword* (Boolean, phrase, and wildcard searching). Sample searches are located on the search page and should be referred to before beginning a search. If you are searching for assets (or searching for your target's address), you will select *Name* from the *Search by* drop-down menu and enter your target's last name and first name into the *Search for* box.

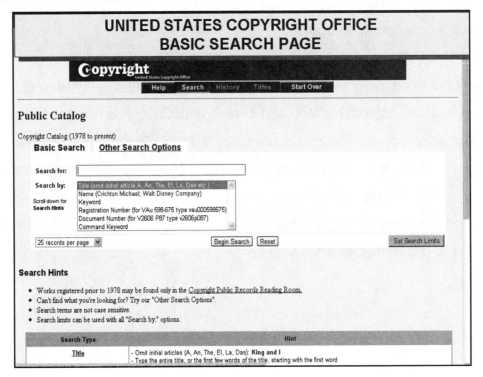

Click the *Other Search Options* tab to access a search form that allows you to conduct targeted Boolean searching with drop-down menus to limit your search to specific fields. For example, you could limit your name search to: *Name Claimant, Name Personal*, or *Name Organization.*

Records from 1870 through 1977 are not available online. You can access them in person at the Copyright Office in Washington, D.C., or by filling out a form (http://linkon.in/bz26QI) to engage the Copyright Office's $200 per hour research service.

BUSINESSES

Business Ownership

As you probably already know, each state has different rules as to what constitutes a regulated business entity and where those entities should register. Most states require registration of Corporations, Limited Liability Companies (LLC), Professional Limited Liability Companies (PLLC), and Limited Liability Partnerships (LLP) at the Secretary of State Office. However, in Maryland, for instance, businesses register at the State Department of Assessments & Taxation. Then there are other states that require Limited Partnerships (LP) to file, and even churches, associations, Limited Liability Limited Partnerships (LLLP), trade names, trusts, sole proprietorships, Partnerships, and Doing Business As (DBA). DBAs are also referred to as Fictitious Business Names (FBN) or Assumed Business Names (ABN). Some of these other business entities we have listed also register at the Secretary of State Office; some of them register at the County Recorder or County Clerk's office instead.

Searching for business information is useful for a variety of tasks:

(1) Identifying business ownership(s) when conducting an asset search

(2) Finding the registered agent's name and address if trying to serve a business

(3) Finding a business's address and phone number

(4) Linking people from one business to other businesses

(5) Identifying the form of business entity

The amount of information about a business that is available online for free will vary from jurisdiction to jurisdiction. To obtain full information about a business (such as Articles of Incorporation and "Good Standing" certificates), you will usually need to place an order with the government agency (for a fee).

It also varies from jurisdiction to jurisdiction whether you will be able to search online for all types of business entities or just certain ones. If you can search all entities, it varies as to whether you can search all businesses together in one database or you must search individual databases, one at a time.

The search options offered also vary from jurisdiction to jurisdiction. Most business registries are searchable by company name and entity number. Some are also searchable by registered agent name, owner name, or officer name. Some jurisdictions display officer names for free, while others charge for this information.

For multistate searching and to search by criteria not available for free (such as an officer's or owner's name for some jurisdictions), a pay database search will be necessary. See *Chapter Twenty-Eight* for pay database information.

SearchSystems.net has an excellent list (with links) to U.S. business registries for all fifty states, the District of Columbia, and Puerto Rico (http://linkon.in/searchsystemsbizreg) and also to various countries' business registries (http://linkon.in/searchsysforeignbiz).

Residentagentinfo.com (http://www.residentagentinfo.com) has compiled a helpful list of links to the Secretary of State sites in all fifty states, the District of Columbia, Guam, and Puerto Rico, and similar resources in Australia, the United Kingdom, and three of Canada's ten provinces (Ontario, New Brunswick, and Nova Scotia).

Forty-eight states and the District of Columbia provide free web access to obtain a corporation's resident agent, while Indiana and New Jersey both charge to obtain this information online. Indiana, offers Registered Agent information for free by telephone.

Many companies are incorporated in Delaware so it's important to learn how to use **Delaware's Division of Corporations** site (https://corp.delaware.gov). It allows you to search for free by clicking *Search for a Business Entity* and then entering an *Entity Name* or *File Number*. You can also search with a partial *Entity Name,* but the results list will be incomplete if there is a large number of results. For example, a search for *Universal* returns a list of only fifty entities of the "999 matches found" that begin with *Universal*. The site's results page for entities searched includes its *Entity Name* and *File Number*. After you choose an entity from the list, the *Entity Details* page displays its *Incorporation Date/Formation Date*, *Entity Kind*, *Residency*, *Registered Agent Name*, *Address*, and *Phone Number*.

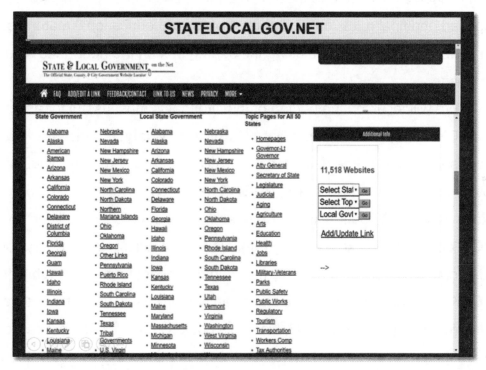

When it comes to Fictitious Business Name (FBN) filings, every county and city offers different amounts of information and different methods for accessing and searching the information. Some jurisdictions may not offer FBN searches at all. When the FBN databases can be searched for free, it varies as to whether you can search by the FBN only or also by the owner's name.

To find links to the county's or city's agency website that handles FBN filings (usually a Clerk or Recorders Office), use the **State and Local Government on the Net** website (http://www.statelocalgov.net). Click the name of the state from the *State Government* column and then scroll down to *Counties* or *Cities* to click the one you're interested in. You will need to browse the county's or the city's website to find the Recorder's (or Clerk's) office.

Locating Information About Public Companies, Executive Compensation, and Stock Ownership

The federal government's official Securities and Exchange Commission (SEC) site (https://www.sec.gov) offers all types of information relating to public companies and individuals connected to those companies, such as SEC filings, public statements, proposed and final rules, enforcement actions, and educational materials. All this can be keyword/phrase searched using the search box on the right-hand side of their homepage.

We will focus on the portion of the site that is most useful for asset searches, the **SEC's EDGAR (Electronic Data Gathering, Analysis, and Retrieval system)** database, which is a free database of 21 million public company filings and exhibits, provided in "real time." Originally, **EDGAR** searches were limited to company name, ticker symbol, CIK (Central Index Key), and a few other options. Then, in 2006, **EDGAR** offered full-text searching (http://linkon.in/edgarpubco) by keywords, phrases, and people's names, etc., but only for the most recent four years. While this has made **EDGAR** more useful, it would be significantly more useful if full-text searching were available for all years. Pre-2006, when we couldn't conduct full-text searches by personal names (and other keywords), we had to know the names of the companies that our subject was involved with, making the search very difficult, if not impossible at times.

To begin searching **EDGAR**, click *Filings* from the **SEC's** homepage and then select **EDGAR** *Search Tools* (or use this direct URL: http://linkon.in/edgarsearchtool).

At the *Search Tools* page, you are provided with many databases, all offering different search options and dates of coverage. We'll focus on the three that are the most useful to our asset searching (shown in the next illustration):

- *Company or fund name, ticker symbol, CIK (Central Index Key), file number, state, country, or SIC (Standard Industrial Classification)*
- *Full text (past four years)*
- *Boolean and advanced searching, including addresses*

Note: The *Central Index Key (CIK)* is the unique identifying number the SEC assigns each company) and the *Standard Industrial Classification* is the government's numerical classification system that describes a company's business.

For asset searching, you would typically use the *Full text (past four years)* database if you needed to discover the amount of your subject's executive compensation (if your subject is at a public company) because this is where you can search by keywords, including a subject's name. A search by personal name will also help you discover if your subject owns stock in public companies. However, this applies only if your subject owns five percent or more of a public company (because they are the only ones required to file a Schedule 13-D with the **Securities and Exchange Commission** (**SEC**), or in some cases, a Schedule 13-G (a "beneficial owner's report").

After you choose the *Full text (past four years)* database from the *Search Tools* page (http://linkon.in/edgarsearchtool), you are first taken to a basic search page which allows you to enter your keywords, phrases, personal names, etc. into the *Search For Text* box. Take note of the *Advanced Search Page* link to the right of that box. Click that link to create more sophisticated searches, such as limiting your search to a specific filing type (choose one from the *In Form Type* drop-down menu*)* and adding a date range, a *Company Name*, a *CIK*, or an *SIC* to your search. We recommend leaving these last three criteria blank so you can capture as many results with your subject's name as possible.

Unlike **Google**, **EDGAR** requires you to type the *AND* Boolean connector in between your keywords and phrases and you MUST type it in upper case. (As explained earlier, **Google** treats the *AND* Boolean connector as a default connector, so it is inserted behind the scenes when you leave a space between words and phrases.) The other two Boolean connectors, *OR* and *NOT*, also must be upper case. If you wish to conduct a successful full-text search, be sure to review **EDGAR's** *Full-Text Search Frequently Asked Questions (FAQ)* (http://linkon.in/edgarfulltextfaq).

As shown in the next illustration, we searched for our subject's last name *Engelman AND "executive compensation"* (**EDGAR** recognizes phrase searches when you surround your words with quotation marks).

SEC EDGAR "FULL-TEXT (PAST 4 YEARS ONLY)"

We also chose *DEF 14A* from the *In Form Type* drop-down menu because we learned from **EDGAR's** *Researching Public Companies Through EDGAR: A Guide for Investors* (http://linkon.in/researchedgar) that this is one of the forms where a company executive's compensation would be listed. We retrieved results for this search, but when we clicked on any one of the filings to view it, we are NOT taken to the page with our keywords. Instead we must scan the filing to find our keywords. Fortunately, there is a work-around to scanning through an entire document and that is the "Find" function, explained on page 28, which allows you to jump right to the page where your keywords appear (and they will be highlighted).

One of the newer changes to the **EDGAR** site is an addition of a *Boolean and advanced searching, including addresses* database, which allows you to search "full-text" for filings back to 1994. The reason we place "full-text" in quotation marks is because it's not actually full-text. Instead, it's a search of the <u>header</u> information from the **EDGAR** index. This is very different from the *Full text (past four years)* database, discussed earlier, which searches the full text of every word of every filing (including exhibits).

To search this index, select *Boolean and advanced searching, including addresses* from the **EDGAR** *Search Tool page* (http://linkon.in/edgarsearchtool) or use this direct URL: http://linkon.in/historiced. After you click the link, you are taken to a page where you are "Welcome[d] to the archive of historical **EDGAR** documents...[to] enter complex queries to retrieve all but the most recent day's **EDGAR** filings" back to 1994 (shown in the next illustration).

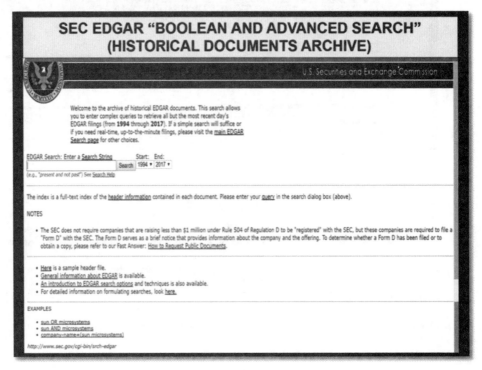

If we "full-text" search the *archive of historical **EDGAR** documents* (shown in the next illustration), using the same search that we used in the earlier *Full text (past four years)* database search ("*executive compensation*" AND *Engelman*), we retrieve no results because, apparently, the header doesn't include the phrase "*executive compensation.*"

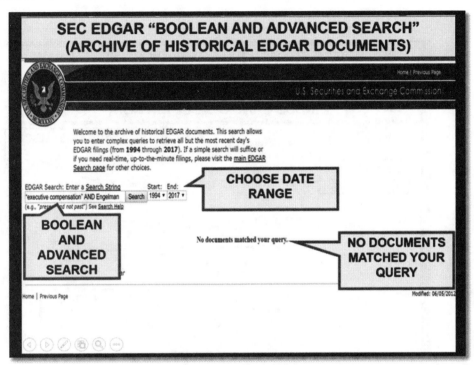

When we revised our search to just *Engelman*, we did retrieve results, showing us that this database can be searched by personal names in addition to company names, but not the actual full-text of documents. To find documents about *Engelman*'s executive compensation, we would need to sift through them until we found the relevant document.

The last of the three databases we'll discuss is the *Company or fund name, etc.,* database. Select it from the **EDGAR** *Search Tools* page (http://linkon.in/edgarsearchtool) or use this direct URL: http://linkon.in/edgarcompanysearch. Be sure to click *More Options* once you reach the *Company* database to avail yourself of the additional search options shown in the next illustration.

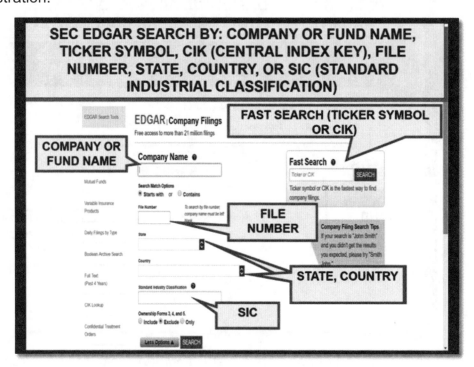

You can search by *Company Name* or *File Number.* (If you search by *File Number*, leave the *Company Name* blank.) You can also conduct a *Fast Search* (shown on the right side of the *Company Name* search form) to search by *Ticker* symbol or *CIK* (see page 267, for information about *CIK).* You can also search by a *Standard Industrial Classification* number (see page 267, for information about *Standard Industrial Classification* numbers. Finally, you can add a *State* and/or *Country* to your *Company Name* search or to your *Standard Industrial Classification* search, or leave all the search boxes blank and just select one state or country from the drop-down menu to retrieve all filings from that state or country.

SEC Info (http://www.secinfo.com) offers free searching of U.S. Securities and Exchange Commission filings back to 1994. Searching at **SEC Info** is much like the **EDGAR** *Boolean and advanced searching, including addresses* database, which allows you to search the header information from the **EDGAR** index and not actually full-text. The following search options are available: *Name* [company and personal], *Symbol*, *Industry*, *Business*, *SIC Code*, *SEC CIK*, *Accession Number*, *File Number*, *Topic*, *City*, and *ZIP Code*. While you can search the site (and receive a list of results) without registering, free registration is required to view the full-text of the filings returned by searches. One useful feature of this site is the ability to set up free alerts to follow a company or person. Simply check the box to the left of *Send me notifications of all future filings involving* [company or person] from your results page.

     Morningstar, once free, but now a fee-based service, offers real-time, full-text searching of current U.S. Securities and Exchange Commission **EDGAR** filings, filings back to 1994, and pre-EDGAR filings back to 1966 (http://www.morningstar.com). The site's database also includes annual and interim reports for more than 44,000 companies in more than 126 countries. At the fee-based **Morningstar** site, automated company alerts are available.

Note, however, that **Morningstar** (aka **Morningstar Investment Research Center**) can still be accessed for free using remote access to many public libraries' subscription. Check your public library website to see if your library subscribes. See page 175 for details on how to access **Morningstar** (and other expensive databases) for free by using your public library's remote access. Many public libraries list their remote access databases by category (in addition to title), so review your public library's category list to learn which company-related databases it offers. The next illustration is from the Metropolitan Library System of Oklahoma City/County and it lists many company databases, such as **Morningstar Investment Research Center**, **Mergent Online**, and **Business Source Premier**.

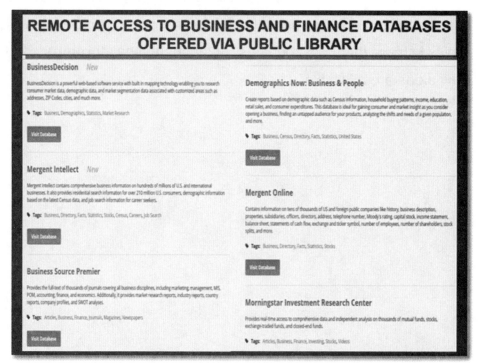

Locating Information About Company Employee Benefits Plans

Regardless of their size, companies and organizations that sponsor an employee benefit plan (e.g., pensions, 401Ks, profit-sharing) subject to The Employee Retirement Income Security Act of 1974 (ERISA; 29 U.S. Code § 18, *available at* http://linkon.in/1wcxxFq) must file IRS Form 5500. The law requires that Form 5500 and select Schedules be "open for public inspection." This includes public and private companies, and (since 2009) non-profit organizations. There are 2.6 million Employee Retirement Income Security Act (ERISA) Form 5500s, covering 1.3 million plans and 1 million plan sponsors.

To search these plans, see the U.S. Department of Labor (USDOL) Employee Benefits Security Administration's **Form 5500/5500-SF Filing Search** (http://linkon.in/efasterisasearch). Searching is by *Plan Name*, *Sponsor Name*, *Plan Administrator, EIN,* etc. Searching can be conducted using full or partial names.

Form 5500 usually contains information on the number of participants in a plan, benefits offered, and so on. Schedule I includes the total assets for the plan and any liabilities. Information on the assets held by any single plan participant is not included. However, establishing that an individual's employer offers a pension plan alerts you to include questions about that account in a discovery request (or you may need to file a motion to compel the individual to disclose information about their personal balance in the plan). Also, if an individual is the sole employee of a company with a benefits plan that requires filing Form 5500, then you can infer that whatever balance is shown in the plan belongs to the individual. Single-participant plans are common among professional corporations (e.g., doctors, lawyers).

FreeErisa.com (http://freeerisa.benefitspro.com/) offers a searchable database of the last three years of Form 5500 filings. Free registration is required. You can use a full or partial *Company Name* to search the filings. Results can be filtered by state or ZIP Code, which is not an option on the USDOL site. The *Deluxe Search* subscription, priced at $59.95 per year, offers additional criteria by which you can search the database. These additional criteria are most useful to benefits managers and advisers (rather than attorneys who are searching for assets).

Chapter Sixteen

VITAL RECORDS

Vital Records: Births, Deaths, Marriages, Divorces, and Social Security Numbers

Information from vital records can be used for all sorts of reasons when you are trying to find a missing person or gather background information about a person. For example, when you are searching for a woman, you will need to know her maiden name and married name (or names) to conduct a complete search, so finding her marriage and divorce records can be extremely useful. In addition to entering your subject's name into a database search form, sometimes a database requires you to also enter the subject's date of birth or Social Security Number to complete the search, so finding birth records and Social Security Numbers becomes imperative.

Although vital records are filed at government agencies, and are thus "public records," they are not always considered public. For example, many states have confidentiality laws that prohibit you from requesting a copy of a vital record (especially birth certificates) unless you are requesting your own (or your parent's, spouse's, or child's).

Even if a vital record is public, whether they are available for free on the Internet varies widely from jurisdiction to jurisdiction, from state to state, and even from county to county and city to city within the same state. Also, the location of vital records varies widely; some are kept at the state level, others at the county level and others at the federal level. Dates of coverage are another aspect about public records that varies widely. For these reasons, we can't always rely on finding our public record information through official government resources, so that's when we resort to trying to find vital record information at publicly available sites (e.g., genealogy sites or historical society sites) or at pay investigative research sites.

Over 400 U.S. state, federal, and local agencies have even outsourced the function of providing online access to vital records. When you are visiting U.S. government agency sites, you might encounter **VitalChek** (http://www.vitalchek.com), which is a "one-stop shop" where you can purchase vital records. A limited number of U.S. territorial agencies and agencies in Canada, Mexico, and the United Kingdom are also affiliated with **VitalChek**.

If you cannot find a vital record for free, you might have to resort to a pay investigative database. But even then, you might not obtain the information you are seeking because most pay investigative databases are only displaying a birth month and year for both births and deaths and only a partial Social Security Number, unless you are pre-authorized to see the full dates and numbers. (See *Chapter Twenty-Eight* for more information.) You usually won't find any marriage or divorce information in a pay investigative database.

There are several online directories, discussed in the next section, which are helpful to discover if these vital records are available online from government or non-government sources. Check several before deciding a vital record is not online.

How To Find Vital Records Using Online Directory Sites

To find a link to a vital record database, you can use **Search Systems** (http://publicrecords.searchsystems.net) by scrolling down the homepage (see page 160 in *Chapter Ten*), selecting *Birth Records, Death Records, Marriage Records,* or *Divorce Records* from the *Search By Category* list, and then selecting a state. You can also find a particular vital record link by selecting a jurisdiction on the homepage (see page 162 in *Chapter Ten*), and then scrolling through all of that jurisdiction's list of public records until you find what you want. The list will be rather long since it includes more than just vital records. The next illustration shows the result when we selected *Death* and then *California.* Though we only selected *Death*, **Search Systems** provides an overview of all California official state vital records.

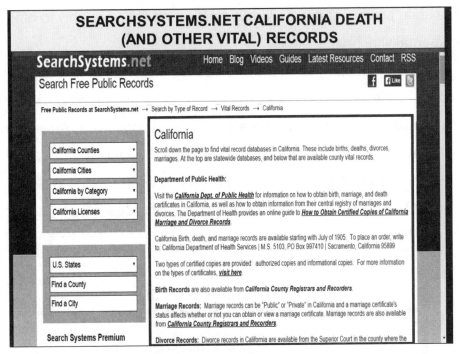

As you scroll down the page, you can select a statewide or county vital record link. The links are to governmental sites and non-governmental sites, such as genealogy sites or historical society sites.

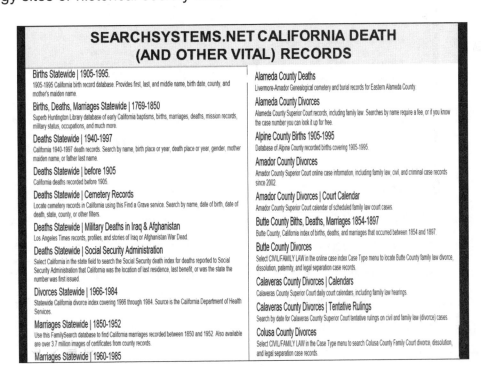

BRB Publications (http://linkon.in/1nTLiKc) provides free links to public records, including vital records. You will need to select a state from the list and then select a state agency or a county, but most of the links are only to official governmental vital record sites.

Various genealogy sites provide access to vital records databases while other sites only provide links to vital records. Some of these sources are free and some require payment. One of the best fee-based genealogy sites, **Ancestry.com** (https://www.ancestry.com), <u>can</u> be searched for free though, but only if your public library subscribes to it and you visit the library in-person. (See *Chapter Twelve* to learn more about how to access **Ancestry.com** and other fee-based databases for free, via your public library.)

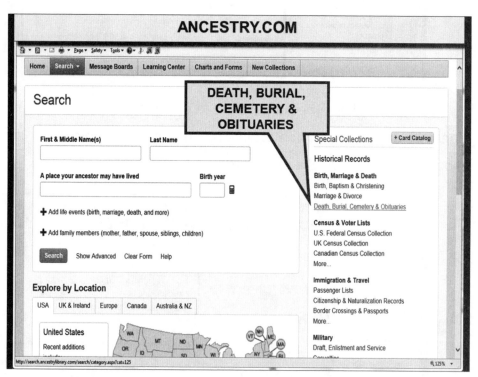

Ancestry.com (https://www.ancestry.com) allows you to cast a wide net over multiple types of vital records (births, deaths, baptisms, divorces, military records, census, etc.), world-wide. You can enter a name on the homepage, but to narrow your search to death-related resources only, click the *Death, Burial, Cemetery & Obituaries* link (as shown in the prior illustration). Enter your subject's name and other information (e.g., *Month*, *Day*, or *Year* of *Death* or *Birth*; *Location*) into the search menu (as shown in the next illustration). You can even enter a *Keyword* to your search. If you are positive about the information you entered, you can place a check in the *Match all terms exactly* box (at the top of the menu) as we did (see the next illustration).

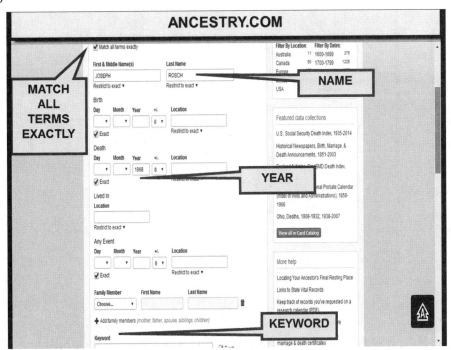

Once you receive your results (as shown in the next illustration), you can narrow them by death records, for example, by clicking the *Social Security Death Index* link. Although the Social Security Admininstration now refers to the *Social Security Death Index* as the **Limited Access Death Master File–LADMF,**

Ancestry.com still refers to it as the *Social Security Death Index*. You can also narrow your results by sliding the search filter bar (as shown on the left side of the next illustration) to *Exact,* or you can expand your search by sliding the search filter bar to *Broad*.

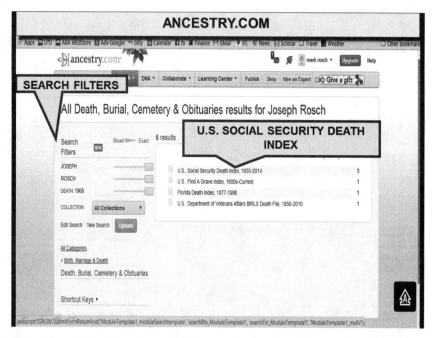

Full Social Security Numbers are only displayed for people who have passed away over ten years ago (see next illustration). See pages 288—295 to learn how to obtain full Social Security Numbers (for a fee) for all deaths.

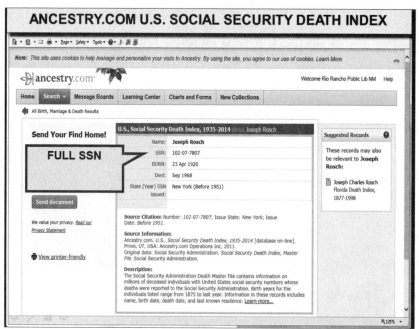

RootsWeb (http://home.rootsweb.ancestry.com) is owned by **Ancestry** and offers free information about genealogy research and provides links to state, regional, and local historical societies and libraries where birth and death, and other vital records might be available (either online or with a visit to the actual place). (**RootsWeb** offers a state resources page (http://linkon.in/1tBxArN), where you can review what's available state by state (shown in the next illustration).

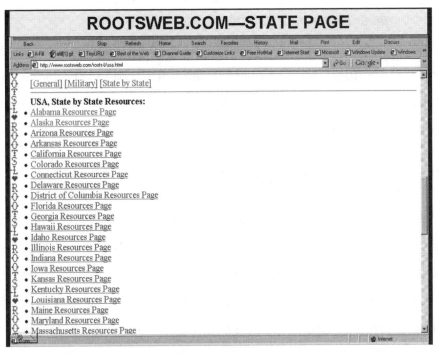

There are also "volunteer project databases hosted at **RootsWeb**, such as obituary and cemetery records and family trees, which might be useful for finding someone's vital records or useful if you are trying to locate names of potential heirs. The state resources pages found at **RootsWeb** also provide links describing how to obtain vital records from various government agencies. After choosing a state from the list on the *State by State Resources* page (http://linkon.in/1tBxArN), scroll all the way down to *Vital Records* and select the type of record that you need (except for some states like California and New Mexico—where you'll choose *Data* and then *Vital Records*). You might also find vital records in some of the other categories, such as *Cemeteries, Census, Local Guides, Newspapers,* or *Obituaries.*

The **Family Search** site (http://linkon.in/1tBBjWo) provides free access to vital records databases for forty-six states, the District of Columbia, and numerous foreign countries. The following is a sample of a few of the available databases:

- *California, Birth Index, 1905-1995*
- *Illinois, Births and Christenings, 1824-1940*
- *New York, Deaths and Burials, 1795-1952*
- *Virginia, Births and Christenings, 1853-1917*

While these databases contain millions of records (each) they do not appear to be complete. Although many of our test searches turned up exactly the results we expected, other tests did not turn up births or deaths of individuals known to have been born or died in that specific jurisdiction during the database's coverage range.

MARRIAGE AND DIVORCE RECORDS

When you are trying to find a missing person, an important step is to make sure you know what name they are currently using and what names they have used in the past. Marriage and divorce records can be useful to learn this information.

California marriage and divorce records are a prime example of how access to vital records can vary even between counties within a state. On the *California Vital Records* page found at **Search Systems** (http://linkon.in/1pRvYcf), there are divorce record links to just thirty-one county superior court sites (out of California's sixty-eight counties). Some offer free databases (e.g., Solano County) while others only offer pay (e.g., Los Angeles). Some offer no searchable database at all. Most of the county court sites' databases only have more recent divorce records (e.g., Los Angeles has 1983-present). Some databases allow you to narrow the search to divorce only but many do not, so you will be searching through all the court cases. Some divorce and marriage links are to non-governmental sites, but these are mostly for older records (e.g., from pre-1900 up to 1984).

Texas marriage and divorce records are a prime example of records once kept at the county level now being kept at the state level. There are two places to obtain the Texas state marriage and divorce records for free online. The first place is the official state website, but the records are not in a user-friendly searchable database.

Instead, the records must be downloaded and then opened in Excel. As of June 3, 2017, Texas marriage records are available for the years 1966-2014 and can be found at http://linkon.in/txmarriage. Divorce records are available for the years 1968-2014 and can be found at http://linkon.in/txdivorce. (Each year's records are held in a separate file.) Earlier records are found at individual county websites.

The second place to obtain Texas marriage and divorce records for free is at **Courthouse Direct** (http://www.courthousedirect.com). For searchability, **Courthouse Direct** is better than the state's site because it provides user-friendly searchable databases, but it appears that **Courthouse Direct** no longer keeps these databases up-to-date, so they are only useful for historical research. **Courthouse Direct's** database of Texas marriage records (1966-2003) can be found at http://linkon.in/aKFh1R and its database of divorce records (1966-2003) can be found at http://linkon.in/cQe9Fx. Both the marriage and divorce databases allow you to include a date range to narrow down your results. Oddly, when searching the divorce database, the date range also applies to the marriage date included in the record. So, if a couple divorced between 1966 and 2003, but married before 1966, searching the divorce database for the bride or groom's last name can return a wedding date as early as 1925 as well. For a fee, **Courthouse Direct** (http://www.courthousedirect.com) provides access to other public records in Texas and other states such as grantor grantee indexes and images of real property records, including deeds, mortgages, liens, oil & gas leases, abstracts of judgment, releases, bankruptcies, etc.

To determine whether other states post marriage and divorce records on the Web or if they are available from other non-official sources, visit the directories noted earlier in this section, such as **FamilySearch.org** (http://linkon.in/1tBBjWo), which includes the following databases (and numerous others) in its collection (https://www.familysearch.org/search/collection/list):

- *Florida, Marriages, 1830-1993*
- *North Carolina, Marriages, 1759-1979*
- *Wisconsin, Divorce Index, 1965-1984*

If you do not find the information you are interested in at one of the directories, try running a search engine search for the name of the jurisdiction and the words *divorce records*, or if you are looking for marriage records, use those words as your keywords along with the jurisdiction's name.

BIRTH RECORDS AND BIRTHDAYS

After the terrorist attacks on September 11, 2001, it became harder to find free databases displaying a person's birthday. Before September 11, 2001, databases containing California and Texas birth records, for example, were hosted free at **RootsWeb** but have now been removed. After September 11, 2001, **Vitalsearch Worldwide** removed both their free California birth (and death) records databases from the Internet, but then in early 2003, added them back, but for a fee. Their California birth records are from 1996-2009 and 1905-1995 (http://linkon.in/vitalsearchbirth). According to the site, "Under existing California law specifically Health and Safety Code Sections 102230 et seq. the databases can only be accessed by such persons who will use it for law enforcement or prevention of fraud. In order to be granted access, you would first need to apply and qualify."

Currently, the best source of various free archival birth record databases is **FamilySearch.org**, discussed earlier in this chapter (http://linkon.in/1tBBjWo). The next illustration shows a list of birth (and other vital record) indices, from the U.S. and other countries. Most of the U.S. records are from state and county records. In our test searches of the *California Birth Index, 1905-1995*, we found our subjects' dates of birth.

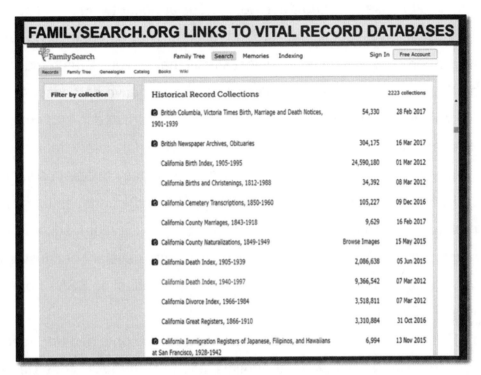

Besides searching specific collections at **Familysearch.org**, you can also search all its vital record databases together (https://familysearch.org/search), but you will typically get an overwhelming number of results. Filtering your results sometimes helps to bring the results down to a more manageable number, but not always. See page 292 for details on how to search all **Familysearch.org's** vital record databases together.

RootsWeb's state pages, **Search Systems**, or **BRB Publications** (all discussed earlier in this section) also include links to numerous official and unofficial sources for birth records.

You can also visit your public library to search its **Ancestry.com** subscription database for free to find birthdays (and other vital records). Finally, you can locate your subject's birthday by subscribing to fee-based investigative databases (such as **TLOxp**), as discussed in *Chapter Twenty-Eight*.

It is often useful to know someone's Social Security Number (SSN) when you are conducting investigative/background research. For example, if you are looking for a missing person, knowing your subject's SSN makes your search much easier because you can run a reverse SSN at a pay investigative database. A reverse SSN search will more likely turn up the person you are interested in and not someone who has the same name. Some databases, such as criminal history databases, require that you search by name and SSN. But, it's not that easy to obtain someone's SSN.

Full SSNs for people (both living and deceased) cannot be found free on the Internet, unless the number appears on an older public record, such as a lien or a bankruptcy docket. Even this method is getting less prevelant because some states, such as California and New York, are retroactively redacting SSNs from older public records (**PACER** does not).

Full SSNs for people who are deceased can be obtained (for a fee) by certified subscribers to the Social Security Administration's **Limited Access Death Master File** (**LADMF**), which was formerly known as the **Social Security Death Master File** or the **SSDMF** (https://www.ssdmf.com). (Full SSNs are part of a decedent's death record.) Certified subscribers are individuals, entities such as banks, insurance companies, etc. and their employees, and also entities such as pay investigative database vendors and some of their certified subscribers. (See pages 288—295 for information about new laws restricting access to death records and full SSNs of deceased people.)

Full SSNs for people who are still <u>living</u> can be obtained from some pay investigative database vendors if you are a "certified" subscriber. If you are not a certified subscriber, you will only see a truncated SSN (the first five digits). (See pages 488 and 496 for information about pay investigative database vendors and certified subscribers.)

Each time a search is performed, pay database vendors require users to attest that they have a permissible use to access full SSNs under the Gramm-Leach-Bliley Act, (GLBA) 15 U.S.C. 6802. (See pages 493–494 to learn about the GLBA's permissible uses.)

If you already know your subject's full SSN, you can always use it for a reverse search at a pay investigative research database, but the search results will still only display a truncated SSN, unless the searcher is a certified user.

As noted earlier, when the pay investigative research databases display a truncated SSN they show the first five digits. Meanwhile, the government's pay **PACER** bankruptcy docket database displays the last four digits. Therefore, even if you do not have access to full SSNs from a pay investigative research database or the **LADMF**, if the individual you are researching has filed for bankruptcy, you can combine the last four digits of their truncated SSN from their bankruptcy docket with the first five digits of their truncated SSN from the pay investigative research database to learn their full SSN.

DEATH RECORDS (AND DECEDENTS' SOCIAL SECURITY NUMBERS)

Before spending the time and money to find or investigate someone, first make sure they are still alive. State laws are quite strict about who can obtain someone else's death record, so the official state sources are usually not the best route to take. Even if you could meet the state's requirements, you would have to know in which state your subject might have died and then proceed with a state-by-state search if you did not locate the records in the first state.

Doing a national search through the official **LADMF**, is a more reasonable way to search deaths through multiple jurisdictions (https://www.ssdmf.com). However, the subscription cost is quite high at $900.00 per year for one user and up to $5000 for 26+ simultaneous users. The database is updated weekly. It contains over 86 million death records reported to the Social Security Administration (SSA), going back to 1936. Most records in the database include a full SSN, name, date of birth, and date of death. The SSA warns users that it does not have a death record for all persons; therefore, it does not guarantee the veracity of the file. Thus, the absence of a particular person's name is not proof this person is alive.

Aside from the high cost, the amount of information in the database (and thus its usefulness) has been shrinking over the past few years. On October 31, 2011, approximately 4.2 million "protected state records" received from sources such as family members, funeral homes, hospitals, and financial institutions were removed from the database. So, now the database is composed of only deaths reported directly to the SSA. The exclusion of information from these sources will also mean approximately 1 million fewer names will be added to the **LADMF** each year. Also, on October 31, 2011, the SSA stopped selling records with full SSNs to third-party vendors (but continued to display them to their own subscribers). Then, on March 26, 2014, Section 203 of the Bipartisan Budget Act of 2013 (Pub. L. 113-67) went into effect, which limited the display of a person's death record in the **LADMF** until three years after a person's death, except to certified users (https://linkon.in/nossnsfor3yrs). This Public Law can be found at 42 U.S.C. 1306c (https://linkon.in/3yrdeathindaccess) To become certified, a user must pay a certification processing fee of $200 and must fall within the provisions of 15 C.F.R. §1110.102(a) (https://linkon.in/15cfr1110102a), which mandates that:

> (1) Such Person has a legitimate fraud prevention interest, or has a legitimate business purpose pursuant to a law, governmental rule, regulation, or fiduciary duty, and shall specify the basis for so certifying;

> (2) Such Person has systems, facilities, and procedures in place to safeguard the accessed information, and experience in maintaining the confidentiality, security, and appropriate use of accessed information, pursuant to requirements similar to the requirements of section 6103(p)(4) of the Internal Revenue Code of 1986...

Certified users who are searching the **LADMF** through their own organization's subscription to the **LADMF**, such as employees at an insurance company, will be able to see all death records from all years and the full SSN for each returned result. Certified subscribers to certified pay investigative database vendors will also be able to see all death records from all years and full SSNs (see page 488 for details).

When the SSA removed the 4.2 million state records from the **LADMF** and also stopped selling records with full Social Security Numbers to many vendors that had offered the records for free (e.g., the Mormon Church-affiliated **FamilySearch.org** site at https://familysearch.org/search, **Rootsweb**, and **Ancestry.com**), **FamilySearch.org** at first maintained the older database they had purchased from the SSA, which included both the 4.2 million records removed by the SSA <u>and</u> full Social Security Numbers that the SSA had removed.

When we ran test searches on June 3, 2017 in **FamilySearch.org's** *United States Social Security Death Index* collection (http://linkon.in/famsearchdeath) they included death records from 1962 through February 28, 2014, but the SSNs no longer were displayed. When we re-ran our test searches on September 5, 2018, we did not find death records beyond February 28, 2014. We are unsure if **FamilySearch.org** is no longer able to purchase death records from the SSA to post them online for free (without SSNs). Even if they can purchase the database from the SSA, **FamilySearch.org's** database would be three-years behind the SSA's. However, as we'll soon explain, **FamilySearch.org** does manage to show deaths that have occurred since February 28, 2014 to the present.

Recently, **FamilySearch.org** began requiring all users to set up an account to access its data, but they do offer it for free. As of this writing, the genealogy web site **Findmypast.com** (https://www.findmypast.com/) does still offer a search of the **Social Security Death Index** that includes Social Security Numbers, but only for deaths through 2012 (free registration required). It does not appear that this site contains any death records from the SSA after 2012. In theory, they should not be displaying SSNs for any years.

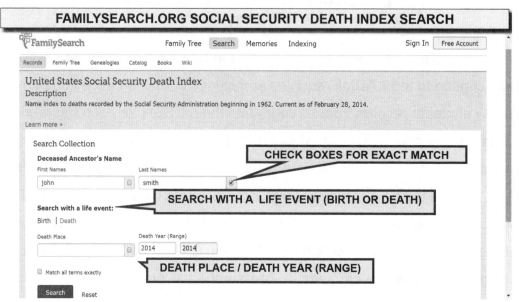

To only search **FamilySearch.org's** *United States Social Security Death Index* collection, you will need to use this URL: http://linkon.in/famsearchdeath (we no longer find a link to it on the site). As shown in the prior illustration, to search, you would enter names into the *First Names* and *Last Names* search boxes (or just the *Last Names* search box). Checking the check-box to the right of the one (or both) of the *Names* search-boxes forces the database to search only for exact matches. If you leave one or both check-boxes unchecked, the returned results can include names that are similar to the names you've entered. Note that names entered into the *First Names* field may also appear as middle names in your search results. If you choose the *Death* option from **FamilySearch.org's** *Search with a life event*, as we did, you are then offered two more ways to refine your search: (1) *Death Place* and (2) *Death Year (Range)*. We entered the same years (2014) into the *Death Year (Range)* boxes because we were sure of the exact year of death, but we left the *Death Place* blank.

After your results are displayed you can enter a place of death into the *Death Place* box (on the *Refine your search* column on the left).

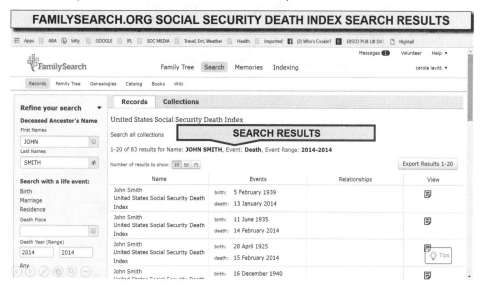

Earlier we mentioned that **FamilySearch** does manage to show current deaths even though the SSA won't sell them death records until three years after a death. The way **FamilySearch.org** can manage to show us current deaths (and other information) is by collecting billions of records from other sources, such as census records, state agency records, obituary databases, or **Findagrave.com**. (**Findagrave.com's** records are gathered by volunteers who visit gravesites and compile lists to upload to **Findagrave.com**. See page 297 for more information.) **FamilySearch.org** then compiles all these records into its *Search Historical Records* database (https://familysearch.org/search). (None of the records from these "other" sources contain full SSNs, however.)

So, if you don't find a death record at **FamilySearch.org's** *United States Social Security Death Index* collection (because it is too recent or because it's missing even from the **LADMF**), you should also search **FamilySearch.org's** *Search Historical Records* database (https://familysearch.org/search), as shown in the next illustration.

FAMILYSEARCH.ORG: SEARCH HISTORICAL RECORDS

You search **FamilySearch.org's** *Historical Records* database in much the same way as the **FamilySearch.org's** *United States Social Security Death Index* collection. Even though the *Names* search boxes are labeled as *Deceased Ancestor's Name*, be advised that you <u>can</u> search the records of people who are still alive.

This database's *Search with a life event* limiter allows you to refine your search with a variety of types of information, but, unfortunately, not all of the records that **FamilySearch** has added to its database necessarily contain all the same information as the next record. So, for example, if you know your subject's death place and decide to include it in your search, you might not receive any results if the record does not include the death place. If you don't find your subject, delete some information and conduct a broad first and last name only search and then match other information you have about your subject with information in the search results.

This database's *Search by relationship* allows you to refine your search by adding a *Spouse*, *Parents,* or *Other Person's* name, but we recommend that you do not include these when searching for death records because that information might not be included in the record.

As noted earlier, various pay investigative research database vendors subscribe to the **LADMF** as certified users. If you have a subscription to one of these databases, such as **TLOxp** (see pages 496–509), the $5 summary report will indicate if someone is deceased. But if you want to conduct a deceased-only search at **TLOxp**, this is free to subscribers. However, the death record will not display a full SSN unless you are a "certified" subscriber (effective August 24, 2018, **TLOxp** subscribers who work from a home offices are no longer considered certified and cannot view SSNs).

Ancestry.com offers searchable access to the *United States Social Security Death Index* 1935-2014 that includes Social Security Numbers for some older deaths. You can pay to subscribe to **Ancestry.com** or you can access it for free if your public library offers **Ancestry.com** at the library. See page 181 for information about accessing **Ancestry.com** for free by visiting your public library (in-person).

State and Local Death Records

Many state and local governments also maintain death indices. State and local government death indices have become even more important now that the Social Security Administration removed approximately 4.2 million records from the **LADMF** and will no longer be accepting new state and local death records for inclusion in the **LADMF**. However, as noted earlier, state laws are quite strict about who can obtain someone else's death record, so this is usually not the best route unless you are trying to obtain a record of a close relative or your reason for accessing the record meets the requirements of that state's laws. For this reason, we often use genealogical sites, such as **RootsWeb.com** to search death records. Most of these sites will not include recent death records, however. Select a state from **RootsWeb.com's** state resources page (http://www.Rootsweb.com/roots-l/usa.html) and scroll down to *Vital Records* (but for California, click on *Data* and then scroll down to *Vital Records*). **RootsWeb** offers a searchable database of 9,366,786 California deaths from 1940 through 1997 (http://bit.ly/cadeaths). (For a fee, you can search California death records from 1940-2000 and 2001-2009 at **Vitalsearch** (http://linkon.in/vitalsearchdeath).

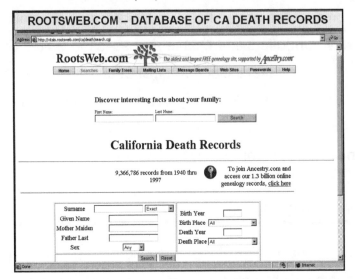

RootsWeb also offers a searchable database of 3,963,456 Texas death records from 1964 thru 1998 (http://linkon.in/rootswebtxdeath), 2,921,383 Kentucky death records from 1911 thru 2000 (http://linkon.in/rootskydeath), and 401,960 Maine death records from 1960 thru 1997 (http://linkon.in/rootsmainedeath).

DeathIndexes.com (http://www.deathindexes.com; see next screenshot) provides links, by state, to local and state archival death indices and cemetery records in all 50 states and the District of Columbia. Some examples include:

- *District of Columbia Deaths, 1874-1959 at FamilySearch*
- *Illinois, Cook County Deaths, 1878-1922*
- *New York Deaths and Burials, 1957-1962*

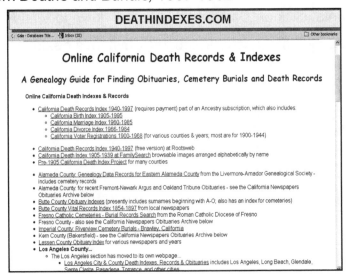

GRAVESITES

If the resources we've already discussed haven't helped you to determine whether your subject is deceased, you may be able to glean this information by finding their gravesite.

Findagrave.com

Findagrave.com (http://www.findagrave.com) can be searched to find the gravesite locations of nearly 200 million people. Originally, you could search the database with as little as a *Last* name but also add a *First* and *Middle* name as well. A check box also allowed you to instruct the site to include a *Maiden name* in your search results. You could further narrow your results by adding *Year Born*, *Year Died*, and *Cemetery Location*.

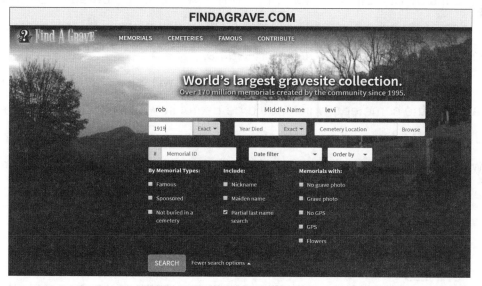

Findagrave.com's search was upgraded in November 2017 to include other optional search and sorting criteria. You now can also search by a *Partial Last Name* (and even a partial first name even though there is no checkbox for that) or by a *Nickname*. To choose these options, click into the appropriate checkboxes. In a test search, we entered a partial first name and a partial last name—*rob levi*. This retrieved a long list of results. Adding *1919* as the *Year Born* reduced the list to just eight results. (See next illustration.)

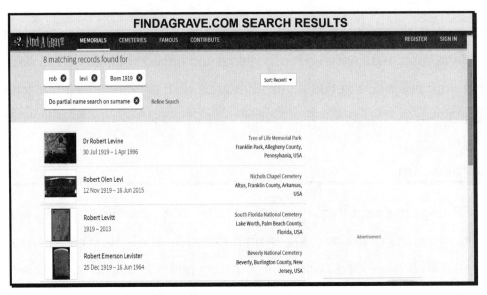

There was one result for *Robert Levitt*, which was the person we were searching for. You can click the *Sort* drop-down arrow (see prior illustration) to re-sort the results by *Cemetery* or *Recently Added* (*Name* is the default). On the homepage, you also could have clicked the *Order by* drop-down arrow to order results by *Name, Death Date, Birth Date,* or *Cemetery Name.*

The amount of information in each result will vary, but most show the name and location of the cemetery, which could be useful in your search for living relatives. Once you find which city your subject is buried in, you can move on and search for that city's newspaper database, which might include an obituary for your subject and names of relatives to search for and contact. (See page 175 for information on finding free newspaper databases.)

OBITUARIES

If you still haven't been able to ascertain whether your subject is deceased from the resources discussed already, you may be able to glean this information by finding their obituary. Obituaries often list names of living relatives, which could be useful, especially if you need to find heirs.

Tributes.com (http://www.tributes.com) contains a searchable database of over 95 million death records dating back to the 1930s, which are retrieved from "funeral home partners across the country and the Social Security Administration's Death Index (SSDI)." We do not know if **Tributes** is a certified user of the **SSDMF** (see page 290). If they are not, then this database will now only include death information from funeral home partners.

On the homepage, you can search by first and last name and state. When we searched *Marilyn Goldsmith* and *New York*, we received one result—a 2004 record that listed *April 17, 2004* as the date of death and *Staten Island* as the last city of residence. When we left off the first name, and searched only the last name, *Goldsmith,* and *New York*, we received 64 results. But, none included the *April 17, 2004* record that we found in the initial search. When we searched *Goldsmith,* and left off both the first name and state, we received twelve results, but none included the *April 17, 2004* record we found in the initial search. The *April 17, 2004* record should have appeared in all three result lists. It appears that it's best to search with a full name and state. Some **Tributes.com** obituaries contain more information than others.

Selecting *Advanced Search* (see next illustration) allows you to add additional criteria, including a *City*, or *Keywords* that might appear in the obituary, or the *Date of Death* (by using the drop-down menu shown in the next illustration). Using the *Advanced Search*, you could even search only with a first name if you added in other clues about the person. For example, we searched for *Marilyn* and *Staten Island* and 2000-present and found 59 results, including the same *April 17, 2004* record in the prior illustration.

Legacy.com

Legacy.com (http://www.legacy.com) collaborates with more than 1,500 newspapers in the U.S., Canada, Australia, New Zealand, the U.K., and Europe to display their obituaries. You can search with a *last name*, *first name*, *state*, *country*, *date range of death* (using the drop-down menu shown in the next illustration), or *keyword* that might appear in the obituary.

When we searched *Marilyn Goldsmith, New York,* and chose *All* (for the date), we found our subject's obituary, who died on April 6, 2014, that we had not found using **Tributes.com** discussed previously. It included her husband's name, *Will*, and the fact that she was a *poet*. In a test of the keyword search, we learned it is hit or miss because when we re-ran the exact previous search and added the keyword *Will*, we retrieved no results. But, when we added the keyword *poet*, we retrieved the correct result. In another test search, we left off *Marilyn Goldsmith's* name entirely, used the keyword *poet*, and chose *New York* and *All* (for the date), this retrieved over 1,000 results. Adding just the first name *Marilyn* to this search (no last name) narrowed the results to four, one of whom was our subject's. Thus, you can search with no name or just a first name if you add in other clues about the person.

Public Library "Free Remote Access Databases" Might Include Obituaries

Obituaries can sometimes be found for free by visiting your public library's website and remotely accessing (for free) various obituary databases and newspaper databases that include obituaries. (See page 175 for more information.)

Chapter Seventeen

TELEPHONE/ADDRESS DIRECTORY WEB SITES

Finding and Investigating People and Companies Using Telephone/Address Directory Web Sites

There are many free and pay telephone/address directory websites that list businesses and people in the United States and abroad. The pay sites are usually updated more often (e.g., daily) than the free sites. Telephone/address directories can help you find one or more of the following pieces of information:

- Telephone number (landline and sometimes cellular)
- Home address
- Company address
- E-mail address
- Neighbors' names and contact information

Many of the directories have both regular lookups (by name) and reverse lookups (e.g., by phone number, area code, ZIP Code, or address).

It is a good idea to be familiar with a few free telephone/address directory websites. This way, if you strike out at one, another might come through. Also, it's a good idea to compare information from a few sites before reaching any conclusions. If you don't find your answer at a free website, try visiting your public library's website and use your library card to remotely access **RefUSA** or **AtoZ Database** (for free), if they offer access to those sites (see pages 176–181).

Pay investigative research databases, such as **TLOxp**, **Accurint**, and **PeopleMap**, are excellent sources for current telephone numbers and addresses because their databases are updated daily (see pages 496–509 for details about **TLOxp**). The information might come from utility companies reporting new hook-ups, magazines reporting a change of address, etc.

There are non-traditional ways of finding a person's address by searching free public record databases, such as deed transfers or even a docket database, such as **PACER** (see pages 185–202). If the docket includes a recently filed complaint against your subject, it might include their most recent address.

Finally, **Google** and other general search engines such as **Bing** and **Yahoo!** can be searched (and reverse searched) to find contact information; all you have to do is enter a name and, depending on your research needs, enter the word *phone* or *cell* or *fax* or *e-mail* into the search engine's query box. If the search engine finds that the name and keywords you've searched for are located on a publicly available Web page, that e-mail address or telephone, cell, or fax number (and possibly a physical address) will be returned in your Web search results, just like any other information listed on a Web page. You can run a reverse search by entering a phone, cell or fax number, or an e-mail or physical address into the search engine's query box to try to determine the owner's name.

In the next section, we'll discuss three free telephone/address directory sites, **411.com** (http://www.411.com), **AnyWho.com** (http://www.anywho.com), and **WhitePages.com** (http://www.whitepages.com). While they have many similar search options, each has some unique features, which we'll point out. In some instances when we have used identical test searches, we found different information at each one (and sometimes no information at one, but information at the other). For example, **WhitePages.com** and **AnyWho.com** both found Mark Rosch's address and phone number. Meanwhile, **411.com** found his address and phone number, and also provided a particularly useful additional option for finding information about his neighbors.

AnyWho.com (http://www.anywho.com), with its compilation of millions of consumer and business phone and address listings, is updated weekly. To search by a person's name, first click the *People Search* tab and then enter as little as a last name into the *Find a Person* search menu. If you retrieve too many results, add in other criteria, such as a first name (or initial), a *City, State, or ZIP*. From this same menu, you can also perform a reverse search *By Address* or *By Phone Number*.

You can perform other searches by clicking one of the following tabs located on **AnyWho.com's** homepage:

- *Yellow Pages*: search by a company's name, business category, or reverse phone number.

- *Reverse Phone Lookup*: search by telephone number to learn the name and address of the owner of that number. **AnyWho.com** states that cellular phone numbers are not available, but when we entered Mark Rosch's, it came back with a correct result (probably because it began its life as a landline). When results are displayed, you are offered a large blue button to *View Full Profile*. Clicking this button does display some additional information, such as the age of the returned owner, cities where that person has lived, and possible relatives. However, the *Full Profile* is only available after purchasing from **Intelius**. (See page 306 for more information on **Intelius**.)

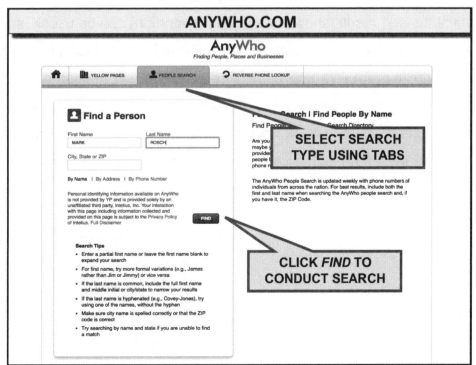

After you enter a name and click the *Find* button, **AnyWho.com** displays the full address and phone number if it is available in its database.

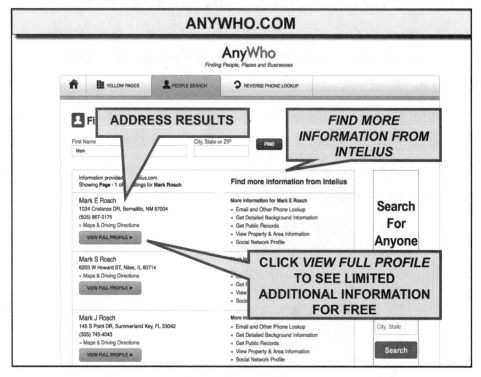

If you click on any of the links listed beneath *Find more information from Intelius*, you will be taken to **Intelius** (or by the time you read this, another pay database like **US Search** could be listed). Some of the information shown for free on the initial "teaser" result (shown in the next illustration) can be useful, so don't be afraid to click on the link and use the free information. For example, after viewing Mark's address at **AnyWho.com**, the **Intelius** teaser information about where Mark had lived in the past and the names of some of his relatives could help you verify that you had found the correct Mark Rosch (if you knew something about him to begin with). Not all the information is correct, however. For example, he never lived in Mountain View, California.

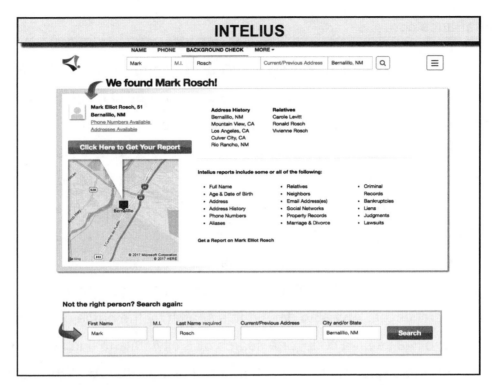

We do not, however, suggest that you click any further, because you will be asked for your credit card information to obtain more information. The fee charged by **Intelius**, **US Search**, and other similar databases that don't require you to be pre-approved before accessing their information, will be costlier (and the information probably less fresh) than databases that require you to be pre-approved before accessing their information (such as **TLOxp**, **Accurint**, and other databases that we discuss in *Chapter Twenty-Eight*). See page 512 for more information about **Intelius** and **US Search**.

Although **AnyWho.com** is owned by "The Real Yellow Pages," it goes out of its way to inform users (on its help page at http://www.anywho.com/help/about) that, "The personal identifying information available on **AnyWho** is provided solely by **Intelius**, Inc. and is derived from Public Records, Publicly Available Information and Commercial Records …" and that only "Yellow Pages listings (searches by category or name) are obtained from yp.com." (See page 314 for information regarding The Telephone Records and Privacy Act of 2006.)

WhitePages.com (http://www.whitepages.com), similar to **AnyWho.com**, offers the ability to search U.S. people or companies by name to find their addresses and phone numbers. It also offers a reverse phone or reverse address search to identify the name connected to that phone number or address. However, **WhitePages.com** also offers several unique searches not offered by **AnyWho.com**.

Like **AnyWho.com**, **WhitePages.com** offers *Reverse Area Code* and *Reverse ZIP Code* lookups (hidden at http://www.whitepages.com/more_searches) that allow you to search by a ZIP Code or area code to find out what city (or cities) corresponds to the ZIP or area code. But, **WhitePages.com's** also offers two *Area Code* and *ZIP Codes* searches that **AnyWho** does not: a search by the name of a city/state, or the ZIP Code to find its area code; or a search by a city/state to find its ZIP Code.

WhitePages.com offers another useful feature that **AnyWho** does not, which is its *International* search, used to locate international calling codes and international phone directories. (You won't see the *International* link until you scroll beyond the *Area & ZIP Codes* link.)

The basic *Person* search on the homepage requires only a last name, but you will probably get too many results if you don't add in other criteria, such as a first name (or initial), or a city, state, or ZIP Code.

The initial result (see next illustration) shows your subject's name, an estimated age (usually a four-year age range), other names associated with your subject, a partial address (city/state), and a partial list of other possible cities where your subject has lived.

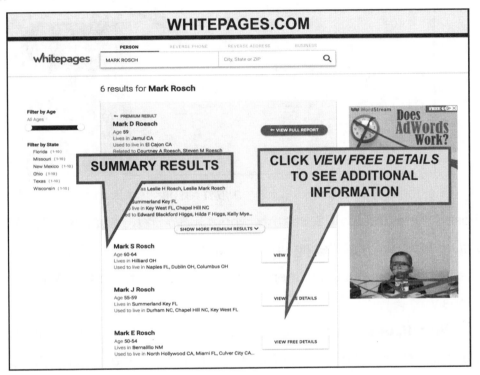

Clicking the *View Free Details* button displays available information that may include the address and phone number (as seen in the next illustration).

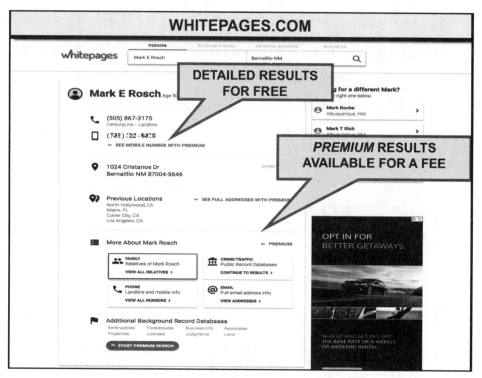

Clicking any of the links for *Premium* results leads to a series of pages similar to those at **Intelius** and **US Search**, where a *Single Report* costs $19.95 but a *Premium Membership* offering unlimited searches is only $9.95 (per month). We offer the same caveat about using them as we mentioned in the **AnyWho.com** section previously.

WhitePages brought back correct information in our test reverse telephone number searches. When we ran Carole's landline number, it correctly identified: the owner's name, age and address; the carrier's name and city/state; and the fact that the number was a landline.

When we ran Carole's cellular number, it also brought back a mix of correct and incorrect information (the address information and one of the other phone numbers associated with the results were outdated, as shown in the next illustration), but we were impressed that it correctly identified her cellular number as a cellular number, considering it began as a landline that she ported over to a cellular number. Many other databases still list it as a landline.

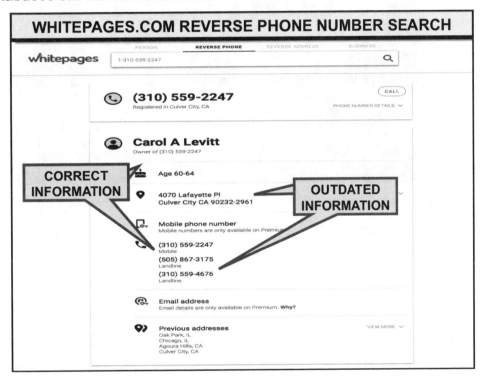

Whitepages.com no longer provides information on the currency of the data it provides. In the past, the site indicated that they were "continually updating" their data, but it also went on to say, "[g]enerally speaking, listing information … is 60-90 days old." It is possible that the information is now only updated yearly.

411.com

Like **AnyWho.com** and **WhitePages.com**, **411.com** offers a name search, along with a reverse phone number, business name, and address search. The different searches are accessible by clicking the labels just above the search box near the center of the homepage (see next illustration).

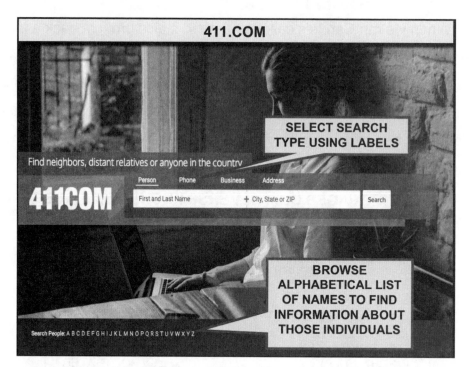

411.COM

Find neighbors, distant relatives or anyone in the country

411COM

| Person | Phone | Business | Address |

First and Last Name | + City, State or ZIP | Search

SELECT SEARCH TYPE USING LABELS

BROWSE ALPHABETICAL LIST OF NAMES TO FIND INFORMATION ABOUT THOSE INDIVIDUALS

Search People: A B C D E F G H I J K L M N O P Q R S T U V W X Y Z

You can also browse an alphabetical list of names by clicking on any of the letters seen at the bottom of the previous illustration (although we can't imagine why anyone would when there's a name search available).

If you scroll to the area beneath the alphabetical list (not shown in the previous illustration), you will find links to *Area Code* and *ZIP Code* lookups similar to the ones found at **Whitepages.com**. If **411.com** is beginning to sound a lot like **Whitepages.com**, that's because they are owned by the same company.

Just like searches at **Whitepages.com**, name searches at **411.com** display summary results, with additional details available by clicking the *View Free Details* button (see next illustrations).

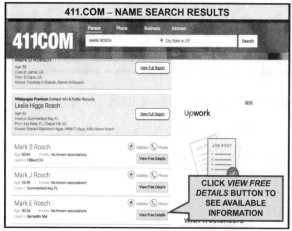

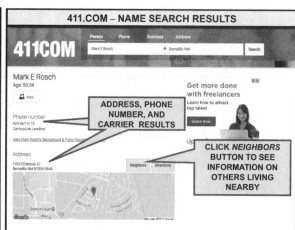

Oddly, **411.com** offers some very useful additional information, beyond name and address, that **Whitepages.com** used to offer but no longer does.

After you run a name search at **411.com**, you get the added option of a *Neighbors* button (as seen in the previous illustration).

Clicking it generates a list of neighbors' names and addresses who live in close geographic proximity to your subject. No phone numbers are included. You could run a separate search for each neighbor, by name, to get their respective phone numbers if you wanted to contact them by phone.

If your target has moved or is avoiding you, you could use a list like this to contact those neighbors to see if they have any helpful information. Luckily, **ReferenceUSA** makes compiling such a list a little bit easier because it offers a similar option that includes neighbors' names, addresses, and phone numbers in a single search. See pages 176–181 to learn how to access **ReferenceUSA** using your public library's remote access databases.

Infobel.com (http://www.infobel.com) provides links to the Web-based telephone directories of over 200 countries.

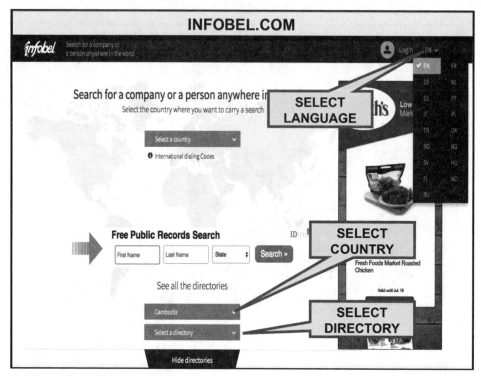

Choose a country and directory in that country to search and **Infobel.com** will link you to the that local online phone directory. These directories are maintained by the local phone companies, so search functions and parameters (including available search language) vary widely from site to site.

You can also set a language for the **Infobel** page using the drop-down menu in the upper right-hand corner. This language preference only effects the language on the **Infobel** page—not the languages on the directories to which it links.

Restrictions on Obtaining Phone Record Information (Call Logs)

There was a time when information brokers would obtain confidential telephone records (call logs) about their subject by contacting the phone company (or other utility company) and pretending to be that individual—a strategy known as "pretexting." Other information brokers might have obtained these records by paying a phone company employee for the information, while still other brokers managed to gain unauthorized Internet access to their subject's account via a phone company's Web page or purchased the records from an Internet-based data broker who trafficked in these records.

Recognizing that "call logs may include a wealth of personal data … that may reveal the names of telephone users' doctors, public and private relationships, business associates, and more," the Telephone Records and Privacy Act of 2006 was passed to criminalize obtaining telephone records by the means listed in the prior paragraph (18 U.S.C. 1039, *available at* http://linkon.in/confiphonerecs). The original law, Public Law No. 109-476, can be found at http://linkon.in/calllogpublaw.

The law stated that "call logs are typically maintained for the exclusive use of phone companies, their authorized agents, and authorized consumers." If anyone offers to sell you this information, you should reject the offer because the law and the penalty also apply to anyone "knowing or having reason to know such information was obtained fraudulently." The penalty ranges from a fine, to not more than 10 years imprisonment, or both. However, the law does not apply to "any lawfully authorized investigative, protective, or intelligence activity of a law enforcement agency of the United States, a State, or political subdivision of a State, or an intelligence agency of the United States."

The telephone listing sites and other databases we have discussed so far do not obtain telephone numbers and addresses and other information, such as names of those associated with the same phone number or the subject's age, from the telephone company's "call logs." Instead, these sites obtain their information from:

- Publicly available sources (e.g., Yellow or White Pages phone books)
- Public records
- Other sources that the subjects themselves voluntarily divulged their information to, such as warranty cards, rebate forms, sweepstakes entries, and the like

Chapter Eighteen

CRIMINAL BACKGROUND INFORMATION

Locating criminal records information online, whether for free or a fee, is hit or miss because there is no national criminal records database available to the general public or legal professionals. We've been told by some law enforcement officials that even the FBI's **National Crime Information Center (NCIC)** database (available to federal and local criminal justice agencies, as well as some select, authorized, non-criminal justice agencies) is not a complete collection of criminal records information. The **NCIC** relies on local law enforcement agencies and courts to report information for inclusion in the **NCIC** database. Our law enforcement sources have told us that agencies in smaller jurisdictions often do not enter warrants for criminals if the jurisdiction is unwilling or unable to pay for the criminals' extradition back to their jurisdiction for trial.

That said, there are numerous sites on the Internet that purport to offer a "Full Nationwide Criminal Records Search" or something similar. This is an impossibility if for no other reason than New York does not sell its criminal history information to any third-party vendor. While these vendors might have some records from every state, they cannot have all records from every state.

Individual resources covering different jurisdictions can provide some information about arrests, criminal convictions, or incarcerations.

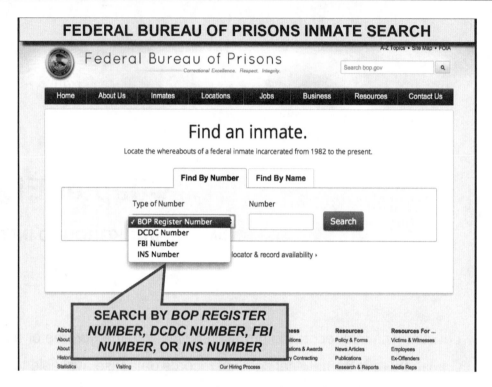

The **Federal Bureau of Prisons' Federal Inmate Locator**

(http://www.bop.gov/inmateloc/) can be used to search for federal inmates using their *BOP Register Number, DCDC Number, FBI Number, INS Number*, or name (a full first and last name are both required). The site includes information on all federal inmates from 1982 to the present. Information regarding federal inmates released prior to 1982 can be obtained by sending a request to the **National Archives and Records Administration** (**NARA**). See http://www.bop.gov/inmateloc/about_records.jsp for details.

State and Local Criminal Records

Corrections.com (http://linkon.in/1ul8e0U) provides links to the Departments of Correction in all fifty states. That does not mean that every state provides a searchable database of inmates. Even in those states that do offer such searchable databases, the criteria by which you can search and the amount of information displayed will vary from state to state. For example, Illinois makes inmate information available online (http://linkon.in/iloffsearch), with searches available by *Last Name*,

Birthdate, or *IDOC* number, while California's database (http://inmatelocator.cdcr.ca.gov/) can be searched by an *Inmate Number* or *Last Name*. The addition of a *First Name* or *Middle Name* is optional. The **New York State Department of Corrections and Community Supervision** inmate database (http://linkon.in/1vlT4ed) can be searched with just a *Last Name.* Adding additional criteria (e.g., a full or partial *First Name, Birth Year*) to narrow your search is optional.

VineLink.com (http://www.vinelink.com) allows you to find out when an offender has been arrested, or released, or is scheduled to appear in court.

It has data from all states and the District of Columbia. The opening screen prompts you to select a state in which to search. Coverage varies for each state, so after you select a state, click *Discover More State Resources* to learn which counties in that state are not providing information to **VINE**. Searching is uniform in all jurisdictions covered. You can search by *Offender ID* or by name search, but with a name search you must search with *Last Name* and at least the first letter of the first name. You can also add a *Date of Birth* or *Age Range* if you have this information. Results will display: *Offender ID, Date of Birth, Age, Race, Gender, Custody Status,* and *Location of Offender.* After finding the individual in the database, the victim (or anyone) may register to receive a phone call or e-mail before an offender's release date. The site's acronym **VINE (Victim Information and Notification)** reflects the system's original purpose of protecting crime victims by providing them with notification of the release date or transfer of offenders.

Free Inmate Locator (http://www.inmatesplus.com/) has compiled links to the forty-one states that offer free information on and photographs of incarcerated inmates. Click the name of the state you're interested in from the alphabetical list to access the **Free Inmate Locator** resource page for that state. Information on the state-specific pages includes a link to the state's inmate locator or its Department of Corrections site (if no free inmate locator is available), as well as links to the county-level resources in that state to search jail inmates. The site also includes a link to the **Federal Bureau of Prisons' Federal Inmate Locator** database, discussed earlier.

Some law enforcement agencies place their booking logs on the Web, while others provide lists of delinquent parents or jail escapees, all for free. For an example of an online booking log, see the **Los Angeles County Sheriff's Inmate Information Center** (http://app4.lasd.org/iic/ajis_search.cfm). For an example of an online list of "Most Wanted" delinquent parents, click the *Most Wanted* link at the **Los Angeles County Child Support Services Department's** site (http://cssd.lacounty.gov/wps/portal/cssd). For an online database of escapees, see the **Florida State Department of Corrections' Inmate Escape Information Search** (http://www.dc.state.fl.us/EscapedInmates). To determine if similar information is available in other jurisdictions, try a search engine search with appropriate keywords (e.g., *"San Diego" county california warrants search*).

State Criminal History Reports

For a fee, many states make criminal history reports about third parties available to individuals with a permitted business use for accessing the information. The reports are usually generated by the state police or court system for a fee. The availability, process, and cost vary from jurisdiction to jurisdiction. **Internet For Lawyers** (http://www.netforlawyers.com/page/criminal-record-reports) has compiled a list of links to the official state sources for these reports in the states where they are available.

Fee-Based Sources for State and Local Criminal Records

In addition to the collection of state and local-level links to searchable inmate databases, **Search Systems** offers access to criminal record information on a "pay as you go" basis. Criminal records searches by state are $6.95, and a "nationwide" search is $14.95. See page 514 for more information on the coverage of these records.

BRB Publications' Public Record Retriever Network database of public records vendors (http://www.prrn.us/content/Search.aspx) includes numerous companies that provide *ad hoc* access to (or in-person retrieval of) criminal records in multiple jurisdictions.

Sex Offender Records

Wonder if your new neighbor is a sex offender? The U.S. Department of Justice (DOJ) **National Sex Offender Public Website** (http://www.nsopw.gov/) offers one-stop access to registries from fifty states, American Samoa, Guam, U.S. Virgin Islands, the District of Columbia, Puerto Rico, and portions of Indian Country.

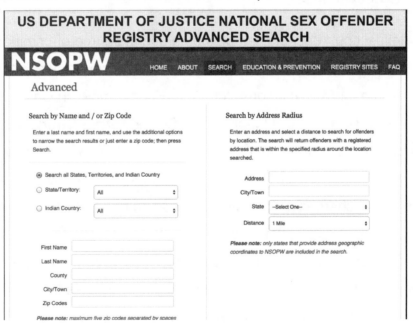

You can conduct a basic name search by using the search boxes located in the upper right-hand corner of the homepage. The search requires a *Last Name* and (at least) a first initial of your subject's *First Name* to conduct a search through all the participating jurisdictions. Click the *search by location* link to conduct either a *Search by Address Radius* search or an *Advanced Search*. On the *Advanced Search* page, you can choose to *Search all States, Territories, and Indian Country*, or select a single state or territory to search from the *State/Territory* drop-down menu, or select a single tribe to search using the *Indian Country* drop-down menu. You can also search by *County*, *City*, or *ZIP Code*. A separate *Address Radius Search* allows you to search for registered offenders within a *1*, *2*, or *3* mile radius of the address you enter.

It's important to note that the DOJ has only created an overlay of the existing sex offender databases maintained by each jurisdiction. The DOJ has not created a master national database of sex offenders that it maintains separately. Additionally, the search form covers data from only 116 of the 566 federally recognized Indian nations.

You can also find direct links to the sex offender registries in all fifty states, the District of Columbia, Guam, Northern Mariana Islands, Puerto Rico, U.S. Virgin Islands, and 130 Indian tribes online by visiting the **FBI State Sex Offender Registry** website (http://www.fbi.gov/hq/cid/cac/registry.htm).

Criminal Court Dockets

Criminal court dockets can also be a useful source of criminal history information. Some state and local courts provide online access to their criminal dockets—some for free and some for a fee. For example, in California, criminal appellate dockets are available for free at the **California Courts** website (http://appellatecases.courtinfo.ca.gov). These dockets are searchable by *Case Number*, *Party*, *Attorney*, or *Case Caption*. On the other hand, **Los Angeles County Superior Court** charges a small fee ($4 to $4.75 depending on volume) to access its trial-level criminal dockets database (http://linkon.in/1FP27f1). Use a public record portal or directory site like **Search Systems** (http://www.searchsystems.net) or **BRB Publications** (http://linkon.in/1nTLiKc) to locate court sites in various jurisdictions.

At the federal level, the Appellate Courts and also the District Courts (which serve as the trial-level courts) both provide access to dockets through **PACER** (See *Chapter Thirteen* for information on searching **PACER** and other sites for federal dockets).

As high-profile social campaigns that have worked to curb Driving Under the Influence (DUI) or Driving While Intoxicated (DWI) have gained momentum, some jurisdictions have created searchable online databases to publicize these charges and convictions.

In New Mexico, for example, the state courts offer a free, searchable database of DWI (and domestic violence) convictions back to 1991 (http://www.nmcourts.gov/caselookup/app; then select the *DWI Search* tab after completing the access verification process). This site provides access to New Mexico District Court, Magistrate Court, and Municipal Court data. Municipal court data is limited to DWI convictions (and criminal domestic violence) from September 1, 1991 to date. Searching by full name (*Last Name First Name*) retrieves the defendant's year of birth and driver's license number (if available). Checking the check box next to one of the cases and clicking the *View Selected Cases* link displays the case number, court, charge, the disposition, disposition date, and a link to the full docket.

Some law enforcement agencies, like the **Hillsborough (FL) County Sheriff's Office,** do not break out DWI arrests in a separate database, but rather include DWI arrests in the booking log files with all other arrests (http://www.hcso.tampa.fl.us/PublicInquiry/ArrestInquiry). The Sherriff's online booking log can be searched with as little as a *Last Name*. Additional criteria, including *First Name*, *Race*, *Date of Birth, Booking Date*, or *Release Date,* can be added to narrow down your results.

To locate DUI/DWI databases in your jurisdiction, try a search engine search for relevant keywords (e.g., *dui OR dwi database search [your location]*). You might also add in additional keywords like *arrest* or *conviction* to narrow your results.

Chapter Nineteen

FINDING EXPERTS
AND VERIFYING THEIR CREDENTIALS

Before you begin your search for an expert witness, it's often a good idea to do some background reading about the subject for which you need that expert witness. This can also help you find experts by identifying the leading authors in the field. Instead of traveling to a library to perform a literature search, you can view library book catalogs (by title, subject, and author) over the Internet, and you can also tap into libraries' valuable databases remotely to search for academic papers and journal articles (as noted on pages 175–181) and download the articles for free. Similarly, many academic papers and other journal articles can be accessed through **Google Scholar** (see pages 332–333) or **Microsoft Academic Search** (see page 334), but not always for free.

Finding Experts by Searching Free National Expert Witness Directory Databases

There are many types of free sites where you can find experts. A logical place to begin a search is at a national expert witness directory database. These sites may include the expert's profile, *curriculum vitae* (CV), deposition transcripts, references, trial transcripts, and articles.

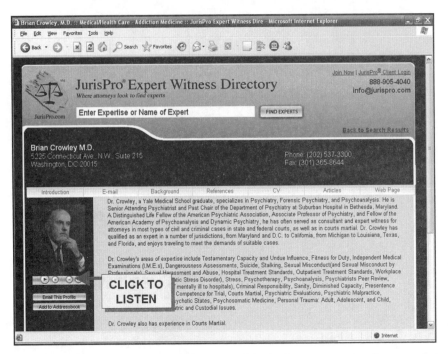

JurisPro.com (http://www.jurispro.com) is a free expert witness database with some unique features. The site gives you the ability to view experts' photographs and listen to the experts introduce themselves in their own voices. The expert's *CV*, *Background*, *Publications*, and *References* are also included, in addition to a link to the expert's own website (where applicable) and an e-mail contact form. Some experts have even uploaded video clips.

ALMexperts.com (http://www.almexperts.com/advsearch) has a database of expert witnesses searchable by *First Name*, *Last Name, Location, Company Name, Area of Expertise*, or *Keyword*. Search results can include the experts' *Profile*, *Resume*, picture, link to their website, *Educational/Licenses* information, and an e-mail contact form.

Experts.com's (http://www.experts.com/Expert-Witnesses/Search) directory lists experts in over 1,200 categories of expertise. Search criteria are similar to that of **JurisPro** and **ALMExperts**, but the search results offer less detail than those two sites. Results include a profile of the expert, contact information, links to the expert's website and CV, the expert's e-mail address, and links to books or articles they've authored, in addition to a postal mail address, phone (and sometimes fax) numbers. While the site has reportedly added audio, we have not found any experts taking advantage of this option in test searches.

MoreLaw (http://www.morelaw.com/experts/) also has a free directory of experts that is browseable by state and city, and area of expertise, and it is searchable by *Name*, *Company*, *Email,* and *Description*, among other criteria (http://www.morelaw.com/experts/search). Results include the least amount of information of the directories discussed here. Profiles include contact information, website and e-mail links, and a description of the expert's areas of expertise. See page 428 for other ways to locate experts using **MoreLaw**.

Finding Experts by Using a Search Engine, or by Searching Social and Professional Networking Sites

To locate an expert in a specific field using a search engine, enter the phrase *"expert witness"* (in quotation marks) or the word *expert*, along with any other keyword or phrase that describes the expertise for which you're searching, such as *"child custody",* into the query box. This will often turn up the websites of expert witnesses in that particular area, or lead to sites where experts you may be interested in have been mentioned.

Experts may also be participating in social and professional networking sites such as **LinkedIn**, **Facebook**, **Twitter**, or **Google+**. See pages 356–416 for more information on conducting searches at these sites.

Finding Experts by Searching Law Association Websites

Many specialty law association websites sponsor expert witness directories. Accessing them usually requires paid membership in the association.

The **Defense Research Institute** (**DRI**; http://www.dri.org) offers an expert witnesses database free to its members (who are all defense attorneys) searchable by expert *Name*, *Expertise*, and *Locale*.

TrialSmith (formerly known as **DepoConnect**; http://www.trialsmith.com/ts) is a subsidiary corporation of the Texas Trial Lawyers Association. TrialSmith offers a database where plaintiff's attorneys can access an online litigation bank with more than a half-million deposition transcripts and millions of other database items that reference experts and case topics (http://linkon.in/YnyLU3). Access to TrialSmith's collection is available only to the plaintiff's bar. Annual subscription fees vary depending on membership in one of the site's more than 100 partner associations. Most member/affiliate plans start at free, for the site's Basic Plan, and go up to $1,099 per year for the Firm Plan. Non-members of any of **TrialSmith's** partner associations pay from $199 to $1,199 annually, depending on the level of membership. Per-search charges also vary depending on the level of membership.

Many state and county bar associations offer expert witness directories on their websites, often for free. For example, the **Illinois State Bar Association** (http://www.isba.org/experts) offers a browseable list of experts organized by category, while the **Los Angeles County Bar Association's** database, **Expert4law** (http://www.expert4law.org), offers a directory of experts, private judges, consultants, researchers, and others searchable by *Keyword*, *Category*, *Name*, or *Company*.

Finding Experts by Searching Other Association Websites

Another useful way to locate an expert, especially when needing one with an unusual expertise, is to get a referral from an association based on the particular field of expertise with which you are dealing. There's an association for every field, or so it seems, and those associations know who the experts are in their respective fields. If you know the association's exact name, use a search engine to find its website. If you don't know the exact name of the association (or if you are unsure whether one even exists), you can still use a search engine and enter the topic of the association (e.g., *banana*) and the word *association*. (By the way, there are at least five associations related to the banana.)

Associations Unlimited and **Guidestar** are two other useful databases from which you can keyword search for an association.

Associations Unlimited (formerly titled **Encyclopedia of Associations**) is a searchable database that contains listings for organizations around the world, ranging from local Chambers of Commerce to large national organizations like the American

Medical Association. It also includes IRS information on nonprofit organizations. Some libraries provide their library cardholders free remote access to this database.

Guidestar (http://www2.guidestar.org/search) contains information on more than 1.8 million non-profit associations searchable by keywords. Results can be further filtered by *State* or *City*, *Cause Category*, or *Revenue* (as reported on the most recent Form 990). Access to basic information from the results (e.g., *Summary*, *Program + Results*, *Financials*, *Operations*) is available with a free registration. Click the green *Forms 990* button in the upper right-hand corner of the listings page to access the last three most recent years of filed tax forms. When available, information in the *Operations* section can be most useful in identifying potential experts or in supplying referrals to potential experts. Additional information (e.g., comparative historical financial data, *Officers, Directors, Trustees and Key Employees* including titles and compensation) is available for $125 or free to paid subscribers. Subscriptions begin at $83 per month (when paid annually) for "Premium Search" access. Additional filter criteria are also available with paid membership.

For medical experts, the **American Medical Association (AMA)** site (http://www.ama-assn.org) is a good starting point to find information about nearly every one of the 814,000 licensed physicians in the United States. The AMA's **DoctorFinder** is located at http://linkon.in/1tzlza6. Click on the *DoctorFinder* link, and then read the disclaimer and click *Accept*. You can search by *Last Name* or by *Specialty*. You also have the option of adding a *First name, City, ZIP Code* or *State* to either type of searches. Basic background and contact information is provided.

You won't find any discipline information at the **AMA** database, but you might find some if you visit the **Association of State Medical Board Executive Directors DocFinder** site (http://docfinder.docboard.org/docfinder.html). This site simultaneously searches sixteen states' physician license databases and two osteopathic license databases. Discipline information is sometimes included in results but varies by jurisdiction. There are also links to the medical licensing boards in thirty-three states and the District of Columbia, as well as nine state osteopathic licensing boards where you can search for information individually.

Another way to identify experts is to locate companies in the industry in which you need an expert. This is useful when you need to find an expert knowledgeable about a specific product but you don't know who manufactures it, or you are looking to locate an expert from a particular company's rival. **ThomasNet.com** (http://www.thomasnet.com) is a manufacturing supplier directory that allows you to search for companies by keyword.

The search box on the homepage defaults to retrieving *Product/Service* results. You can also use tabs across the top of the homepage (e.g., *Product Sourcing*, *Industry News*) to search these separate resources.

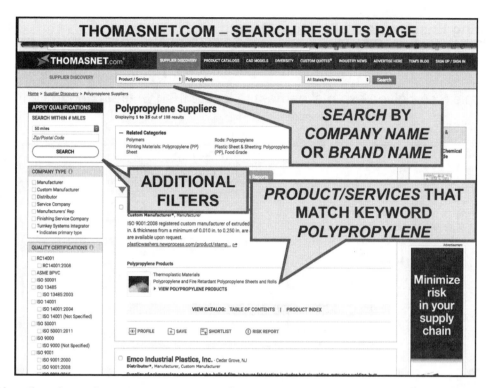

THOMASNET.COM – SEARCH RESULTS PAGE

Use the drop-down menu next to the search box at the top of the results page to display *Company Name* or *Brand Name* results that match your keywords. Additional filters (e.g., geographic, *Company Type*, *Quality Certifications*) are also available in the left-hand column.

Finding Experts by Searching a College or University Website

College professors often make good expert witnesses. If you plan to hire or depose experts who are professors, go to the university's website to review their CV, courses they've taught, and articles or books they've published. Links to college and university homepages can be found at **Wikipedia** (http://linkon.in/2tli6cU). Often the institution will have a search page to locate experts among its faculty that is searchable by subject or name. For example, **Florida State University's College of Medicine** (http://linkon.in/H6My3M) lists its faculty's specialties and links to those professors who have Web pages that include their CV, list of research projects, and publications, etc. Similarly, the University of Texas at Austin offers a university-wide database of *Faculty/Staff* at https://directory.utexas.edu/advanced.php. It can be searched by *Name*, *College/Department*, and *Title*, among other criteria.

When you need experts in a specific area, you can perform literature searches by topic (or by given experts' names) to locate their writings and to verify their expertise.

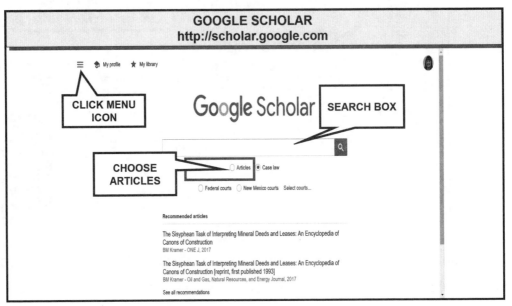

Google *Scholar* (http://scholar.google.com) is an excellent source for locating journal articles and other scholarly publications authored by experts. It is a specialized search that retrieves results from a database that is separate from the regular **Google Web** search database. It includes "articles, theses, books, abstracts and court opinions, from academic publishers, professional societies, online repositories, universities and other websites" (see http://linkon.in/aboutgooglescholar).

To search **Google** *Scholar's Articles*, first click into the *Articles* radio button on **Google** *Scholar's* homepage beneath the search box (see previous illustration) and then enter your keywords into the search box.

To create more targeted, sophisticated searches, access the *Advanced Search* menu by clicking the menu icon (the three horizontal bars shown in the left-hand corner of the previous illustration). This will then display a drop-down menu with an *Advanced Search* link that you would click to display the *Advanced Search* menu (see the next illustration).

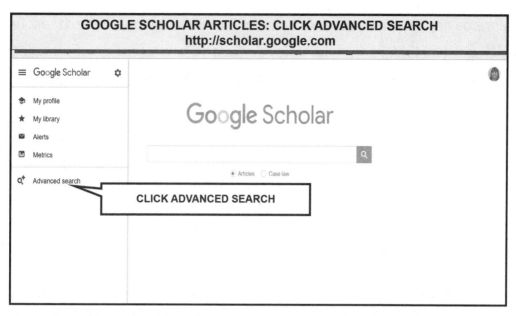

Using the *Advanced Search* menu, you can enter a phrase into the *with the exact phrase* search box or create Boolean searches for articles that contain:

- *all of the words,*
- *at least one of the words,* or
- exclude words by entering them into the *without the words* search box.

You can specify whether you want your search terms to appear *anywhere in the article* or only *in the title of the article*. You can also target your *Advanced Search* by author or publication, as well as specifying a date range (of years) from which you want to see results.

Google *Scholar* also offers free *Alerts* if you want to follow a particular expert, or topic, or both. To learn how to create a **Google** *Scholar Alert,* see page 470. (**Google** *Scholar Alerts* are a separate product from **Google.com's** *Alerts.* **Google.com's** *Alerts* are discussed on page 95. You could set up *Alerts* using both products for a more comprehensive *Alerts* result.)

An important distinction between **Google** *Scholar* and "regular" **Google** search results is that some of the content listed in *Scholar* search results is not available for free. While some of the results do link to free PDF or Web versions of the articles, many more link to an abstract or some other type of descriptive page that includes the ability to purchase access to the article from the journal that published the article.

Before paying for an article, check one of the other literature search resources listed in the next list that might offer the article for free:

- Your library's remote databases of full-text, free newspaper and magazine articles (see page 175)

- **IngentaConnect** (http://www.ingentaconnect.com) offers a database of abstracts of over 5 million articles, chapters, and reports from 13,000 professional and academic publications. This collection can be searched and viewed free of charge. However, to access the full text of any article you must purchase it from the site by credit card (prices vary).

- The **U.S. National Library of Medicine** offers databases of publications on medical topics that can be searched by topic or by a specific expert's name (http://www.nlm.nih.gov).

- **Microsoft Academic Search** (http://academic.microsoft.com) boasts a database of over 120 million publications on a variety of topics (mostly hard science) from millions of authors.

While you can conduct a keyword search for a potential expert by name or a specific medical condition, **Microsoft Academic** is built to go beyond keyword searches and to "understand" complex concepts. It **"employs natural language processing to understand and remember the knowledge conveyed in each document...[and] semantic inference to recognize the user's intent and to proactively deliver results relevant to the user's intention."**

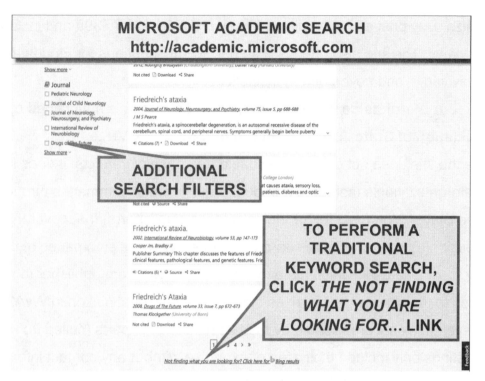

MICROSOFT ACADEMIC SEARCH
http://academic.microsoft.com

ADDITIONAL SEARCH FILTERS

TO PERFORM A TRADITIONAL KEYWORD SEARCH, CLICK *THE NOT FINDING WHAT YOU ARE LOOKING FOR...* LINK

Additional filters are available on the left-hand side of the search results page to narrow your results further by *Author*, *Affiliation*, *Field of Study,* or *Journal*. If, however, this semantic search isn't delivering the results you want, you can always click the *Not finding what you are looking for? Click here for Bing results* link at the bottom of the search results.

Finding Experts Through Jury Verdict, Settlement, Case Law, and Brief Bank Websites

Sometimes the best way to find experts is by searching through documents (such as jury verdicts, settlements, case law, and brief banks) where they have been mentioned as the expert of record.

MoreLaw.com (http://www.morelaw.com/verdicts) provides a free jury verdicts and settlements database. You can search using keywords describing your case to locate experts who have previously testified in cases similar to one that you are handling; or you can conduct a field search to retrieve results using the name of the *Defendant(s) Expert(s)* or the *Plaintiff(s) Expert(s)*. You can also filter results by State.

Law.com's VerdictSearch.com is a pay database of over 180,000 jury verdicts (http://www.verdictsearch.com). Annual subscription prices are based on law firm size. Day passes are available to any practitioner for $395 and include 75 full case views. The site also offers state-specific subscriptions for Florida, New Jersey, Pennsylvania, and seven other jurisdictions.

JuryVerdicts.com (http://www.juryverdicts.com) is maintained by the **National Association of State Jury Verdict Publishers** (NASJVP). While the site does not offer a searchable database of verdicts, it does link to the sites of the organization's members that publish jury verdict summaries throughout the United States. You must follow the links to the publisher(s) that cover the jurisdiction(s) in which you're searching. Fees to access summaries of the cases, jury verdicts, or awards in which the experts testified vary from publisher to publisher. Access to the site's expert witness directory is free (http://linkon.in/WwYVSp). However, it is only browseable by the last names of experts (culled from jury verdicts). The listings only include their area of expertise without any contact information. The only link provided is to information about the verdict's publisher so you can contact them to purchase a copy.

Expert witnesses also might be mentioned by name in case documents (see the *Chapter Thirteen*) or case law (see the discussion of **Google** *Scholar's* case law search capabilities on pages 463–472). For an in-depth discussion of searching free and low-cost case law and docket resources (and other legal research resources) on the Internet, see Carole A. Levitt and Judy K. Davis, *Internet Legal Research on a Budget* (ABA LPD Publishing, 2014, *available at* http://linkon.in/1jbLQZn).

Verifying Experts' Professional or Trade Licenses

For more information on verifying an expert's professional or trade license, see page 425.

Expert Witness Background Research Services

As more information has become more readily available (to both sides) about individual expert witnesses, the necessity to conduct this kind of due diligence into the background research of your own witnesses, as well as the opposition's, has increased. If you are not inclined to go through all of the research steps outlined in this chapter to vet your own expert or to prepare to question the opposition's, the **Expert Witness Profiler** (http://linkon.in/nJ18tV) service can create a detailed background research report for you.

The profiles are custom-created by a team of professional expert witness researchers using a combination of publicly available resources and proprietary databases not readily available to most lawyers. The research team is comprised of over twenty-five legal professionals specially trained to use advanced research tools and techniques to locate difficult-to-find information about expert witnesses.

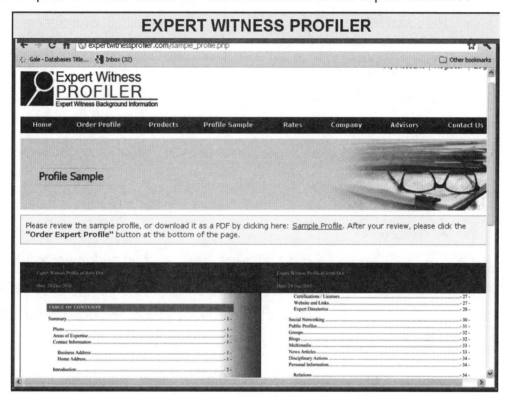

The site offers three levels of reports on expert witnesses:

- *Expert Witness Profile* ($495, 5-day turnaround)
- *Expert Challenge Study* ($125, 3-day turnaround)
- *Preliminary Screening Report* ($25, 2-day turnaround)

Reports can be expedited for an additional fee.

The most comprehensive of the reports, the *Expert Witness Profile*, includes detailed information about the expert witnesses' professional, personal, and litigation backgrounds. These expert witness profiles are created by scouring numerous sources, including:

- Testimonial history
- Challenge (Daubert/Frye) history
- Disciplinary history
- Licensing and certifications (including verification)
- Educational background (including verification)
- Professional background
- Associations and memberships
- Personal information (such as the expert's political persuasion, interests, and opinions posted on various Websites)
- Publications
- Teaching and research
- Patents, trademarks, and copyrights (if relevant)
- References in news, blogs, social networking, or discussion groups
- Rates
- Names of references
- And more

Where available, the *Expert Witness Profile* also includes access to expert witness transcripts, briefs (including memoranda in support of or in opposition to motions to exclude testimony), and other relevant supporting documents. Depending on the expert, profiles can run dozens to hundreds of pages in length.

As members of the company's board of advisors, we helped devise the research methodology used to create the reports. Additionally, we have performed quality control reviews on a number of reports and we were impressed with the volume and breadth of information returned by the **Expert Witness Profiler** researchers, not to mention their thoroughness and depth of research.

Additional documents, such as trial transcripts, deposition testimony, etc., may also be ordered (when available) for an additional fee.

Chapter Twenty

SEARCHING SOCIAL NETWORKING SITES

One of the most talked-about areas of content growth on the Internet continues to be the social networking sites (also referred to as social media). The term "social network" was coined in the mid-1950s by sociologist J. A. Barnes to describe interactions between people in the real world. When applied to the Web, it refers to websites where individuals with similar personal and/or professional interests can create an online "profile" and share information about those interests so others can read about them and interact.

For attorneys, the information individuals share via social media sites can be very useful for background and investigative research about parties, witnesses, current and potential clients, seated and potential jurors, attorneys and judges, and as a source of evidence.

Even pay databases like **TLOxp** have added searches of social networking information to their product offerings. (See the discussion on page 499 for more details.) You can get a head start on uncovering this information for free, though, if you know how to coax the information out of the sites.

Friendster (http://www.friendster.com) was one of the first sites to be referred to by the "social network" label. However, later arrivals, such as **Facebook** (http://www.facebook.com), **Myspace** (http://www.myspace.com), and **Google+**

(http://plus.google.com), have become better-known social networking sites. Most of these sites give users the ability to post text, pictures, sound, and video to their profiles. Many offer the ability to communicate directly via one-on-one or group messaging/chat. Some include the ability to create a blog.

Newer still are sites like **Instagram** (http://www.instagram.com) and **Pinterest** (http://www.pinterest.com) that allow users to share pictures.

Social networking sites were originally the domains of the 20-and-under crowd, but a report by the Pew Research Center found that in 2016 (the most current year for which data are available) 69 percent of American adults use social networking sites ("Social Media Fact Sheet," *available at* http://linkon.in/2qiw30K). Pew found that American adults preferred **Facebook** by a wide margin, calling it "the most-widely used of the major social media platforms," with 68 percent of American adults reporting having a **Facebook** profile. Pew also noted that, "its [**Facebook's**] user base is most broadly representative of the population as a whole."

The next most popular social networking site was **Instagram** with 28 percent of American adults reporting, followed by **Pinterest** at 26 percent, **LinkedIn** at 25 percent, and **Twitter** at 21 percent. Pew also noted that 56 percent of these online adults reported having profiles at multiple social networking sites ("Social Media Update 2016, *available at* http://linkon.in/2qfcvwj). Notable, too, is that Pew does not, as it had in previous years, include **Myspace** in its survey any longer.

Participants in these online social networks tend to share personal information very freely in their profiles. Often this is because they forget that their intended audience members (e.g., their online friends) are not the only people who can see their profiles. Depending on how these users set up their accounts, their profiles might be open to a viewing audience as wide as everyone on the Internet.

A much-reported survey from the American Academy of Matrimonial Lawyers (AAML) found that 81 percent of their members cited "an increase in the use of evidence from social networking websites" between 2005 and 2010. Two-thirds of those respondents indicated that "**Facebook** [was] the primary source of this type of evidence," with **Myspace** following with 15 percent, **Twitter** at 5 percent, and other choices listed at 14 percent. ("Big Surge in Social Networking Evidence Says Survey of Nation's Top Divorce Lawyers," *available at* http://linkon.in/1z70mGv).

But family law is not the only area of law where this trove of information and evidence can be applied. Recently, attorneys have been able to find information in social networking profiles that has made a difference in the outcomes of other types of civil cases and criminal cases. Since 2011, e-discovery vendor X1 Discovery has reviewed "state and federal court cases with written decisions available online," looking for cases that "involved social media evidence in some capacity." For example, for the month of January 2017 alone, they "counted over 1,200 cases accessible through Westlaw and/or Google Scholar for January 2017" in which evidence from social media was a factor in the case. (John Patzakis, "Criminal Conviction Overturned Due to Failure to Authenticate Social Media Evidence," http://linkon.in/2r5DSKi [February 8, 2017]). This represents a significant increase over the X1 Discovery's past surveys.

A similar survey covering April 2014 found 112 cases (published on Westlaw) in which evidence from social media was a factor in the case. (John Patzakis, "Evidentiary Challenges to Social Media Evidence Now Routine When Best Practices Not Utilized," http://linkon.in/1vymNzP [May 6, 2014]). By comparison, in the first half of 2012 Patzakis discovered 319 cases, which was a significant increase over the same period in 2011. (John Patzakis, "Mid-Year Report: Legal Cases Involving Social Media Rapidly Increasing," http://linkon.in/13EiUON [July 23, 2012]).

Even when relatively new, social media evidence played a persuasive role in cases. For example, Santa Barbara, California, prosecutors said information a woman posted about her partying lifestyle on **Myspace** was the difference between a judge ordering a prison sentence rather than probation in a drunken driving crash that killed her passenger. One attorney recently told us that his wife (also an attorney) was able to locate an elusive individual and serve her based on information the individual had posted in her **Facebook** profile. Another attorney was able to locate a missing witness using **Myspace**, even though the witness did not have a profile—her young daughter did. (See page 43 for information regarding admissibility of information from social networking profiles.)

Beyond trial lawyers using information from a party's or witness's social networking profile as evidence, they have also used information from a judge's profile to get judges disqualified from cases (primarily based on bias). Law firm recruiters and even judges have been known to use social networking sites to sift through profiles of potential hires. Be sure to familiarize yourself with federal and state labor laws that might affect your use of these profiles for hiring.

LAWYERS HAVE AN ETHICAL DUTY TO BE AWARE OF SOCIAL NETWORKING SITES AS A POTENTIAL SOURCE OF EVIDENCE

Lawyers should be advised that they cannot ignore evidence from social media. Hopefully, by now you are aware of the ABA's recent changes to Comment [8] of its Model Rule of Professional Conduct 1.1 (http://linkon.in/1xjst3u), which instructs that lawyers "should keep abreast of changes in the law and its practice, including the benefits and risks associated with relevant technology." This implies that lawyers should be familiar with social networking sites and how they could be useful in matters they are handling. As of this writing, thirty-one states have adopted this comment.

Some state Bar associations have gone one step further, specifically advising lawyers that they "have a general duty to be aware of social media as a source of potentially useful information in litigation, to be competent to obtain that information directly or through an agent, and to know how to make effective use of that information in litigation." (The New Hampshire Bar Association Ethics Committee, *Social Media Contact with Witnesses in the Course of Litigation - Advisory Opinion 2012-13/05*, http://linkon.in/1opSdr5 [June 20, 2013]). Similarly, the State Bar of California issued Formal Opinion 2015-193 (http://linkon.in/2qN61qe), citing ABA Model Rule 1.1's Comment 8, as well as stating:

> Attorneys who handle litigation may not ignore the requirements and obligations of electronic discovery

Interestingly, this appears to be a softening of the language issued in the original Interim Opinion (http://linkon.in/calinterimop), in which the Bar stated:

> "Attorneys who handle litigation may not simply ignore the potential impact of evidentiary information existing in electronic form."

CONDUCTING JURY RESEARCH

In a twist on researching a party's or witness's social networking profile to use as evidence at trial, more and more lawyers are conducting juror research (in the courtroom and outside the courtroom) during jury selection. They use information they find for peremptory strikes or to identify favorable jurors. (For example, we were recently retained to conduct social media background research on potential jurors in a multimillion dollar personal injury case.)

If you are researching jurors inside the courtroom, be sure to do it outside their view to avoid tipping off jurors that you are investigating them. They may think you're invading their privacy and this could result in ill will toward you or your client.

In addition to investigating jurors' backgrounds during jury selection (to challenge them for cause), lawyers have investigated seated jurors to learn about their interests so they can weave those interests into openings and closings.

Even after trial, lawyers should continue to monitor former jurors' online activity, looking for potential evidence of juror misconduct that could justify a new trial. See *Newman v. Vagnini*, No. 15-CV-1363-JPS (E.D. Wis. Apr. 3, 2017) *available at* http://linkon.in/vagnini.

One of the earliest cases reported to include social media research as part of jury selection occurred in 2007, during the federal terrorism case against now-convicted "dirty bomber" Jose Padilla, when a team of defense lawyers conducted online juror research with their laptops during *voir dire* while sitting at a back table in a Miami federal courtroom. According to one potential juror's own posts on social media, lawyers discovered she had lied on her jury questionnaire. It turned out this potential juror posted that she was under investigation for malfeasance at the time, according to Linda Moreno, a Tampa, Florida, solo trial lawyer who served as a jury consultant for one of Padilla's co-defendants. After the judge was informed, she dismissed the juror (see http://writ.news.findlaw.com/ramasastry/20100730.html).

In contrast, a New Jersey state trial judge did not allow attorneys to conduct online background research of potential jurors in court. The judge asked an attorney who was using his laptop to access the courthouse's Wi-Fi if he was researching jurors. When the attorney responded that he was, the judge instructed the attorney to stop. *Carino v. Muenzen*, No. A-5491-08T1 (N.J. Super. Ct. App. Div. Aug. 30, 2010) *available at* http://linkon.in/carinonogoogle, *cert denied Carino v. Muenzen, 13 A.3d 363, 205 N.J. 96 (2011) available at* http://linkon.in/carinodenied.

The attorney appealed the decision after losing the case. His client, Carino, contended "that the trial judge abused his discretion during jury selection by precluding his attorney from accessing the internet to obtain information on prospective jurors." He argues that the trial judge deprived him of "the opportunity to learn about potential jurors…one of the most fundamental rights of litigation." The appellate court found that the trial judge should have allowed Carino's counsel to use his computer in the courtroom during jury selection, stating: "Despite the deference we normally show a judge's discretion in controlling the courtroom, we are constrained in this case to conclude that the judge acted unreasonably in preventing use of the internet by Joseph's counsel." However, the appellate court found that there had been no prejudice because the attorney did not point to a single juror who was unqualified and didn't claim he would have exercised a peremptory challenge. The appellate court also noted that the attorney could have done online research outside the courtroom because it took two days to pick jury.

In *Oracle v. Google*, Judge Alsup proposed an order to ban lawyers from researching jurors' Internet presence. *Oracle v. Google*, No. C-10-03561, Document 1573 (N.D. Cal. March 25, 2016), *available at* http://linkon.in/jurorggoogleoracle. The judge based his juror research ban on three reasons:

- First, if they knew lawyers were researching them, Judge Alsup feared that jurors would stray from the court's admonition to refrain from conducting Internet searches on the lawyers and the case.
- Second, if the lawyers' research uncovered certain juror preferences, the lawyers might shape their trial arguments and witness examinations to make improper personal appeals to the jurors based on those preferences.
- Third, the judge wanted to protect the privacy of the *venire*.

If counsel did not agree with the proposed order, the judge stated that he would inform the jurors they were being researched by counsel. The lawyers agreed to the ban.

While Judge Alsup acknowledged that it is ethical for counsel to conduct Internet searches on prospective jurors and view their public social media profiles, he said, "That such searches are not unethical does not translate into an inalienable right to conduct them." He then discussed ABA Formal Opinion No. 466, where the ABA considered the extent to which an attorney may conduct Internet searches of jurors and prospective jurors without running afoul of ABA Model Rule 3.5(b), which prohibits *ex parte* communication with jurors (see page 410). In that Formal Opinion, the ABA said judges may limit the scope of the searches that counsel could perform regarding the juror's social media "[i]f a judge believes it to be necessary, under the circumstances of a particular matter."

For other ethics opinions about what constitutes ethical online research of jurors, see pages 407 and 412.

SERVICE OF PROCESS VIA SOCIAL NETWORKING SITES AND OTHER ELECTRONIC MEANS

Some courts are even allowing service of process via social media and other electronic means. This could include e-mailing service or posting service to a person's known social networking profile, or, as in one case, anywhere on the Web where the person being served could find it during a search engine search for their own name (e.g., if the person being served "Googles" him/herself and finds the service of process notice).

When petitioning spouses in two separate family law matters were able to demonstrate to the court that while their (former) spouses were evading contact or could not be reached through traditional or substitute methods of service, but were still actively posting updates to their social networking accounts and interacting with their "friends" online, the courts allowed the petitioners to serve the opposing parties via a post on their Facebook (or similar) social networking accounts or by other electronic means. See *Mpafe v. Mpafe* Hennepin County, MN No. 27-FA-11-3453, *available at* http://linkon.in/1vnXdyA. See also *Noel v. Maria*, F-00787-13/14B, NYLJ 1202670317766, at *1 (Fam., RI, Decided September 12, 2014), *available at* http://nylawyer.nylj.com/adgifs/decisions14/091714gliedman.pdf.

The following is the court's order in the *Mpafe* case:

> IT IS HEREBY ORDERED THAT: It shall be considered sufficient service for Petitioner to serve Respondent by publication on the internet. All information and timing requirements that would go into a newspaper shall be posted online. Petitioner may choose the format in which they believe it is most likely that Respondent will receive notice. This may include but is not limited to the following:
>
> - Contact via any facebook, myspace, or other social networking site,
> - Contact via email,
> - Contact through information that would appear through an internet search engine such as Google.

Elsewhere, in *WhosHere, Inc. v. Gokhan Orun, d/b/a WhoNear, Who Near, whonear.me*, Civil Action No. 1:13 cv 00526 AJT-TRJ (E.D. Va. February 20, 2014), *available at* http://linkon.in/1FMzrmG, federal Magistrate Judge Thomas Rowles Jones, Jr. granted plaintiff's motion to serve defendant (located in Turkey) via e-mail,

Facebook, and **LinkedIn.** In this trademark infringement case, plaintiff was able to demonstrate that attempts to serve defendant via traditional methods recognized by the Hague Convention had failed. Plaintiff was further able to substantiate that specific e-mail addresses and social networking profiles were linked to defendant. Rowles goes into great detail to explain why he believed that, in this case, service via e-mail and social networking profiles satisfied the Federal Rules of Civil Procedure (Fed. R. Civ. P. 4(f)(3), *available at* http://www.law.cornell.edu/rules/frcp/rule_4).

In *Federal Trade Commission v. PCCare247 Inc.*, Case No. 12 Civ. 7189 (PAE), *available at* http://linkon.in/1wxXzUb, District Judge Paul A. Engelmayer similarly ruled that service via e-mail and **Facebook** on defendants based in India would be appropriate under Fed. R. Civ. P. 4(f)(3).

Recognizing the trend of people having an active online life (even if they cannot be located in the real world), Utah has revised its Motion for Alternate Service (http://linkon.in/utaltserv) to allow for alternate service via Facebook, Twitter, or text message "[o]nly if they [a plaintiff/petitioner] first gets the permission of the judge. The way to ask for permission is to file a Motion for Alternative Service. In the Motion, the plaintiff/petitioner must clearly describe all the things they have done to try to find and serve the defendant/respondent and why those efforts didn't work."

In the Motion for Alternative Service, the plaintiff/petitioner must explain which method(s) they think are most likely to give the defendant/respondent actual notice of the court case...Utah law allows the judge to order other methods to notify someone, including:

- Utah Press Association's Legal Notices (utahlegals.com) webpage
- text messaging,
- email,
- social media (Facebook, Twitter), or
- a combination of these methods

WHY A CIVIL SUBPOENA WON'T GET YOU INFORMATION FROM A SOCIAL NETWORKING SITE

Most lawyers would prefer to obtain their subject's social media account content directly from the social media company, rather than trying to obtain it from the subject through a discovery request. However, lawyers who serve a civil subpoena on a social media company will categorically be denied access to the content based on the 1986 Stored Communications Act (SCA), 18 U.S.C. § 2701 et seq, *available at* https://www.law.cornell.edu/uscode/text/18/2701. (They may be able to access the "customer records"—the name of the account holder, which we'll discuss on page 352.)

The SCA, 18 U.S.C. § 2701 *et seq*, is quite long and confusing, so we will paraphrase it here (and later quote several sections *verbatim*). To further explain the Act, we will discuss selected courts opinions addressing whether the SCA applies to social networking companies. This will include one of the leading opinions, *Crispin v. Audigier*, 717 F.Supp.2d 965 (2010, C.D. CA), *available at* http://linkon.in/CrispinvAudigier. Also, we will discuss **Facebook's** interpretation of the Act.

Obtaining "Customer Content" from a Social Networking Site

Sections 2702(a)(1) through (2)(B) of the SCA, *available at* https://www.law.cornell.edu/uscode/text/18/2702, state that a person or entity that provides "an electronic communication service" or "remote computing service to the public" are prohibited from knowingly divulging the "contents of a communication" to a person or entity while the communication is in electronic storage by that service or carried or maintained on that service. Section 2702(a)(3) states that "a record or other information pertaining to a subscriber to or customer of such service (not including the contents of communications covered by paragraph (1) or (2))" cannot be knowingly divulged to any governmental entity.

Because the SCA was enacted before the advent of **Facebook**, **Myspace**, or other social networking sites, and even before the World Wide Web, *Crispin* and various other courts have simply analogized social media companies to "electronic communication service and remote computing service to the public" to make the Act apply, thus preventing social media companies from divulging the contents of an account holder. **Facebook** has interpreted "contents of a communication" to mean "ex: messages, Timeline posts, photos."

Facebook makes this clear in a *Help* page article titled "*May I obtain any account information or account contents using a subpoena?*" (http://linkon.in/XWGVkB). In the *Help* page article, **Facebook** cites the SCA as the reason that it will not divulge a profile owner's "content of communications" even with a civil subpoena, stating unequivocally that:

> Federal law does not allow private parties to obtain the content of communications (ex: messages, Timeline posts, photos) using subpoenas. See the Stored Communications Act, 18 U.S.C. § 2701 *et seq.*

The following is § 2702(a) of the SCA, *available at* https://www.law.cornell.edu/uscode/text/18/2702:

> (a) Prohibitions.—Except as provided in subsection (b) or (c)—
>
> (1) a person or entity providing an electronic communication service to the public shall not knowingly divulge to any person or entity the contents of a communication while in electronic storage by that service; and
>
> (2) a person or entity providing remote computing service to the public shall not knowingly divulge to any person or entity the contents of any communication which is carried or maintained on that service—
>
> (A) on behalf of, and received by means of electronic transmission from (or created by means of computer processing of communications received by means of electronic transmission from), a subscriber or customer of such service;
>
> (B) solely for the purpose of providing storage or computer processing services to such subscriber or customer, if the provider is not authorized to access the contents of any such communications for purposes of providing any services other than storage or computer processing; and
>
> (3) a provider of remote computing service or electronic communication service to the public shall not knowingly divulge a record or other information pertaining to a subscriber to or customer of such service (not including the contents of communications covered by paragraph (1) or (2)) to any governmental entity.

However, there are many exceptions listed in §§ 2702(b), 2702(c), and 2703, *available at* https://www.law.cornell.edu/uscode/text/18/2703, under which providers of remote computing service or electronic communication service can divulge the "contents" or the "customer records."

As previously stated, one of the leading cases discussing whether the SCA applies to social networking companies is *Crispin v. Audigier*, 717 F.Supp.2d 965 (2010, C.D. CA), *available at* http://linkon.in/CrispinvAudigier. The *Crispin* court held that the § 2702(b) exceptions (see below) do not allow social media companies to divulge the "contents" (the communications) of a social media account to a private attorney, even with a civil subpoena.

> Section 2702(b): Exceptions for disclosure of communications.—A provider described in subsection (a) may divulge the contents of a communication—
>
> (1) to an addressee or intended recipient of such communication or an agent of such addressee or intended recipient;
>
> (2) as otherwise authorized in section 2517, 2511(2)(a), or 2703 of this title;
>
> (3) with the lawful consent of the originator or an addressee or intended recipient of such communication, or the subscriber in the case of remote computing service;
>
> (4) to a person employed or authorized or whose facilities are used to forward such communication to its destination;
>
> (5) as may be necessarily incident to the rendition of the service or to the protection of the rights or property of the provider of that service;
>
> (6) to the National Center for Missing and Exploited Children, in connection with a report submitted thereto under section 2258A;
>
> (7) to a law enforcement agency—
>
> (A) if the contents—
>
>> (i) were inadvertently obtained by the service provider; and
>>
>> (ii) appear to pertain to the commission of a crime; or
>
> [(B) Repealed. Pub. L. 108–21, title V, § 508(b)(1)(A), Apr. 30, 2003, 117 Stat. 684]
>
> (8) to a governmental entity, if the provider, in good faith, believes that an emergency involving danger of death or serious physical injury to any person requires disclosure without delay of communications relating to the emergency.

In this case, magistrate Judge McDermott denied plaintiff Crispin's motion to quash subpoenas served by defendant on **Facebook** and **Myspace**. Judge McDermott concluded that the SCA did not apply to social networking companies such as **Facebook** and **Myspace** because:

> that Act reaches only electronic communication service ("ECS") providers and third-party businesses are not ECS providers as defined in the statute. Judge McDermott also concluded that the SCA prohibits only the voluntary disclosure of information by ECS providers, not disclosure compelled by subpoena. Finally, Judge McDermott found that the SCA prohibits only the disclosure of communications held in "electronic storage" by the ECS provider, and that the materials were not in electronic storage as that term is defined in the statute.

However, District Court Judge Morrow disagreed with magistrate Judge McDermott's interpretation of the SCA and found that the SCA <u>did</u> apply to **Facebook** and **Myspace**. She held that certain elements (e.g., private messages) of a user's **Facebook** or **Myspace** profile were protected from a civil subpoena under the SCA and that those companies could not divulge private messages. She cited many cases and the legislative history of the SCA, which indicated the law's intent was to protect electronic communications meant to be private, such as private Bulletin Board System (BBS) or e-mail messages, from scrutiny. In quashing the defendant's subpoenas seeking private messages from the plaintiff's **Facebook** and **Myspace** accounts, Judge Morrow analogized private messages sent via social media to messages sent via e-mail and messages posted to private BBSs.

However, as to the subpoenas seeking **Facebook** wall postings and **Myspace** comments, Judge Morrow remanded the matter so that a fuller evidentiary record regarding plaintiff's privacy settings could be determined before deciding whether to also quash the subpoena for these postings and comments. The court said it wasn't clear whether "the general public had access to plaintiff's **Facebook** wall and **Myspace** comments, or access was limited to a few." This implies that if the record showed "access was limited to a few" (such as *Friends* only) the subpoena would be quashed, and if it was open to the general public, it would not be quashed. But, if the plaintiff's **Facebook** wall and **Myspace** comments were open to the public, the defendant wouldn't have had to subpoena them in the first place, leaving us to conclude access must have been limited. The evidentiary hearing on this issue was never published, leaving us to ponder what a "few" means.

Obtaining "Customer Records" from a Social Networking Site

Obtaining a "customer record" is an important tool for lawyers to prove who owns an account when trying to get a social networking profile admitted into evidence, especially if the profile owner has used a pseudonym. As explained in the SCA, a customer record refers to the name of the customer/subscriber on the account, "not the contents of [their] communications..."

Many court decisions have held that § 2702(c)(6)'s exception does permit social media companies to divulge customer records to private attorneys via a subpoena because this exception says the customer record may be divulged "to any person other than a governmental entity," among others. (Note that 18 U.S.C. 2702(c)(4), shown below, and 18 U.S.C. 2703, *available at* https://www.law.cornell.edu/uscode/text/18/2703, provide governmental entity exceptions.)

> Section 2702(c) Exceptions for Disclosure of Customer Records.—A provider described in subsection (a) may divulge a record or other information pertaining to a subscriber to or customer of such service (not including the contents of communications covered by subsection (a)(1) or (a)(2))—
>
> > (1) as otherwise authorized in section 2703;
> >
> > (2) with the lawful consent of the customer or subscriber;
> >
> > (3) as may be necessarily incident to the rendition of the service or to the protection of the rights or property of the provider of that service;
> >
> > (4) to a governmental entity, if the provider, in good faith, believes that an emergency involving danger of death or serious physical injury to any person requires disclosure without delay of information relating to the emergency;
> >
> > (5) to the National Center for Missing and Exploited Children, in connection with a report submitted thereto under section 2258A; or
> >
> > **(6) to any person other than a governmental entity.**
> > [emphasis added]

Facebook refers to a customer record as "account information," "basic subscriber information," or "subscriber information (not content)" (http://linkon.in/XWGVkB). To learn how to obtain a customer record from **Facebook**, see its *"May I obtain any account information or account contents using a subpoena?" Help* page (http://linkon.in/XWGVkB). It reads in part:

> Account Information
>
> Facebook may provide the available basic subscriber information (not content) where the requested information is indispensable to the case, and not within a party's possession upon personal service of a valid subpoena or court order and after notice to affected account holders.
>
> If you are domiciled within the U.S. or Canada, the subpoena must be a valid federal, California or California domesticated subpoena, addressed to and served on Facebook, Inc. If you are domiciled outside the U.S. or Canada, the subpoena or court order must be addressed to and served on Facebook Ireland Limited.
>
> Any such subpoena or court order should be limited in scope to seek basic subscriber information only, and set out the specific accounts at issue by identifying them by URL or Facebook user ID (UID). Names, birthdays, locations, and other information are insufficient.

See page 41 for a discussion of the *Tienda* case, where the customer record (which used a pseudonym) and "the internal content of the **Myspace** postings — photographs, comments, and music — was sufficient circumstantial evidence to establish a prima facie case such that a reasonable juror could have found that they were created and maintained by the appellant." (The court in *Tienda* referred to a customer record as a "subscriber report" when discussing it in relation to **Myspace**.

Courts Regularly Admit (and Compel Parties to Produce) Social Networking Content as Evidence

Even though social networking companies will not respond to a civil subpoena, private attorneys can still use the traditional discovery rules to request that a party (or non-party) turn over information from their accounts. If the person refuses, courts are usually willing to issue an order compelling the person to grant access to the information, assuming the court deems it relevant.

In *Romano v. Steelcase*, 2010 NY Slip Op 20388 (September 21, 2010), *available at* http://linkon.in/1xr3NbK, Steelcase asked for an order granting access to the plaintiff's current and past **Facebook** and **Myspace** postings—including all deleted pages and related information. Steelcase argued that the public portion of the plaintiff's **Facebook** profile showed her engaged in an active lifestyle that was inconsistent with the nature and extent of injuries she claimed to have suffered. The plaintiff cited her personal privacy and the fact that her profile(s) were not available publicly as reasons that she should not have to turn them over. The judge did order the plaintiff to turn over the content of those profiles, stating:

> To deny Defendant an opportunity [to] access to [sic] these sites not only would go against the liberal discovery policies of New York favoring pre-trial disclosure, but would condone Plaintiff's attempt to hide relevant information behind self-regulated privacy settings.

See page 366 for details about downloading **Facebook** accounts.

The courts are not granting unfettered access to information in these profiles, though. You still must prove that information in the profile would be relevant to the matter at hand. You can't request content from social networking profiles as part of a "fishing expedition" for evidence. In *Abrams v. Pecile* 2011 NY Slip Op 03108 (April 19, 2011), *available at* http://linkon.in/1nn1QKo, which was a conversion case, the trial court granted the defendant's request for access to the plaintiff's private **Facebook** account to determine her "finances, education, immigration status, and educational background." The Appeals Court unanimously reversed that access, stating:

> …no showing has been made that "the method of discovery sought will result in the disclosure of relevant evidence or is reasonably calculated to lead to the discovery of information bearing on the [conversion] claims.

(We have collected these and several of the other more-often-cited cases that involve evidence from social networking sites. You can find links to their full decisions and/or orders at http://linkon.in/nvtPSa.)

Conduct Your Social Networking Research Prior to Making Your Discovery Request

Prior to making a discovery request for your subject's social networking accounts, we recommend that you conduct research to ascertain whether your subject even has any accounts. This way, if any accounts are public, you can browse through them and download any damning evidence. This prevents your subject from deleting the account or any part of it (such as certain posts or photos) after they receive your discovery request.

If you find an account but cannot browse through it because it is private, at least you can inform your subject's attorney that you know that their client has an account. Hopefully, your subject's attorney has educated your subject about the duty to preserve to avoid a spoliation charge, and that your subject refrains from deleting the entire account (or any part of it).

One of the most widely referenced social networking spoliation cases is *Lester v. Allied Concrete*, Case numbers CL08-150 and CL09-223 (May 27, 2011, Virginia Circuit Court of the City of Charlottesville), *available at* http://linkon.in/Zi7CCn. In Lester's wrongful death suit, his lawyer, Matthew B. Murray, found a photo of Lester wearing a T-shirt that read "I ♥ hot moms" in Lester's **Facebook** profile and advised him to "clean up" his account (thinking that the photo was potentially damaging evidence). However, counsel for the defense had already found that photo, printed a copy of it (and others), and requested them via interrogatories. In the meantime, Lester deactivated his account, then reactivated it and deleted sixteen photos—including the one that could have been potentially damaging evidence. At trial, Attorney Murray allowed Lester to testify that he did <u>not</u> have a **Facebook** account—which Murray (and the defendant's attorney) knew to be false. The court held both Lester and his attorney Murray accountable for spoliation, sanctioning Murray $542,000 and Lester $180,000 to cover Allied Concrete's attorney's fees and costs relating to the spoliation issue. Facing disciplinary action from the Bar, Murray retired.

SEARCHING SOCIAL NETWORKING SITES TO LOCATE PROFILES AND THEIR CONTENTS

Facebook

Facebook (https://www.facebook.com) contains self-created profiles of nearly 2 billion people around the world. Over 1.2 billion of those users access **Facebook** each day. Approximately 47 percent of those daily users access the service via a mobile device. When the site initially became available to the general public, members were broken down into "networks" based on their attendance at specific schools, employment at specific workplaces, etc. Over time, those pre-defined networks have become less and less important. Each day, users share posts that include their thoughts, feelings, opinions, activities, and location. They also share approximately 350 million photos per day (Salman Aslam, "Facebook by the Numbers: Stats, Demographics & Fun Facts," http://linkon.in/2s58CeP [January 24, 2017]). Profiles include clues about the owner's interests such as the *Groups* they've joined, and *Events* they've liked or attended. The information that's shared publicly was once all searchable, although **Facebook** did not make the mechanics of how to search obvious.

Facebook has recently discontinued many of those "non-obvious" search features, such as searching by email address and phone number to locate someone's **Facebook** profile. The company did retain a few non-obvious searches.

Discontinuing searching by email address and phone number was spurred by revelations that political data mining firm Cambridge Analytica scraped publicly available information from an estimated 87 million **Facebook** profiles for political marketing purposes during the 2016 U.S. Presidential election. (Reports estimate that 71 million of those profiles were of U.S. residents.) Recent reports also indicate that the practice was widespread among other third-party actors seeking to cull data (for various reasons) from the profiles of **Facebook's** 2 billion users. More details are available on our website (https://linkon.in/no-fb-email-search).

One useful fact for background and investigative researchers is that most **Facebook** users create their profiles using their real names. Another is that the information in their profiles might not be as "private" as they think, depending on the restrictions the user sets in their *Privacy Settings*.

Search Facebook by Name to Locate Profiles

Conducting a simple name search, using the search box at the top of the **Facebook** screen, will often turn up the profile of your investigation target. However, this search box only appears if you are logged into a **Facebook** account of your own. It is no longer possible to search for users by name without being logged into your own account. To their credit, **Facebook** has put the search box at the very top of their interface, labeled *Search*.

When a user creates a new account, certain preferences are automatically set by default. For example, your friends list is set to "public," your profile can be indexed by search engines, you can be tagged in any post, the site suggests that your friends tag you in images, and so on. Other defaults, such as who can see your future posts or who can see posts you're tagged in, are set to "Friends." However, **Facebook** users can change their *Privacy Settings* at any time to limit how their profiles can be searched by going to their account and making changes or even on the fly by changing their privacy settings per post (by using the drop-down menu to the right of *Newsfeed* and selecting *Friends*, *Public*, *Only me*, etc.). The two things that can't be changed are the ability to be searched by name by any other **Facebook** user and that searcher's ability to see at least part of your profile, including your primary **Facebook** photo, and any other information you have left public.

Introduced in 2013 with much fanfare, **Facebook's** *Graph Search* allowed you to also use the search box to create very targeted conceptual searches of the information users posted to their profiles. It was originally meant for searches like *Friends who like to ski* or *Restaurants liked by my Friends.* However, the *Graph Search* functions could also be used to create queries to locate background and investigative research information about any **Facebook** user—even those we were not *Friends* with or otherwise connected to (as described in the next few potential sample searches). It was possible to retrieve *Graph Search* results from **Facebook's** search box up until late 2016.

While it's no longer possible to retrieve *Graph Search* results from the **Facebook** search box, you can still create your own *Graph Searches* by forming them in the address bar of your browser using **Facebook's** *Graph Search's* search syntax and search parameters. Searches are formatted this way:

http://www.facebook.com/search/[USERID]/[PARAMETER].

For example, if we wanted a list of potential witnesses to an occurrence at a particular business, we could create a **Facebook** *Graph Search* to locate users who reported working at that business—in this example, *El Pinto Restaurant* in Albuquerque, NM. To do so, we would enter this URL in our browser's address bar:

https://www.facebook.com/search/52188973194/employees.

The subject's *USERID* must be the user's numeric profile id and not their custom, vanity URL (if the user created one). See page 361 for more information on identifying **Facebook** profile user IDs.

Similarly, we can search for **Facebook** photos taken at *El Pinto Restaurant*, like this:

https://www.facebook.com/search/52188973194/photos-of

This sample search will retrieve all of the photos tagged as being taken at *52188973194,* which is the numeric profile-ID of *El Pinto Restaurant* in Albuquerque, NM. It doesn't matter who took them, or when. As long as they are publicly available to be viewed on **Facebook**, this search will retrieve them.

We can also narrow that search down to a particular month, like this:

https://www.facebook.com/search/52188973194/photos-of/2016/oct/date-2/photos/intersect

This search returns only those photos of tagged with *El Pinto's* User ID, posted in October 2016.

Or we can search for all locations where a target individual checked in, like this:

https://www.facebook.com/search/650396649/places-visited/

Note that all of the parameters must be lowercase and even though you are not entering this search into the **Facebook** search box you must be logged into <u>your</u> **Facebook** account to view the results.

We have assembled a more detailed list of search parameters at http://www.netforlawyers.com/page/fb-graph-search-parameters.

Third parties, such as **SearchIsBack.com** (www.searchisback.com)**,** have created their own interfaces to submit *Graph Searches* to **Facebook**.

.

This site presents a series of search forms and drop-down options that help you formulate targeted searches, such as a *Search for: All People, Gender: Male, Current Company: John Deere, Name: Kirby* (as shown in the previous illustration). You must be logged into your **Facebook** account to view results.

Note that **Facebook** announced that it is ending support for these third-party interfaces. However, **SearchIsBack** still works, but only partially. For example, when we tried this search recently, it returned results for *Males* named *Kirby* but not necessarily ones whose *Current Company* was *John Deere.* When we hit our back button, we noticed that *John Deere* had been stripped out of the *Current Company* search box, indicating that **Facebook** has disabled **SearchIsBack's** *Current Company* search.

If a **Facebook** user URL for your target looks like this, *https://www.facebook.com/profile.php?id=52188973194*, the profile's user ID is the string of numbers that follow the identifier: *?id=* (in this example *52188973194*). Not all **Facebook** profiles display their user ID, however. Some users have created a custom, vanity URL, such as *https://www.facebook.com/ElPintoRestaurant*, to identify their profile.

For a profile URL where the user has created a custom, vanity URL, visit a site like **FindMyFBid.com** (http://findmyfbid.com) and enter that vanity URL into the *Find numeric id* box to retrieve the user ID number. Despite the site's name, you can use it to retrieve anyone's **Facebook** ID number.

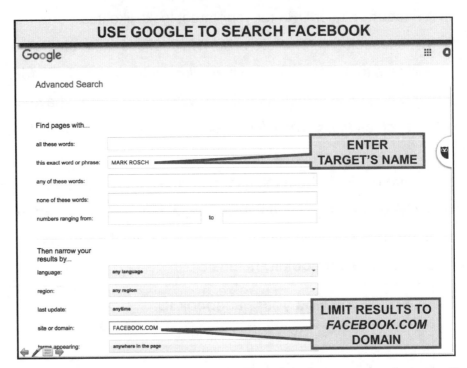

Instead of using **Facebook** to search **Facebook**, you can also use **Google's** *Advanced Search* page to create a search for your target's name and limit **Google's** results just to the *Facebook.com* domain (as seen in the previous illustration).

Similarly, it can sometimes be just as effective to conduct a simple search engine search for *Target's Name* and *Facebook* (e.g., *Mark Rosch Facebook*) to retrieve a link to the individual's profile, if one exists, as it is to search directly at **Facebook**.

Be aware that **Facebook** account owners can use one of **Facebook's** *Privacy Settings* to decide whether they "want search engines outside of **Facebook** to link to [their] profile." If this is set to "no" these types of search engine searches will not return links to those profiles.

If you have been unable to identify a **Facebook** profile using any of the methods discussed so far, there is something of a work-around that allows you to determine whether someone has created a **Facebook** profile—or at least if there is a profile associated with (one of) their known e-mail addresses or phone numbers. This method works even if they have limited who can search for them using these criteria in the **Facebook** search box (as discussed on page 356). To do this, we exploit a feature of **Facebook's** login page and its user verification process. So first, you need to be logged out of your own **Facebook** account.

Once you're logged out, enter the known e-mail address or phone number of your target into the *Email or Phone* login box on the login page. (Note: Phone numbers are a login option because **Facebook** users are prompted for a phone number as part of the registration process.) You are not trying to gain access to, or hack into, the account (if one exists), so you will leave the *Password* box blank. Then click the *Log In* button.

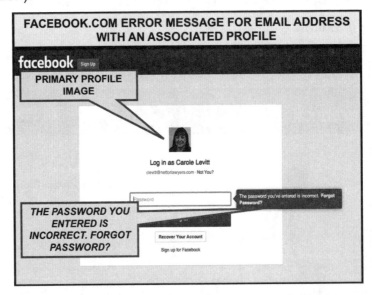

FACEBOOK.COM ERROR MESSAGE FOR EMAIL ADDRESS WITH NO ASSOCIATED PROFILE

If there is no **Facebook** profile associated with the e-mail address or phone number you entered, you will receive this message, "*The email [or phone number] you've entered doesn't match any account. Sign up for an account.*", (as seen in the previous illustration).

FACEBOOK.COM ERROR MESSAGE FOR EMAIL ADDRESS WITH AN ASSOCIATED PROFILE

However, if there is a **Facebook** profile associated with the e-mail address, you will receive a different message, as seen in the previous illustration. It will read, *The password you've entered is incorrect. Forgot Password?* The message will also include the name and primary photo associated with the account, so if you know what the target looks like, you will be able to verify that they probably have a profile. Then you can request their profile content with confidence. This is also helpful in challenging individuals who claim not to have a profile.

Oddly, if you run this search for a phone number that is associated with a profile, you'll see the same *The password you've entered is incorrect.* message as the previous search—which verifies that there is a profile associated with that phone number—but you will not see the primary profile image or the subject's name.

Searching Facebook (and Other Social Networking Sites) by Pseudonym

If you have been unable to locate the profile of your target by name, phone number, or e-mail address in a **Facebook** search (or any other social networking site), try searching by their known pseudonym. To learn how other lawyers have been able to authenticate profiles with pseudonyms and get them admitted into evidence, see page 41.

Searching Facebook Live Video

In April 2016, Facebook introduced the **Facebook Live** video streaming capability that allows users to broadcast a live video to their *Friends/Followers* via **Facebook** mobile apps. You cannot create a *Graph Search* for past **Facebook Live** video streams.

If you are able to locate your target's **Facebook** Profile, you can browse through all of their posts and you might be able to view the old/completed **Facebook Live** videos they have produced, depending on the target's overall *Privacy Settings*. Click on any videos that you can see to play the video and view the comments that viewers made during the live video. (Note that individual videos can carry different levels of sharing, e.g., *Public*, *Friends*, *Friends Except*, *Specific Friends*.)

If you are logged into your **Facebook** account, you can view all public **Facebook Live** videos currently streaming at https://www.facebook.com/livemap/. Clicking on any dot on the map allows you to view that video.

If a judge compels a party (or non-party) to turn over his or her **Facebook** account to the opposition (in a civil action), **Facebook** recommends that the compelled person use **Facebook's** *Download Your Information* tool (*available at* http://linkon.in/XWGVkB):

> Parties to litigation may satisfy party and non-party discovery requirements relating to their Facebook accounts by producing and authenticating the content of communications from their accounts and by using Facebook's "Download Your Information" tool, which is accessible through the Settings drop down menu.

> If a person cannot access their content, Facebook may, to the extent possible, attempt to restore access to deactivated accounts to allow the person to collect and produce their content. However, Facebook cannot restore account content that had been deleted. Facebook preserves account content only in response to a valid government requests. [sic]

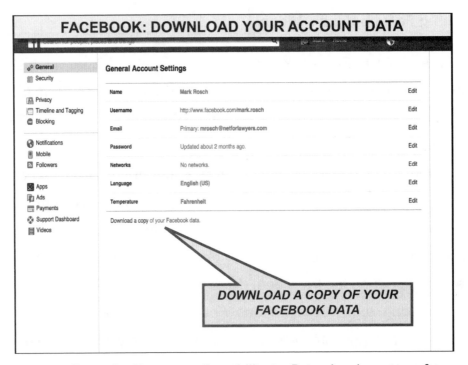

Facebook offers all of its users the ability to *Download a copy of your Facebook data*. To access this tool, visit http://www.facebook.com/settings while logged into your account. At the bottom of the list of *Settings* that you can customize is a link labeled *Download a copy of your Facebook data*. Click that link to begin the process of downloading a history of all your activity on **Facebook**.

FACEBOOK: DOWNLOAD YOUR ACCOUNT DATA

Search for people, places and things   Mark   Home

Download Your Information
Get a copy of what you've shared on Facebook.

Start My Archive

What's included?
- Posts, photos and videos you've shared
- Your messages and chat conversations
- Info from the About section of your profile
- And more

START MY ARCHIVE

About   Create Ad   Create Page   Developers   Careers   Privacy   Cookies   Terms   Help

On the subsequent page, click the *Start My Archive* button to generate the file that contains your posts, photos, videos, messages, chats, and the description in the *About* section of your profile, among other information from your account. You will receive an initial e-mail message informing you that the archive has been requested and a subsequent e-mail with a link to download the archive. Archive files can take minutes, hours, or days to generate, depending on the amount of information available for a specific account and the volume of archives requested at any given time.

FACEBOOK: SAMPLE OF ACCOUNT DATA CONTAINED IN ARCHIVE

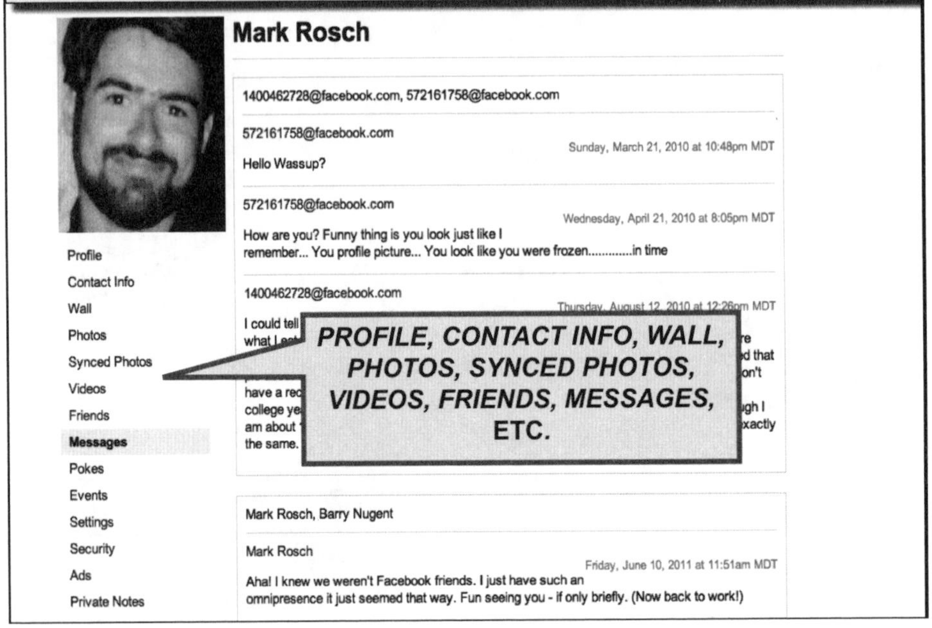

This illustration shows an example of some of the account data included in the **Facebook** account archive.

Opposing parties who are required to produce information from their **Facebook** profiles can be instructed on how to initiate this process in order to produce the requested information.

Google+

In June 2011, **Google** launched its fourth or fifth foray into social networking with **Google+**. Initially, **Google+** was its most successful attempt, boasting more than 1.1 billion users (individuals and companies) by February 2014. (Cendrine Marrouat, "Google+ Now Has 1.15 Billion Registered Users," Social Media Slant, Feb 12, 2014, *available at* http://linkon.in/1ohXldX). There are some who attribute this growth to **Google** "forcing" new **Gmail** account users to accept an accompanying **Google+** account. **Google** discontinued the practice in September 2014, and since then, the service's growth has slowed down. Despite the fast growth in users, **Google+** never experienced the level of engagement that **Facebook** achieved. In late 2016, it was reported that Google+ had just 375 million active users, of whom less than 10 percent

(27 million) visit **Google+** in a given month. (Statistic Brain Research Institute, *Google Plus Demographics & Statistics*, September 4, 2016, *available at* http://linkon.in/2l9EwB2).

Google+ mixes some familiar elements from existing social networks with new features. Ironically, some of **Google+'s** new features have now been adopted by **Facebook** (such as creating groups of friends), while others, such as hosting free videoconferences on the fly, which have not been adopted by any other social networking site. Up until mid- 2014, most people created their **Google+** profiles using their real names because **Google** insisted on it, warning: "Your account may be suspended if we determine your profile name violates our user conduct and content policy" (http://support.google.com/plus/answer/1228271). That rule changed on July 14, 2014 (http://linkon.in/googlenewnamerule) when Google announced, "There are no more restrictions on what name you can use." However, **Google+** advises that some profile names, such as ones that impersonate another profile name, might violate **Google+** guidelines.

Google+ users have the option of making any of their postings *Public* or available only to specific people with whom they have created a relationship on **Google+**. It's these *Public* posts that will be available in search results.

The public portions of most profiles include whatever biographical information the user has provided in the *About* section (such as work and education history, contact information, and location information), as well as *Public* posts (if any), and the list of people that the user has connected with on **Google+**. Users can also upload *Photos*, and *Videos*.

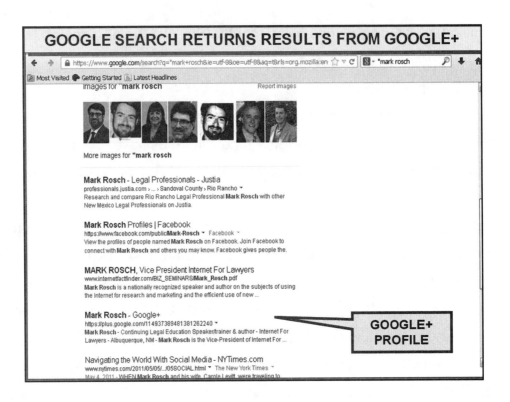

GOOGLE SEARCH RETURNS RESULTS FROM GOOGLE+

Google no longer maintains a dedicated search page for **Google+** profiles. The publicly available content of **Google+** can be searched without being logged into a **Google+** account using the **Google** Web *Search* interface. Searches for individuals by name will usually display their **Google+** profile in the first page of **Google** results— but not always. Adding the keyword *Google+* after your target's name is more likely to return not only the subject's personal **Google+** account, but also any *Company pages* associated with the target's name.

You can limit results to **Google+** by visiting **Google's** *Advanced Search* page, entering your subject's name into the "all the words" search box and narrowing the results to the specific **Google+** site/domain. You would do this by entering *http://plus.google.com* into the *Then narrow your results by site or domain* box on **Google's** *Advanced Search* page, as discussed on page 77 Note that even though **Yahoo!** and **Bing** recognize the *site*: domain limiter, they do not do as good a job at returning results only from the *plus.google.com* domain.

You can also create an even more targeted search by using **Google's** little-known proximity connector (*AROUND(#);* discussed on page 58). For example, if you wanted to search **Google+** for profiles of managers who work at John Deere's Headquarters in Johnston, Iowa, you would structure the query this way:

site:http://plus.google.com works AROUND(3) Deere manager lives AROUND(3) Iowa

Some of the other limiters on the *Advanced Search* page (e.g., *Last Update*) will work properly to retrieve results from **Google+**, while others (e.g., *File Type, Language*) will not.

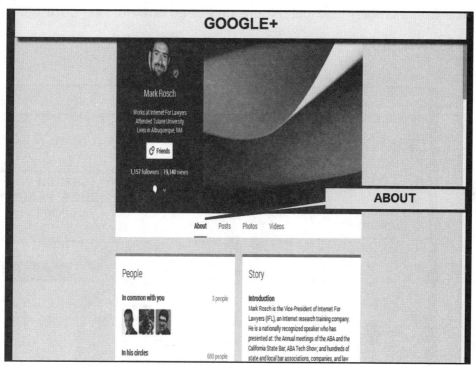

Even when you're logged into your own **Google+** account, the site now offers fewer search options and filters than it did in the past. A search box appears at the top of the screen allowing you to keyword or name search. Results are returned in categories—*People & Pages, Posts, Collections*, or *Communities*. A *Collection* is a series of *Posts* grouped together by the user who posts them. A *Community* is a group of members usually dedicated to discussing a particular topic. Any **Google+** user can create a *Community*. Previously, there had been another half dozen or so other categories you could use to narrow down your results list.

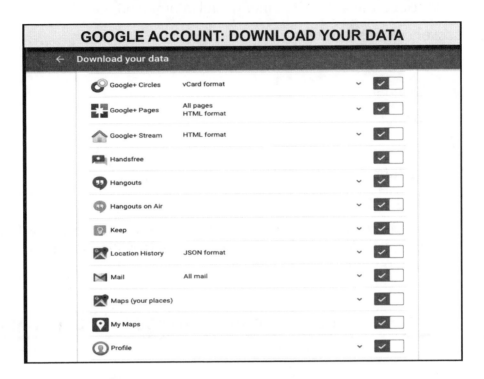

You can export **Google+** data (and other data, such as your *Bookmarks*, *Mail*) into an Archive from various services in your **Google Account**, including **Google+**, by visiting https://takeout.google.com/settings/takeout, but you must be logged into your account. For **Google+**, you can download:

- *Profile*
- *Hangouts*
- *Google+ Circles*
- *Google+ Stream*
- *+1s*
- *Google+ Pages*

Because **Google** integrates many of its other products besides **Google+** into a **Google Account,** there may be other useful information you should consider including in a discovery request, including:

- *Mail*
- *Calendar*
- *Contacts*
- *Drive*
- *YouTube*
- *Google Photos*
- *Location History* (users can opt-in to use their phone's GPS functions to report their location to Google to receive location-based information like traffic reports)

Once the user selects the data they want to archive from their account, they can opt to have a link to the archive file sent to them via e-mail.

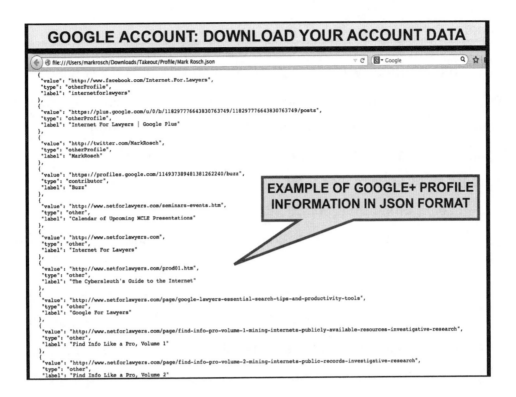

GOOGLE ACCOUNT: DOWNLOAD YOUR ACCOUNT DATA

file:///Users/markrosch/Downloads/Takeout/Profile/Mark Rosch.json

```
{
"value": "http://www.facebook.com/Internet.For.Lawyers",
"type": "otherProfile",
"label": "internetforlawyers"
},
{
"value": "https://plus.google.com/u/0/b/118297776643830763749/118297776643830763749/posts",
"type": "otherProfile",
"label": "Internet For Lawyers | Google Plus"
},
{
"value": "http://twitter.com/MarkRosch",
"type": "otherProfile",
"label": "MarkRosch"
},
{
"value": "https://profiles.google.com/114937389481381262240/buzz",
"type": "contributor",
"label": "Buzz"
},
{
"value": "http://www.netforlawyers.com/seminars-events.htm",
"type": "other",
"label": "Calendar of Upcoming MCLE Presentations"
},
{
"value": "http://www.netforlawyers.com",
"type": "other",
"label": "Internet For Lawyers"
},
{
"value": "http://www.netforlawyers.com/prod01.htm",
"type": "other",
"label": "The Cybersleuth's Guide to the Internet"
},
{
"value": "http://www.netforlawyers.com/page/google-lawyers-essential-search-tips-and-productivity-tools",
"type": "other",
"label": "Google For Lawyers"
},
{
"value": "http://www.netforlawyers.com/page/find-info-pro-volume-1-mining-internets-publicly-available-resources-investigative-research",
"type": "other",
"label": "Find Info Like a Pro, Volume 1"
},
{
"value": "http://www.netforlawyers.com/page/find-info-pro-volume-2-mining-internets-public-records-investigative-research",
"type": "other",
"label": "Find Info Like a Pro, Volume 2"
```

EXAMPLE OF GOOGLE+ PROFILE INFORMATION IN JSON FORMAT

While some useful information can be found here, be aware that some of the categories of information, like the *Profile*, are provided in a JavaScript format (JSON) that may require the use of specialized software to be easily read.

LinkedIn (http://www.linkedin.com), a professional networking site, can be used by attorneys in much the same way that they use social networking sites (to find missing people and obtain background information about people). Like **Classmates.com**, those using **LinkedIn** want to be found—thus, they tend to use their real names. This makes the **LinkedIn** site an ideal tool for finding people.

In 2018, **LinkedIn** reported 562 million users (https://about.linkedin.com/), with 252 million visiting the site in a given month (http://fortune.com/2017/04/24/linkedin-users/).

LinkedIn used to allow you to search without being logged into an account. All you had to do was visit https://www.linkedin.com/ and enter a first and last name into the *Find a colleague* search boxes. **LinkedIn** would then show you a results list and let you view profiles. But now, the results list is obscured by a pop-up that asks you to *Join* or *Sign In*. If you do neither and just click *Search*, **LinkedIn** does one of two things: (1) it might show you a results list, but it won't let you see any profiles or (2) it won't even show the results list, but just asks you to sign in or join.

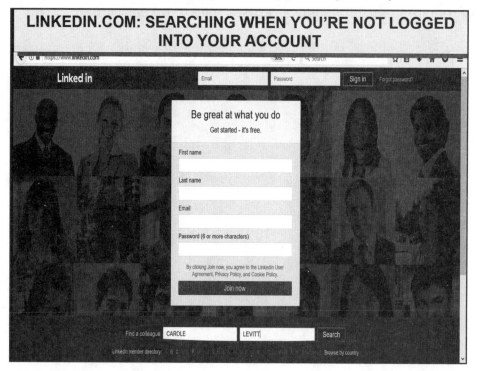

So, to view profiles, you now must be logged into your own **LinkedIn** account. But even then, you might not see much because individual profile owners can set their **LinkedIn** privacy settings to limit the amount of information people to whom they are not directly connected to can see.

Once you log into your account, you can search for profiles using the *Search* box on the top left side of the page. Although it's not obvious, in addition to entering a personal name into the *Search* box, you could instead enter a company name or even keywords or phrases (in quotation marks) with Boolean connectors. **LinkedIn** recognizes the *OR* and *NOT* Boolean connectors. Like at **Google**, these Boolean connectors must be capitalized for **LinkedIn** to recognize them as connectors. **LinkedIn's** Boolean connector default is *AND* (so you do not need to type that connector). Also, when you click into the search box, a drop-down menu appears allowing you to filter by *People*, *Jobs*, or *Posts*.

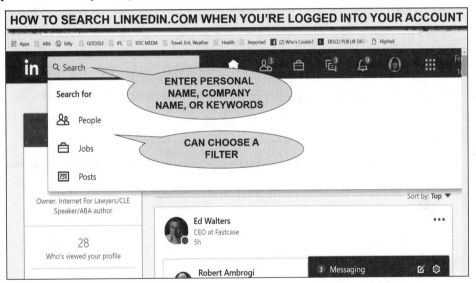

Once you have run your search at **LinkedIn** and retrieve results, you are presented with options to create more sophisticated, targeted searches. For instance, if you click the *More* link a drop-down list appears for you to limit your search by *Companies*, *Groups*, or *Schools*. You can also, use the *People Filters* (to the right of *More*) to filter by *Locations*, *Connections*, or *Current Companies.*

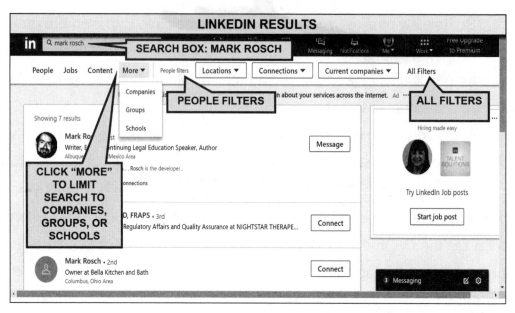

Additionally, you can click *All Filters* to expand the filtering choices by *Past Companies, Title, Industries, Languages,* etc. If you were searching for an electronic discovery expert witness who is also an attorney, you could enter *"electronic discovery"* OR *ediscovery* into the *Search* box and then enter *lawyer* into the *Title* filter box. (Instead of entering *lawyer* into the *Title* filter box, you could enter *lawyer* into the *Search* box as keyword along with the search terms *"electronic discovery"* OR *ediscovery*.)

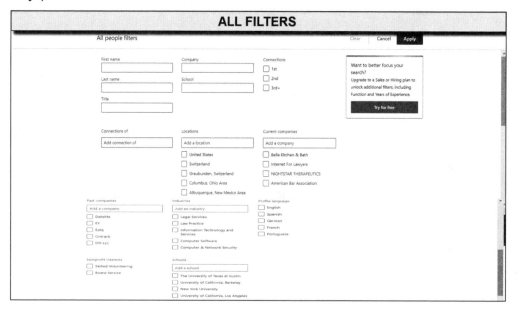

One important caveat: Of all the major social/professional networks, **LinkedIn** is one of the two that, by default, <u>does</u> alert its users about who has viewed their profile. (**Classmates.com** is the other.) When you are logged into your own account and view the profile of another user, **LinkedIn** will report your name, title, employer, and geographic location (from your profile) to that user as someone who has viewed his or her profile.

LINKEDIN.COM PRIVACY SETTINGS

in

⊕ Account   ⊘ Privacy   ☐ Communications

Profile privacy	**Profile privacy**	
Blocking and hiding		
Data privacy and advertising	**Edit your public profile**	Change
	Choose how your profile appears in search engines	
Security		
	Who can see your connections	Change
	Choose who can see your list of connections	Connections
	Viewers of this profile also viewed	Change
	Choose whether or not this feature appears when people view your profile	Yes
	Sharing profile edits	Change
	Choose whether your network is notified about profile changes	No
	Profile viewing options ——— **PROFILE VIEWING OPTIONS**	
	Choose whether you're visible or viewing in private mode	
	Notifying connections when you're in the news	Change
	Choose whether we notify people in your network that you've been mentioned in an article or blog post	Yes

Luckily for searchers who do not want to leave a trail, **LinkedIn** gives you the ability to turn this option off. To do so, click the *Me* drop-down menu (under your profile picture in the upper right-hand corner of your profile) and click on *Settings & Privacy*. On the subsequent screen, click the *Privacy* tab at the top of the screen, and then *Profile viewing options*. You can then choose from two l f anonymity. You can opt to leave just private profile characteristics (e.g., *Som University*);); or you can opt for *Private Mode*, leaving no tra you visit the other user (e.g., *Anonymous LinkedIn Member view your **LinkedIn** profile, the highest level of information your profile will be the level of information you have opted (even if visitors have selected to leave a higher level of inf

380

Download Your LinkedIn Account Data

LinkedIn offers users the ability to download two different types of archives—
Fast file only and *Fast file plus other data*. The latter contains more information and
would be more useful for evidentiary purposes than the former.

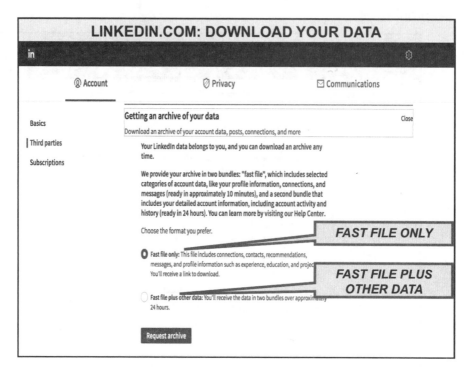

The more comprehensive of the two account archives (which is more likely to
be useful for evidentiary purposes than the other), can be requested by visiting
https://www.linkedin.com/psettings/member-data while logged into your **LinkedIn**
account, clicking into the *Fast file plus other data* radio button, and then clicking the
Request archive button. Once requested, you will receive an e-mail, "within
minutes…with a link where you can download certain categories of personal
information…including your messages, connections, and contacts…." Other
information takes longer to compile and export (a second e-mail, with a link to
additional information, could take up to 24 hours to receive).

Both portions of the archive are delivered as a series of .CSV files that can be viewed with any spreadsheet software (like Excel) and includes:

- *Inbox Communications* – all of the messages that are in the *Messages*, *Sent*, *Archive*, and *Trash* (if not emptied) folder

- *Contacts* – contacts imported into LinkedIn

- *Login Attempts* – includes I.P addresses used and date, time, and type of login (e.g., from *Website* or *Third Party* app)

- *Photos* – photos shared through the account

- *Likes* – updates (including articles, shared pictures, etc.) liked by the account

- *Search History* – list of recent searches

- *Registration info* – the date the account was registered, the IP address registered from, and the name of the member who invited the user to join **LinkedIn**, if there was one

- *Connections* – 1st *Degree Connections only*

- *Email addresses* – history of all of the e-mail addresses that have ever been associated with the account

As promised, the link to download the first group of .CSV files arrived within five minutes of requesting the archive. Note that lists like *Contacts* and *Connections* are in no discernible order. They also do not include additional useful information, such as the date the contact or connection was added.

Despite being one of the original sites to be described as a "social network," **Myspace** (https://myspace.com) has fallen out of favor with users who have largely migrated to other sites. The site's 2011 re-launch, with entertainer Justin Timberlake as a part-owner, now heavily favors musical performers and their songs over more general content. As of March 2017, **Myspace** reportedly had 50.6 million active users. (Statistic Brain Research Institute, *Myspace Statistics*, March 30, 2017, *available at* http://linkon.in/2raAVYK).

The basic user profile includes pre-defined categories of information, into which members can add their own information. It is not necessary to create a **Myspace** account to be able to browse or search through the "public" profiles on the site. Click the *Search* link in the upper left-hand corner of the homepage to begin searching.

The search defaults to the *AND* Boolean connector. Phrase searching is not recognized.

Results are displayed in columns separating:

- *Articles*
- *Songs*
- *Videos*
- *Artists*
- *Albums*
- *People*
- *Mixes*

Any information that members add to their public profile would be visible to anyone else who visits that profile—including the list of *Connections> People* [they're connected to], and a city/state location. A list of the user's *Top 8 Connections* is also displayed. Hovering over any of the *Top 8* reveals information about their profile, including their *Full Name* (which may often be their real name), *UserName* (which is often a pseudonym), and a link to their profile.

Many people register with their real name, but when they create their profile, they realize that they should not (or prefer not to) display it on their profile and select a pseudonym as their *UserName*—but that won't really help mask their identity, since the *Search* box retrieves both the *Full Name* and the *UserName.* However, **Myspace** users can change the *Full Name, UserName*, or the e-mail address associated with their account.

Because the majority of profiles are not "private," you can access a large number of profiles to see if your subject has created a **Myspace** profile. If you locate your subject's profile, you will be able to view some of the information they have posted about themselves, who they've connected to, and who has connected to them.

Beware of shortcomings in the way search results are displayed. For example, when we searched for *David Dadon* and clicked the *People* link to scroll through all the results that were supposed to be for *David Dadon*, there were many results for individuals with names that were similar (and not so similar) to our search term. Users with the *DisplayName David Dadon* didn't show up until the fifty-third entry on our results list of 713 people. The lack of Boolean connectors, other than the default *AND*, and the lack of phrase searching, makes it impossible to create sophisticated, targeted searches.

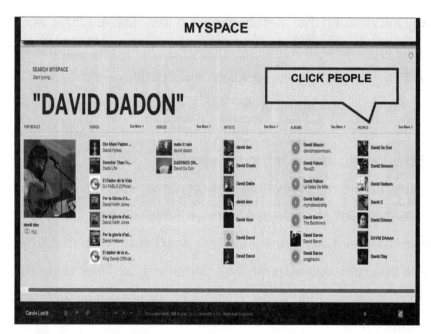

As discussed on page 77, however, you can use **Google's** *Advanced Search* page to create a more sophisticated search and limit **Google's** results just to the *Myspace.com* domain.

Myspace does not offer its users the option to download their entire profile like **Facebook**, **Google+**, and **LinkedIn**.

Classmates.com (http://www.classmates.com), which offers many of the same functions as **Facebook** and **Myspace**, predates those other sites and was launched long before the social network label was applied to websites. **Classmates.com's** database claims over 70 million members from over 100,000 schools located in the United States and Canada.

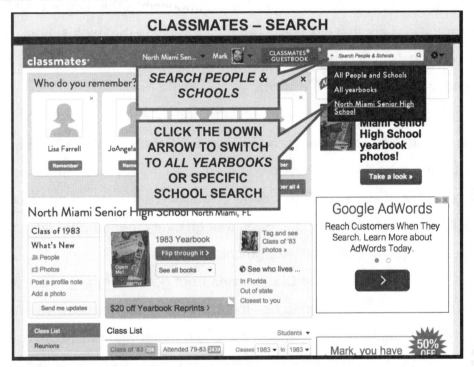

To search the **Classmates.com** database, you must first create an account of your own. Creating an account requires that you supply:

- *First name*
- *Last name at graduation*
- *Last name [now] (optional)*
- *Email*
- *Graduation year*
- *Graduation high school*

Once you're logged into **Classmates.com**, you are not limited to searching just the school in your profile. You can search the entire database from the search box located in the upper right-hand corner of the page. The default search is to *Search*

People & Schools. You can enter your target's name to retrieve matches from the entire 70 million-plus users. The **Classmates.com** database is particularly useful because it asks registrants for their *Last name at graduation*—allowing one to search for women using their maiden names and possibly learning their married names.

Displayed results include the information required to create an account, including the individual's name (including their current name if you searched for a woman using her maiden name), name and location of the high school they graduated from, and the years that individual reported attending that high school. Clicking on a search result displays the individual's photo (if they have added one to their profile) but little other additional information.

Clicking the down-arrow on the left-hand side of the search box gives you the option of switching your search to *All People & Schools*, *All yearbooks*, or to the specific high school you indicated you graduated from (that is, the one you listed when you created your account). The site no longer offers the robust advanced search capabilities it offered in the past. Even though every member provides one, e-mail addresses cannot be used as search criteria.

Because people using **Classmates.com** generally <u>want</u> to be found (by their fellow classmates), they tend to use their real names. This, coupled with the availability of maiden names, makes the site popular with private investigators. Taking full advantage of this site requires a $39 annual fee (often discounted to a fraction of that amount).

Note that if you are logged into your own profile, the default privacy setting is to automatically leave information that you have viewed your subject's profile. To turn this off, click: (1) the gear icon in the upper right-hand corner, (2) *Account* from the drop-down menu, (3) *Privacy*, and (4) *Visit profiles anonymously* in the *Share my activity with others* section.

Microblogging Sites (e.g., Twitter)

"Microblogging" sites are a more recent development in the online social networking scene. As the name implies, microblogging sites consist of short posts—very short. **Twitter** (http://www.twitter.com), the most popular microblogging site, limits posts (known as "tweets") to just 140 characters. It has more than one billion registered users, although a little less than a third are active on a monthly basis. Microblogging sites are even easier to update than the "traditional" social networking sites already discussed. These posts often address the answer to the question "What's happening?" and can include detailed information about the individual poster's daily activities. Increasingly, users are posting links to, and commentary about, news stories and current events. Reviewing their posts, and other information in their profiles, can reveal important indicators of an individual's interests, points of view, or even political leanings. This information can be very useful to attorneys conducting juror research, for example.

For those not logged into an account, the link to **Twitter's** simple search form has been banished from the site's homepage. However, you can still conduct searches without being logged in, but you will need to use this direct URL: http://twitter.com/search-home. There, you can keyword search through the millions of individual tweets—from (roughly) the last two weeks. Once you identify your target's profile, you can see the entirety of their list of tweets back to their first tweet.

Note that the **Internet Archive's Wayback Machine** captures many individual **Twitter** profile pages. This archived version of your subject's tweets might contain deleted tweets that would not show on the "live" list you can view directly at **Twitter**. (See page 134 for more information on using the **Wayback Machine**.)

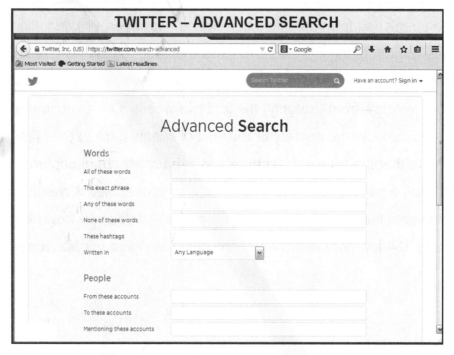

Those not logged into an account can also use **Twitter's** *Advanced Search* page to create more sophisticated, specific searches by using this direct URL: https://twitter.com/search-advanced.

The site's default Boolean connector for simple searches is *AND*, but the site also recognizes the *OR* connector, phrase limitations (by surrounding the phrase with quotation marks), and the ability to exclude a word or phrase by using the same syntax as when searching with **Google** (the minus sign). The *Advanced Search* page includes numerous Boolean search options, similar to **Google's** *Advanced Search* page, to locate tweets with *All of these words*, *Any of these words*, *None of these words*, and *This exact phrase*. You can "mix and match" the search options on the *Advanced Search* page to create more targeted searches.

One unique feature of **Twitter** search is that even as you're browsing through results, the site continues to run your search in the background. If new results are found that match your search criteria, **Twitter** notifies you with a pop-up box at the top of the results list indicating the number of new results found. Clicking the pop-up adds the new results to the top of the list.

Entering an individual's name into the search box on the simple search page or the *All of these words* box on the *Advanced Search* page will yield a set of *Top People* results. These results can include accounts that utilize a pseudonym but do not make direct reference to the owner's real name.

For example, entering *Michael Ausiello* into the search box on the simple search page yields two accounts for TV critic Michael Ausiello: his own **Twitter** account (with the user name *@MichaelAusiello*), as well as the official account for his website TVLine.com (with the user name *@TVLine*). Even though Ausiello's name is not mentioned in the description of the *@TVLine* **Twitter** account, it appears that he must have used it when creating the *@TVLine* account.

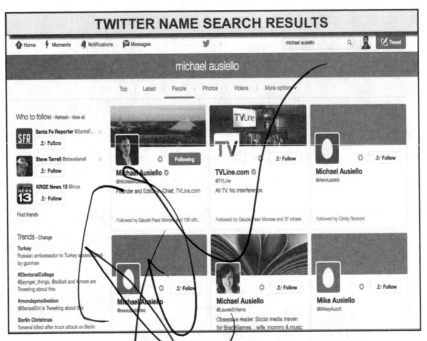

TWITTER NAME SEARCH RESULTS

Other results for our *Michael Ausiello* search include various inactive accounts and one (*@LaurenEHlems*) using "Michael Ausiello" as its Profile Name/Headline. As you sift through your results list, remember that many people may share the same name. So be sure to match other descriptive or identifying information about the person for whom you're searching with your search results (e.g., photo, their location).

Farther down the *Advanced Search* page, in the *People* section, you can use the following search options to locate tweets: *From these accounts*, *To these accounts*, or *Mentioning these accounts*. The *People* heading for this section can be a bit misleading because you cannot search by a person's real name. Instead, to get good results in the *People* section, you need to search using the "user name" that an individual tweets under. Many people use a pseudonym as their screen/user name for their **Twitter** accounts.

It is often easy to uncover the pseudonyms under which your targets tweet, by simply searching for your target by their real name in the *All of these words* or *This exact phrase* field boxes on the *Advanced Search* page because many will have used their real names to create their **Twitter** accounts. While these people were probably not trying to hide their true identities, it's not always this easy to uncover a pseudonym when someone is trying to hide their identity. Also, consider that a person may use the same screen name on multiple online services. Identifying a screen name at **Twitter** can be useful in tracking that person's activity across multiple sites (or vice versa—find their pseudonym at another online site they use and try using it at **Twitter**).

Some people might actively hide their identity by creating a **Twitter** account using a false name and e-mail address when they register and by using a pseudonym for their Profile Name/Headline and user name. If someone creates their **Twitter** account using a false name and also uses a pseudonym as their user name, it's probably impossible to identify this person's account without a court order to determine additional information about that user (e.g., connection location, IP address).

Twitter's *Advanced Search* page also includes a *Dates* section. The *Dates* search can be used in conjunction with other search criteria on the *Advanced Search* page to create more targeted searches. For example, you could search for tweets *From these accounts* (searching by user name), with *Any of these [key]words*, and limit the date range during which the tweets were posted. Our test searches have been able to retrieve tweets as far back as 2007 from a specific account that included a specific keyword using this method.

The *Advanced Search* page's *Places* search is not as useful as it first appears, because it only works for general locations—like a city or town. Precise addresses cannot be entered.

However, all tweets do contain geographic location data embedded in them. While this location information is not displayed for a tweet unless the user opts-in to do so, the information is still stored by **Twitter** as part of the tweet. It is possible to search for tweets using a more precise location if you use **Twitter's** secret geographic search instruction.

Performing Precise Geographic Searches Using Twitter's Simple Search Box

Twitter's secret geographic search instruction is *geocode:*. To create a search using it, you must enter this instruction into **Twitter's** simple search box followed by the latitude and longitude of the location you want to use as your center point, like this:

geocode:latitude,longitude

Luckily latitude and longitude coordinates are easier to find than you might think.

They can be located by doing a **Google Maps** (http://maps.google.com) search for the location you're interested in identifying.

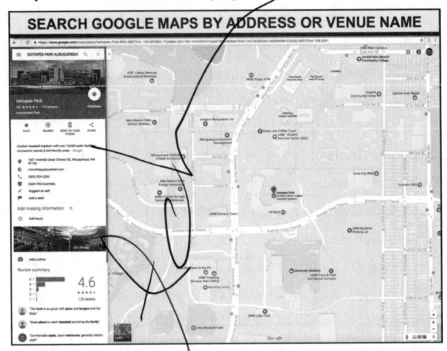

For example, we can enter *Isotopes Park Albuquerque, New Mexico* into the search box on **Google Maps'** homepage to retrieve a map showing the venue's location.

LATITUDE/LONGITUDE FROM GOOGLE MAPS SEARCH RESULTS

place/Isotopes+Park/@35.0697244,-106.631294,17z/data=!3m1!

You can copy the latitude and longitude coordinates for the venue embedded in the URL of the results page (*35.0697244,-106.631294*; shown in the previous illustration), to create a geographical search in the search box on **Twitter's** simple search page, like this.

geocode:35.0697244,-106.631294

The prior search will retrieve results only from that specific geographical location. You can expand the radius of the search by adding a proximity variable, like this;

geocode:35.0697244,-106.631294,1mi

This new search will return tweets sent within a one mile radius of the geographical point you defined in your search.

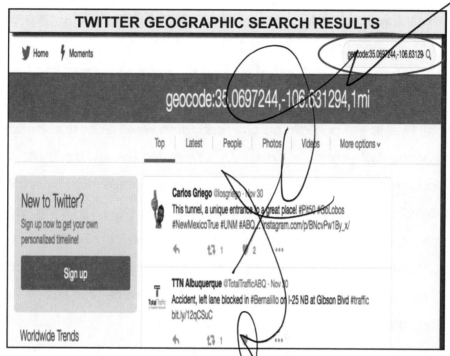

The default results list will display the *Top* tweets that match the location you've entered. You can also click to see the *Latest* tweets, as well as *Photos*, *Videos*, or *People* who also meet your location criteria.

You can further limit your search to a specific date range by including **Twitter's** date-limiting instruction, like this:

since:YYYY-MM-DD and *until:YYYY-MM-DD*

A combined location, radius, and date search would look like this:

geocode:35.0697244,-106.631294,1mi since:2017-02-01 until:2017-02-09

This new search will return tweets sent between February 1, 2017 and February 9, 2017, within a one-mile radius of the geographical point you defined in your search.

You could also add specific keywords to your search, like this one, which is looking for tweets within a one mile radius of Isotopes Park in Albuquerque, between February 1, 2017 and February 9, 2017, that include any (or all) of the keywords *auto*, *car*, *truck*, *accident*, or *crash:*

auto OR car OR truck OR accident OR crash geocode:35.0697244,-106.631294,1mi since:2017-02-01 until:2017-02-09

You could also search for tweets from a particular user at, or near, a specific location, but you must know their **Twitter** username. To retrieve all tweets sent by user *@MarkRosch* within a two-mile radius of Isotopes Park in Albuquerque, you would structure your search this way:

from:MarkRosch geocode:35.0697244,-106.631294,2mi

All **Twitter** search results lists are displayed in reverse chronological order. Almost all tweets are public. You can read them whether or not you are logged into a **Twitter** account of your own. When you're viewing tweets, it's important to remember that if you are logged into your own account, you should NOT click the follow button in your subject's profile (to automatically receive their tweets). Doing so will send them an e-mail informing them that you have followed them on **Twitter**.

Other popular microblogging sites like **Tumblr** (http://www.tumblr.com) and **Plurk** (http://www.plurk.com) do not have the search capabilities of **Twitter**, making them less useful for investigative research.

Like some of the other social networking sites discussed in this chapter, Twitter offers users the ability to download an archive of their account data. To request the archive, you can visit https://twitter.com/settings/account while logged into your account and click the *Request your archive* button near the bottom of the page. A link to download the archive once it's ready is sent to you via e-mail.

The **Twitter** user's archive includes a timeline of all of the tweets contained in the account. Clicking any month on the timeline (seen on the right-hand side in the previous illustration) displays a list of the tweets sent that month. The total number of tweets for the month is displayed at the top of the list.

The archive can be keyword searched using the search box in the upper right-hand corner. Unfortunately, there are no dates (or times) attributed to the tweets that appear in a search results list until you click the *View on Twitter* link that accompanies each result. The archive does not appear to include any tweets that might have been deleted by the user.

Social Networking Sites for Photos and Videos

Instagram (http://www.instagram.com)

Instagram (http://www.instagram.com) is a social networking site focused on sharing images and video. The site reportedly has more than 500 million users, sixty percent of whom are outside of the United States (Statistic Brain Research Institute, *Instagram Company Statistics*, September 1, 2016, *available at* http://linkon.in/2qqDiDZ). One of the primary attractions of the site has been the ability for users to apply digital filters to the images they share, making the images appear as if they were taken by a '70s-era Polaroid camera, sepia-toned, black and white, or otherwise stylized. Users can also record and share 15-second videos. Because **Instagram** started out as a mobile app, the website actually feels a bit like an afterthought—with not very much functionality.

Originally, **Instagram** had no built-in search capabilities. Third-party sites such as **GramFeed** (http://www.gramfeed.com; now **Picodash**, http://www.picodash.com), **Websta** (http://websta.me) (also formerly known as Webstagram.com), **Findgram** (http://www.find-gram.com), and **WorldCam** (http://worldc.am) were created to fill that gap. After adding more search capabilities to its own site, **Instagram** changed the terms of its developer agreement to no longer allow these types of third-party search services. All of these third-party sites then ceased being useful investigative tools.

While the site has added some more search capabilities over time, they are still not as robust as other social networking sites we've discussed. However, you must be logged into your own **Instagram** account to be able to search from their websites.

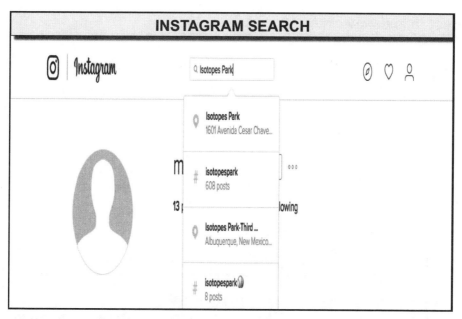

INSTAGRAM SEARCH

You can use the search box at the top of the **Instagram** site to search by keyword, username, hashtag, or place of interest. The previous illustration shows the searches suggested by **Instagram** when we entered *Isotopes Park* into the search box; they include two different physical location descriptions and two hashtags. (The two different location descriptions are caused by the existence of different *Check In* points in the **Instagram** system. In this case, one is the actual physical address of the stadium and the other appears to be a specific vendor located at the stadium. They each display different photo results.)

Displayed results are separated into two categories—*Top Posts* and *Most Recent*. There are no options to filter the results (e.g., by date, by user).

By default, all photos posted to **Instagram** are public. Users can also make their accounts private, so that only people who follow them on **Instagram** will be able to see their photos. If they have made their profiles private, their photos are not returned in search results.

Pinterest is a different kind of social network that provides users with virtual "boards" where they can "pin" images they create or find on the Internet. The boards are usually categorized into topical collections that the user can then share with other users.

Pinterest's value is more as a background research tool to learn about an individual's interests, hobbies, and so on. You do have to be logged into your own **Pinterest** account in order to search the site.

Once logged in, use the search box at the top of the page to search for individuals by name. The default set of results (*All Pins*) utilizes the OR Boolean connector and displays pins that include either the first or last name (or both) of the individual for whom you searched. Click the *Pinners* button above the search results (see previous illustration) to see user name matches for your search terms. Some users are easy to identify in the search results because they have included a photo of themselves in their profile—but not all users have done this.

Like any social networking site, some people use their real name and some use a pseudonym. If you have identified a profile at another social networking site where your target has used a pseudonym, use that pseudonym as a keyword to search **Pinterest** (or at any other social network you are searching for that person) as people often reuse the same pseudonym at multiple sites.

While the primary purpose of **Pinterest** is to collect and share images, users do have the ability to create "secret boards" that can only be seen by the creator and anyone they invite to view the board. Since pictures pinned to secret boards don't show up anywhere else on **Pinterest**, so be sure to ask at deposition or in interrogatories if your subject has any secret **Pinterest** boards.

YouTube (http://www.youtube.com)

YouTube is a free video-sharing website where anyone can create and upload their own videos to share with others or view the videos created and shared by others. From its launch in 2005, **YouTube** has grown into one of the most popular sites on the Web, with an estimated 1.3 billion users. **YouTube** visitors watch approximately 3.25 billion hours of video every month. (Statistic Brain Research Institute, *YouTube Company Statistics*, September 1, 2016, *available at* http://linkon.in/2kT5fEZ). Because the site is meant to publicly display and share video, you can search it without having an account of your own.

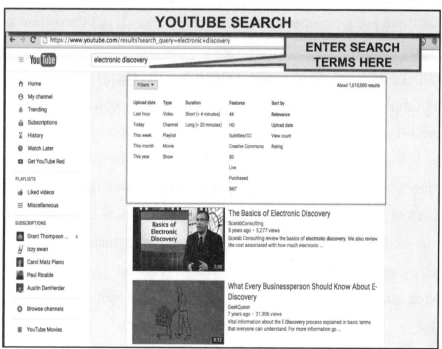

The search box at the top of the **YouTube** homepage allows you to search the site's billions of videos by keyword.

Google acquired **YouTube** in 2006. Just as with **Google**, there are a number of specific search operators and instructions you can use in the search box to narrow down your search results. For example, you can limit your search to:

- an exact phrase by enclosing your keywords in quotation marks (e.g., *"street racing"*),
- a specific time range by including the instructions *hour, today, month, week, year* along with your keywords.

To search for videos involving street racing that were posted within the last month, you would enter the search into the **YouTube** search box this way:

"street racing", month

(Note that you can't define a specific time frame like 2 months or 5 years.)

After you conduct a search, a *Filters* button also appears between the search box and your results list. Available filters include:

- Upload Date
- Type
- Duration
- Features
- Sort by

Note that there are no name or location-based search options offered in the filters.

You can, however, enter a target's name into the search box as a keyword (or phrase). In order to be displayed in search results, their name has to be included in the title or description of a video, or in the name of a **YouTube** channel. (Note that there can be some false positives for these types of searches, where videos are returned in the results even when the name you've searched does not appear in the title or description. This can occur when the name does appear in the title or description of an associated video (e.g., one that is next on a playlist or is recommended in the right-hand side bar). You can eliminate some of these false positives by instructing **YouTube** to limit your keyword to appearing only in the title of returned search results, by using the *allintitle* search instruction this way:

allintitle:"Mark Rosch"

You can also use the *allintitle* instruction with keywords and phrases that are not proper names, such as:

allintitle:"street racing"

The *allintitle* instruction must be all lowercase. There is no space between the colon and the keyword(s) that follow it.

You cannot search for a **YouTube** user by user name or the e-mail address the user used to create the account.

Stephen Nicholls, an independent Web developer, used tools available from **YouTube** to build the location-based **Geo Search Tool** (http://www.geosearchtool.com/). You can enter a street address, intersection, or city name to retrieve **YouTube** videos with location metadata that matches your search. You can use **Geo Search Tool's** *Time Frame* drop-down menu to limit your results to video posted from the *Past Hour* to the *Past Year*, or you can also set a *Custom Date Range.*

The site's *Advanced Search* options allow you to add keywords and/or a radius (from 1 km to 1,000 km) to your search.

HOW TO COLLECT AND ARCHIVE THE CONTENT OF SOCIAL NETWORKING PROFILES

There are several methods to locate, gather, and review the content of social networking profiles for potential evidentiary purposes or other useful information.

You can conduct targeted searches of the major social networking sites to locate any publicly available content posted by or about your research target. While this can be time consuming, it can also be a useful first step in preparing interrogatories, preservation letters, and/or production requests to gain access to the full content of the profile—even "private" posts or messages. Later in this chapter we will walk through steps you can take to locate that public material yourself.

Once the opposition receives your request or is compelled by the court to produce such information, some sites make it easier than others for the profile owner to download their account activity to turn over to you. Methods for users to download account data will be discussed in the site-specific sections later in this chapter.

There are a number of services that have been created for the sole purpose of crawling the publicly available portions of profiles and storing copies of them as they change over time. The advantage to using one of these services is that the collection and archiving of the information is done automatically, the archives are searchable, and the vendors (generally) provide some sort of verification and authentication of the captured information. This can all also be accomplished when doing the research and capturing the information yourself, it just takes time. Another advantage these services offer is the ability to manipulate the content as if it was live (e.g., expand comment threads, play videos, and enlarge photos). One drawback to collecting information yourself can be the inability to also collect metadata about the content (e.g., dates, times, GPS information, and computers from which content was posted) that can be equally important as the content itself. The third-party services generally capture this metadata.

There are other services that provide similar services. The following are some the best-known ones:

ArchiveSocial (http://www.archivesocial.com) captures content in its "native format" (e.g., images, videos) and offers the ability to "replay" the content you've captured as if you were viewing it the day it was captured. You can read and expand comment threads, play videos, enlarge photos, and so forth. **ArchiveSocial** also lets you export the archived content in its native format(s), PDF, or HTML. While the service is marketed primarily to the financial services industry and government agencies as a compliance tool, it can also be used for capturing content from opposing parties, and so forth. Prices start at $1,99 per month to capture up 1,000 posts, and other content, from up to 10 social networking accounts. Prices increase for higher volumes of captured information.

Nextpoint (http://www.nextpoint.com) captures available posts from the social networking accounts you target and stores them on **Nextpoint's** secure servers. Data are stored in their native format. This includes not only the posts, but also links to content on other sites (e.g., "videos, news or Facebook posts linked to from archived records") and files embedded in the posts (e.g., PDF, Word, Excel). The captured data are stored on Nextpoint's secure servers. Previously, posted prices began at $295 per month for unlimited captures and storage for a single case. The company now requires you to contact them for pricing. A free trial is available.

PageFreezer (http://www.pagefreezer.com) offers two separate solutions for capturing Web pages and available content of social networking accounts. The first solution is the company's managed account, which is designed to capture multiple-page websites or social media profiles and store them on **PageFreezer's** secure servers. The second solution, **Web Preserver**, is a plug-in for the Chrome Web browser designed specifically to capture single pages locally, on your own computer. (Multi-page captures may be available in future releases.) Both solutions capture content in their native format with date and time stamps for authentication. Captured pages and posts not only look the same as they did when they were captured, but you can also click through the links and be taken to captured versions of the content the link pointed to on the day the content and link was captured. Comment threads can also be expanded and contracted. Content captured with either solution can be keyword searched and exported as native files or PDFs. Pricing for capturing a single social media account is $475. **Web Preserver's** monthly fee includes a set number of captures. Additional captures and sharing features are available at additional cost.

The **X1 Social Discovery** product (http://linkon.in/2r7oPzJ) from search and e-discovery vendor X1 offers search, collection, and retrieval capabilities similar to **PageFreezer**, **Nextpoint**, and **ArchiveSocial**. Two big differences are that where the others are offered as SaaS (Software as a Service), **X1 Social Discovery** is only available as Windows-compatible software that you license for $1,995 per year (discounts are available for multi-year licenses); and where the others' searches are all initiated "in the cloud," **X1 Social Discovery** software must be installed on your local (Windows OS) computer.

Using social networking sites to conduct background and investigative research on opposing parties, counsel, expert witnesses, jurors, and others has the potential of ensnaring attorneys in ethical traps. Whether or not an attorney crosses an ethical line often depends on how access to the information in the profile being viewed was obtained.

There has been much discussion online among legal ethics experts, and at our live seminars, about what sorts of investigative activity is ethical for lawyers to engage in. Despite that more and more attorneys and judges are already mining the wealth of information contained in social networking profiles, more and more bar associations are weighing in on these questions. Next, we've provided a selected list (in approximate reverse chronological order) of some ethics opinions (available as of this writing) that deal directly with the issue of attorneys conducting background and investigative research using information readily available on the Internet—including social networking profiles. We have created a Web page at http://linkon.in/socialmediaresearchethicsopinions to keep the list up to date.

- New York State Bar Association Commercial and Federal Litigation Section Social Media Committee's Social Media Ethics Guidelines (2017) (http://www.nysba.org/socialmediaguidelines17)

- DC Bar Association Ethics Opinion 371 (2016) (http://linkon.in/2qOJl96)

- State Bar of California Formal Opinion No. 2015-193 (http://linkon.in/ca2015-193)

- Philadelphia Bar Association Ethics Opinion 2014-5 (http://linkon.in/phl2014-5)

- Pennsylvania Bar Association Formal Opinion 2014-300 (http://linkon.in/2sDdvsc)

- Massachusetts Bar Association Committee on Professional Ethics Opinion 2014 (http://linkon.in/maethicsop2014)

- American Bar Association Standing Committee on Ethics and Professional Responsibility Formal Opinion 466 (2014) (http://linkon.in/jurorsocmedresearch)

- Oregon State Bar Association Formal Opinion 2013-189 (http://linkon.in/1tvGHzl)

- New Hampshire Bar Association Ethics Committee Advisory Opinion #2012-13/05 (http://linkon.in/1opSdr5)

- Kentucky Bar Association Ethics Opinion KBA E-434 (2012) (http://linkon.in/2qLYROG)

- New York City Bar Association Formal Ethics Opinion 2012-2 (http://linkon.in/nycbarsocmedia)

- San Diego County Bar Association Ethics Opinion 2011-2 (http://linkon.in/xojvmY)

- New York County Lawyers Association Committee on Professional Ethics Formal Opinion 743 (2011) (http://linkon.in/1r1gsiU)

- New York City Bar Association Formal Ethics Opinion 2010-2 (http://linkon.in/rJcilT)

- New York State Bar Ethics Opinion #843 (2010) (http://linkon.in/nyethicop843)

- Missouri Bar Association Informal Opinion 2009-0003 (http://linkon.in/1qQWANH)

- Philadelphia Bar Association Ethics Opinion 2009-02 (http://linkon.in/uEPWox)

- Oregon State Bar Association Formal Opinion 2005-164 (http://linkon.in/1waZqwl)

It's important to note that the majority of these ethics opinions are specific to the jurisdictions from which they originate. Each of these opinions considers slightly different questions, but even when the issues are identical or very similar, not all of these bar associations are in agreement. The ABA and the New York State ethics opinions come the closest to sharing similar conclusions. Be sure to check the ethics opinions in any jurisdictions in which you are licensed to practice law. If your state does not have an ethics opinion on social media ethics, it might be a good idea to read some of the opinions from neighboring states just for guidance.

The following discussion covers a selection of opinions from the ABA and the most populous states.

While not a formal ethics opinion, this collection of social media "best practices" still touches on many of the potential ethical issues lawyers may face when using social networking sites personally or professionally for marketing or research.

The guidelines advise that it is appropriate for attorneys to view the publicly available websites or social networking profiles of represented and unrepresented individuals but caution that ethical issues could arise from those sites that alert users as to who has viewed their profile (in disagreement with San Diego—see page 412). They further advise that attorneys may not contact represented parties to access private portions of profiles but can request access to private portions of the profiles of unrepresented persons as long as the attorney uses no pretext in his or her contact with the person. Additionally, the guidelines remind attorneys that they cannot "order or direct an agent" to contact parties for access to their private profiles if the attorneys themselves are ethically precluded from doing so.

Guideline 5.A informs attorneys that:

> A lawyer may advise a client as to what content may be maintained or made nonpublic on her social media account, including advising on changing her privacy and/or security settings. A lawyer may also advise a client as to what content may be "taken down" or removed, whether posted by the client or someone else. However, the lawyer must be cognizant of preservation obligations applicable to the client and/or matter, such as a statute, rule, regulation, or common law duty relating to the preservation of information, including legal hold obligations. Unless an appropriate record of the social media content is preserved, a party or nonparty may not delete information from a social media account that is subject to a duty to preserve. [footnotes omitted]

Some lawyers interpret Guideline 5.A's language advising that, "A lawyer may also advise a client as to what content may be "taken down" or removed…" to contradict ABA Model Rule 3.4 (see page 417) regarding fairness and not "alter[ing], destroy[ing] or conceal[ing]" evidence.

Guideline 5.D addresses a circumstance that has been brought up in many of the conversations at our live seminars: Can a lawyer view the contents of a represented person's private profile if it was provided to them by someone who was already authorized to see it and did not gain access by pretext or just to turn the information over to the lawyer? While this Guideline indicates it is permissible, it also appears to limit the attorney to only viewing information provided by their client under these circumstances and not any other person (party or witness) when it advises:

> A lawyer may review a represented person's non-public social media information provided to the lawyer by her client, as long as the lawyer did not cause or assist the client to: (i) inappropriately obtain non-public information from the represented person; (ii) invite the represented person to take action without the advice of his or her lawyer; or (iii) otherwise overreach with respect to the represented person.

Guideline 6 is generally in agreement with the ethics opinions discussed here that lawyers may review the public portions of a juror's social networking profiles so long as the lawyer does not contact the juror. Similarly (in most jurisdictions' ethics rules), the lawyer is bound to report any juror misconduct detected in the social networking activity to the court as soon as it is discovered.

State Bar of California Standing Committee on Professional Responsibility and Conduct Formal Opinion No. 2015-193

Unlike the other opinions discussed in this section, the State Bar of California's Standing Committee on Professional Responsibility and Conduct's Formal Opinion No. 2015-193 (http://linkon.in/ca2015-193) does not directly comment on the ethics of using social networking sites to conduct background and investigative research. It does touch on some of the evidentiary issues potentially related to the discovery of such information. The opinion directly considered the question, "What are an attorney's ethical duties in the handling of discovery of electronically stored information?" While not addressing information from social networking sites directly, information from social networking sites does meet the legal definition of "electronically stored information" (ESI). (See 16 CFR § 2.7 (a)(1) *available at* http://linkon.in/1uWCi5h, for the definition of ESI.)

In the opinion, the Committee found that, aside from the duty to produce responsive information in discovery (whatever the format), lawyers have an "ethical duty of competence... [with regards to] new technologies...integrated with the practice of law." For litigators, the opinion continues that, "Attorney competence...generally requires, at a minimum, a basic understanding of, and facility with, issues relating to e-discovery, i.e., the discovery of electronically stored information ("ESI")."

The opinion further stressed that the lack of knowledge itself could be considered an ethical breach in cases requiring discovery of ESI, noting:

> An attorney lacking the required competence for the e-discovery issues in the case at issue has three options: (1) acquire sufficient learning and skill before performance is required; (2) associate with or consult technical consultants or competent counsel; or (3) decline the client representation. Lack of competence in e-discovery issues also may lead to an ethical violation of attorney's duty of confidentiality."

Pennsylvania Bar Association Formal Opinion 2014-300

In Formal Opinion 2014-300 (http://linkon.in/PA2014-300), the Pennsylvania Bar casts one of the widest nets to identify and address the most prevalent issues related to lawyers' use of social networking sites professionally (with the stated, purposeful exclusion of advertising and marketing issues). The Opinion sums up its findings itself on page 2:

> This Committee concludes that:
>
> 1. Attorneys may advise clients about the content of their social networking websites, including the removal or addition of information.
> 2. Attorneys may connect with clients and former clients.
> 3. Attorneys may not contact a represented person through social networking websites.
> 4. Although attorneys may contact an unrepresented person through social networking websites, they may not use a pre-textual basis for viewing otherwise private information on social networking websites.
> 5. Attorneys may use information on social networking websites in a dispute.
> 6. Attorneys may accept client reviews but must monitor those reviews for accuracy.
> 7. Attorneys may generally comment or respond to reviews or endorsements, and may solicit such endorsements.
> 8. Attorneys may generally endorse other attorneys on social networking websites.
> 9. Attorneys may review a juror's Internet presence.
> 10. Attorneys may connect with judges on social networking websites provided the purpose is not to influence the judge in carrying out his or her official duties.

In Formal Opinion 466 (http://linkon.in/jurorsocmedresearch), decided in 2014, the American Bar Association Standing Committee on Ethics and Professional Responsibility considered the question of "whether a lawyer who represents a client in a matter that will be tried to a jury may review the jurors' or potential jurors' presence on the Internet leading up to and during the trial," as well as the question of, "what ethical obligations the lawyer might have regarding information discovered during the review."

This opinion is different from the other opinions cited in this section because it deals with the review of Internet postings made by jurors (or potential jurors), whereas the other opinions deal with the review of Internet postings by non-parties (either represented or unrepresented) or un-represented witnesses.

This opinion rightly applies existing research and communication standards to "electronic social media" or "ESM"—essentially treating it no differently than the types of information that have previously been available. The opinion found that:

- Unless limited by law or court order, a lawyer may review a juror's or potential juror's Internet presence, which may include postings by the juror or potential juror in advance of and during a trial, but a lawyer may not communicate directly or through another with a juror or potential juror.

- A lawyer may not, either personally or through another, send an access request to a juror's electronic social media. An access request is a communication to a juror asking the juror for information that the juror has not made public and that would be the type of *ex parte* communication prohibited by Model Rule 3.5(b).

- The fact that a juror or a potential juror may become aware that a lawyer is reviewing his Internet presence when a network setting notifies the juror of such does not constitute a communication from the lawyer in violation of Rule 3.5(b). [Authors' note: This is most likely to happen when viewing a juror's **LinkedIn** profile, as it is the only major social or professional networking site that actively informs users about visitors to their profiles. As noted earlier, this notification can be turned off.]

- In the course of reviewing a juror's or potential juror's Internet presence, if a lawyer discovers evidence of juror or potential juror misconduct that is criminal or fraudulent, the lawyer must take reasonable remedial measures including, if necessary, disclosure to the tribunal.

For many, the opinion's finding that (unless otherwise prohibited) an attorney may view the publicly available portions of the juror's Web presence is a "no brainer." The opinion's admonition that "a lawyer may not communicate directly or through another with a juror or potential juror" is analogous to the "real life" restriction that lawyers have against communicating with jurors outside of the courtroom and is in line with other opinions that have tackled similar questions. Similarly, the opinion's instruction that, "if a lawyer discovers evidence of juror or potential juror misconduct that is criminal or fraudulent, the lawyer must take reasonable remedial measures including, if necessary, disclosure to the tribunal," is analogous to the lawyer's responsibility to report such relevant information they learn from "real world" sources.

One place where the ABA's opinion diverges from other similar opinions is in instances where the juror might be advised by the social media site that a particular individual (in this case the lawyer or their agent) had viewed the juror's online information. The ABA found that in situations where the juror was thus-notified, "The lawyer is not communicating with the juror; the ESM service is communicating with the juror based on a technical feature of the ESM. This is akin to a neighbor's recognizing a lawyer's car driving down the juror's street and telling the juror that the lawyer had been seen driving down the street."

Previous opinions had taken a decidedly different approach to these types of notifications. For instance, the 2012 New York City Bar Association opinion (http://linkon.in/nycbarsocmedia) found that this type of notification from the ESM would "constitute a prohibited communication if the attorney was aware that her actions" would generate such a notice. The opinion offered, "no position on whether such an inadvertent communication would in fact be a violation of the Rules."

New York County Lawyers Association Formal Opinion 743 (2011) (see page 412) took a similar position as the New York City Bar Association's 2012 opinion, stating: "If a juror becomes aware of an attorney's efforts to see the juror's profiles on websites, the contact may well consist of an impermissible communication, as it might tend to influence the juror's conduct with respect to the trial."

San Diego County Bar Association Ethics Opinion 2011-2

In this opinion, the San Diego County Bar's Legal Ethics Committee (http://linkon.in/xojvmY) considered the question of whether an attorney can send a "friend" request to a represented party using the attorney's real name. "Attorney is concerned that those employees, out of concern for their jobs, may not be as forthcoming with their opinions in depositions and intends to use any relevant information he obtains from these [private] social media sites to advance the interests of Client in the litigation." The committee concluded that, "The rules of ethics impose limits on how attorneys may obtain information that is not publicly available, particularly from opposing parties who are represented by counsel." They continued:

> Social media sites have opened a broad highway on which users may post their most private personal information. But Facebook, at least, enables its users to place limits on who may see that information. The rules of ethics impose limits on how attorneys may obtain information that is not publicly available, particularly from opposing parties who are represented by counsel.

> We have concluded that those [California ethics] rules bar an attorney from making an *ex parte* friend request of a represented party. An attorney's *ex parte* communication to a represented party intended to elicit information about the subject matter of the representation is impermissible no matter what words are used in the communication and no matter how that communication is transmitted to the represented party. We have further concluded that the attorney's duty not to deceive prohibits him from making a friend request even of unrepresented witnesses without disclosing the purpose of the request. Represented parties shouldn't have "friends" like that and no one—represented or not, party or non-party—should be misled into accepting such a friendship. In our view, this strikes the right balance between allowing unfettered access to what is public on the Internet about parties without intruding on the attorney-client relationship of opposing parties and surreptitiously circumventing the privacy even of those who are unrepresented.

New York County Lawyers Association Committee on Professional Ethics Formal Opinion 743 (2011)

In this opinion, the New York County Lawyers Association Committee on Professional Ethics (http://linkon.in/1r1gsiU) directly considered the question, "After *voir dire* is completed and the trial commences, may a lawyer routinely conduct ongoing research on a juror on Twitter, Facebook and other social networking sites?"

In doing so, the Committee synthesizes elements of a number of other opinions summarized in this section into its own (broader) opinion.

They found that it would be proper for attorneys to conduct such juror research both during *voir dire* and trial as long as the attorney does not make contact with the juror, stating:

> It is proper and ethical under RPC 3.5 for a lawyer to undertake a pretrial search of a prospective juror's social networking site, provided that there is no contact or communication with the prospective juror and the lawyer does not seek to "friend" jurors, subscribe to their Twitter accounts, send jurors tweets or otherwise contact them. During the evidentiary or deliberation phases of a trial, a lawyer may visit the publicly available Twitter, Facebook or other social networking site of a juror but must not "friend" the juror, email, send tweets to the juror or otherwise communicate in any way with the juror or act in any way by which the juror becomes aware of the monitoring. Moreover, the lawyer may not make any misrepresentations or engage in deceit, directly or indirectly, in reviewing juror social networking sites.

The opinion goes on to clarify that if the attorney becomes aware of juror misconduct while conducting such searches, the attorney is bound by the same duty to notify the court as if the notice of misconduct was learned in a more traditional manner, stating:

> In the event the lawyer learns of juror misconduct, including deliberations that violate the court's instructions, the lawyer may not unilaterally act upon such knowledge to benefit the lawyer's client, but must promptly comply with RPC 3.5(d) and bring such misconduct to the attention of the court, before engaging in any further significant activity in the case.

Interestingly, the opinion differentiates this duty from lawyers' obligations related to information they might learn about adverse parties while conducting similar research, stating:

> Lawyers who learn of impeachment or other useful material about an adverse party, assuming that they otherwise conform with the rules of the court, have no obligation to come forward affirmatively to inform the court of their findings. Such lawyers, absent other obligations under court rules or the RPC, may sit back confidently, waiting to spring their trap at trial. [footnote omitted]

In this opinion, the New York City Bar's Committee on Professional Ethics (http://linkon.in/rJcilT) considered the question of whether an attorney, or her agent, could send a "friend request" to obtain information from an unrepresented person's social networking profile without also disclosing the reasons for making the request. The attorney, or her agent, would use her real name and profile to send such a request. The committee concluded that there would be no violation of the rules of professional conduct. However, the committee noted that, "[a] lawyer may not attempt to gain access to a social networking website under false pretenses, either directly or through an agent." The committee said:

> Rather than engage in "trickery," lawyers can—and should—seek information maintained on social networking sites, such as Facebook, by availing themselves of informal discovery, such as the truthful "friending" of unrepresented parties, or by using formal discovery devices such as subpoenas directed to non-parties in possession of information maintained on an individual's social networking page. Given the availability of these legitimate discovery methods, there is and can be no justification for permitting the use of deception to obtain the information from a witness on-line. [footnote omitted]

> Accordingly, a lawyer may not use deception to access information from a social networking webpage. Rather, a lawyer should rely on the informal and formal discovery procedures sanctioned by the ethical rules and case law to obtain relevant evidence.

In this opinion, the New York State Bar Association Committee on Professional Ethics (http://linkon.in/nyethicop843) considered the question of whether it was ethical for a lawyer to access the public social networking profiles of parties to a case in order to review the information they might contain. There, the committee said, "A lawyer representing a client in pending litigation may access the **public pages of another party's** [emphasis added] social networking website (such as Facebook or MySpace) for the purpose of obtaining possible impeachment material for use in the litigation." Further, the committee explained:

> New York's Rule 8.4 would not be implicated because the lawyer is not engaging in deception by accessing a public website that is available to anyone in the network, provided that the lawyer does not employ deception in any other way (including, for example, employing deception to become a member of the network). Obtaining information about a party available in the Facebook or MySpace profile is similar to obtaining information that is available in publicly accessible online or print media, or through a subscription research service such as Nexis or Factiva, and that is plainly permitted.[footnote omitted] Accordingly, we conclude that the lawyer may ethically view and access the Facebook and MySpace profiles of a party other than the lawyer's client in litigation as long as the party's profile is available to all members in the network and the lawyer neither "friends" the other party nor directs someone else to do so.

In this opinion, the Philadelphia Bar Association Professional Guidance Committee (http://linkon.in/uEPWox) considered the question of whether or not it is ethical for an attorney to ask a non-lawyer assistant to "friend" an unrepresented witness on a social networking site in order to gain access to the witness's "private" profile in order to gain access to information in the profile. In this scenario, the non-lawyer would use her real name but without disclosing the reasons for making the request.

The opinion concluded that this conduct would violate several rules of professional conduct:

- First, the "proposed course of conduct contemplated by the inquirer [the lawyer] would violate Rule 8.4(c) because the planned communication by the third party [the assistant] with the witness is deceptive. It omits a highly material fact, namely, that the third party who asks to be allowed access to the witness's pages is doing so only because he or she is intent on obtaining information and sharing it with a lawyer for use in a lawsuit to impeach the testimony of the witness."

- Second, even though the attorney is not making the actual "friend" request, because of Rule 5.3 (Responsibilities Regarding Nonlawyer Assistants), the attorney is in violation of Rule 8.4(c) because he is responsible for the "violative conduct" of the person he supervises.

- Third, the proposed conduct violates Rule 4.1 because it "constitutes the making of a false statement of material fact to the witness."

- Fourth, because "the violative conduct would be done through the acts of another third party, this would also be a violation of Rule 8.4a."

Some of the liveliest discussions we have during our live social networking research MCLE presentations revolve around how lawyers can or should advise clients about the content of their social networking profiles.

Some lawyers argue that it would be appropriate to advise a client to remove or delete content from the client's profile, as long as the client maintained a copy of the deleted content (either in print or electronically, offline). Those same lawyers generally argue that it would be appropriate to advise a client to "deactivate" (or some argue even delete) an account, as long as the client kept some sort of copy of the content. These lawyers argue that as long as the content has been preserved (even if not in its original format) and can still be produced to the opposition or court if requested, that no spoliation has occurred. Their rationale for deleting the account (or certain information from an account) or deactivating an account is to not make its existence obvious (or easy to find using the search methods previously discussed in this chapter). If the content of the profile were subsequently subject to a preservation of evidence letter or other discovery request, these lawyers have indicated they would certainly turn it over as required by the rules.

There are others, however, who argue that the deactivating or deleting an account or deleting of content, even if a copy is maintained, would constitute spoliation of evidence based on ABA Model Rule of Professional Conduct 3.4: Fairness to Opposing Party & Counsel (http://linkon.in/1CwcSQO), and corresponding state rules. Rule 3.4(a-b) states:

> A lawyer shall not:
>
> (a) unlawfully obstruct another party's access to evidence or unlawfully alter, destroy or conceal a document or other material having potential evidentiary value. A lawyer shall not counsel or assist another person to do any such act;
>
> (b) falsify evidence, counsel or assist a witness to testify falsely, or offer an inducement to a witness that is prohibited by law;

However, the New York State Bar Association Commercial and Federal Litigation Section Social Media Committee's Social Media Ethics Guidelines (see page 407) advises in its Guideline 5.A that it is permissible to counsel a client to "take down" or "remove" information so long as no laws or rules are broken and the material is preserved in some other format:

> A lawyer may advise a client as to what content may be maintained or made nonpublic on her social media account, including advising on changing her privacy and/or security settings. A lawyer may also advise a client as to what content may be "taken down" or removed, whether posted by the client or someone else. However, the lawyer must be cognizant of preservation obligations applicable to the client and/or matter, such as a statute, rule, regulation, or common law duty relating to the preservation of information, including legal hold obligations. Unless an appropriate record of the social media content is preserved, a party or nonparty may not delete information from a social media account that is subject to a duty to preserve. [footnotes omitted]

One of the most widely referenced deactivation/spoliation cases is *Lester v. Allied Concrete*, where the plaintiff's attorney, Matthew B. Murray, advised his client to "clean up" his **Facebook** account (after the lawyer had found some potentially damaging evidence), at which point the client deactivated his account. *Lester v. Allied Concrete*, Case numbers CL08-150 and CL09-223 (Virginia Circuit Court of the City of Charlottesville), *available at* http://linkon.in/Zi7CCn. As discussed on page 355 attorney Murray allowed his client to testify that that he did not have a **Facebook** account—which the defendant's attorney knew to be false because the defendant's attorney had already found the account and printed off the potentially damaging evidence.

Generally, in these discussions, there is agreement that it is appropriate for a lawyer to advise a client to stop posting information to his or her profiles from that point forward, or to at least refrain from posting any information about the matter in which the attorney is representing the client. There is also usually agreement that it would be appropriate for the lawyer to advise the client to tell the client's friends not to post anything about the client (or the matter).

The Difference Between "Deactivating" and "Deleting" a Facebook Account

Facebook offers users multiple ways to hide their accounts from people who might be searching for their profiles. In addition to using the privacy settings (mentioned on page 356), **Facebook** users can also *deactivate* or *delete* their account. While the two terms sound synonymous, they are not. Deactivating an account is temporary, where deleting an account is permanent. In its *Help* pages (http://linkon.in/2pI1AMG), **Facebook** explains it this way:

If you deactivate your account:

- You can reactivate whenever you want.
- People can't see your Timeline or search for you.
- Some info may remain visible (ex: messages you sent).

If you delete your account:

- You can't regain access once it's deleted.
- We delay deletion a few days after it's requested. A deletion request is cancelled if you log back into your Facebook account during this time.
- It may take up to 90 days to delete data stored in backup systems. Your info isn't accessible on Facebook during this time.
- Some things aren't stored in your account. For example, a friend may have messages from you after deletion.
- Copies of some material (ex: log records) may remain in our database but are disassociated from personal identifiers.

Because deactivated accounts can be reactivated, **Facebook** retains account data (e.g., friends, interests), in case you choose to reactivate.

Chapter Twenty-One

LOCATING IMAGES OF PEOPLE, CONCEPTS, PRODUCTS, OR PLACES

Locating Images by Using Keywords

To find images of people, enter their name into a general search engine that includes an image database, such as **Yahoo! Images** (http://images.search.yahoo.com), **Bing Images** (http://www.bing.com/images), or **Google Images** (http://images.google.com). Image searches also work for places, concepts, or products if you enter descriptive keywords into the image search box. (See pages 103—106 for details about searching **Google Images**, which is our favorite.)

In addition to using general search engines to find images, you can also search sites that specialize only in returning image results, such as **PicSearch** (http://www.picsearch.com).

PicSearch claims to search over 3 billion images. In a test search using Carole Levitt's name through **PicSearch's** search engine, the number of results were paltry and only one was of our subject.

On the other hand, **Google Images** had many more results and they were more relevant. In addition to images of Carole, **Google Images** also included images of books and articles she wrote, images of her colleagues, and even images of

PowerPoint slides from some of her presentations. So, not only does **Google Images** show you what Carole looks like, it practically creates a dossier of Carole, using images instead of text.

After you receive your results from **PicSearch**, you are offered an *Advanced Search* (look very closely; it's almost hidden along the left side of the results list) to filter results by *color*, *size*, *orientation,* and *type*. **Google Images** offers more filtering options.

Other places to find pictures of people are at their own websites, blogs, and social networking profiles (e.g., **LinkedIn** or **Facebook**).

For videos of people (and places, things, or products), you might try searching at **Youtube.com** (https://www.youtube.com). (See *Chapter Twenty* to learn more about searching these sites.)

Locating Images by Searching by Image (Reverse Image Searching)

If you need to find where an image is posted to the Web, for evidentiary purposes, reverse image searching is useful. For example, a trademark attorney could search with their client's marks to see if they are being used without a license. A family law attorney could search with the opposing spouse's photo to see where the opposing spouse has posted his or her image. This is useful if the spouse has posted a profile and image at a social networking or dating site but used a pseudonym. Searching by name would not have uncovered the profile.

Our favorite site for conducting reverse image searches is **Google Image Search** (http://images.google.com) as discussed on page 106.

TinEye.com (http://www.tineye.com) is a dedicated reverse image search engine that functions very similarly to **Google's** *Search by image.* While it claims to search over 19 billion images to find matches, it found far fewer images than **Google's** *Search by image* did in our test searches. However, at over 19 billion images and growing, we expect this to become a more useful resource over time.

Chapter Twenty-Two

FINDING MILITARY PERSONNEL

If you have tried unsuccessfully to sue or subpoena someone, it is possible that person may be in the military and, thus, legitimately unavailable.

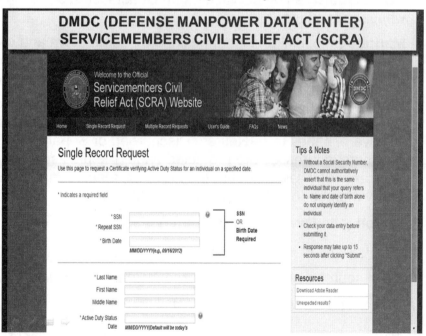

To verify if someone is currently in the military (Army, Navy, Marine Corps, Air Force, NOAA, Public Health, and Coast Guard), you may access the **DMDC (Defense Manpower Data Center) Servicemembers Civil Relief Act** (**SCRA**) website for free and receive instant results (in the form of a downloadable PDF). Previously, it was necessary to write or call to establish an account before searching this database. To verify a single record, see https://scra.dmdc.osd.mil/single_record.xhtml. To verify multiple records you will need to set up a free account (https://scra.dmdc.osd.mil/appj/scra/multiple_record.xhtml). You must search with a minimum of a *Last Name* and either a *SSN* (Social Security Number) or a *Birth Year*, *Month*, and *Day*. (See page 286 for information on locating dates of birth.) Results indicate whether the individual is or is not currently on active duty and or whether the service member (or his/her unit) has received notification of future orders to report for Active Duty. Presumably out of privacy and military tactical concerns, there is no specific information regarding duty station. Some service branches also maintain a personnel locator service that can help track down the location of active duty personnel, but you typically must write or phone for information:

- **Air Force** (http://linkon.in/airforcemail)
- **Army:** As of this writing, the Army's personnel locator webpage is offline.
- **Coast Guard**: As of this writing, the Coast Guard's personnel locator webpage is offline.
- **Marines** (http://linkon.in/marineslocate): scroll down and click the *Personnel Locator* link for instructions on how to request information by phone and mail.
- **Navy** (http://linkon.in/navymail): The **Navy World Wide Locator** helps locate individuals who are either in the Navy (Active Duty and Reserve) or who were in the Navy (Retired, Discharged or Separated). Service members' addresses are protected under the provisions of the Privacy Act and cannot be released, but the Navy will forward mail for $3.50 (no fee for family member or official Government business).

GI Search (http://www.gisearch.com) is a social networking site of 140,000 people who wish to get in touch with others with whom they served in the armed forces. You can search using a *firstname* and *lastname*, *Nickname*, or *Military Status/Affiliation*. You can search with a partial first or last name. Registration is free but not required to search. A military background is not needed to become a member.

Chapter Twenty-Three

VERIFYING OCCUPATIONAL LICENSES OF TRADESPEOPLE AND PROFESSIONALS

In *Chapter Nineteen*, we discussed the importance of, and resources for, researching the licenses of expert witnesses—either your own or the opposition's. And in *Chapter Twenty-Four,* we discuss resources for researching judges' and attorneys' licenses. Just like lawyers, other licensed professionals work hard to achieve the level of education and expertise required to obtain their license and they expend great effort to maintain it. There are, however, some who will claim to hold licenses they have not earned—or that have been taken away from them via disciplinary action. Shockingly, there are others who will claim to be licensed even when they have not put in the effort or met the requirements to be licensed. Thus, it is also important to conduct due diligence research to confirm the licensing of individuals who your clients might be involved with (e.g., potential business partners) or you might even need to verify a current or potential client's license. Finding someone's license can be useful for a variety of other reasons. For example, if a person is evading service of process at their home address, you can try serving them at the address on their license, which is often their work address. Also, if you need to identify someone's employer to garnish wages, their license address could be a good clue.

Finding the right agency or organization to check on someone's license can be daunting because there are so many types of licensing entities. For example, many professionals and trades people, from architects and accountants to plumbers and barbers, are typically licensed by state agencies, while others are licensed by their professional association, and still others, such as stockbrokers and various financial professionals, are licensed by an independent, not-for-profit organization authorized by Congress to protect America's investors—**FINRA** (Financial Industry Regulatory Authority). To make matters more confusing, despite there being national educational standards for many professionals, such as medical doctors, they are still licensed at the state level and not a national level. Luckily, there are several free resources online that have compiled categorized collections of links to licensing databases that we can rely on as jumping-off points.

Directories for Locating Licensing Bodies

Portico has a free *Occupations* page (http://linkon.in/1BJBvMZ) that links to various licensing boards throughout the country. Occupations range from *Artist/Architect* to *Medical Professions* and *Lawyers/Judges*. The collection is probably weakest in the law-related categories. It no longer includes direct links to bar association pages.

Internet For Lawyers (http://linkon.in/pLUdvT) provides links that point directly to the searchable member databases of forty-five state bar associations and the District of Columbia's member database. The site also includes information on getting information from the bar associations in those five remaining states that do not offer online searchable databases. See *Chapter Twenty-Four* for more information on locating attorney licensing and background information.

BRB Publications (http://linkon.in/1uCoiBb) has an extensive collection of free links to *State Occupational Licensing Boards*, browseable by state.

Search Systems (http://www.searchsystems.net) also links to occupational licensing boards. Choose a state and scroll through the alphabetical list of agencies and information sources. You can also choose *Licenses* from the *Type of Record* drop-down menu to retrieve a list of state links (the District of Columbia and Puerto Rico,). Click any state to see the full list of licensing resources in that state compiled in the **Search Systems** collection.

To verify medical licenses (and in some states, doctors' discipline records), use the links found at the **Federation of State Medical Boards'** website (http://linkon.in/1rB6LH6), an organization of seventy-one medical licensing authorities in fifty states, the District of Columbia, Guam, Puerto Rico, the Northern Mariana Islands, and the U.S. Virgin Islands.

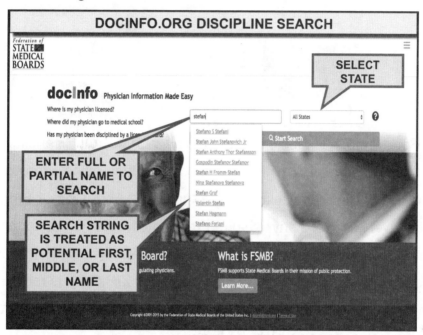

The Federation also operates **DocInfo.org** (http://www.docinfo.org), which provides disciplinary sanction information about "medical doctors, osteopathic physicians and the majority of physician assistants licensed in the United States." Searches can include as little as a partial first or last name (it treats the text you enter as either). The default is *All States*.

When a search result includes disciplinary action for the doctor, the results page will note *Actions Found In [state]* and include a link to that state's licensing entity, but not to the disciplinary action. To narrow your results, can also select a *State* from the drop-down menu.

Another good source of information about medical professionals can be their associations' websites, from the general **American Medical Association** (**AMA**) site to specialty medical association sites. Some include disciplinary, contact, or biographical information, in addition to licensing information.

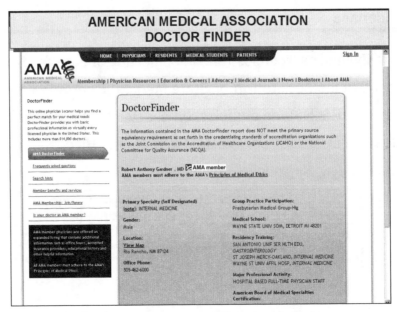

For example, to locate information beyond doctors' licensing status, such as where they graduated from medical school, and their office addresses, visit the **AMA's Doctor Finder** site (http://linkon.in/2uoXgnj). The **AMA Doctor Finder** site searches "virtually" every licensed physician (more than 814,000) or doctor of osteopathy in the U.S. and its possessions, by either *Name* or *Specialty* (whether or not they are a member of the **AMA**). Note that either a *State* or *ZIP Code* is required to conduct a search, so you would have to conduct separate searches in each state in which you believe your target doctor might be licensed.

Results for non-member doctors now include significantly less information than for members (or than those same non-member doctor records contained in the past results). Note that even though the location listed for a result is only the city, state, and ZIP Code where the doctor is located, clicking the *View Map* link (when available) will display a map with the office (or sometimes home) address and a pin indicating the location. Unfortunately, results for the doctors that are displayed do not include any notation about disciplinary action against those doctors.

For other health-related professions, look for licensing boards in the individual states or professional membership organizations, such as the:

- American Chiropractic Association at http://www.acatoday.org (Click the *Find a Doctor* button in the top navigation menu bar.)

- American Dental Association at http://www.ada.org (To search for a dentist by name, visit http://findadentist.ada.org).

The **Financial industry Regulatory Authority (FINRA;** http://www.finra.org; formerly National Association of Securities Dealers, NASD), the licensing and regulatory agency for more than 3,800 securities firms and over 632,000 brokers, is an independent, non-profit organization authorized by Congress—but it is not a government agency. Its primary mechanisms for carrying out its mandate "to protect America's investors by making sure the securities industry operates fairly and honestly" are:

- writing and enforcing rules governing securities firms and brokers;
- examining firms for compliance with those rules;
- fostering market transparency; and
- educating investors.

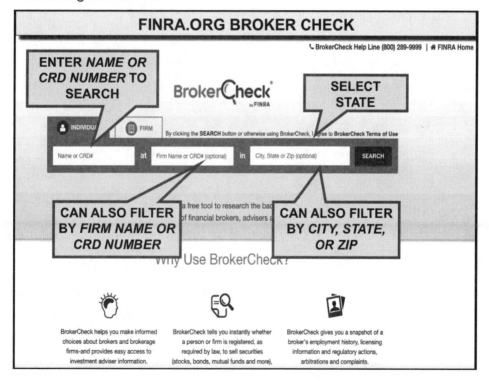

Unlike many regulatory agencies, **FINRA** has placed their license and discipline search prominently on the homepage of their website (see previous illustration). The organization's *BrokerCheck* can be searched by broker's name or CRD number (Central Registration Depository), or firm name. The *BrokerCheck* results for individuals can include:

- employment history
- professional qualifications
- disciplinary actions
- criminal convictions
- civil judgments
- arbitration awards

The *BrokerCheck* results for firms can include:

- information on a firm's profile
- history
- operations
- disciplinary actions
- criminal convictions
- civil judgments
- arbitration awards

Some results for firms might only include a summary of information or disciplinary actions and a link to a *Detailed Report* for additional information.

FINRA is not the only regulatory body for the securities industry, however. Each state, the District of Columbia, Puerto Rico, and the U.S. Virgin Islands have local regulatory agencies. The **North American Securities Administrators Association** (**NASAA**; http://linkon.in/ZqFw7Q) has compiled a list of all of these local regulatory agencies, along with links to the website of each jurisdiction's agency. As the name suggests, **NASAA** members also include the Canadian provinces and territories, as well as Mexico. Links to those jurisdictions' agencies can also be found on this website.

The **Securities and Exchange Commission (SEC)** maintains the **Investment Adviser Public Disclosure (IAPD)** database (http://linkon.in/1CG5KkX) that provides access to the "registration or reporting form ("Form ADV") that the adviser filed." It includes current and certain former Investment Adviser Representatives, Investment Adviser firms registered with the SEC and/or state securities regulators, and Exempt Reporting Advisers that file reports with the SEC and/or state securities regulators. The database is searchable by *Individual Name/CRD#* or *Firm Name or CRD/SEC#*. If you're searching for an individual with a common name, the search can be narrowed down with the addition of a *Firm Name or* geographically by *ZIP Code* and a radial distance from that ZIP Code, ranging from 5 to 25 miles.

Summary Results for individuals can include:

- *Current Employers*
- *Qualifications*
- *Registration History*
- *Disclosure Information*

Disappointingly, the results do not include links to any of the *Regulatory Events* or *Customer Disputes* listed in the *Disclosure Information* section. The best way to locate this more specific information is to run a **Google** search for the name of the adviser and the additional keywords *SEC*, *adviser*, and *sanction*.

Search results for firms include SEC registration status and a link to its current *Form ADV – Uniform Application for Investment Adviser Registration*.

National Futures Association (NFA; http://www.nfa.futures.org/) is another self-regulatory organization covering the "U.S. derivatives industry," including on-exchange traded futures, retail off-exchange foreign currency (forex) and OTC derivatives (swaps). Like **FINRA**, the **NFA** "has developed and enforced rules, provided programs and offered services that safeguard market integrity, protect investors and help [their] Members meet their regulatory responsibilities." Also like **FINRA**, **NFA** has a prominent link on the upper right-hand corner of its homepage to its member search—although you wouldn't know it immediately. Click the *Visit BASIC* button in the upper right-hand corner of the homepage to search by trader or firm name, *NFA ID Number,* or *Pool Name.* (Note that *BASIC* does not describe the depth of returned results, it is an acronym standing for Background Affiliation Status Information Center.)

NFA searches can include:

- *Current Status (includes links to Case Summary similar to a docket and a Narrative Summary with more background and detail)*
- *Regulatory Actions*
- *NFA Arbitration Decisions*
- *CFTC Reparations Cases*
- *Doing Business as*
- *Listed Principals*
- *History*

It should be noted, however, that the *Regulatory Actions* section of these search results apparently do not include **FINRA** or **SEC** actions against the individual searched.

Chapter Twenty-Four

LOCATING AND BACKGROUNDING ATTORNEYS, JUDGES, AND OTHER LEGAL PROFESSIONALS

Contact Information, Biographies, and Directories

There are all kinds of sources to learn about (or locate) attorneys, judges, and other legal professionals, from law journals, legal and general newspapers, commercial directories, court directories, and rating services, to blogs/blawgs and tweets.

But, before using any of those resources, if you are researching an opposing attorney, a potential hire, or even one you are making a referral to, it's always a good idea to first check the status of the attorney's law license and whether any disciplinary action has been taken against that attorney.

For information about attorneys' license status, disciplinary action taken against them, and their contact data, check the appropriate licensing entity in that jurisdiction. While that is often the state bar association, remember that not all bar associations are unified (i.e., mandatory). If the state bar association is unified, then you will most likely find much of this information at the state bar association website. If the state bar association is not unified, but is a voluntary association, then you will need to research a lawyer's law license, contact information, and disciplinary action at the state's attorney licensing entity, which is often a division of the state supreme court or an independent governmental agency or quasi-governmental agency. To learn if a state bar is unified or voluntary, use the bar association list compiled at http://linkon.in/XSolFd. From this list, you can also link to the bar associations' websites.

To make locating the licensing entities easier to locate, we have created a state-by-state directory of attorney licensing databases at the **Internet For Lawyers** website. (http://linkon.in/pLUdvT). The directory links directly to the searchable databases of attorney licensing boards (or to the unified state bar association) in forty-five states, as well as the District of Columbia. The directory also includes information on getting information from the licensing entities in those five remaining states that do not offer online searchable databases. So, remember, for states that do have online directories, but are voluntary bars, do not assume an attorney is unlicensed if his or her name is missing from the association's directory, and the same goes for attorneys in Oklahoma and Virginia because they are allowed to opt out of being included in their bar associations' publicly searchable databases. You will need to telephone or e-mail the bar if you do not find a name in the directory of voluntary bars and Oklahoma and Virginia.

The **Martindale.com** *Legal Directory* (http://www.martindale.com/), **FindLaw's** *Find a Lawyer* directory (http://lawyers.findlaw.com), and **Justia's Lawyer Directory** (http://www.justia.com/lawyers) are three of the major, free, traditional lawyer directories. There are two other directories, **Superlawyers.com** and **Avvo.com,** which also offer lawyer ratings (see page 439 for details). We'll discuss each of these in the next few pages.

From 1868, until the time the Internet became popular, **Martindale-Hubbell** had been a print national lawyer directory and was pretty much the only game in town. Martindale-Hubbell eventually became an online legal directory, **Martindale.com** (http://www.martindale.com). **Martindale.com** (http://www.martindale.com/) is owned by **Internet Brands.com** (https://www.internetbrands.com/our-brands/legal), which also owns a few other lawyer directories, such as the one at **Nolo.com** (which is less robust than **Martindale.com**).

To search or browse **Martindale.com's** directory, enter one or more criterion (*name*, *law firm*, *organization*, *school*, *articles*, or *location*) into the top search box (shown in the next illustration) to find a lawyer anywhere in the world.

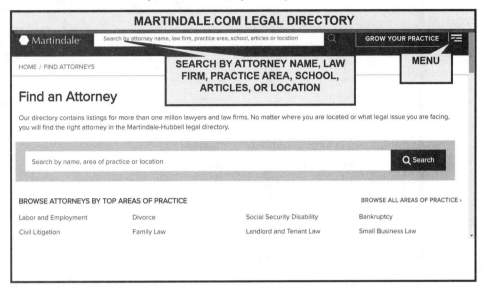

Although you can search by various criterion, it doesn't always work correctly when you try to mix and match the criterion. Our search for *practice area* (*Family Law*), *location* (*Los Angeles*), and *school* (*Pepperdine*), brought back several results, but not all of them included *Pepperdine*.

As you scroll down the homepage, you can instead *Browse Attorneys By Top Areas of Practice* or *Browse Attorneys By All Areas of Practice* (shown in the previous illustration). As you continue to scroll down the page (not shown), you can also choose to *Browse Attorneys By Popular Cities, Browse All Locations,* or *Browse By States*. If you do browse by location, you can also add in a practice area to narrow your results, and if you browse by practice area, you can also add in a location to narrow your results.

The next illustration shows search results for *criminal law chattanooga.* As shown in the in the top left-hand column, we can narrow our search results by *Categories (Law firms, Attorneys,* or *Articles)* or choose from one or more of the *Filters*: *Peer Reviews, Client Reviews, Languages, Law School,* etc. After that, you can *Sort By Name (A-Z* or *Z-A), Peer Reviews, Client Reviews,* or *Peer Awards.*

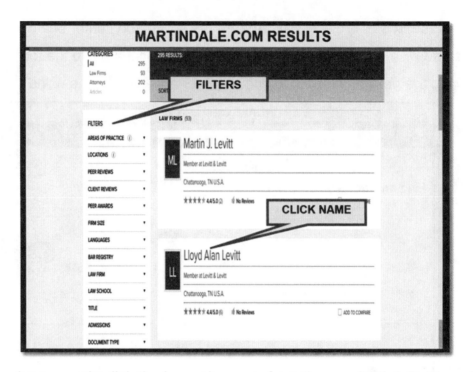

To view a result, click the lawyer's name from the results list. Retrieved results will only display the firm name, city, state, and, if any, *Client Reviews* and *Peer Reviews,* unless a lawyer has paid to be a *Featured Firm.* *Featured Firms* include the firm's address and phone number, links to the firm's website, and a *Contact Us* tab to send an email to the firm from within **Martindale.com**.

Use the Menu icon on the top right-hand side of the homepage to click one of these links*: Law School Alumni, Legal Library, or Bar Associations* (see the illustration before the previous one).

The *Law School Alumni Search* looks useful. You can click on a law school to display a list of their alumni. For instance, you could choose *The John Marshall Law School,* and view the list of over 10,000 alumni. To narrow your search even further, you can choose the same *Categories* and *Filters* discussed earlier and shown in the prior illustration.

The *Legal Library Search* is not a search of libraries or librarians, but a content section divided into these categories: *Legal Alerts/Articles*, *White Papers*, *Court Documents*, and *Presentations*. For the most part, all these categories appear to be articles, although we did find a *Brief* in the *Court Documents* category. We did not see any forms in the *Forms* category and nor did we see any *PowerPoints, video, or audio* in the *Presentations* category.

The *Bar Associations Search* allows you to obtain contact information for all U.S. State Bars and some foreign and international bars. (The site no longer includes its Experts and Services database.)

Nolo's *Find a Lawyer* directory (http://www.nolo.com/lawyers) can only be browsed by *Practice Area* or *Location*.

FindLaw re-designed its *Find a Lawyer* directory, changed the way to search it, and now uses this URL (https://lawyers.findlaw.com). There are two search boxes, which are side-by-side. You can use one or the other, or both simultaneously. The first is *What's your legal issue*? After you click into that box you can type a legal issue into the box or click *Legal Issues* from the *More Options* drop-down menu. A list of issues appears to choose from. The *More Options* drop-down menu also offers *Name Search, Browse Lawyers, Browse Law Firms, Browse Types of Cases,* and *Help*. The second search box, *Location*, allows you to type a city, ZIP Code, or state into the search box. Scroll down the page to browse by *Cities, State, and Counties*. Once you retrieve a list of results, the amount of information to the right of the firm's name varies. Some results only show a link to the *Law Firm Profile* while others also show one or more of the following: a *Law Firm Website* link, a *Contact us* link, and the firm's phone number.You can use one or the other, or both simultaneously.

Once you retrieve a list of results, the amount of information to the right of the firm's name varies. Some results only show a link to the *Law Firm Profile* while others also show one or more of the following: a *Law Firm Website* link, *a Contact us* link, and the firm's phone number. The next illustration shows what happened when we clicked the *Law Firm Website* link. Depending on who designed the lawyer's or law firm's website, it could include a picture of the attorney(s), *Firm Overview*, *Practice Areas*, *Blog*, *Contact*, and *Directions*, etc.

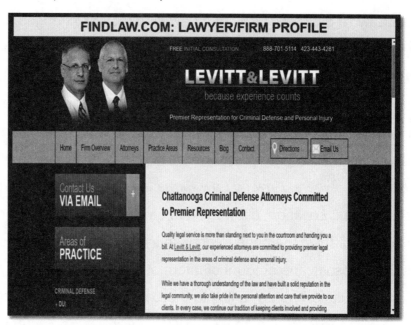

Justia's *Find a Lawyer* directory provides a basic search at http://www.justia.com/lawyers. There are two search boxes at the top of the page. In the first, enter a *Legal Issue or Lawyer Name.* In the second box, a city and state may already be filled in, which is based on your Internet connection, but it can easily be changed. Scroll down the page to browse by *Practice Areas, States, or Cities*. All lawyers have a free listing with basic information and contact information. **Justia** allows lawyers who have a free **Justia** account and an active profile in the **Justia** *Find a Lawyer* directory to rate other lawyers on a scale of 1-10, based upon: *Legal Knowledge, Legal Analysis, Communication Skills*, and *Ethics* and *Professionalism*. Lawyers can "claim" their profiles by clicking *Update your profile now!* This is a free service which allows you create a more complete profile that can include your photo, biographical information, education and experience, websites and blogs, social media profiles, and more.

The following directories also include a rating system for the lawyers listed:

- **Superlawyers.com** (https://attorneys.superlawyers.com/) describes itself as "[a] rating service of outstanding lawyers from more than 70 practice areas who have attained a high-degree of peer recognition and professional achievement. This selection process includes independent research, peer nominations and peer evaluations." When you visit the site, the default is set to *Search Lawyers,* but you can change this to firms by clicking the *Search Firms* tab to the right of the *Search Lawyers* tab. Depending on which tab you chose, enter a lawyer or firm name into the *Name or Legal Issue* search box below the tabs and enter a *Location.* You can also use the same *Name or Legal Issue* search box to search by *Legal Issue.* The *Location* search box must be filled whether you choose the *Name or Legal Issue* search. Instead of entering names (or legal issues) and locations into the search boxes, you can scroll down the page to browse by *Top Cities; State or Region*; or *Practice Area.* There is also an *Advanced Search* link below the *Location* search box. Click that to enter one or more of the following into the search boxes: *First Name, Last Name, Law Firm/Organization.* You can also select a *Law School* or *Practice Area* (or both) from the drop-down menu. Selecting a *Location* from the drop-down menu is required on the *Advanced Search* page. **Superlawyers.com** is owned by Thomson Reuters. .

- **Avvo.com** (http://www.avvo.com/find-a-lawyer) is a directory that also includes a rating system. Ratings are dependent on many factors according to **Avvo**, such as "public data we've collected on each attorney and the information they have provided in their profile…[and] including public records (state bar associations, regulatory agencies, and court records) and published sources on the internet (including attorneys' websites)." **Avvo** states that peer endorsements are also another factor, but not client reviews (see http://linkon.in/avvorate for more detailed ratings information). You can search the directory by entering an attorney or law firm name or a practice area into the left-hand search box and by entering a a location into the right-hand search box or you can scroll down the homepage to browse by practice area, city, or state. **Avvo** joined the **Martindale Legal Marketing Network** in 2018 as part of **Internet Brands**. Once you retrieve a list of results, notice the left-hand column where you can filter by *Free Consultations, Fixed-fee services, No misconduct,* and *Other Languages Spoken.* You can also sort by: *Best match, Best reviewed,* and *Years licensed* (*Most to least* or *Least to most*). We did not find that these options worked very well. When we narrowed our "criminal defense in Detroit" search results to attorneys who spoke Arabic, some of our results included attorneys who did not list Arabic.

All current and former Article III federal judges can be searched at the **Federal Judicial Center's Biographical Directory of Article III Federal Judges, 1789– present** (https://www.fjc.gov/history/judges).

Article III federal judges include judges from the:

- Supreme Court of the United States
- U.S. courts of appeal.
- U.S. district courts
- Court of International Trade
- Former U.S. circuit courts, Court of Claims, U.S. Customs Court, and U.S. Court of Customs and Patent Appeals

There is no similar official, judicial biography directory for Article I judges, which include judges from the United States Court of Appeals for the Armed Forces, United States Court of Appeals for Veterans Claims, United States Tax Court, United States Court of Federal Claims, United States bankruptcy courts, and U.S. territorial courts in the Northern Mariana Islands, Guam, and the Virgin Islands.

To search the **Biographical Directory of Article III Federal Judges**, enter a last name only or a last name, first name (you must use the comma as shown) into the search box, or click a letter of the alphabet to browse through a list of names that begin with that letter.

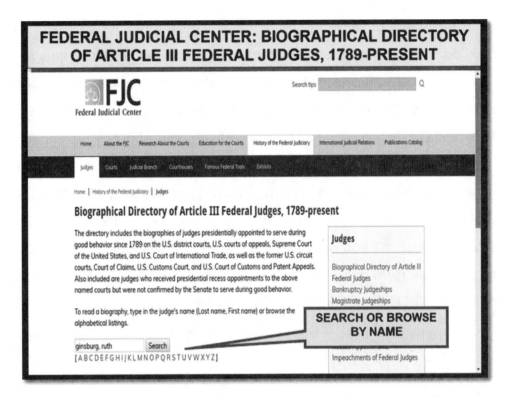

In addition to searching or browsing by name, you can create customized lists of judges based on various criteria, including the name of the president who appointed them, the type of court, dates of service, and demographics (e.g., select criterion from various drop-down menus to discover how many female judges sit in the bankruptcy courts) at https://www.fjc.gov/history/judges/search/advanced-search.

Although it's not an official judicial directory, **Ballotpedia** (http://bit.ly/stlocaljud) fills in some of the gaps of the **Biographical Directory of Article III Federal Judges**, which we just discussed, by offering biographies of:

- Article I federal judges (http://bit.ly/art1judge)
- State and local judges from the municipal and magistrate level up through state appeals courts judges and state supreme courts (https://linkon.in/ballotpediajudges)
    - To view **Ballotpedia's** biographies of state and local court judges, scroll down the list of states until you find the court you are interested in, click it, and then click the judge's name to view the biography.

Ballotpedia does not include a biography for every judge. Its biographies vary in length and depth. **Ballotpedia** also includes biographies of U.S. Supreme Court justices (http://bit.ly/sctballot).

Ballotpedia provides informational articles about courts at each level, "to help readers discover and learn useful information about the court systems and judiciary in the United States" and provides information about the other branches of government and elections. **Ballotpedia** states that its articles are "100 percent written by our professional staff" (https://ballotpedia.org/Ballotpedia:About).

On April 19, 2016, Michael Lissner announced that his site, **CourtListener**, launched its **Judicial Database** (https://www.courtlistener.com/person) of 8,500 federal and state courts judges (Figure17.6). On the *Advanced Judge Search* page (see next illustration), you can search by keywords only or fielded search boxes only (such as *Name, Birth city, School Attended, Appointed by,* and *Political Affiliation*), or a combination of keyword and fielded searching.

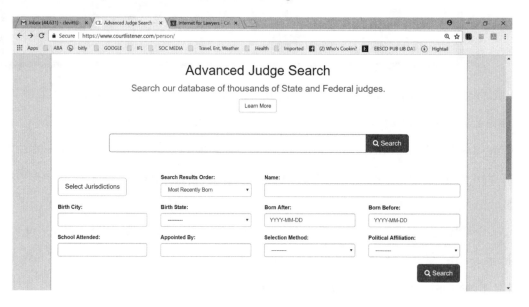

Results include judges' biographical and educational background, judicial and non-judicial positions held, political affiliations, American Bar Association ratings, campaign finance data and judicial portraits (https://linkon.in/courtlistjudicial; see next illustration).

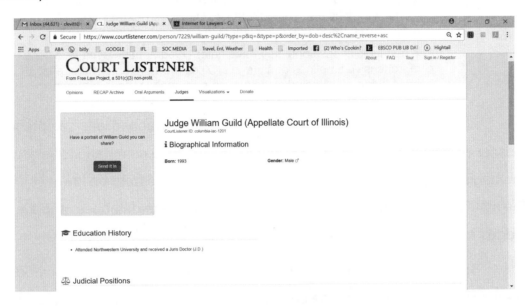

Many profiles also include links to the opinions that the judge has authored (see next illustration).

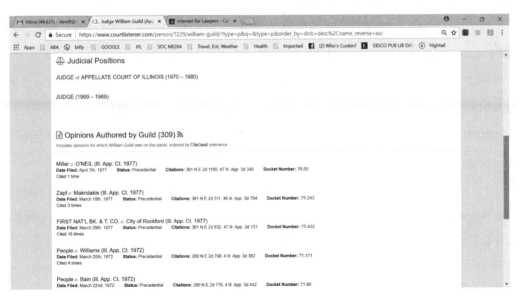

Lissner added the following details about the data being collected (https://linkon.in/courtlistjudicial):

> The judicial positions they have held: The core of this data is a list of courts and dates for each judge, but it also includes details about their specific position, how they were nominated or elected, what the voting outcome was, who appointed them, the clerks they supervised, and nearly a dozen dates about the timing of their nomination process.

> The non-judicial positions they have held: The database aims to include comprehensive timelines of a judge's full career both before and after being a judge. This includes work in other branches of government, in private practice, and in academia.

Although the announcement proclaimed the database was comprehensive, Lissner explained that: "We have been unable to find a comprehensive source of data for magistrate judges or federal bankruptcy judges. The data on lower court judges in the states is poor. Most judges are still missing from the database, and the included judges are missing many data points" (https://linkon.in/courtlistjudicial).

Some states do provide official profiles of their state and local judges (or at least contact information) at the court's official site. For example, profiles of the California Supreme Court's seven sitting justices appear online (http://www.courts.ca.gov/3014.htm).

Also, check your state, local, or specialty bar association for judicial profiles. For example, the **Dallas Bar Association** provides its collection of judicial profiles to all website visitors (http://www.dallasbar.org/node/110). Meanwhile, the **Federal Bar Association** makes profiles of federal judges that appeared in its "Federal Lawyer" magazine available to all website visitors (http://bit.ly/fedbarproind) where they can be searched by circuit or by name.

To locate links to state or local bar associations, see the **ABA Division for Bar Services** site (http://bit.ly/findabar) or **HG.org's** site, which also includes international and foreign bar associations (https://www.hg.org/legal.html).

To locate articles by or about judges and attorneys, there are several places to begin, such as the **American Bar Association (ABA)** *Legal Technology Resource Center's (LTRC)* **Free Full-Text Online Law Review/Journal Search** database (http://tinyurl.com/5talf2d), powered by **Google**. It has over 400 online law reviews and law journals. It also searches select online document repositories hosting academic papers and related publications such as **Congressional Research Service** reports. The search includes several foreign and international law journals. Coverage dates and online availability of the full text of articles varies from publication to publication.

The **Law Review Commons** (linkon.in/lawcommons) is a free and growing collection of law reviews and legal journals in an easily browsable and searchable format. It contains both current and archival content spanning over 100 years. You can conduct advanced searching with keywords and restrict them to a specific field, such as *Abstract*, *Subject*, *Author*, *Title*, etc. You can add a *Date Range* and sort by *Publication Date* or *Relevance*. Many of the law journals are from top law schools.

LegalTrac is a commercial database that indexes articles from legal periodicals and legal newspapers. **LegalTrac** can be searched for free if your public library subscribes to it and offers remote access to you. (To search this site, you would need to visit your public library site and review their list of remote access databases.) **LegalTrac** primarily offers abstracts of the articles, although some are available in full text. (See page 175 for details about public libraries offering free remote access to **LegalTrac** and other general newspaper and magazine sources that may contain articles by or about judges and attorneys.)

Legal newspapers often profile lawyers and judges or feature articles by them. **Law.com** (http://www.law.com) provides online access to articles published in its ALM (formerly American Lawyer Media) local and national legal newspapers. A free *Digital Membership* is required to view the **Law.com** content. This allows you to view certain publications for free; other publications limit you to viewing only five articles in a thirty-day period. But, access to legal news older than six months is only available through an exclusive subscription to their partner, **LexisNexis**. To keyword search, click the magnifying glass icon in the upper right-hand corner of the homepage. You will then be taken to an *Advanced Search* page to enter your keyword(s) and to sort by *Date* or *Relevance*, by *Ascending* or *Descending Direction*, and to apply *Filters.* Also on this page is the option to *Save This Search As An Alert.* Once you click the *Filters* tab, you can choose to filter by *All Practice Areas, Topics, Author Type, Start Date,* and *End Date.*

JD Supra (http://www.jdsupra.com) is an aggregator/publisher/distributor of legal content written by lawyers at federal government agencies, some of the world's largest law firms, as well as lawyers in solo practice. Enter your keywords into the *Search all Docs* search box located in the upper right-hand corner of the homepage. This search defaults to an OR Boolean connector—casting a wider net than most searchers probably mean to. You can narrow your search by conducting a phrase search (accomplished by placing phrases in quotation marks). While these are the site's most obvious search options, they are not the best way to locate articles on the site from a particular author. To locate all **JD Supra** articles by one of the site's contributing authors, use the *Find an Author* drop-down menu at the top of the homepage and select the *See all Subjects* link. This will display a list of articles published on the site in reverse chronological order. However, on the upper left-hand side of that page is a *Search Authors* search box. Note that this search also defaults to the OR Boolean connector, so you may see some extraneous results. Because some authors might use a middle name or middle initial, we do not recommend phrase searching for names. The *Find an Author* drop-down menu can also be used to browse *By Business Matters*, *By Personal Issues*, or by *State.*

To locate articles by or about judges and attorneys, don't overlook **Google** *Scholar*, which offers articles on a variety of topics, including legal. It also offers free alerts if you want to follow a particular judge or attorney (or legal issue). See pages 332–334 and 463 for more information on how to search **Google** *Scholar.*

More and more lawyers and judges are creating blawgs (a play on the word "blogs," used if the blog is law-related). Blawgs may help you learn about a lawyer's practice area or about the lawyer's or judge's personality. To find a blawg (or blog) on a particular topic, visit **Justia's Blawgsearch** (http://blawgsearch.justia.com), which can be keyword searched in addition to browsed by *Categories*.

Another blawg directory is the **ABA Journal's Blawg Directory** (http://www.abajournal.com/blawgs/), which can be browsed *By Topic, Author Type* (e.g., *Associate, Partner, Librarian, Judge*), *Region, Law School,* or *Courts* (http://linkon.in/abablawgbrowse). It can also be keyword searched (http://linkon.in/abablawgsearch) using the search box in the middle of the page beneath *Search the Blawg Directory*.

Just like everybody else, attorneys and judges are using social networking sites like **Facebook**, **Twitter**, and **LinkedIn** both personally and professionally. See *Chapter Twenty* for details about searching social networking sites.

Justia created **LegalBirds** (http://legalbirds.justia.com) to capture law-related posts on **Twitter** and build a directory of their authors. The keyword search no longer works. (It used to split results into two sections: one section of lawyers who included that keyword in their **Twitter** biography and a second section of tweets that included that keyword.) The site's collected tweets, and other information, can no longer be name searched (to locate tweets sent by a particular person or mentioning that person). So, what's left? You can browse **Twitter** accounts by *Categories and Practice Areas* and by *All, Lawyers, Law Librarians,* or *Academics*. You can also view *Recent Tweets*. For more information about blogs, see pages 172. For more information about microblogging (Twitter), see page 387.

Chapter Twenty-Five

LOCATING INFORMATION VIA A
FREEDOM OF INFORMATION ACT (FOIA) REQUEST

When information from federal government agencies is not available anywhere, try a Freedom of Information Act (FOIA) request. Enacted in 1966, FOIA gives any person the right to obtain any federal agency records—with exceptions. Some records are protected from mandatory disclosure by the law's nine exceptions or by six special law enforcement exclusions.

In brief, the nine exceptions listed in 5 U.S.C. § 552(b)(1)-(9) (http://www.law.cornell.edu/uscode/text/5/552) are:

1. national defense or foreign policy documents designated as "Classified";
2. documents which are "related solely to the internal personnel rules and practices of an agency;"
3. documents which are "specifically exempted from disclosure by statute" other than FOIA, but only if the other statute's disclosure prohibition is absolute;
4. "trade secrets and commercial or financial information obtained from a person and privileged or confidential;"
5. "inter-agency or intra-agency memorandum or letters" which would be considered privileged in civil litigation;
6. "personnel and medical and similar files the disclosure of which would constitute a clearly unwarranted invasion of personal privacy;"
7. "records or information compiled for law enforcement purposes," but only if one or more of six listed results would occur;
8. documents which are related to "an agency responsible for the regulation or supervision of financial institutions;" and
9. maps and other information related to the location of oil wells.

To facilitate FOIA requests, the **U.S. Department of Justice (DOJ)** has created all kinds of information on FOIA, and more recently, added videos to accompany many topics, such as:

- *What is FOIA?* (https://www.foia.gov/about.html)
- *How do I make a FOIA Request?* (https://www.foia.gov/how-to.html)
- *Where to make a FOIA request* (http://www.foia.gov/report-makerequest.html)

If you are already visiting the website of the agency you believe would hold the documents you seek, look for a link labeled *FOIA* for information about the type of records that the agency holds and the contact information for filing a request.

For state-level FOIA information, visit the **National Freedom of Information Coalition** (NFOIC) site for up-to-date information about all aspects of FOI in each state and the District of Columbia, including contact information and links to their resource pages (http://www.nfoic.org/state-foi-resources). The NFOIC site also links to the Freedom of Information laws in all fifty states and the District of Columbia (http://www.nfoic.org/state-freedom-of-information-laws) and state sample FOI request letters for all fifty states (http://www.nfoic.org/state-sample-foia-request-letters).

Chapter Twenty-Six

POLITICAL CAMPAIGN CONTRIBUTIONS

Why Search Political Campaign Contribution Websites?

It can be useful to search political campaign contribution websites for all kinds of reasons. For example, in the case of a missing person, you might be able to uncover their home address or their employer's name to track them down at work. If you are conducting juror research, this is one way to potentially learn about a juror's political persuasion, where they live, and their occupation. You might also be able to search by the name of an opposing attorney to discover if the attorney has contributed to the campaign of the judge you are both appearing before. This may be grounds for a recusal by the judge to avoid the appearance of impropriety.

FEC's Individual Contributor Database

The **Federal Election Commission (FEC)** (http://www.fec.gov/finance/disclosure/norindsea.shtml) tracks federal political campaign contributions over $200. The basic search allows only for a *First* and *Last* name search, but only the last name is required.

FEDERAL ELECTION COMMMISSION INDIVIDUAL CONTRIBUTOR DATABASE

Clicking the *Advanced Search* link from the basic search page (or using this direct URL: http://www.fec.gov/finance/disclosure/advindsea.shtml) gives you the ability to narrow your results with additional search criteria about your subject (as seen in the previous illustration), such as their *City*, *State* (you can use more than one criteria), *Zipcode*, *Employer*, and *Occupation*. You can also filter by a date range or for contributions that fall within a particular *Amount Range*.

FEDERAL ELECTION COMMMISSION INDIVIDUAL CONTRIBUTOR SEARCH RESULTS

FEDERAL ELECTION COMMISSION

Individual Contributions Arranged By Type, Giver, Then Recipient

Contributions to All Other Political Committees Except Joint Fundraising Committees

Contributor Name	City	State	ZIP Code	Employer	Occupation	Committee Name	Transaction Date	Amount	Image Number
SHEEN, MARTIN	LOS ANGELES	CA	90049	THE WEST WING	ACTOR	TROUTMAN, NANCY ELIZABETH 'BETH' VIA BETH TROUTMAN FOR CONGRESS	06/14/2004	2000.00	24971938304
SHEEN, MARTIN	LOS ANGELES	CA	90049	THE WEST WING	ACTOR	TROUTMAN, NANCY ELIZABETH 'BETH' VIA BETH TROUTMAN FOR CONGRESS	06/14/2004	2000.00	24971938303
SHEEN, MARTIN	MALIBU	CA	90265		ACTOR	CAPPS, LOIS G VIA FRIENDS OF LOIS CAPPS	09/26/2000	1000.00	20036181603
SHEEN, MARTIN	MALIBU	CA	90265	WARNER BROTHERS TA	ACTOR	GEPHARDT, RICHARD A VIA GEPHARDT FOR PRESIDENT, INC.	12/01/2003	2000.00	25990164803

Total Contributions: 7000.00

INCLUDES EMPLOYER AND OCCUPATION

CLICK THE CANDIDATE (OR COMMITTEE'S NAME TO DETERMINE THEIR PARTY AFFILIATION

CLICK *IMAGE NUMBER* TO SEE FILING AND ADDITIONAL INFORMATION

To uncover your subject's political party affiliation, click the candidate's name (or the name of the committee) listed to the left of your subject's name on the results page. This will identify which party the candidate (or committee) is affiliated with, which will probably also be your subject's party affiliation. To uncover your subject's address and employer name, click the link to the right of your subject's contribution amount (it will be a long number) found in the summary results. Be aware that this takes you the FEC's Schedule A form which will list three contributors per form, so you will need to scan the page to find your subject's name, as seen in the next illustration.

FEDERAL ELECTION COMMMISSION INDIVIDUAL CONTRIBUTOR SEARCH RESULTS

Transaction ID: 50707

B.
Full Name (Last, First, Middle Initial)
Robert Sheehan

Mailing Address
4 Times Sq

City
New York

State: NY   Zip Code: 10036-6518

Date of Receipt
M M / D D / Y Y Y Y
10 15 2003

FEC ID number of contributing federal political committee.

Amount of Each Receipt this Period
1000.00

Name of Employer
Skadden Arps Slate Meagher & Flom

Occupation
Attorney

Receipt For: 2004
X Primary   General
Other (specify) ▼

Election Cycle-to-Date ▼
1000.00

Transaction ID: 45147

C.
Full Name (Last, First, Middle Initial)
Martin Sheen

Mailing Address
6916 Dume Dr

City
Malibu

State: CA   Zip Code: 90265-4227

Date of Receipt
M M / D D / Y Y Y Y
12 01 2003

FEC ID number of contributing federal political committee.

Amount of Each Receipt this Period
2000.00

Name of Employer
Warner Brothers TV

Occupation
Actor

Receipt For: 2004
X Primary   General
Other (specify) ▼

Election Cycle-to-Date

FILING INCLUDES CONTRIBUTOR'S ADDRESS

SUBTOTAL of Receipts TFs Page (optional) ....

TOTAL This Period (last page this line number only) ....   ▶

FEC Schedule A   (Revised 1/2001)

You can also use the *Advanced Search* page to search by an employer name to learn which of their employees made political contributions and to which candidates.

The National Institute on Money in State Politics's **Followthemoney.org** site (https://www.followthemoney.org/) has aggregated campaign contribution information for state, federal, and even some local elections. For details about what types of data is available (e.g., contributions to candidates, parties, committees) and for which years, see http://linkon.in/2uzzQvE.

To begin a search on **Followthemoney.org**, click *Start Here* to open the *Ask Anything* pop-up seen in the next illustration.

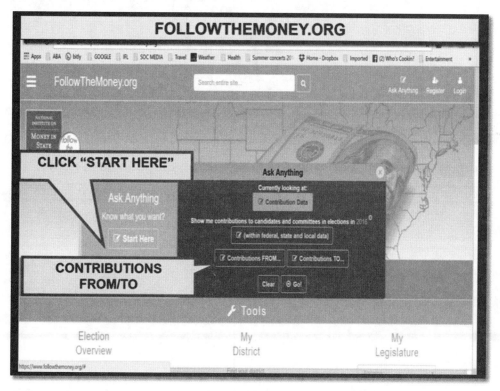

Then click either the *Contributions FROM* search option to search by an individual contributor's name or the *Contributions TO* option to search for contributions to a particular *candidate, ballot measure(s), PACs*, etc. Besides a contributor name search, the *Contributions FROM* tab offers seaches by *industry, location*, etc.

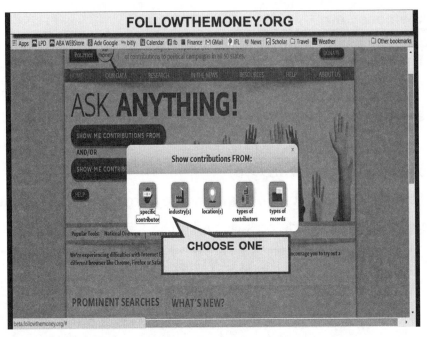

In the previous illustration, we see the pop-up that follows clicking on the *Contributions FROM* search option. Click the *specific contributor* button on this pop-up to bring up the search form where you can enter your subject's name.

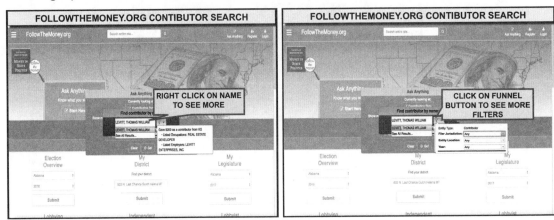

After you type in a name, a drop-down menu with a list of names and a funnel button will appear to the right of the names. If you click the thumbtack button, a filter menu appears that you can use to narrow the list by *Filer Jurisdiction*, *Entity Location*, or *Year.*

To view details about a contributor, left-click their name and then click the *Go!* button in the subsequent pop-up window.

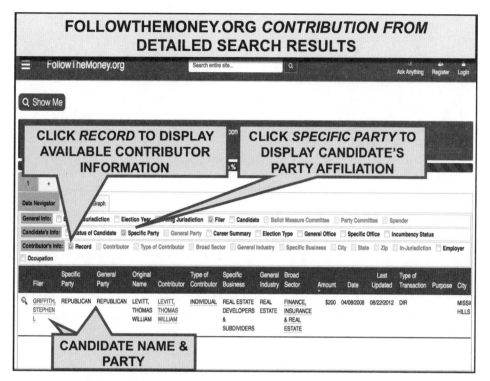

The results page will look blank until you click the *Record* checkbox in the *Contributor's Info* row near the middle of the page. This will display how much the contributor gave to which candidate (or committee) and the contributor's occupation and employer, among other information. To display the candidate (or committee's) party affiliation, click the *Specific Party* checkbox in the *Candidate's Info* row. Unlike the **FEC** database, there is no address listed for the contributor.

Individual State's Campaign Contribution Sites

Individual states typically have databases similar to the **FEC's** (or at least a list that you could download and search) to track contributions to state political campaigns in their respective states. To find a specific state's political contribution database, visit **Search Systems** (http://publicrecords.searchsystems.net) and choose a state. Look for an entry under *Campaign Finance* or *Campaign Contributions*. The information about contributors will vary from state to state. For example, the California campaign contributor database (http://dbsearch.sos.ca.gov/ContributorSearch.aspx) only shows the contributor's city, state, and ZIP Code but Alaska's database shows the full addresses (http://linkon.in/1zHLZZC).

Chapter Twenty-Seven

USING CASE LAW DATABASES TO GATHER BACKGROUND INFORMATION ABOUT PEOPLE, COMPANIES, ETC.

CASE LAW DATABASES

While most attorneys use case law databases for legal research, we very often use them to gather factual or background/investigative information about:

- Expert witnesses
- Opposing parties
- Current and potential clients
- Judges
- Lawyers
- Companies
- A client's potential business partner

While all state supreme court cases and U.S. Supreme Court cases are published and will be found in case law databases, you need to be aware that case law databases do not include every case from other courts, because:

- Many cases never go to trial (they might get dismissed or settled).
- Even if a state case goes to trial, most state trial cases are not published.
- Not all state appellate cases are certified for publication by the court.
- Not all federal trial-level cases or federal appellate cases are certified for publication by the court.

If a case is not certified for publication by the court, sometimes case law database vendors do choose to include them in their databases anyway (with a "not certified for publication" or "not to be published" notation). While some courts do not permit you to cite to these cases for your legal arguments or briefs, this has no effect on using the information for background research.

> To gather as complete a picture as possible about people, companies, etc., you will also need to also research dockets (see *Chapter Thirteen*).

Because some research cannot be charged back to a client, such as research about that client, a potential client, a judge, or a lawyer, you will probably want to search a free case law database. Whether you use a free or pay case law database, most of the searches we will describe in this chapter can be conducted at either type of database.

Since everyone has free access to **Google** *Scholar* and to **Fastcase's** *App*, and because this book primarily covers methods to search for free, we will use these two case law databases as our primary examples of how to search federal and state case law for free. We will also briefly discuss a new free government site, **govinfo.gov** (this site does not capitalize the "g" in govinfo), which searches federal cases only (and many other federal resources).

For those who want even more details on searching **Google** *Scholar*, please see *Internet Legal Research on a Budget* (ABA LPD, 2014; 2nd edition expected January 2019), authored by Carole A. Levitt and Judy K. Davis (http://linkon.in/1jbLQZn).

For those who prefer to use their pay subscription to **Lexis**, **Westlaw**, or **Bloomberg,** or their free subscription to **Casemaker*** or **Fastcase***, you will find substantial documentation at each of their sites. *Internet Legal Research on a Budget* also includes substantial documentation about searching **Casemaker** and **Fastcase**. In certain types of searches, such as field searching, we would suggest using your free **Casemaker** database or even a pay database instead of **Google** *Scholar* or **Fastcase's** *App*. (See page 480 for a field search example using **Casemaker**.)

*With the exception of California, every state bar association provides access to either **Casemaker** or **Fastcase** as a member benefit. (It's possible that California may adopt **Casemaker** or **Fastcase** in 2018, so be sure to check http://www.casemakerlegal.com/consortiumpartner.aspx and https://www.fastcase.com/bar-associations.) Some local and specialty bar associations and other legal entities (such as the Los Angeles Law Library) do the same. To learn if you have free access, check the website of your bar association or other legal entities that you belong to. If you do not have free access to **Casemaker** or **Fastcase** as a benefit of membership in an organization you belong to, individual subscriptions are available for a fee.

In 2009, **Google** added free case law and law review/journal articles to its existing *Scholar* articles database. In this chapter, we will only focus on the case law portion of **Google** *Scholar* (http://scholar.google.com). For information about searching *Scholar's* articles database, see pages 332–334.

Because **Google** has provided little documentation on how to search case law using *Scholar*, we have conducted numerous test searches to determine the functionality and limits of the database discussed in this chapter.

Scholar's database is composed of cases from multiple sources, such as **Cornell LII**, **Justia**, **Public.Resource.org**, and official court sites, so you may find duplicates of the same case in its database. Google states that it does not guarantee its coverage to be complete or accurate. If a particular case is not available online in full-text format, search results will only include a citation. *Scholar* contains cases from the following courts:

- U.S. Supreme Court back to 1791
- All U.S. state appellate and state supreme courts back to 1950
- U.S. federal district, appellate, tax, and bankruptcy courts back to 1923
- Court of Claims from 1929 to 1982 (when the court was abolished)
- Court of Customs and Patent Appeals from 1929 to 1982 (when the court was abolished)
- Customs Court from 1949 to 1980 (it was replaced by the Court of International Trade)
- Court of International Trade from 1980 to present (it replaced the Customs Court)
- Board of Tax Appeals from 1924 to 1942 (it became the Tax Court)
- Tax Court from 1943 to the present (it replaced the Board of Tax Appeals)

To search **Google** *Scholar* cases, you can enter your search into the home page search box as shown in the next illustration. Then you would select the *Case law* radio button beneath the search box.

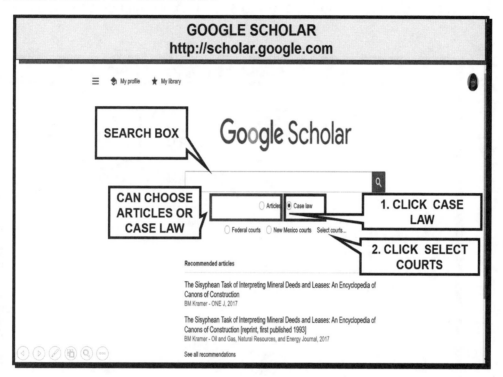

A *Federal Courts* radio button will then appear and usually the state court where **Google** detects your Internet connection is coming from (such as *New Mexico* as shown in the previous illustration). A *Select courts* link will also appear, which you click if you want to select other courts instead. Once you choose *Federal Courts* or the state court shown on the home page, such as *New Mexico* (you can only choose one), you can enter your keywords into the search box and click the magnifying glass icon.

If you click the *Select courts* link (as seen in the previous illustration), click into the checkboxes (shown in the next illustration) for the courts you want to search, or click *Select all* from the *State courts* or the *Federal courts* (or both) to search all of those courts. You can click *Clear all* to deselect all the checked boxes, which allows you to then choose one or more courts to search. You will need to then click *Done*.

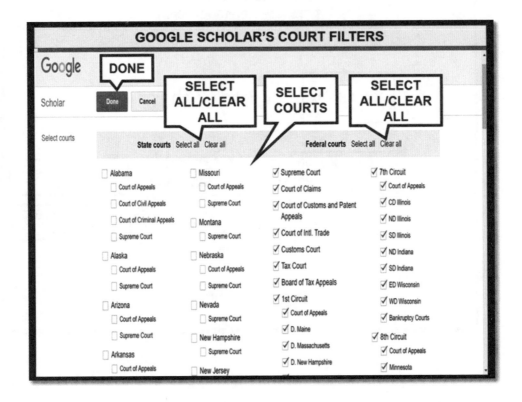

Once you have selected your courts and clicked *Done*, you will then see a page (as shown in the next illustration) with a basic search box and instructions to *Please enter a query in the search box above*. The court you selected (e.g., *Texas*) will be highlighted in red in the left-hand column. You could enter keywords, phrases, Boolean connectors, and Proximity connectors into this basic search box, just like you would at **Google.com**.

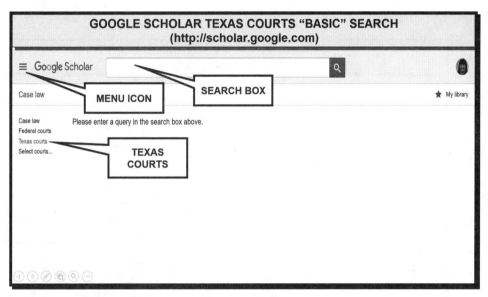

But, if you prefer to conduct an *Advanced Search*, click the unlabeled Menu icon, which is indicated by three horizontal bars located on the top left of the **Scholar** homepage (shown in the prior illustration) and then click *Advanced Search* (as shown in the next illustration).

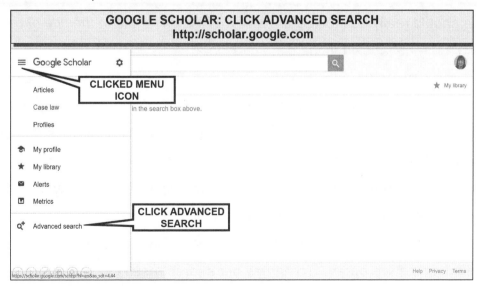

In the next illustration, even though we selected *Case law* (and NOT *Articles*), the *Advanced search* menu is labeled *Find articles*. Nevertheless, this is the correct place to search case law. It appears that **Google** never bothered changing the menu name from *Find articles* to *Find Case law.* Nor did **Google** change any of the *article* search labels or *article* radio button labels with *Case law* labels, so we will explain how each search label and radio button label should have been labeled so they make sense for your *Case law* searching.

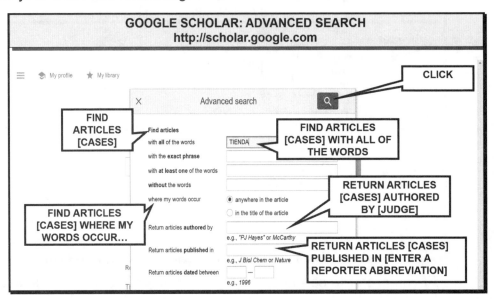

Beneath *Find articles where my words occur,* notice the two radio buttons labeled *anywhere in the article* and *in the title of the article*. These are examples of where **Google** failed to replace *article* labels with *Case law* labels. A*nywhere in the article* should really be labeled *anywhere in the case* and *in the title of the article* should really be labeled *in the case caption*.

In the previous illustration, we selected *Texas* courts, entered a name, *Tienda,* into the *with all of the words* search box, and then left the *where my words occur anywhere in the article [case]* radio button clicked into (which is the default) to find all cases mentioning *Tienda.* Some of our 196 results included *Tienda* in the case caption (as a party name) while others included *Tienda* anywhere in the case (and not as a party). For example, in one of our results, *Garza v. State,* a witness "told investigators that Abraham Martinez Tienda, who had been in Garcia's Bar on the evening of the shooting, shot the woman." To narrow our search results to cases where *Tienda* appears only in the case caption (as a party), and not just anywhere in the case, we clicked the *in the title of the article [case caption]* radio button and retrieved just fifteen cases.

Return articles authored by should really be labeled *Return cases authored by judge*. If you enter a judge's name into this search box, you will retrieve cases where that judge either wrote the opinion, dissented, concurred, etc.

Return articles published in should really be labeled *Return cases published in a particular reporter*. Test searches indicate that when you restrict your search to *Case law*, the *Return articles [cases] published in [a particular reporter]* field allows you to search for the abbreviation of case reporters—e.g., A.2d, SW 3d, and so on. (Entering a full case citation retrieves no results.) Typically, you would use this field in combination with a keyword search (e.g., a party name) or a phrase search (e.g., a case title). For instance, when you know a certain case was published in a certain Reporter (e.g. SW 3d), but you don't know the full citation, enter *Tienda* into the *with all of the words* search box and *SW 3d* into the *Return articles [cases] published in [a particular reporter]* box. When we left the default to *where my words occur anywhere in the article [case],* we retrieved thirty-four cases. But when we clicked into the *title of the article [case caption]* radio button, we retrieved two cases.

Return articles dated between should really be labeled *Return cases dated between*.

To do background research about a specific attorney (e.g., Robert Pulone) to learn whether he has been the attorney of record (in a published case) before Judge Vogel in California, use the *Advanced search*, select *California* as your court, and enter *Vogel* into the *Return articles [cases] authored by* search box and enter *Robert Pulone* into the *with all of the words* search box.

You could also add the keyword *attorney* into the *with all of the words* search box if you were getting results for someone with that name who was not the attorney of record (e.g., a party or an expert witness). If you were certain that *Robert Pulone* did not use a middle name or middle initial, you could enter his first and last name into the *with the exact phrase* search box. If you knew that *Robert Pulone* always used a middle name (or middle initial), you could enter his first, middle, and last name into the *with the exact phrase* search box. There was one result for our *Robert Pulone* and Judge *Vogel* search. To read the full case, click the case name.

To learn what published cases a known expert witness has been involved in, enter the name into *with the exact phrase* search box (or into the *with all of the words* search box) the same way we did in our previous *Robert Pulone* search. You could also add the keyword *expert* into the *with all of the words* search box, if you retrieve too many irrelevant results. If you need to locate an expert who has a certain expertise, then search using keywords to describe that expertise (e.g., *accident reconstruction*).

To see if a certain person or company has been a party in a published case, enter the person's first and last name (e.g., *Genoveva Anaya*) or the company's name (e.g., *Nike*) into the search box labeled *with the exact phrase* and select *in the title of the article [case caption]* from the *where my words occur* drop-down list. You can search one or multiple courts. In this case, we selected **California** to search for *Genoveva Anaya* and received one case result. If you find no results, you might enter the names into the *with all of the words* search box in case your party uses a middle name or middle initial that you are unaware of.

To search by citation, enter the citation (in Bluebook style) into the exact phrase search box and select *anywhere in the article [cases]* from the *where my words occur* drop-down list. (As noted earlier, even though a case citation is not an "article," the results will include cases if you clicked into the *Case law* radio button on the home page.) The results will include your case but also all cases that cite your case. If you are trying to limit the search to only the case you entered a citation for, you might think you could do this by selecting *in the title of the article [case caption]*, but you will receive a message informing you that *Your search did not match any articles [cases]*.

Once your case results are displayed, you can manipulate them by using the filtering and sorting options on the left-hand column (see next illustration).

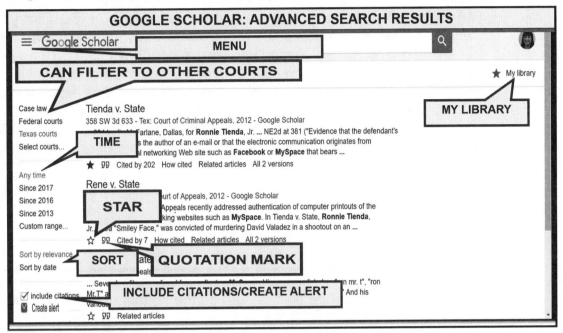

- *Case law:* This shows your search results are from *Case law.*
- *Federal Courts:* Click this to change your search results to *Federal Courts.*
- *Texas Courts*: This is the state that you selected to search.
- *Select courts*: This allows you to select different courts from the court filter menu shown earlier.
- *Any time*: This allows you to choose a year or create a custom date range (years only).
- *Star* icon: If you hover over the *Star* icon, you will see the label *Save.* When you click the *Star* icon, this will save the result in *My Library,* but only if you are logged into your **Google** account.
- *Quotation Mark* icon: If you hover over the *Quotation Mark* icon, you will see the label *Cite.* When you click this icon, the Bluebook citation is created, which you can easily copy and paste it into a document or import into a bibliographic manager, if you have one.
- *Sort by relevance/Sort by date*: By default, results are sorted by relevance. If you click *Sort by date,* this sorts from newest to oldest (you can't reverse this from oldest to newest).
- *Include citations*: You have the option of including or excluding cases where **Scholar** only has a citation to a case instead of the full-text.

- *Create Alert:* This allows you to set up a continuous, automatic search, which we'll discuss later. The *Alert* link also appears as an option on the Menu drop-down list, which you can reach by clicking the Menu icon (three horizontal bars on the top, far left-hand side of any Scholar page, which we explained earlier). This is where you can review or cancel your saved *Alerts.*

- *My Library:* This brings you to the *Showing all articles in your library* page, which lists all cases and articles you saved when you clicked the *Star* icon. Then, next time you are logged into your account, you can click on *My Library* at the top of the *Scholar* home page (see the first illustration at the beginning of this *Scholar* section) to review your list of saved cases (and articles) and click any that you wish to read again—without having to re-run your search. *My Library* is also found in two other places: (1) in the Menu drop-down list and (2) in the upper right-hand corner of any search results page.

- Change your *Case law* search to an *Articles* search simply by clicking *Articles* from the Menu drop-down list.

Google Scholar: Alerts

Scholar offers a free *Create alert* feature on the bottom of the search results page, as shown in the prior illustration. If you set up an alert, **Google** runs your search continuously through *Scholar* and sends you an e-mail alert about cases (or articles) retrieved based on your keywords and chosen court(s). The alert defaults to your current search and court(s), but you can revise the alert by typing in other keywords/phrases. You cannot revise the courts from the *alert* menu. You would have to return to your search results and revise the courts there. *Alerts* can be set up even if you do not have a **Google** account and the *alert* can be sent to any email address; a **Google** *Gmail* address is not required. However, **Google** will require you to acknowledge you are not a robot, ask you some questions to prove it, and then you will see this notice: *A verification email has been sent to [the email you provided]. You will not receive alerts on this topic until you click the link in the verification email and confirm your request.*

After you click a case result, you can read the full-text in what *Scholar* calls— aptly enough—the mode. All your keywords are highlighted in yellow, but you can remove the highlighting by clicking the X in the upper right-hand corner. In the next section, we'll explain what happens when you click *How Cited*.

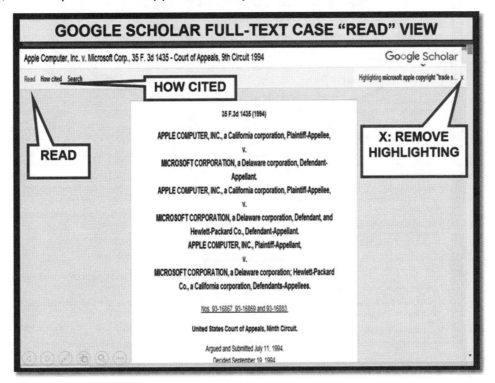

Before relying on the decision of a case, make sure the case has not been overruled or reversed by using the *How cited* feature at **Google** *Scholar*, as shown in the next illustration.

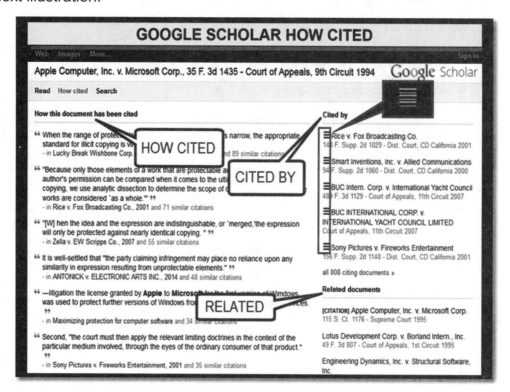

Even if *Scholar* includes cases in your results that have not been certified for publication, these cases are NOT included in *Scholar's How cited* (the same is true for **Casemaker** and **Fastcase**), so be sure to run the party name through the *Scholar* (or **Casemaker** and **Fastcase)** case law database as if they were keywords or phrases and include a date range (using the year your case was decided and the current year). This will basically be a self-created citator. See a further explanation on page 477.

Be aware that *Scholar* does not offer the type of editorial enhancements that you may be used to from **Shepard's**, **Keycite**, or **BCite**. *How this document has been cited*: (on the left-hand column) displays a few sample cases with a snippet of text to show where your case is mentioned. The cases listed under *Cited by* (on the top portion of the right-hand column) are all the cases in *Scholar's* database that cite your case. The horizontal bars located to the left of the case name indicate "depth of treatment"—the more bars, the more this case discusses your case. For example, three bars indicate a case with deeper treatment of your case, while no bars indicate there is very little discussion of your case; it might just be mentioned in passing. Cases listed beneath *Related documents* (on the bottom portion of the right-hand column) do not cite your case, but *Scholar's* algorithm thinks they may be similar enough to your case.

Fastcase *App*

Fastcase offers a free federal and state case law and statute *App* for iPhone, iPad, and Android mobile devices. The *App* is a lighter version of **Fastcase's** full Web database. (The full Web database includes additional materials, such as federal and state regulations, and more sophisticated search features.) The **Fastcase** *App* and the **Fastcase** full Web database offer the same date coverage. They are similar to **Google** *Scholar's* date coverage (see page 462*).* The *App* is free to download and search, but you will need to create a free account (using your e-mail address) and create a password before you can search the *App*.

At the bottom of the *App* (see next illustration), there are four options:

- *New Search*

- *Recent*: If you have a paid subscription or member-benefit access to **Fastcase**, this option displays the recent searches you performed using **Fastcase's** Web interface so you can automatically perform the same search on your mobile device through the *App*.

- *Saved*: If you have a paid subscription or member-benefit access to **Fastcase**, any case that you marked as a *Favorite* using **Fastcase's** Web interface will automatically be synced to your **Fastcase** *App*. It can then be retrieved when you click this option in the *App*.

- *Settings*: Using the *Settings* option, you can choose to display results by: (1) **Title** [party names] only, (2) *Title plus most relevant paragraph*, or (3) *Title plus first paragraph*) and the *Results* [number of] *per page*.

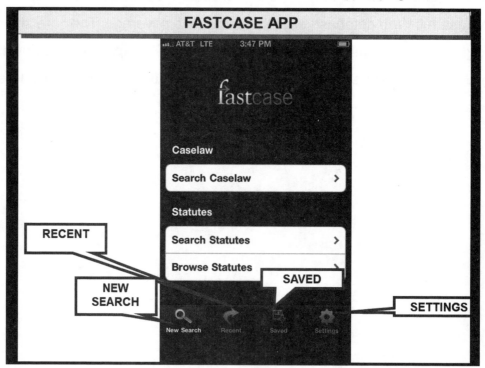

Fastcase *App's* search syntax (keywords, phrases, Boolean and proximity connectors, etc.) is the same as the **Fastcase** Web interface's search syntax, as shown in the next illustration. (You can also search both the *App* and the Web interface by citation; simply type the citation as a string of keywords.)

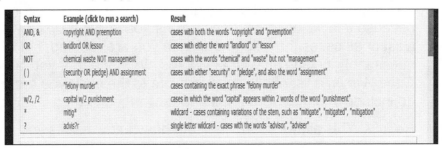

Syntax	Example (click to run a search)	Result
AND, &	copyright AND preemption	cases with both the words "copyright" and "preemption"
OR	landlord OR lessor	cases with either the word "landlord" or "lessor"
NOT	chemical waste NOT management	cases with the words "chemical" and "waste" but not "management"
()	(security OR pledge) AND assignment	cases with either "security" or "pledge", and also the word "assignment"
" "	"felony murder"	cases containing the exact phrase "felony murder"
w/2, /2	capital w/2 punishment	cases in which the word "capital" appears within 2 words of the word "punishment"
*	mitig*	wildcard - cases containing variations of the stem, such as "mitigate", "mitigated", "mitigation"
?	advis?r	single letter wildcard - cases with the words "advisor", "adviser"

The next illustration shows that we clicked *New Search* to search the judge name *Mosely* as a keyword and also added the keywords *Myspace* or *Facebook* because we want to learn if this judge is likely to admit profiles from social media sites as evidence. Researching a judge's prior opinions (a process often referred to as "analytics") that are the same or related to issues in your case could provide insight into how that judge might rule on your case.

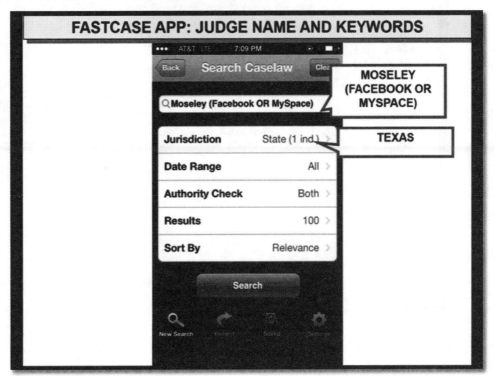

We can then choose one or more of the following options:

- *Jurisdiction*: This allows you to select one or more jurisdictions to search.

- *Date Range*: If left blank, all available dates are searched.

- *Authority Check*: This is the closest tool to a "cite check" product that **Fastcase** provides (Note: they disclaim it is a cite check product, probably because it lacks editorial treatment). If you choose *Display Cited Generally*, a list of all cases that cite to the case you are reading, but which do <u>not</u> necessarily include all your keywords, will appear. If you choose *Display Cited Within*, a list of all cases that cite to the case you are reading, which <u>do</u> include your keywords, will appear.

- *Results*: This allows you to indicate how many results you want displayed.

- *Sort By*: You can sort results by *Relevance*, *Decision Date*, or *Short Name*.

We have chosen to have our case results display the case title and the most relevant paragraph, for our sample search (see next illustration). Notice the *Tienda v. State* case is from 2010 and the *Authority Check* shows 0/0.

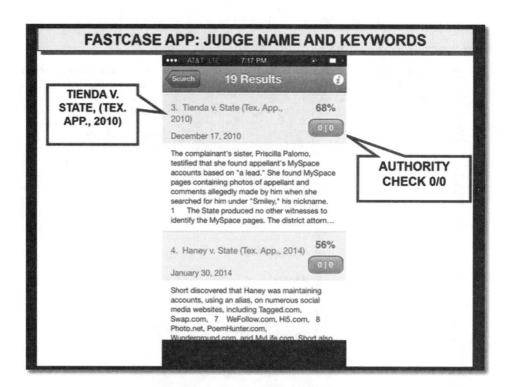

After we click the case caption to view the full text of this case (see the next illustration), we learn that Judge Mosely affirmed the trial court judge's decision to admit **Facebook** and **Myspace** profiles into evidence. We also learn that this is a *Do not publish* case, which means it lacks an official reporter citation, and for that reason it is not in Fastcase's *Authority Check*. So, the 0/0 doesn't necessarily mean that no subsequent cases have cited this 2010 *Tienda v. State* case. As explained on page 472, this is when we create our own citator, to learn if any subsequent cases have cited this 2010 *Tienda* case. For this "citator" search, we typed the party's full name, *Ronnie Tienda*, into the search box, added the keywords *Myspace* or *Facebook*, and restricted our search to Texas courts and the U.S. Supreme Court. Our results showed us that the 2010 case was appealed, affirmed, and ordered published. Many other cases subsequently cited the 2012 *Tienda* and it became one of the leading cases for admitting social media profiles into evidence.

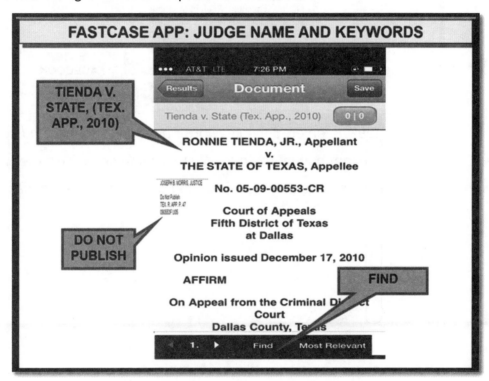

If you click the *Find* tab at the bottom of a case (see prior illustration), it will display a *Find* search box, as shown in the next illustration. You would use this feature to enter a keyword or phrase into the *Find* box to be brought to the page (or pages) where that keyword or phrase is located. The keyword or phrase could be one of your original keywords or phrases or it could be other keywords, phrases, or even a person's name, etc. Once your scanned word or phrase is found, it will be highlighted.

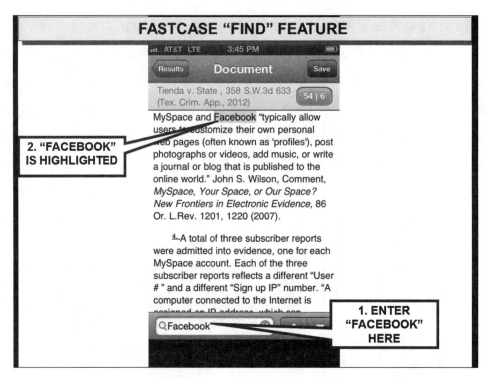

FASTCASE "FIND" FEATURE

In this example, we entered the keyword *Facebook* into the *Find* search box of the 2012 *Tienda* case that had affirmed our 2010 *Tienda* case. This way we can avoid reading the entire case and quickly view just the *Facebook* evidence discussion.

In December 2018, **govinfo** will replace its predecessor site, the **Federal Digital System** (**FDsys**). The *United States Courts Opinions* collection at **govinfo.gov** (https://www.govinfo.gov) is "a collaborative effort between the U.S. Government Publishing Office (GPO) and the Administrative Office of the United States Courts (AOUSC) to provide public access to opinions from selected United States appellate, district, and bankruptcy courts. The content of this collection dates back to April 2004, though searchable electronic holdings for some courts may be incomplete for this earlier time period" (https://www.govinfo.gov/help/uscourts). The **govinfo.gov** site explains that the "secure transfer of files to GPO from the AOUSC maintains the chain of custody, allowing GPO to authenticate the files with digital signatures" (https://www.govinfo.gov/help/uscourts). In addition to the federal Appellate, Bankruptcy, and District court opinions, **govinfo.gov** also offers opinions from the Court of International Trade.

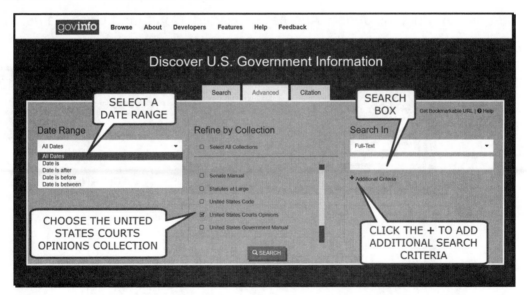

Opinions at **govinfo.gov** can be searched by going to https://www.govinfo.gov, and then clicking *Advanced* (as shown in the preceding illustration). Then, scroll down the *Refine by Collection* list to choose the *United States Courts Opinions* collection. You can now click the arrow beneath *Date Range* to select from the drop-down list of dates (or leave it blank to search all dates). Then, beneath *Search In,* enter keywords or a metadata field search (e.g., *partyname:hatch*) into the search box beneath *Full-*

Text To search by other criteria, click the arrow to the right of *Full-Text* and click another criterion from the drop-down list, such as *Citation, Party name*, etc. You can add more search boxes by clicking *Additional Criteria* (below the search box). The collection can also be browsed if you go back to https://www.govinfo.gov and click the *Browse* link on the top horizontal bar. Then choose: *A-Z, U, United States Courts Opinions*, a year, and then browse numerically by docket number from most recent to oldest.

Field Searching at Casemaker and Other Databases

Fastcase's *App* and its Web version do not offer field searching and, as explained earlier, **Google** *Scholar's* fields are not tailored to case law, so if you prefer to conduct field searches (e.g., by entering a name into the designated attorney or judge field box), you will probably prefer **Lexis**, **Westlaw**, **Bloomberg**, or **Casemaker**.

In the next illustration, you can see all the options for field searching offered by **Casemaker**, from the *Judge*, *Attorney*, *Keyword*, *Court,* and *Case Name,* to *Cite, Date Decided*, *Docket No.*, and *Panel*.

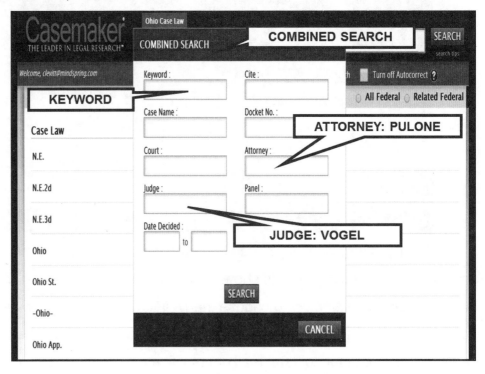

Chapter Twenty-Eight

PAY INVESTIGATIVE RESEARCH DATABASES

What Are Pay Investigative Research Databases?

Most of the free public records and publicly available information sites we have discussed so far collect information on just one topic (such as death records, or real estate records, or news), or focus on a single jurisdiction. Usually, they also have limited search protocols. If you need to collect various types of information or information from various jurisdictions (or both), searching free resources site by site would be very laborious and often not worth your time. Instead, you should opt to use one of the major pay investigative research databases such as (1) **TLOxp** (http://www.tlo.com), (2) **LexisNexis Public Records Database** (**SmartLinx**), (3) **LexisNexis Accurint**, (4) **Westlaw** (whose parent company is **Thomson Reuters**) **PeopleMap**, and (5) **Thomson Reuters CLEAR**. (Longtime users of this book will notice that we have eliminated **Merlin** from this chapter because it has been subsumed by **TLOxp** and no longer exists as a separate database.)

These databases collect information from as many sources (see pages 481–486) and jurisdictions as possible and then integrate all of it into one large searchable database. Your results will allow you to create a dossier about your subject.

These databases are not available to the general public. They are only available to legal professionals, governmental agencies, law enforcement, and certain industries such as insurance and banking. All subscribers are required to be vetted to obtain a subscription. Note that "legal professionals," in the context of this chapter, refers to lawyers, investigators, paralegals, and law librarians who do <u>not</u> work in governmental agencies or in law enforcement, because pay investigative research database vendors offer different subscription contracts (with access to more information) to legal professionals employed by government agencies and law enforcement personnel.

The major pay investigative research databases that legal professionals use provide more sophisticated search protocols than free investigative and public record sites and even "general public" pay databases. The major pay investigative research databases also tend to be more up to date.

All the databases noted on page 481 include information from national, federal, and state sources, but **TLOxp** offers some additional California-only databases. There are other vendors that offer one state-only or regional-only databases. A law librarian in Oregon recommends what she describes as a "regional-only database," **OPENonline.com** (http://www.openonline.com), which covers Oregon, Idaho, California, Nevada, Washington, Michigan, and Ohio. The "regional" label seems somewhat odd, considering it's a mix or Western and Mid-western states and national databases. It was founded in "1992 through a partnership between private industry and the Ohio State Bar Association …" and provides background checks, employment screening, and drug test services …" according to its site (https://www.openonline.com/Solutions/Investigative).

A database favored by Texas lawyers is **PublicData.com** (http://www.publicdata.com), which also has records for other (but not all) states besides Texas. See http://bit.ly/publicdatacoverage to learn about which records and which states are available for each type of search. For example, **Publicdata.com's** *Drivers Licenses Search* (search by name, or date of birth, or license number) only offers current information for Texas and Florida records, while its professional license database covers twelve states.

In this chapter, we will use **TLOxp** (http://www.tlo.com) to illustrate how to search a pay investigative research database. We're doing this because all of the databases noted earlier in this chapter have very similar information and search protocols. Additionally, **TLOxp** is more "attorney-friendly" in terms of access to full Social Security Numbers and full dates of birth (see page 496) and has pricing plans that are more transparent than most other vendors, making it easier to discuss in greater detail. Contact your local **LexisNexis, Westlaw**, or **Thomson Reuters** representatives for more information on what access you would have and your cost. We recommend that you request a trial subscription and test each of the databases, using your own name, so you can better compare results to assess which one will work best for your needs.

Although it is not a comprehensive pay investigative research database, we will also discuss some of **Search Systems'** *Premium Databases,* to search evictions, bankruptcies, judgments, tax liens, criminal records, and watch lists.

Because their free "teaser" information could be of some use, we will also look at two pay investigative research databases geared to the general public that do not require that the researcher be vetted prior to use (**Intelius** and **US Search**).

When Should You Use a Pay Investigative Research Database?

Use a pay investigative research database when you need to:

- Access public records that are not free on the Web.

- Conduct a unified search of publicly available information, public records, and non-public information (e.g., information from credit headers).

- Search simultaneously through all or multiple jurisdictions for one record type.

- Search simultaneously through multiple record types in one, all, or multiple jurisdictions.

- Find relationships between people.

- Find relationships between a person and various public records associated with that person.

- Find a full Social Security Number (see pages 487–489 and 491 to learn about limitations of finding a full Social Security Number).

- Find a full date of birth (see pages 286 and 491 to learn about limitations of finding a full date of birth).

- Conduct a sophisticated search using one or more clues you have about a person, such as their name (sometimes even just a first name can be searched if you can add other identifying information); Social Security Number (full or partial); date of birth; estimate of the person's age; or a previous or current phone number, city, state, or ZIP Code.

- Find your subject when all the free resources have not been useful.

What Types of Records Are Found in Pay Investigative Research Databases?

The following records and information might be found in pay investigative research databases (and at most databases, you can also use one or more of these information types as your search criteria):

- Addresses (current and past)
- Associates (e.g., individuals who may have worked or owned property with your subject)
- Bankruptcy records
- Birth dates (often truncated to only the month and year, unless you have been approved to view the full date) (see pages 487 and 496)
- Business profiles
- Cellular phone numbers
- Company ownerships (usually corporate, but could include other forms of ownership)
- Credit headers
- Criminal records, including sex offenders, arrests, and wants and warrants
- Crisscross (reverse) directories to search by telephone or Social Security Numbers or by address (e.g., physical or e-mail) instead of just by name
- Death dates
- Driver's license information
- E-mail addresses
- Employer name
- Evictions
- Liens, judgments, and UCCs
- Marriages and divorces
- Names (maiden and married) and aliases (note that some "aliases" are merely accidental misspellings)
- Neighbors of your subject
- Personal property (could include watercraft, motor vehicles, aircraft registrations, and FAA certifications)
- Professional licenses (e.g., contractors) and permits/licenses for controlled substances, hunting/fishing, and concealed weapons
- Real estate records (could include assessor or tax data, and even mortgages)
- Relatives of your subject
- Social Security Numbers, unless you have been approved to view full Social Security Numbers (see page 489)
- Telephone numbers (landlines) (current and past)
- Vehicle registrations
- Voter's registration

Some pay databases provide other enhancements, such as a graphical presentation of the results to help visualize connections or an e-alert feature to notify you when someone's information has changed. Note that the amount of information (and whether it is available at all) will vary from jurisdiction to jurisdiction and from database vendor to database vendor.

Where Do Pay Investigative Research Database Vendors Obtain Their Data?

Depending on which pay investigative research database you are using, the data listed in the prior section might come from one or more of the following sources:

- Public records (e.g., bankruptcies and real estate assessor records)

- Publicly available information (e.g., telephone and address listings from telephone companies and, more recently, information scraped from websites, blogs, and even social networking sites such as **Myspace**, **Facebook**, and **LinkedIn**)

- Proprietary information (which is a catch-all category for information investigative database vendors purchase from sources they typically won't divulge, such as your address and phone number, which you provided to a utility company or a local restaurant that delivers food to your home)

- Credit Headers, which refers to non-public, non-financial information such as addresses, phone numbers, full Social Security Numbers, and full dates of birth, which are derived from credit reports (see pages 487–489 for an explanation about who qualifies to receive full Social Security Numbers and full dates of birth in search results, and page 489 for an explanation of credit headers)

Pay Investigative Research Databases Are Relational Databases

In addition to collating various types of records associated with your subject, most pay investigative research databases also employ a "relational" component that shows relationships between your subject and your subject's neighbors, associates, relatives, and companies. This relational feature makes it easier to create a more comprehensive dossier about your subject. Discovering the names and contact information for people who have a relationship with your subject, and then reaching out to them, can be useful if you need to:

- Learn the whereabouts of your subject if your subject has gone missing
- Uncover background information about your subject
- Find information about their assets, etc.

With that said, these relational databases have limitations of their own. Typically, they only link people who:

- Share the same last name <u>and</u> with whom they have lived with during the past thirty–forty years (the date coverage is, generally, only back to the mid-1980s for most pay investigative databases)
- Have different last names but with whom they have lived with during the past thirty–forty years
- Currently or previously have owned real estate together, regardless of names

Thus, these databases might miss some crucial relationships. For example, a "complete" report on your subject might not include names of the subject's parents or siblings if the subject hasn't shared an address or owned real estate with them since the mid-1980s.

Pay Investigative Research Database Vendors Restrict Access to Social Security Numbers

When we first began using online databases to search public records (back in the 1980s), we were able to search by name to learn a subject's full Social Security Number and full date of birth. This full access lasted for many years. After the 9/11 terrorist attacks in 2001, and after some database data breaches, many pay investigative research databases tightened access to full Social Security Numbers and full dates of birth, showing only partial information for both. For example, **Lexis's Accurint** would only approve full Social Security Number access for those attorneys whose primary function was collections work, and then at some point, **Accurint** changed its policy and said it would decide whether subscribers were entitled to full access after they performed a site visit of the subscriber's office (to ascertain the subscriber was a legitimate subscriber and that their office met certain security standards). **Westlaw** and **Thomson Reuters** require site visits.

TLOxp (http://www.tlo.com) did not require a site visit unless a subscriber wanted access to full dates of birth and full Social Security Numbers (and driver's license numbers). But, beginning January 1, 2017, all **TLOxp** subscribers were required to submit to a site visit. (**TLOxp** subscribers pay a nominal fee for this site visit and are later reimbursed.) Thus, all **TLOxp** subscribers had the same access to full dates of birth and Social Security Numbers (and driver's license numbers). However, effective August 23, 2018, we received notice that, "The last four digits of Social Security numbers will be masked. Driver license numbers will be masked." No explanation was given until we called and were informed that home-based subscribers were the only ones who were losing this access.

Pay investigative research databases had always allowed you or any other subscriber to search by a full Social Security Number if you already knew it, but unless you were approved to name search to access the full Social Security Number, the number still did not display in your results. Of course, if you were searching with the full Social Security Number, then you already knew the full Social Security Number, so not seeing it displayed wouldn't matter. **TLOxp** and various other databases allow you to search by a partial Social Security Number, but you must also add in at least a last name.

Although searching with a full Social Security Number usually will return more targeted results, this is not always the case, especially because certain records fail to include a full Social Security Number. However, more sophisticated relational databases (see page 487) will often be able to link all of a person's records together, even if some of those records typically do not include a Social Security Number (such as a driver's license), by using other matching criteria.

Credit Headers: What Are They, Who Has Access to Them, and Why Do They Make a Database Better?

Credit Headers are the non-financial, "personally identifying" information from a credit report, compiled by credit bureaus (e.g., Experian, TransUnion, and Equifax). The information consists of a subject's name, address, telephone number, full Social Security Number, and full date of birth and is found at the "head" (that is, the "top") of a credit report (hence the name "credit headers"). It's important to note the information does <u>not</u> include a subject's credit/financial information or credit score.

Credit Headers are considered by many researchers to be the most "fresh" (up-to-date) information about a person, which makes them incredibly useful to the database vendors who purchase them from the credit bureaus to add to their pay investigative databases.

Credit Header information is considered "non-public" because it is neither a "public record" (because it is not held by a government agency) nor "publicly available" (because it is not freely available to the public).

The United States Code governs "consumer reports" and "consumer reporting agencies," both of which sound suspiciously like "credit reports" and "credit bureaus." However, pay investigative research database vendors state that the reports you retrieve from their databases are <u>not</u> consumer reports and do not constitute a consumer report under the Fair Credit Reporting Act (FCRA)—probably because they do not include a subject's credit/financial information or credit score. The pay investigative research databases also warn subscribers that their reports may not be used to determine the eligibility for credit, insurance, employment, or any other purpose regulated under the FCRA. For more information on the FCRA and related state laws, see pages 246–247.

489

A Consumer Report is defined in 15 U.S. Code § 1681a (d) (See https://www.law.cornell.edu/uscode/text/15/1681a) as:

> (d) Consumer Report.—
>
> (1) In general.— The term "consumer report" means any written, oral, or other communication of any information by a consumer reporting agency bearing on a consumer's credit worthiness, credit standing, credit capacity, character, general reputation, personal characteristics, or mode of living which is used or expected to be used or collected in whole or in part for the purpose of serving as a factor in establishing the consumer's eligibility for—
>
>> (A) credit or insurance to be used primarily for personal, family, or household purposes;
>>
>> (B) employment purposes; or
>>
>> (C) any other purpose authorized under section 1681b of this title.

A Consumer Reporting Agency is defined in 15 U.S. Code § 1681a (f) (See https://www.law.cornell.edu/uscode/text/15/1681a) as:

> (f) The term "consumer reporting agency" means any person which, for monetary fees, dues, or on a cooperative nonprofit basis, regularly engages in whole or in part in the practice of assembling or evaluating consumer credit information or other information on consumers for the purpose of furnishing consumer reports to third parties, and which uses any means or facility of interstate commerce for the purpose of preparing or furnishing consumer reports.

Those pay investigative research database vendors that do include credit header information in their databases have installed an extensive approval process to ensure that subscribers are not selling information to identity thieves (or others who should not have access to the information). In addition to submitting to a site visit, if you want to become a subscriber you must fill out an application and provide copies of your law license, business license, driver's license, and letterhead.

Because **Westlaw's PeopleMap** and pay investigative databases that are geared to the general public, such as **Intelius** and **US Search**, do not include credit header information, their databases do not necessarily provide the most up-to-date contact information and would not be able to provide full Social Security Numbers or full dates of birth to their subscribers. (It is possible, however, that they might be able to retrieve full dates of birth and up-to-date contact information from sources other than credit headers, but not full Social Security Numbers.)

Part of your application process for **LexisNexis**, **CLEAR**, and **TLOxp** includes attesting that you fall within one of the "General Exceptions" of the Gramm-Leach-Bliley Act (GLBA), 15 U.S.C. 6801-6802 (http://linkon.in/cofH3Z), which is discussed in the next section.

Gramm-Leach-Bliley Act (GLBA), 15 U.S.C. 6802(e)

Pay investigative research database vendors do not dispute that they and their subscribers must comply with the Gramm-Leach-Bliley Act (GLBA), 15 U.S.C. 6801-6802, *available at* http://linkon.in/cofH3Z, which protects access to a consumer's non-public personal information (which includes credit header information) found at financial institutions (which includes credit bureaus). To read the full text of the original 1999 act (where it is titled "Gramm-Leach-Bliley Act"), see http://linkon.in/bpnCDt.

Section 6801, which is titled "Protection of nonpublic personal information," states:

> (a) Privacy obligation policy
>
> It is the policy of the Congress that each financial institution has an affirmative and continuing obligation to respect the privacy of its customers and to protect the security and confidentiality of those customers' nonpublic personal information.
>
> (b) Financial institutions safeguards
>
> In furtherance of the policy in subsection (a) of this section, each agency or authority described in section 6805 (a) of this title, other than the Bureau of Consumer Financial Protection, shall establish appropriate standards for the financial institutions subject to their jurisdiction relating to administrative, technical, and physical safeguards—
>
> (1) to insure the security and confidentiality of customer records and information;
>
> (2) to protect against any anticipated threats or hazards to the security or integrity of such records; and
>
> (3) to protect against unauthorized access to or use of such records or information which could result in substantial harm or inconvenience to any customer.

Access to non-public personal information (e.g., credit header information) is, however, allowed to those who fall within one of the "General Exceptions" of Section 6802(e)(1)–(e)(8) of the GLBA, *available at* http://linkon.in/cofH3Z. (See page 493 to read this section of the GLBA.) Thus, if financial institutions (a term which, as noted earlier, includes credit bureaus) come within a GLBA General Exception, they can extract non-public, personally identifiable information from credit reports to sell to investigative pay database vendors, who in turn can sell the information to subscribers (such as lawyers) if they also come within one of the GLBA General Exceptions. Subscribers must attest that they fall within one of the GLBA General Exceptions each time they conduct a search, not just in their original application. A violation of the privacy laws of the GLBA may subject a company, individual, or management to criminal penalties pursuant to 15 U.S.C. 6821 and 15 U.S.C. 6823.

Those who are in the legal profession and wish to access credit headers through one of the pay investigative research databases should read the GLBA. You will usually be choosing Title 15, Sections 6802(e)(3)(B), 6802(e)(3)(D), 6802(e)(3)(E), or 6802(e)(8) of the General Exceptions when you search.

> **(e)** General Exceptions
>
> Subsections (a) and (b) of this section shall not prohibit the disclosure of nonpublic personal information—
>
> > **(1)** as necessary to effect, administer, or enforce a transaction requested or authorized by the consumer, or in connection with—
> >
> > > **(A)** servicing or processing a financial product or service requested or authorized by the consumer;
> > >
> > > **(B)** maintaining or servicing the consumer's account with the financial institution, or with another entity as part of a private label credit card program or other extension of credit on behalf of such entity; or
> > >
> > > **(C)** a proposed or actual securitization, secondary market sale (including sales of servicing rights), or similar transaction related to a transaction of the consumer;
> >
> > **(2)** with the consent or at the direction of the consumer;
> >
> > **(3)**
> >
> > > **(A)** to protect the confidentiality or security of the financial institution's records pertaining to the consumer, the service or product, or the transaction therein;
> > >
> > > **(B)** to protect against or prevent actual or potential fraud, unauthorized transactions, claims, or other liability;
> > >
> > > **(C)** for required institutional risk control, or for resolving customer disputes or inquiries;
> > >
> > > **(D)** to persons holding a legal or beneficial interest relating to the consumer; or
> > >
> > > **(E)** to persons acting in a fiduciary or representative capacity on behalf of the consumer;…
> >
> > (8) to comply with Federal, State, or local laws, rules, and other applicable legal requirements; to comply with a properly authorized civil, criminal, or regulatory investigation or subpoena or summons by Federal, State, or local authorities; or to respond to judicial process or government regulatory authorities having jurisdiction over the financial institution for examination, compliance, or other purposes as authorized by law.

Now that you've read this portion of the act, you will probably agree that the General Exceptions are quite vague and are a prime example of "legalese."

Typically, each database vendor provides a verbatim list of GLBA General Exceptions (see the next illustration) after you log into their database, and you must select one General Exception (which **TLOxp** refers to as Permitted Use) for each search that you conduct.

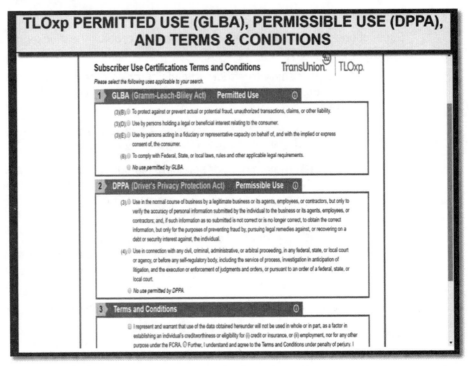

If you have no GLBA-authorized purpose for a specific search, you can select the *No use permitted by GLBA* option. This will still allow you to access information from the investigative research databases, but all credit header data will be excluded from your search results. (However, data that predates the GLBA might appear in your search results, but remember, it will be old information and not necessarily all that helpful.) The prior illustration also shows a list of *DPPA* [Driver's Privacy Protection Act] permissible use options, which you also must select from. (See page 152 for the text of DPPA).

Most database vendors refuse to offer an opinion about what the General Exceptions mean in the legal profession context, except for **Merlin** (before it was subsumed by **TLOxp**). For example, **Merlin** explained that:

- "persons holding a legal or beneficial interest relating to the consumer" meant that its subscribers could access credit headers found in **Merlin's** database if they were "locating beneficiaries & heirs and locating owners of unclaimed goods."

- "for use to protect against or prevent actual or potential fraud, unauthorized transactions, claims, or other liability" meant that its subscribers could access credit headers found in **Merlin's** database if they were involved in "fraud prevention, insurance claims investigations/subrogation, locating fraud victims."

- "for use to comply with Federal, State, or local laws, rules, and other applicable legal requirements" meant that its subscribers could access credit headers found in **Merlin's** database if they were involved with "child support enforcement, legal process service, locating witnesses & victims, or locating former patients."

Sometime after we wrote the last edition of this book and prior to this current edition, we noticed that **TLOxp** removed its *Permissible Use* drop-down menu (shown in the next illustration), which had looked suspiciously like the now defunct **Merlin's** GLBA interpretations, leaving us with no written guidance for interpreting the nearly unintelligible GLBA exceptions.

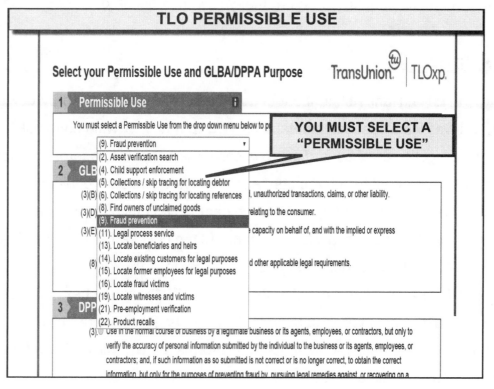

Pricing and How to Become a Subscriber to Pay Investigative Research Databases

Prices and pricing models vary from one pay investigative research database vendor to the next. Some offer flat-rate pricing, while others offer a "per search" fee. Most also charge a monthly subscription fee. **TLOxp** never charged a monthly subscription fee, until it instituted a $25 monthly "spend" as of January 1, 2017. The $25 is applied against your searches, so if you rack up $50 worth of searches in a month, you will only pay $50 and not $75. But, if you don't search at all one month, for example, you will still be charged $25.

Many of the databases also will run "batch" processing jobs for a set fee if you want them to conduct a large number of searches for you. Typically, to run a batch job, you will need to provide a spreadsheet to the vendor with whatever information you have about your subjects (their Social Security Numbers might be required). In addition to *Batch Processing*, **TLOxp** offers *Batch Monitoring*, which automatically alerts you to changes about those subjects you submitted to **TLOxp** for *Batch Processing*. You can pre-select the type of information (phone, address, place of employment, bankruptcy, or death) that you want monitored.

TLOxp

In 2011, Hank Asher, the founder of **Accurint** (now owned by **Lexis**), launched a new investigative research database, **TLOxp** (http://www.tlo.com). Like most of the pay investigative databases, **TLOxp** is comprised of public records, publicly available information, proprietary information, and credit headers and requires that you get credentialed to use it. **TLOxp** offers free demonstrations of its database and free trials.

After Asher's January 2013 death, **TLOxp** declared bankruptcy. The credit bureau **TransUnion** acquired **TLOxp**, on December 16, 2013.

While **TransUnion** doubled the prices of **TLOxp** searches in January 2015, and then did so again as of January 1, 2017 (most searches are now $5.00), its prices still remain reasonable for the amount of information you will retrieve (for most subjects) and the time saved, especially if you need to acquire a dossier-type report (which **TLOxp** labels a *Comprehensive Report*) about your subject. This *Report* is priced at $20.00 (in addition to the $5.00 charge you already incurred by conducting the original search). The *Deceased* search, *Phone Email Report* and *Vehicle Sightings* search are free, but it will cost you anywhere from $20.00–$50.00 to retrieve a *Vehicle Sightings Report* (prices vary according to date coverage). **TLOxp** also offers flat-rate pricing and "per seat" pricing.

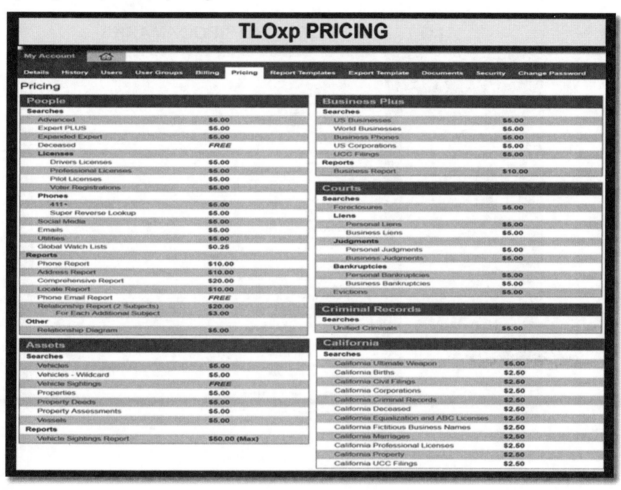

Searching **TLOxp** is easy despite its use of more sophisticated search techniques than any free public records sites. We like the way their *Comprehensive Report* is presented, especially the *Table of Contents* (see next illustration), which shows the types of information a *Comprehensive Report* gathers. It can be used to create background dossiers, find people's addresses and phone numbers, locate real and personal assets, uncover criminal histories, and much more.

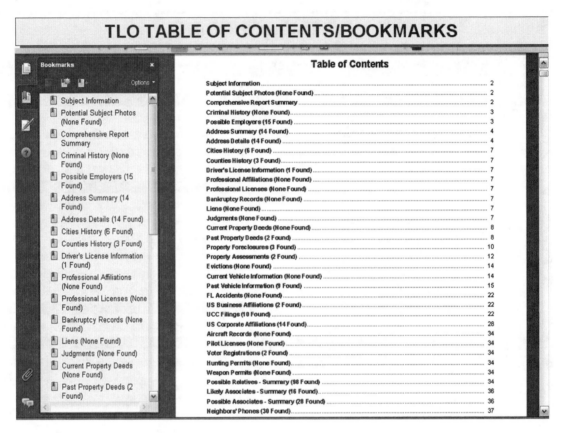

The homepage displays six broad categories, with narrower categories to search. Each of the narrower categories offers unique search menus. The availability of data varies from jurisdiction to state.

- *People*: This includes *Deceased* records, *Phones* (old and current landline and cellular numbers and reverse searches), *Address Report, Licenses* (*Drivers, Professional, Pilot*, and *Voter Registrations), Social Media* (searchable by email address only), *Emails, Utilities* (recently added), *Global Watch Lists,* and other records not listed on the homepage but searchable if you choose to perform one of the three *People* searches: *Advanced, Expert Plus*, or *Expanded Expert*, which we will explain later in this chapter.

- *Business Plus:* This includes *US Businesses, World Businesses, Business Phones, US Corporations,* and *UCC Filings.*

- *Courts:* This includes *Foreclosures, Liens* (*Personal* and *Business*), *Judgments* (*Personal* and *Business*), *Bankruptcies* (*Personal* and *Business*), and *Evictions.*

- *California*: This category of records comes from the former **Merlin** database; it includes some historical-only information (e.g., *Births, Deceased,* and *Marriage* records) and current information (e.g., *Civil Filings, Corporations, Criminal Records, Equalization and ABC Licenses, Fictitious Business Names, Professional Licenses, Property,* and *UCC Filings.* Its *Ultimate Weapon* is a pre-search to locate information on your subject in any of the California databases just listed. The results will show you which databases have information and you can then purchase some or all of the complete results.

- *Assets*: This includes *Vessels* (recently added to **TLOxp**, but only for U.S. merchant vessels and U.S. recreational vessels that are at least five tons.), *Vehicles* (vehicle registrations for thirty-nine states (New York and Alaska are not current), the District of Columbia, and Puerto Rico, current driver's license information for only Florida and Texas, and *Sightings* (nationwide), *Properties* (Deeds and Assessments), which, although not listed, could also include mortgages.

- *Criminal Records:* The *Unified Criminals* records could include state, local, or federal criminal records, registered sex offenders, warrants, and arrests.

As noted earlier, there are three ways to perform a broad *People* search. First is the *Advanced* search (see next illustration), which costs $5.00.

The *Advanced* search menu allows you to search by one or more of the following criteria:

- *Last Name*, *First Name*, *Middle Name*
- *Address* (*street, building, community*)
- *ZIP*, *ZIP 9*, *City*, *County*, or *State*
- *Phone*
- *Date Range Seen at Address*
- *Radius from location*
- *DOB* (date of birth)
- *Age Range*
- *SSN* (Social Security Number)—*Full, First 5 digits, or Last 4 digits*
- *DL* (Driver's License), *Email*, *Domain*, or *IP* (Internet Protocol address);
  A *Domain* name search may help you create a list of employees at a specific company.
- *TLO Person ID*; each person in **TLOxp's** database is assigned a unique number, called the *TLO Person ID*. Once you find your subject's record, make a note of their *TLO Person ID* because it is the best way to search for that subject if you need to do so again. If you choose to search by a *TLO Person ID*, no other search criterion is permitted.

Our search results brought back thirty-two potential results, with each result showing us some summary information about each person. Once you have homed in on which person you think is the correct result, select the *View Full Record* (see next illustration) to view more personally identifying information, such as possible phone numbers, relatives, and e-mail addresses, which will help you better ascertain whether this is, indeed, your subject. There is no extra charge for this. To retrieve something more like a dossier of your subject, click the *Run Comprehensive Report*. You will then incur a $20.00 charge.

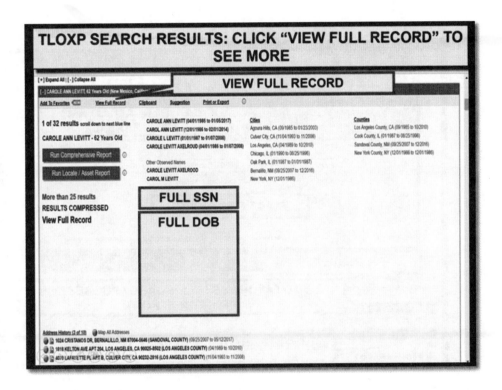

The second way to search the *People* category is *Expert Plus* (see next illustration), which offers only one search box, where you can search with keywords and phrases, like a **Google**-type search. Using the *Expert Plus* option, *we* searched for *MARK CAROLE "LOS ANGELES (COUNTY) CA" "BERNALILLO NM" "OAK PARK IL."* For those who are not used to such **Google**-type searches, this means we searched for the keywords *MARK AND CAROLE AND* the phrases *"LOS ANGELES (COUNTY) CA" AND "BERNALILLO NM" AND "OAK PARK IL."* We also checked off the *Exact First Name* box. Notice that we did not even use a last name for either person.

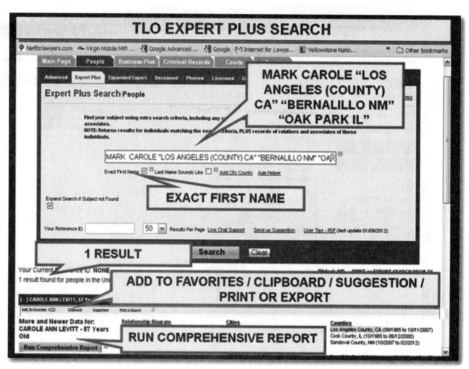

Our *Expert Plus* search brought back only one result and it was the exact result we were looking for (Carole Levitt). Notice the horizontal bar towards the bottom, *Add To Favorites / Clipboard / Suggestion / Print or Export.* If you choose *Print or Export* your search results can be exported to PDF, RTF, or TXT, and you can change the font size and page orientation of your document. *Add To Favorites* is a newer feature which allows you to store records or reports for later review. You can also run a *Relationship* search to compare two people who you have added to your *Favorites.* Selecting *Clipboard* allows you to keep a copy of this result. Selecting *Suggestion* allows you to submit a suggestion to customer support.

To learn more about your subject, select *Run Comprehensive Report.* The information in Carole Levitt's *Comprehensive Report* went back to about 1985. The current address and current phone numbers were correct. One notable exception, however, was that her current mobile phone number was listed as a landline. It originally was a landline but was ported over to a mobile service in 2004. Some investigative databases have caught the change but most have not. Only one prior address was incorrect, but other investigative databases also show this incorrect address (it is her ex-husband's prior work address).

The menu for the *Expanded Expert* search option (see next illustration) allows you to search for a person and add in *Any combination of multiple addresses, states, cities, counties, neighborhood names or building names* and multiple names of *Subject's Relatives and/or Associates.*

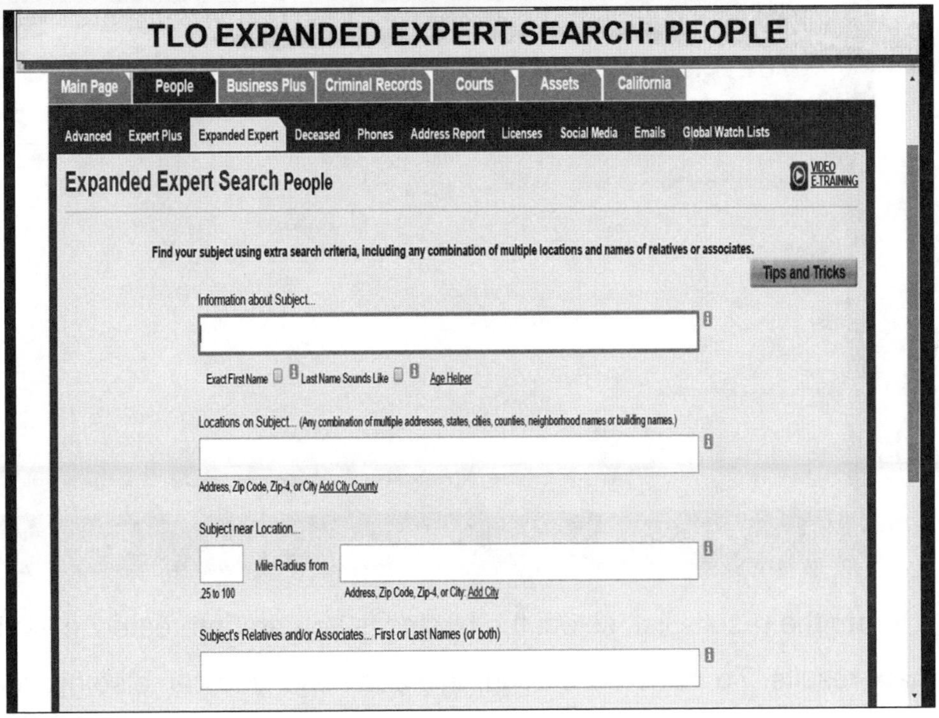

The *Address Report* offers current and historical known details associated with a specific address, including Individuals, Businesses, Assets, and Filings, in one comprehensive report. The cost of this report is $10.00.

TLO offers five *Business Plus* databases. The most comprehensive is the *U.S. Businesses* database ($5.00 to search). After you choose *U.S. Businesses*, an

Advanced Search US Businesses search menu appears (see next illustration), which allows you to search by one or more of the following:

- Business Name; Personal Name by Last Name, First Name, Middle Name;
- Address;
- Phone Number;
- FEIN; D-U-N-S Number;
- Ticker Symbol;
- SSN (Social Security Number)—Full, First 5 digits, or Last 4 digits; and
- Domain Name.

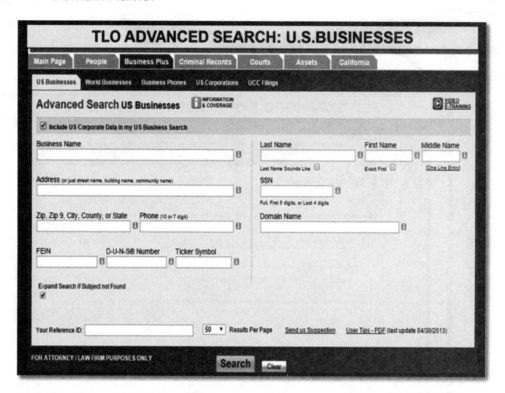

From the results list, select the business you are interested in to view some summary results. To learn more about this business, you can also generate *a Business Report* (priced at $10.00) for that business. The *Report* will include a company profile that lists subsidiaries, officers, directors, and employees. It also could include public filings (liens, judgments, UCC filings, and bankruptcies), corporate assets (vehicles and aircrafts), and property information (foreclosures and evictions).

The *Assets* databases include *Vehicles, Vessels, and Properties.*

- The *Vehicles - Advanced* Search menu allows you to search by *Name* (*Personal or Business*), *Address, SSN, VIN,* or *Tag Number.*

- *The Vehicles - Wildcard* Search (see next illustration) allows you to enter a *Partial Tag* (License Plate Number), *Vehicle Doors, Vehicle Category, Color Category, Make, Model,* etc., to find the owner of a vehicle in thirty-nine states, Puerto Rico, and the District of Columbia.

Our partial tag search (*JSG*) for a *4-Door Silver Toyota Avalon* in *NM* brought back four results. One of the results was for the vehicle for which we were searching.

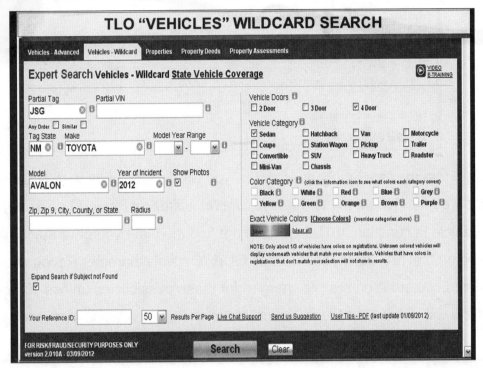

TLOxp offers a nationwide *Vehicle Sightings* proprietary database (which means we don't know where the information comes from) that is quite interesting: It allows you to search for the sightings of vehicles by license plate number. You can search with a full or partial *License Plate* number and choose one state or *All States.*

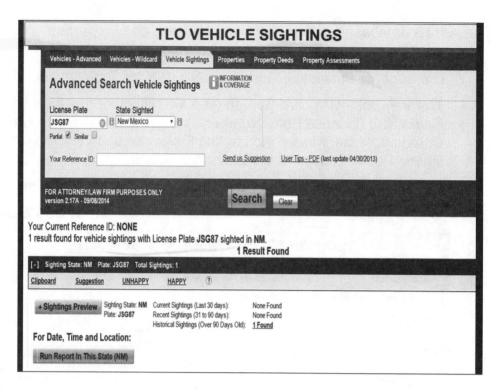

From the free *Sightings Preview*, you will be able to learn if **TLOxp** has *Current (last 30 days)*, *Recent (31 to 90 days)* and/or *Historical (over 90 days old)* sightings of the vehicle in question. If **TLOxp** does not find the plate you entered, it might show you some that are similar because its OCR (Optical Character Recognition) is not 100 percent accurate. You are not charged for these possibilities unless you click the *Run [Vehicle Sightings] Report* tab, which is shown in the previous illustration as *Run Report in This State (NM)* (because we only searched New Mexico). The *Vehicle Sightings Report* displays a picture of the vehicle at the time of the sighting, as well as the exact date, time, and location (latitude/longitude with a link to maps) of the sighting.

There are three property databases in the *Assets* section of **TLOxp** (*Properties, Property Deeds,* and *Property Assessments*). The *Property Deeds* results show mortgage information while the *Property Assessments* results show tax assessments (which could be much different from actual market value). Each search costs $5.00. The $5.00 *Properties* search is a combination of the *Property Deeds* and *Property Assessments* search but only requires the search criteria to be entered once.

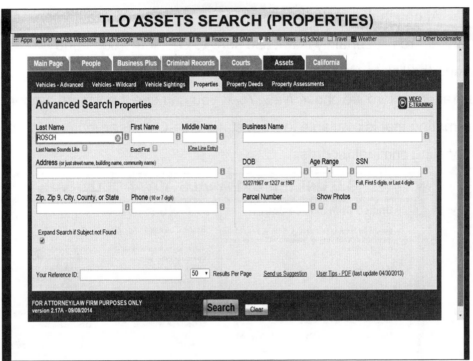

The *Properties* search can be conducted by:

- *Name* (personal or business);
- *Address, Phone Number;*
- *DOB* (*Date of Birth*);
- *Age Range;*
- *SSN* (*Social Security Number*); and
- *Parcel Number.*

You can check off whether you want the results to *Show Photos* (if available) of the property (sometimes this will include photos of the interiors). Our *Date of Birth* test search did not yield correct results but our test searches for all other criteria did, including a search only by telephone number.

Once you retrieve results from your *Properties* search, you can click the Map icon (which might not work for every address) or the *Build an Address Report for this Address* icon.

TLOxp's *Unified Criminals Search* allows you to search criminal, sex offender, arrest, and warrant records all in one search by entering up to three name variations (aliases or a woman's maiden name, for example) into the search boxes.

Although this "unified" search might imply that it is a comprehensive criminal record search, it certainly is not. Be sure to check the coverage for each state by clicking the link to *Coverage Info* and choosing a state. For instance, in the next illustration, where we chose *New York*, you can see the limited amount of criminal information that is available for that state. See *Chapter Eighteen* for more information on locating criminal records.

TLO UNIFIED CRIMINALS ADVANCED SEARCH

Unified Criminals Search

Search for records including Criminal, Sex Offend[er] locations of your subject. Results will be returned criteria entered.

State Coverage

Please note, a complete list of criminal records does [not include] various sources and is growing every day. For details

Click here for a PDF of full state coverage

Please Choose One or More States Below To View

☐ National	☐ Hawaii
☐ Alaska	☐ Iowa
☐ Alabama	☐ Idaho
☐ Arkansas	☐ Illinois
☐ Arizona	☐ Indiana
☐ California	☐ Kansas
☐ Colorado	☐ Kentucky
☐ Connecticut	☐ Louisiana
☐ District of Columbia	☐ Massachusetts
☐ Delaware	☐ Maryland
☐ Florida	☐ Maine
☐ Georgia	☐ Michigan
☐ Guam and Northern Mariana Islands	☐ Minnesota

Criminal Data Coverage

State Coverage for New York

Cattaraugus County Warrant	Prison Release Records
Chemung County Warrant	Rosendale Most Wanted
Dept of Corrections	Rosendale Police Dept. Warrants
Elmira Most Wanted	Saint Regis Mohawk Tribe Sex Offender Registry
Fulton City Arrest	Sex Offender Registry
Greenburgh County Most Wanted	Steuben County Warrants
Ithaca County Most Wanted	Steuben Most Wanted
Madison County Warrant	Ulster County Warrants
Oneida County Arrest	Walden Most Wanted
Oneida County Warrant	Warren County Warrants
Oneida Most Wanted	Warren Most Wanted
Onondaga Arrest	Wayne Most Wanted

☐ North Carolina	☐ Rhode Island
☐ North Dakota	☐ South Carolina
☐ Nebraska	☐ South Dakota
☐ Nevada	☐ Tennessee
☐ New Hampshire	☐ Texas
☐ New Jersey	☐ Utah
☐ New Mexico	☐ Virginia
☑ New York	☐ Virgin Islands
☐ Ohio	☐ Vermont
☐ Oklahoma	☐ Washington
☐ Oregon	☐ Wisconsin
	☐ West Virginia
	☐ Wyoming

You can search by one or more of these options: *Name, Height Range, Race, DOB, SSN, Age Range, ZIP, City, County,* or *State.* The next illustration shows a name search (e.g., *Last Name, First Name, Middle Name* [or *Initial*]). You can even perform a search without using a last name, but you will need to add in more search criteria. For example, we searched by first name, middle initial, and date of birth and found our subject. If you search by last name, it must be the full and correct last name but **TLOxp** is more forgiving with first names. In a last name/first name test search, when we entered the first name *Steve,* the results brought back records for the correct subject, including records where he was booked under *Steven.* In addition, a search for that same subject, but with the spelling of his first name as *Stephen,* brought back the correct records even though he had never been booked with that spelling of his first name. In addition, up to two dates of birth can be entered and up to six counties where you suspect your subject has lived or has a criminal record.

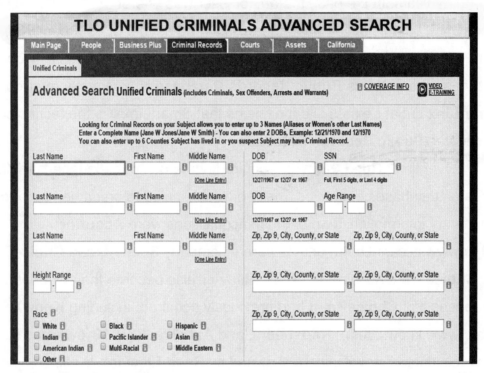

Each type of **TLOxp** search includes an "on-demand" training e-video, which we found useful. Law enforcement can use **TLOxp** at a reduced rate.

As we mentioned earlier in this chapter, we will not be illustrating the other major pay investigative databases, but for those who are curious, we are providing some history about them.

In addition to its legal research databases, **LexisNexis** (whose parent company is **Reed Elsevier**) has offered public records at **Lexis.com** (http://www.lexis.com) for over thirty years. In the past, the *ad hoc* user was offered a "pay as you go" option via **LexisONE**, but this option no longer exists (and neither does **LexisONE**). Since 2011, **LexisNexis** has required an annual subscription to access its **Public Records Database**. **LexisNexis Public Records Database** is commonly referred to as **SmartLinx** but at **Lexis's** site it explains that SmartLinx® is the technology that powers the **Public Records Database**.

Over time, **Reed Elsevier** acquired numerous once-independent investigative research database companies, many of which included credit header and other proprietary information. Two of those acquisitions were **Accurint** (http://www.accurint.com) and its parent company **Seisent**, and **ChoicePoint**. With the **ChoicePoint** acquisition, **Reed Elsevier** also became the owner of other databases that **ChoicePoint** had previously acquired, including **KnowX** (http://www.knowx.com), **Rapsheets**, and **AutoTrackXP**. **KnowX** and **Rapsheets** (now rolled into **KnowX**), are still owned by **Reed Elsevier**. While some of the **Reed Elsevier** acquisitions are still accessible as separate databases (with the same familiar search interfaces that each of their subscriber bases are used to using), at some point we predict that they will all probably be integrated into one database.

In late 2008, **Reed Elsevier** sold **ChoicePoint Government Services LLC** (which included **CLEAR®**) and **AutoTrackXP** to **Thomson Reuters**.

Thomson Reuters marketed these acquisitions as **ChoicePoint CLEAR**, but only gave access to the law enforcement market. The product is now called **CLEAR** and has been made available to legal professionals outside of law enforcement (http://linkon.in/thomclear).

There are many vendors promoting their databases on the Web as "people-finding/background research" databases, but they do not include information from credit headers. These "non-credit header" databases, in contrast to the "credit header" databases discussed earlier in this chapter (**TLOxp**, etc.), appear to be geared more to members of the "general public" who might only have an occasional use for this information and don't want to go through a pre-approval process (or probably wouldn't even qualify). Because these non-credit header database vendors lack credit header information, their information is not as up to date as credit header databases (most likely). The amount of information these vendors provide pales in comparison to the "credit header" databases we have discussed in this chapter.

Yet, we mention them in this book because many of our seminar attendees have encountered links to these non-credit header database vendors as they surf the Web and question us about their usefulness. We also mention them in this book because we sometimes find their free "teaser" information useful and you might, too. (The "credit-header" pay investigative research databases discussed earlier do not offer any information for free.)

Some examples of these non-credit header databases are **Intelius** (http://www.intelius.com) and **US Search** (http://www.ussearch.com), both of which are owned by the same company, **PeopleConnect, Inc.**, **PeopleFinders** (http://www.peoplefinders.com), and **PeopleSmart** (https://www.peoplesmart.com).

If you've performed a phone number search at the free **Whitepages.com** (http://www.whitepages.com) site, you used to see a link in your search results for *Background Information*. Clicking this link would take you to **US Search/Intelius**. In 2011, **Whitepages.com** shifted its allegiance from **US Search/Intelius** to **PeopleFinders**, and then in 2012 switched its allegiance once more, but this time to **PeopleSmart**, and as of this writing, it's unclear which company is supplying their information.

To give you an example of a non-credit header database and its free teaser results, we'll explore **Intelius** in the next section.

You can access **Intelius** by entering a name and state into the *People Search* advertisement on **Search Systems'** homepage (http://publicrecords.searchsystems.net), or you can visit the **Intelius** site directly at https://www.intelius.com. (See pages 159 for information about **Search Systems**.)

After running an **Intelius** *People Search* for *Carole Levitt*, the free summary "teaser" results displayed two different records for her. One record listed her as *Carole A. Levitt* and the other as *Carole Ann Levitt*.

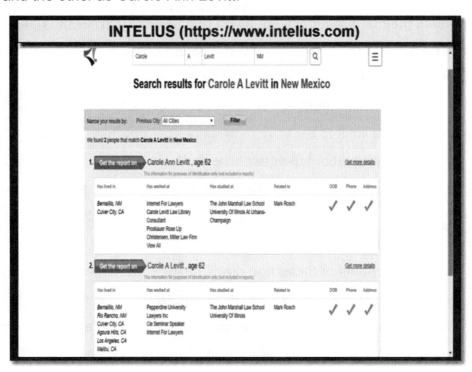

The first record displayed only the last two cities in which she's lived (both correct) and dated back to 1993 to the present. If you click the *View All* beneath *Has worked at,* a total of eight places of employment are listed, back to 1985, but two were incorrect. The second record displayed five cities where she lived back to 1985 (four were correct) and displayed four places of employment back to 1985 (but only two were correct; one was a partial name and the other was a description of the type of work Carole does). The second record covered a date range from 1989 to the present. Both records correctly displayed her age, listed only one relative (her husband) and listed the same two schools she attended. When we ran the same search a few years earlier, there were six variations of her name and names of five relatives (her former and her current husband, her current brother-in-law, her former father-in-law, and one mystery relative). If you were looking for background information about your subject's age, places of employment, cities lived in, or schools attended, it's possible that this teaser information will be useful and even possibly sufficient for your needs.

As soon as you click *Get more details,* you are offered a *People Search Report*, *People Search Report Plus,* or a *Background Report,* which will cost between $2.95 and $49.95. The *Background Report*, at $49.95, seems very high compared to **TLOxp's** $20.00 *Comprehensive Report.* We have compared both *Reports* and found **TLOxp's** to be the superior product. **Intelius's** prices are discounted if you agree to their *Special Price.* In our opinion, these *Special Prices* are ploys to wring more money out of searchers who don't read the fine print informing them that the *Special Price* includes *Intelius Premier Plus,* which will add an automatic monthly membership charge of $29.95 to your credit card. For example, when we clicked the 25% off *Special Price* for the *People Search Report*, this is what we learned we were about to agree to:

> I agree that my 7-day trial of the Intelius Premier Plus starts when I complete this purchase, and then converts to a paid membership after 7 days, unless I cancel. If I cancel within 7 days and have not yet used the background check voucher, I will be charged an additional $7.95. If I use the background check voucher during the 7-day trial, my paid membership will begin immediately upon voucher use. Once my paid membership starts, it will automatically renew for the same term each time it reaches its expiration date, unless I cancel. I will pay $29.95 for each renewal term. I can cancel my membership anytime by accessing my account online or by calling (888) 445-2727, and my benefits will continue through the then-current term. I agree that there are no refunds or credits and that tax will be added where applicable.

A *Background Report* could include all or some of the following information about a person: address; phone number; real estate ownership; selected lawsuit information (bankruptcies, marriage and divorce records, criminal records, tax liens, and judgments); licenses; birth and death records; names; addresses and phone numbers of neighbors and of associates; relatives; and others linked to the same addresses as the subject. There are no business name searches available in this database.

Like **Intelius, US Search** (http://www.ussearch.com) allows you to view some teaser information from your search results for free. Our search for *Carole Levitt* at the **US Search** site brought back nearly identical results as **Intelius**. Also like **Intelius, US Search** had *Special* and *Regular Pricing,* with similar prices for reports and memberships.

Should Legal Professionals Use Databases Like Intelius or US Search?

For those who frequently need to access investigative databases, a subscription to one of the major databases may turn out to be less expensive and include more up-to-date results (since they include information from credit headers), and much more information (such as mortgages).

Search Systems Premium

While we primarily use **Search Systems** for its free links to public record sites (see page 159), it also offers its own *Premium* (pay) databases which you might consider using when you only need to search for discrete pieces of information about your subject (instead of a dossier-type report about our subject). **Search Systems** does not require an application process or an annual or monthly subscription. You only pay per search. Like **Intelius** and **US Search**, **Search Systems'** *Premium* databases do not include information from credit headers. You will need to agree to all the terms listed in their Registration Agreement and provide your credit card information to use the *Premium* databases.

You can access any of **Search Systems'** *Premium* databases from **Search Systems'** homepage at http://publicrecords.searchsystems.net (see the illustration on page 159).

The following are the *Premium* databases offered by **Search Systems**:

- *National Security* database (searching over 75 national, international, and state databases for known terrorists, casino cheats, Interpol fugitives, NCIS & FBI most wanted, debarred parties, sanctioned parties, and persons involved in government fraud, federal banking law violations, money laundering, and illegal imports)

- *Bankruptcy, Judgments, and Tax Liens* database

- *Tenant Screening* database (eviction records)

- *Criminal Records* database (including sex offenders)

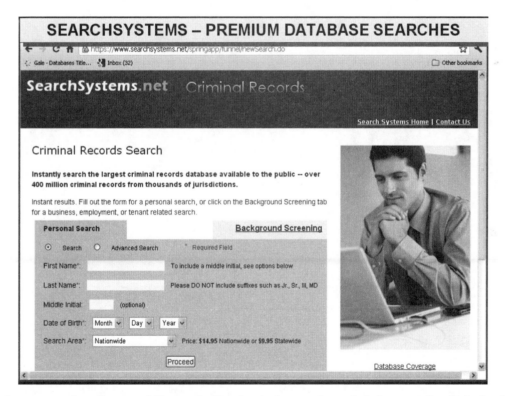

An example of one of **Search Systems'** premium databases, its *Criminal Records* database (prior illustration), offers a *Nationwide* search for $14.95 and a *Statewide* search for $6.95. To their credit, **Search Systems** does a good job of explaining the limitations of these kinds of criminal records searches by providing a state-by-state list of the resources included in each state's search (http://bit.ly/ssyscrim).

INDEX

A (cont.)

American Bar Association
  Blawgs Directory
    Podcasts, 102
  California
    Rule 1.1 Comment [8], 342
  Division for Bar Services
    Bar Association Links, 444
  Journal
    Blawg Directory, 447
  Legal Technology Resource Center, 445
  Preview of United States Supreme Court Cases
    Briefs (Free), 226
  Social Networking Research
    Ethics Opinion, 405, 410
American Lawyer. *See* ALM
American Medical Association, 329, 428
Ancestry.com
  Genealogy site, 280
  LADMF, 282
  Library Edition, 181
  Public Libraries Free Database, 280
  Social Security Death Index, 282
AND
  Boolean Connector, 55
Anywho.com, 305
AOL, 49, 124
Apps Launcher
  Google.com, 86
Archive.org, 133, 134, 143, 144
  Affidavit, 146
  Blocking Collection, 140
  Dynamic Web Pages, 142
  Evidence
    Affidavit, 146
  Evidence Admitted, 143
  Evidence Not Admitted, 146
  Full-Text Search, 138
  Missing Content, 140
  Removing Content, 140
  Robots.txt, 140
  Social Networking Sites, 140
  Twitter, 387
Archived Web Pages
  Archive.org, 133, 134
  Archive-It, 147
  Bing, 133
  Google, 133, 134
  Yahoo, 133
Archive-It, 147
ArchiveSocial, 403
Area Code Directories, 303, 308
Argument Audio (Free)
  CourtListener, 226
  Courts, 226
  National Archives Catalog, 225
  U.S. Supreme Court, 222, 224, 225, 226
    Oyez, 226
Argument Transcripts (Free)
  U.S. Supreme Court, 222, 224

A (cont.)

Army Personnel
  Locator Services, 424
AROUND(n)
  Proximity Connector, 58
Arrest Records, 499, 508
Articles
  Academic, 334
  Attorneys, 445
  Google Scholar, 332
  Journals/Magazines, 176
  Judges, 445
  News, 176
  Public Library
    Free Remote Access, 176
Asher, Hank, 496
Assessor Records, 507
Assets, 245, 485, 505, 507
  401K Plans, 274
  Aircraft, 253
  Bank Accounts, 245
  Businesses, 263, 505
  Copyrights, 257
  Corporate, 505
  Employee Benefit Plans, 274
  Financial (Unclaimed), 252
  Intellectual Property, 257
  Money (Unclaimed), 252
  Patents, 257
  Pension Plans, 274
  Personal Property, 245
  Profit-Sharing Plans, 274
  Real Estate, 249, 507
  Stock, 266
  Trademarks, 257
  Vehicles, 505
  Vessels, 256
Associates, 485, 487, 503
Association of State Medical Board Executive
  Directors
    DocFinder, 329
Associations, 328
  Bars, 328
  Encyclopedia of, 328
  Federal Bar Association, 444
  Non-Profits, 329
    Form 990, 329
  Texas Trial Lawyers Association, 327
Assumed Name Filings, 263
Asterisk
  Proximity Connector, 58
  Wildcard Search, 60
AtoZdatabases
  Free Remote Access, 177

B (cont.)

C (cont.)

R (cont.)

S

CLEseminars.com offers CLE webinars presented by some of the best-know experts in the areas of law practice management, technology, and ethics. Each one hour webinar features practical lessons you can immediately put to work in your practice.

All of our webinars feature live chat access so you can ask the presenters any questions you might have.

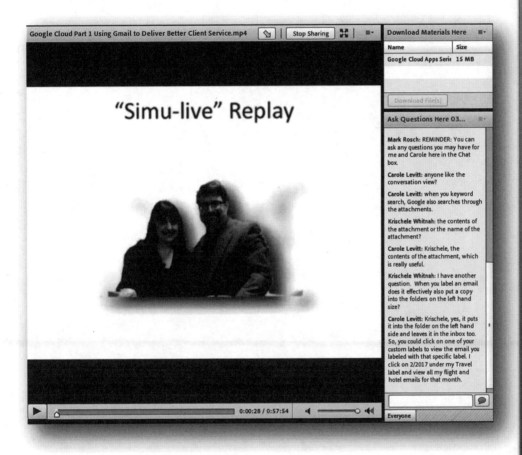

Our webinars are delivered directly to your desktop, laptop, or mobile device using the latest Adobe Connect webinar technology. (Most attendees don't even have to download or install any software.)

Registration is easy – requiring no user name or password.

CLE Credit is available in 20+ states. See the upcoming webinar schedule and jurisdictions where credit is available at http://www.CLEseminars.com.

Presenters Include

Jennifer Ellis

Andrew Elowitt

Lenné Espenschied

John Federico

Debbie Foster

Roy Ginsburg

Barron Henley

Jim Jesse

Irwin Karp

Dennis Kennedy

Robert LeVine

Carole Levitt

Britt Lorish

Jim Robinson

Mark Rosch

Jennifer Ramovs

Cynthia Sharp

Allison Shields

Daniel Siegel

Ernest Svenson

Paul Unger

Free Online Expert Witness Directory
www.JurisPro.com

JurisPro Expert Witness Directory
Clearly conveying the abilities of expert witnesses.

"JurisPro should be among one of your first stops when locating expert witnesses on the Internet."

-American Bar Association, Legal Technology Center

Run by practicing attorneys, JurisPro is a free resource to find or evaluate an expert witness in thousands of categories. When you come to JurisPro (www.JurisPro.com), you may:

Visit the expert's website.

E-mail the expert with any questions.

Contact the expert directly.

Learn the expert's background as an expert witness (# of times testified, % for the plantiff or defense, etc.)

Read the expert's articles.

Contact the expert's references.

E-mail the expert's profile to your client or to other attorneys.

Dr. James R. Dobbs, Ph.D., P.E. Benedict Engineering Co., Inc.
3660 Hartsfield Road
Tallahassee, FL 32302

Phone: (850) 576-1176 ext 135
Fax: (850) 575-8454

Email this Profile

Click To Listen

| Intro | Web Page | E-mail | Background | Articles | References | CV |

Dr. Dobbs is an engineer experienced in failure analysis, including corrosion, fracture, and fatigue of metals, plastic, glass, wood and other materials; and analysis of product failures including automobile restraints, medical devices and machinery. He is also experienced in the areas of vehicular accident reconstruction, including automobile, trucks, trains and motorcycles; pedestrian accident reconstruction, including vehicular, slip, trip and fall; and industrial accident reconstruction, including forklifts, cranes and machinery.

Benedict Engineering Company, Inc. focuses on forensic engineering (accident reconstruction) and consulting engineering and is also involved in the research, development and design of products and systems. Our engineering team represents a variety of engineering disciplines; mechanical, biomechanical, biomedical, civil, safety, industrial, metallurgy and materials. This diversity enables us to reconstruct a variety of types of accidents; automobile, truck, aircraft, boat, train, bicycle, ATV, product, roadway design, electrocution, fire and explosion, slip/trip and fall, "black box" (EDR) and more. The BEC services include investigation and documentation of the scene, engineering analysis, and creating all types of graphics in-house to support the engineering analysis during testimony in deposition and trial.

See and hear the expert to know how the expert presents him or herself.

Download or print the expert's full curriculum vitae.

If you cannot find the expert you are looking for online, contact us at 888-905-4040. Our group of attorneys will help find your expert, free of charge. There are no referral fees, ever.

JurisPro is a Better Business Bureau Company.

For expert witnesses, visit and bookmark
www.JurisPro.com

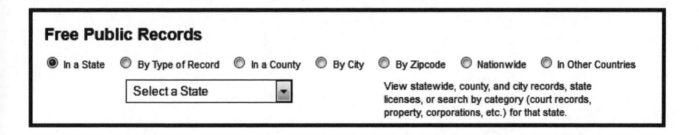

INTERNET FOR LAWYERS

HOME | ABOUT US | LIVE MCLE | ONLINE MCLE | ARTICLES | CALENDAR | BOOKS | BLOG | CONTACT US

Search

THE LATEST INTERNET RESEARCH TIPS

Read the latest strategies, tips and new resources available for integrating the Internet into your law practice in our newsletter.

LegalBoard, the Keyboard for Lawyers, In Practice
03/31/2017

USB Device Promises Unlimited Storage
03/27/2017

Size Matters to Google | Increasing File Size Limit for Incoming Email Attachments
03/03/2017

Internet Legal Research on a Budget
by Carole A. Levitt & Judy K. Davis

Learn to Locate and use:

· Legal portals and directories (government, academic, and commercial)

Home > Search Engine Features Compared

Search Engine Features Compared

In Bing Boolean connectors Google search engines Yahoo!

Share this chart:

Share / Save 🅕 🐦 ↑   You +1'd this

Search Engine	Default Boolean Connector	Other Boolean Connectors Recognized	Proximity Connector	Search Term Limit	Cached Pages	Field Searches	Search Limiters
Google	AND	OR, |, -	AROUND(n), " ", *	32 (previously had been 10 terms)	Yes	domain, intitle, inurl, link, site, among others	date, filetype, language, site, usage rights
Yahoo!	AND	AND, OR, -, ( ) (See this article for details about Yahoo!'s use of OR.)	" ", *	unreported (may be unlimited)	Yes	domain, intitle, inurl, site, among others	Creative Commons license, language, file type, date, site
Bing (Formerly Microsoft's Live Search)	AND	AND, &, OR, |, -, ( ) (See this article for details about Bing's use of OR.)	" ", *	10 terms (previously had been reported as 150 characters)	Yes	domain, inbody, intitle, site	feed, hasfeed, language, locaton, site